Bentonville

Civil War America

Gary W. Gallagher, editor

—— The Final Battle of ——
Sherman and Johnston

Bentonville

Nathaniel Cheairs Hughes, Jr.

THE UNIVERSITY OF NORTH CAROLINA PRESS

CHAPEL HILL AND LONDON

Manufactured in the United States of America

The paper in this book meets the guidelines for permanence
and durability of the Committee on Production Guidelines for
Book Longevity of the Council on Library Resources.

Library of Congress Cataloging-in-Publication Data

Hughes, Nathaniel Cheairs. Bentonville : The Final Battle of
Sherman and Johnston / by Nathaniel Cheairs Hughes, Jr.

p. cm.—(Civil War America)

Includes bibliographical references and index.

ISBN 0-8078-2281-7 (cloth : alk. paper)

1. Bentonville (N.C.), Battle of, 1865. I. Title. II. Series.

E477.7.H84   1996   95-47875

973.7'38—dc20   CIP

00   99   98   97   96   5   4   3   2   1

In memory of

T. R. Hay and Stanley F. Horn

Contents

Maps

Illustrations

Preface

As a boy I began reading about the Army of Tennessee. When I encountered Bentonville, the final fight for those Confederates, it seemed to be mentioned just in passing, yet it was a major battle. That puzzled me. Eventually I came to learn that for many historians and aficionados, indeed for the soldiers themselves, the saga of that ill-starred army had ended at Nashville. Whereas pages might be devoted to Perryville or Chickamauga, a paragraph would suffice for Bentonville. Even Stanley Horn, who loved the Army of Tennessee very much, allotted Bentonville only one page.

Why was this? Nashville and Franklin were bitter episodes, and what followed seemed not only anticlimactic but painful. Soon I too felt compelled to hurry past those terrible pages and close the book. I still do. But an appreciation of the Civil War requires attention to the dark leaves of 1865 as well as to the bright blossoms of 1861.

William J. Hardee led me to Bentonville. I had done my master's thesis about Hardee's pre–Civil War career, but before I committed to his Civil War career as a dissertation topic, I wanted to know how things turned out. So, in the winter of 1955–56, I began a seminar paper on Bentonville, Hardee's last battle. My professor, Fletcher M. Green, encouraged me, partly because another of his students, John G. Barrett, had just completed a fascinating doctoral study of William T. Sherman's Carolinas Campaign.

When winter broke, I abandoned the letters and diaries in the Chapel Hill and Duke libraries and went with my wife Bucky to visit the battlefield itself. Go see Mr. Rose first, advised some wise local when I asked directions. So I did. Herschell V. Rose, Johnston County court clerk, showed enormous patience. Unknown to me, the newly hatched expert, I was talking with a man who had spent nearly a lifetime studying the battle. I learned much and a forty-page paper resulted. Later it was sharply contracted and incorporated in *Hardee*. Still later the surviving copy of the Bentonville seminar paper was loaned to one of my own students and disappeared, a fate I should have anticipated.

I found myself returning to the Bentonville battlefield whenever I happened to be in eastern North Carolina, which proved more often than I might have imagined in 1955. My three sons and I were all stationed at Camp Lejeune, off and on, over a thirty-year span, and my wife and I always have liked the Carolina coast for vacations. So I would go back, drawn to the site.

All along I believe I knew I would do a longer study of the battle, someday. Andrew Wyeth expressed my feelings well: "To make an old thing I've seen for years seem fresh is much more exciting to me." I committed myself finally to write a full account of Bentonville after publishing *Belmont*, the story of the first battle of the Army of Tennessee. I wanted to fast-forward in my research to 1865, see how things turned out with other men I had come to know. Such an effort also promised a sort of symmetry to my work. Besides, as I remembered, the desperation, the futility, of the struggle called Bentonville could serve almost as a metaphor for the Confederacy itself.

By March 1865 no longer did southern soldiers or their leaders speak—or think—of the parallel with George Washington and the first glorious American Revolution. No longer did they believe that God stood squarely beside the Confederacy. A Lafayette McLaws might write his wife two days after the battle, "Our men were confident to the last, although they knew their opponent outnumbered them very largely and were in fact enthusiastic for the fight,"[1] but McLaws knew that the situation was hopeless, as did Hardee and Joseph E. Johnston.[2] It was a last call to duty, a final sacrifice for a failed nation—obligations more readily understood in the nineteenth century.

So Bentonville stands for something very sad from the Confederate point of view and quite glorious from the Union, and that should make for strong irony, I suppose. But one must be careful. Irony and metaphor can lead the historian down other paths. The task is to take basketfuls of yellowed paper and faded script and use these fragments of evidence to provide order and sense to things that seem irreconcilable and confused. What follows may sound authoritative, but the reader must remember it is only the historian's practiced voice. Any battle study is deficient, because history itself is deficient. What follows is only an effort to provide narrative structure to a chaotic event, clouded by time.

It helps, of course, to follow in the footsteps of others. Participants Wade Hampton and Henry Slocum wrote accounts of Bentonville, as did Jefferson C. Davis's chief of staff, Alexander C. McClurg, and many others. Forty years ago Jay Luvaas, current professor of military history at the Army War College, wrote a balanced and interpretative account for the *North Carolina Historical Review*. Then a college freshman, Erik France, fifteen years ago, created an intriguing war game entitled *Bentonville*. The essay France tucked beneath his make-believe pieces of cardboard is first-rate, a model of insight, of economy of language. More recently Weymouth T. "Hank" Jordan, Jr., compiler of the magnificent set of histories of the Confederate regiments of North Carolina, has prepared a brief but informative monograph about Bentonville.

The reader must know at the outset that a major problem confronts all Bentonville historians—where are the official reports of Hardee and Alexander Stewart and William Loring and Braxton Bragg and many others? Only a handful of Confederate official reports have been published; only a handful appear to have been written. This is discouraging and confounds attempts to present a balanced account and analysis.

On the other hand, perhaps the greatest joy in writing history is to meet people who share your interests and to make new friends. Luvaas and Jordan graciously gave me their time and encouragement. Hank Jordan, moreover, read the manuscript and offered a host of suggestions and pages of new information. He pointed out many items that required correction and others that needed rethinking.

Erik France took a special interest in my project and generously shared material. He read the entire manuscript and more than once guided me out of swamps. Indeed, his "tactical sketches" served as the basis for the maps appearing in this study.

John C. Goode, director of the Bentonville State Historic Site, walked the battlefield with me, spending hours attempting to orient me in the woods and fields alongside the wandering Goldsboro road. Goode directed me to new sources and read every chapter and answered every phone call.

No one knows the Bentonville battlefield better than Mark Bradley and Nancy S. King. Either Mark or Nancy could draw an outline of Edward Walthall's double trench line blindfolded. From the beginning they generously shared their knowledge. Nancy even splashed deep into a Bentonville swamp, sawed off a section of briar, and mailed it to me so I would know at firsthand what the soldiers meant when they used the term "impenetrable undergrowth." They both read the manuscript and made suggestions that substantially improved its credibility and readability.

I am indebted to those who aided me, particularly France, Goode, Bradley, King, and Jordan. They improved my work. Any errors of fact or interpretation, of course, are my sole responsibility.

Many other people contributed to this project, and without their help, kindness, and good humor my attempts would have been handicapped, if not totally frustrated. I wish to thank personally Gary J. Arnold, Ohio Historical Society, Columbus; Louise Arnold-Friend, U.S. Army Military History Institute Library, Carlisle, Pennsylvania; Dr. John G. Barrett, Lexington, Virginia; Solomon Breibart, Charleston, South Carolina; Dr. Norman D. Brown, University of Texas at Austin; William H. Brown, North Carolina State Archives, Raleigh; Dr. William P. Buck, Birmingham, Alabama; Virginia J. H. Cain, Woodruff Library, Emory University, Atlanta, Georgia; Becky Cape, Lilly Library, University of Indiana, Bloomington; Nan Card, Rutherford B. Hayes Presidential Center, Fremont, Ohio; Albert E. Castel III, Hillsdale, Michigan; Neal Coulter, Bill Prince, and Ray Hall, Lupton Library, University of Tennessee at Chattanooga; Robert S. Cox, William L. Clements Library, University of Michigan, Ann Arbor; Douglas R. Cubbison, Madison, Alabama; Richard Dalton, Davis Library, University of North Carolina, Chapel Hill; Phil Germann, Historical Society of Quincy and Adams County, Quincy, Illinois; Dr. Joseph T. Glatthaar, University of Houston, Houston, Texas; Dennis Kelly, Kennesaw Mountain National Park, Marietta, Georgia; Dr. Richard F. Knapp, Historic Sites Section, State of North Carolina; Brenda M. Lawson, Massachusetts Historical Society, Boston; Eileen McGrath, North Carolina Collection, Louis R. Wilson Library, University of North Carolina, Chapel Hill; A. Torrey McLean, North Carolina Department of Environment, Health, and Natural Resources, Raleigh; W. E. Meneray, Howard-Tilton Memorial Library, Tulane University, New Orleans, Louisiana; Harold L. Miller, State Historical Society of Wisconsin, Madison; Mark Moore, Raleigh, North Carolina; Ed Morris, North Carolina State Archives, Raleigh; Roy Morris, Chattanooga, Tennessee; Jim Ogden, Chickamauga and Chattanooga National Military Park, Fort Oglethorpe, Georgia; T. Michael Parrish, Austin, Texas; Susan Ravdin, Bowdoin College Library, Brunswick, Maine; E. Cheryl Schnirring, Illinois State Historical Library, Springfield; R. Hugh Simmons, Paoli, Pennsylvania; Dr. Richard J. Sommers, U.S. Army Military History Institute Library, Carlisle, Pennsylvania; Cindy Stewart, Western Historical Manuscript Collection, University of Missouri at Columbia; Gordon Whitney, Spring Hill, Florida; Mac Wyckoff, Virginia National Military Park, Fredericksburg; Dewitt Yingling, Little Rock, Arkansas; and Mel A. Young, Chattanooga, Tennessee.

For their role in making their material available and for assistance beyond the call of duty, I am grateful to the staffs of the Ohio Historical Society; the Southern Historical Collection, University of North Carolina, Chapel Hill; Manuscript Division, William R. Perkins Library, Duke University, Durham; Lupton Library, University of Chattanooga, Chattanooga, Tennessee; Indiana Historical Society, Indianapolis; Illinois State Historical Library, Springfield; U.S. Army Military History Institute, Carlisle, Pennsylvania; Indiana State Library, Indianapolis; and the North Carolina State Archives, Raleigh.

Author's Note

NOTHING DEMONSTRATES the inconclusiveness of written history more than turning up a critical document after you have put a subject to bed and pulled the covers up tight. Thus discovery, which should be the delight of inquiry, can become its dismay.

Recently, Terry L. Jones, the author of *Lee's Tigers*, offered to help me as I edited the prison letters of Maj. N. F. Cheairs, CSA. Jones is preparing a biography of Maj. Campbell Brown—who was a staff officer of Lt. Gen. Richard S. Ewell and a neighbor of Cheairs at home in Spring Hill, Tennessee—so he volunteered to check Brown's diary (George W. Campbell Papers, Library of Congress) for any references to Major Cheairs. In the process, he found an entry Brown had made in Charlottesville, Virginia, on January 26, 1866. Once I read it, I knew that the entry had to be included in my study of Bentonville, then already in press. It must be included both for the sake of completeness and because it affects some of my conclusions, particularly regarding the effectiveness of the Confederate cavalry preceding the battle.

Since it was too late to incorporate the gist of Brown's entry in my narrative by the time it came to my attention, I offer the text of the entry here, in full.

Gen. Johnston gave an account to Col. [Benjamin S.] Ewell & myself at Richmond last week, of the battle of Bentonville. Sherman was moving in two columns, by roads which Johnston's maps represented as twelve miles apart (really only three) at Bentonville. Hardee had encamped the second night before at a point represented as twelve miles from Bentonville—really twenty two. He was directed to join the Army of Tennessee at Bentonville that night. The order reached him at daylight, but he did not march till near noon, for some reason & his troops being from the coast of Carolina & unused to march, he did not get up till noon next day. Hampton had been directed to check the enemy so as to give time to deploy our lines, but not enough to make them come into line. But the mistake in distance & consequent delay of Hardee made it necessary to hold the enemy so hard that he formed his lines and the advantage of attacking the head of his column was lost.

The road here ran along one edge of a large plantation, most of which had been for some time uncultivated & had grown up in brush pine. At the farther side of this plantation from the point where Sherman's column entered it, a strip of a hundred acres had been in cultivation, next the woods. Here Gen. Johnston took his position with the road on his right flank and his line formed so that as it advanced it would gradually cross the road & drive the enemy into the woods—thus: Hardee was on the left—Bragg on the right with his flank in the woods beyond the road, and swampy ground in its front. The enemy came up and formed three lines—one in the open field, a second in the brush pine and a third at the farther edge of the field, in the woods. They overlapped our line and it became necessary to delay while Hardee extended to his left so as to get on their flank. When this was done the line advanced. The enemy's first line was broken, and driven into their second which was entrenched half a mile in rear. Our line advanced in as much order as could be kept, moving deliberately and when they came near the enemy's works, Hardee, being afraid that the experience of the Tennessee Army might make them shy of charging works, rode to the front and *led* them on. They went over the second line without a check, and on nearing the third line found the enemy had formed in front of their works to meet them. This line was driven into its works also, and then Hardee, being afraid that he might be repulsed if he attacked in disorder[,] halted to reform. Meanwhile Bragg had been repulsed & Hardee could go no further.

Gen. Hoke afterwards told Gen. Johnston that finding the enemy entrenched beyond a marshy piece of ground in his front, he had moved round to the right so as to take them in flank and was about to attack, when Gen. Bragg found it out, ordered him back to his first position & made him go square up in front against the enemy's works. Gen. Johnston remarked that it was a great mistake to have two commanders (Bragg & Hoke) for one divn., but added as he had come into Bragg's Dept. & taken command there he did not feel that he had a right to relieve him from command. Col. E. said Bragg was unfit to handle troops in the field at any rate. To this Gen. Jn. assented.

The Cavalry was to have attacked the enemy's right rear, but got on the opposite side of a creek from it and never got into the fight at all.

I told Gen. Johnston of the surprise Gen. [Albert Milton] Barney had expressed at Wade Hampton's not doing more with his Cavalry. He [Johnston] said he did not think there had been any genius shown in the handling of our Cavalry—that being on several roads confronting Sherman's advance guard they never seemed to think when they would make a fight on one road of bringing reinforcements from another—but rather seemed to regard each body of troops as fixed to its own road. Jeb Stuart had been greatly abused, but he had never seen any one he considered his [Stuart's] equal in our Cavalry service. I asked if Forrest were not superior to him. He said Forrest could do more with bad material than any one else, but he did not make soldiers—he had fought without them better than could have been expected.

It had been his [Johnston's] intention to fall back immediately after the battle, but having a good many dead & wounded, he staid [*sic*] to bury the dead & care for the hurt. Meanwhile a creek in his rear, usually fordable, got up &, if Sherman had shown boldness, he would have been in a good deal of trouble. But the latter held off, & was very cautious.

Bentonville

1

Sherman's Web Footted Boys in Blew

SHERMAN LOOKED AHEAD—always. When he made the grand gesture of presenting Savannah, Georgia, to Abraham Lincoln as a Christmas gift on December 22, 1864, Sherman knew well that his next operation could be as important—really more important—than his spectacular March to the Sea. Gen. Ulysses S. Grant, supreme commander-in-chief of all Union armies, wanted to unite their two armies quickly and overwhelm Gen. Robert E. Lee's Army of Northern Virginia. He had thought that this could be done most efficiently by transporting Sherman's 60,000 men to Virginia by sea. The startling news of George H. Thomas's magnificent victory over John Bell Hood at Nashville, however, "has shaken me in that opinion," Grant wrote. Perhaps Sherman could accomplish more by remaining "where you are than if brought here, especially as I am informed . . . that it would take about two months to get you here, with all the other calls there are for ocean transportation." Sherman agreed, in part. Shipping the army by sea "will cost more delay than you anticipate," he wrote. Moreover, such a movement might "very much disturb the unity and *morale* of my army, now so perfect."[1]

As an alternative, Sherman proposed to Grant that he might cut loose from his base at Savannah and smash through the heart of the Carolinas, supplying his army from the countryside. Let me "succeed here," Sherman appealed. "I do sincerely believe that the whole United States, North and South, would rejoice to have this army turned loose on South Carolina, to devastate that State in the manner we have done in Georgia, and it would have a direct and immediate bearing on your campaign in Virginia."[2] Simultaneously Sherman wrote Army Chief of Staff Henry W. Halleck, "I think the time has come now when we could attempt the boldest moves, and my experience is, that they are easier of execution than more timid ones, because the enemy is disconcerted by them."[3]

On January 2, 1865, Grant, influenced heavily by the virtual destruction of Hood's Army of Tennessee at Nashville, approved Sherman's plan—his trusted lieutenant might proceed with his campaign through the Carolinas. Sherman was jubilant. "I feel confident," he assured Grant, "that I can break up the whole railroad system of South Carolina and North Carolina, and be on the Roanoke [River], either at Raleigh or Weldon, by the time spring fairly opens."[4]

Using the month of January 1865 to refit and reposition his army, Sherman turned over Savannah to Gen. John G. Foster and faced north. Grant, wishing to assist Sherman in any possible way, ordered a second major effort to reduce Fort Fisher and Wilmington—this time the attack would be led by the able Maj. Gen. Alfred H. Terry.[5] As additional insurance for the success of Sherman's venture, Grant ordered Maj. Gen. John M. Schofield and 21,000 men from Tennessee, sending them by rail and boat via Cincinnati, Ohio, and Annapolis, Maryland, to the North Carolina coast. Both Terry (at Wilmington) and Schofield (at New Bern) were to be placed under Sherman's command.[6] Now Sherman could move directly through the Carolinas knowing that heavy infantry support would be near at hand. He knew too that the massive element of maneuver represented by the coastal forces of Schofield and Terry would complicate drastically any Confederate combinations to oppose him. Indeed, Sherman's secret operational scheme was to move north from Savannah and seize Columbia, South Carolina. From Columbia he would angle northeast to destroy the arsenal at Fayetteville, North Carolina. Then, as quickly as possible, he would link up with Schofield and Terry at Goldsboro, North Carolina. Goldsboro would provide an excellent base of communications. It was connected by rail to Wilmington and New Bern, from which Terry and Schofield, respectively, would be en route.[7] Also, it was within striking distance of the capital of North Carolina (Raleigh). The Wilmington and Weldon Railroad, furthermore, ran north from Goldsboro to Petersburg, providing the most expeditious route for Sherman if he were to attempt direct support for Grant's army besieging Richmond. Options abounded.

From Savannah to Goldsboro would be a journey of 425 miles through enemy country, a land of legendary swamps and rivers "swollen and spread into lakes by winter floods." Sherman knew that his men could succeed and believed that the campaign would take only six weeks. He told Grant: "I would undertake at one stride to make Goldsborough, and open communication with the sea by the New Bern railroad, and had ordered Col. W. W. Wright, superintendent of military railroads, to proceed in advance to New

Bern, and to be prepared to extend the railroad out from New Berne to Goldsborough by the 15th of March."[8]

Sherman's march through South Carolina in February 1865, although beset with difficulties and fraught with risk, succeeded in textbook fashion. The skill and ease of his accomplishment thrilled his admirers and appalled his enemies. To this day it remains a model campaign, a masterpiece of indirection. Lt. Gen. William J. Hardee, the veteran Confederate commander at Charleston, later admitted that when he "learned that Sherman's army was marching through the Salkehatchie swamp, making its own corduroy roads at the rate of a dozen miles a day or more, and bringing its artillery and wagons with it, I made up my mind that there had been no such army in existence since the days of Julius Caesar."[9]

With lightning speed Sherman pushed north from Savannah—one wing of his army threatening Augusta, Georgia, the other Charleston, South Carolina. The confused Confederates attempted to defend both points, fatally dividing their scant resources. But Sherman bypassed both objectives and interposed his army between the two enemy forces. Not allowing the Confederates time to concentrate, Sherman captured Columbia, the capital of South Carolina, on February 17, then turned his army east toward Cheraw, South Carolina. The outmaneuvered Confederates lost the advantage of internal lines of communication. Hardee abandoned Charleston, intending to march its garrison north to Wilmington, thence by train west to Greensboro, North Carolina. Hardee's plans and hopes were shattered, however, when the combined Union forces of Schofield and Terry captured Wilmington on February 22, 1865. Fearing encirclement Hardee changed route and raced toward Cheraw himself, entering the city just ahead of Sherman. The Confederates attempted to defend Cheraw, quickly constructing a "remarkably strong bridge-head for artillery and infantry." It was to no avail. Leading elements of Sherman's Seventeenth Army Corps under an audacious division commander, Maj. Gen. Joseph A. Mower, pressed hard against Cheraw's defenses. When Hardee learned that the Left Wing of Sherman's army had entered Chesterfield, South Carolina, and crossed Thompson's Creek, he knew that he was outflanked and Cheraw was lost. He abandoned the city on March 3.[10] Sherman pushed on relentlessly, through Cheraw, across the Pee Dee River, and into the state of North Carolina.[11]

North Carolina would be treated differently, Sherman promised. "It may be of political consequence to us." Moderation would be the watchword. Foraging would be forbidden, and the people of North Carolina would be paid for supplies required by the army. Maj. Gen. Oliver O. Howard, commanding Sherman's Right Wing, had been distressed over the outrages of the soldiers in South Carolina and went so far as to dismount most of his foragers.[12] Maj. Gen. Henry W. Slocum, Left Wing commander, issued an order to his men reminding them "that the State of North Carolina was one of the last States that passed the ordinance of secession, and that from the commencement of the war there has been in this State a strong Union party." Furthermore, Slocum admonished his troops, "it should not be assumed that the inhabitants are enemies to our Government, and it is to be hoped that every effort will be made to prevent any wanton destruction of property, or any unkind treatment of citizens."[13]

North Carolina greeted the invading army with rain, torrents of rain. It began to fall on March 9, the day after the Federals stepped over the state line. "The earth seemed to melt beneath our feet," complained brigade commander Benjamin D. Fearing. "After a few wagons had passed over [the road,] the whole bottom seemed to give out, and in places, if wagons left the roadway, they sank to the wagon body in the quicksand." The rain grew heavier and "destroyed what little of the road was left." Officers and men worked through the night in "mud from one to three feet deep." They had no choice but to corduroy the roads as they went, gathering fence rails, cutting small trees, and arranging them crosswise in layers over the roadbed, "but what was particularly discouraging, our corduroy of rails or poles would itself sink down and necessitate a reconstruction."[14]

Sherman's men, of course, took enormous pride in their arduous trek. Division commander John W. Geary spoke for many: "upon the mud and swamps the people of South Carolina depended mostly for its defence, but Yankee ingenuity and stout arms have accomplished what Southern impudence and imbecility pronounced *impossible*."[15]

The disorganized and numerically weak Confederates, on the other hand, seemed unable to use the mud and slush to their advantage. They continued to fall back before Sherman's advance, allowing the leading elements of the Federal army to enter Fayetteville unopposed on Saturday, March 11. To Sherman's surprise, Hardee did not attempt to defend the city. Instead, he retreated across the Cape Fear River and burned the bridge behind him. It proved a nuisance to the pursuing enemy, nothing more. Federal gains, on the other hand, proved significant. Sherman's rapid approach denied the rebels the opportunity to save the cache of war material assembled in the old Federal arsenal.[16]

Once Sherman had secured Fayetteville and driven the Confederates from the northern bank of the Cape Fear, he set his engineers to work, destroying "the vast amount of machinery which had formerly belonged to the old Harper's Ferry U.S. Arsenal." Then all buildings—machine shops and foundries—were knocked down and burned under the careful eye of Col. Orlando M. Poe, Sherman's chief engineer.[17]

While work details systematically wrecked the arsenal, Sherman rested most of his men. Early Sunday morning, March 12—almost as if a homecoming gift from Uncle Billy himself—a shrill whistle startled the Union troops. They rushed to the bank of the Cape Fear. From there they saw the army tug *Davidson* steaming upriver. Piled high on its decks were sacks of mail and newspapers for which they hungered. They greeted the tug with cheers. After six weeks in the wilderness they were once again in communication with a friendly world. During the next two days more transports arrived at Fayetteville bringing sugar, coffee, oats, shoes—but no clothing. A nearby gristmill was put in working order, and foragers quickly gathered corn to grind. For two nights by torch light the old wheel creaked and groaned, providing bread substitute for the next leg of the march. While at Fayetteville Sherman inspected his army thoroughly, "weeding out" the sick, the injured, those who could not keep up. They numbered only 300, however.[18] Once these troops had embarked on boats for Wilmington, Sherman turned his attention to the crowds of refugees and freed slaves following the army (General Howard estimated 4,500 with his wing alone).[19] Sherman directed that they also be loaded aboard.[20]

Truly a magnificent army remained in Fayetteville—"Sherman's web footted boys in blew" (as Lorenzo N. Pratt, Battery M, 1st New York Light Artillery, proudly characterized them).[21] This was arguably the finest army (Union or Confederate) assembled during the Civil War. Sherman already had screened it twice—first in Atlanta, before the March to the Sea, and again in Savannah. Astonishingly few physically unfit men had to be removed.[22] On March 15, 1865, Sherman had approximately 60,000 infantry and artillery divided into two wings, each composed of two corps of 13,000 men. The artillery consisted of sixteen field batteries—sixty-eight guns, equally divided between twelve-pounder Napoleons and three-inch rifled cannon.[23] Although they traveled as lightly as they dared, Sherman's two columns required some 2,500 supply and ordnance wagons and about 600 ambulances. Six mules drew each wagon, six horses each gun. Maj. Gen. Judson Kilpatrick's 4,400 cavalrymen escorted the expeditionary force into North Carolina.[24]

Sherman's Right Wing was commanded by Maj. Gen. Oliver Otis Howard, a soldier of vast experience commonly known then and since as "the Christian soldier." Howard was unquestionably loyal to Sherman and was respected universally for his integrity, his courage, and his unflagging attention to duty. Howard's corps commanders were good soldiers. Combative, magnetic John A. Logan led the Fifteenth Army Corps. His choice for their corps emblem was simple, direct, and businesslike: the cartridge box. The passionate true believer, Maj. Gen. Francis "Frank" Preston Blair, Jr., commanded the Seventeenth Army Corps. Blair was a devoted friend of Sherman's, a member of a powerful political family, and the man many credited for holding Missouri in the Union. Blair had selected for his corps' badge the arrow—for "its swiftness, in striking where wanted, and in its destructive power when so intended." His men often fashioned these arrows from silver spoons and wove them on their hats. One did not ask where they procured the spoons.[25]

Sherman knew well that between Logan and Blair "there existed a natural rivalry. Both were men of great experience, courage, and talent. Both were politicians by nature and experience." Both were proven combat commanders. They could lead men—even inspire them—and they were known as aggressive field commanders, quick to attack or counterattack. Representing the best of the "civilian generals," neither had much use for West Pointers. This, of course, posed a problem for Howard, but Howard was a professional soldier and an "old army man" to the marrow of his bones. He could manage these outspoken, independent, strong-willed subordinates if anyone could. He demanded their best and cared less for their opinion of him than the results of their work. Sherman was "never disappointed with Howard."[26]

The heart of Howard's Right Wing was the Army of the Tennessee, once the pride of James B. McPherson. Composed of the Fifteenth and Seventeenth Corps, the Army of the Tennessee was a veteran western army.[27] The 31st Illinois and the 7th Iowa regiments, for instance, had fought at Belmont in November 1861 and had continued through the trials and triumphs of four years of hard marching and fighting. Some of Howard's men had followed Grant from Fort Donelson to Shiloh to Vicksburg to Missionary Ridge; others had accompanied Sherman from Shiloh to Chickasaw Bluffs to Atlanta. The Fifteenth and Seventeenth Corps had confronted the Confederate Army of Tennessee on many fields but had missed out on the dazzling Union victories at Franklin and Nashville. They still had a score to settle with the boys of A. P. Stewart and Hardee and Johnston.

The Left Wing was different. Its commander, Maj. Gen. Henry Warner Slocum, was different. There was "something independent, even perverse, about him. He wore only a mustache in an army that decreed whiskers."[28] This thirty-eight-year-old New Yorker had taken charge of a country school at age sixteen. According to his friend Howard, Slocum then and there had displayed traits that he made a habit—"self-control, just dealing, constant patience and unquestioned example."[29] In 1848 Slocum entered West Point where he excelled. Phil Sheridan would remark gratefully: "Good fortune gave me for a room-mate a cadet whose studious habits and willingness to aid others benefited me immensely." Howard, an underclassman who roomed on the floor below, observed Slocum carefully: "His individuality especially impressed itself upon me. He expressed himself openly, when it cost so much to do so, as an opponent of human slavery."[30]

Slocum became an artillery officer upon graduation but soon was stifled by repetitive garrison routine at Fort Moultrie, South Carolina, so "he kept his active mind occupied by reading law." He resigned from the army in 1856 and became an attorney in Syracuse. He also served as county treasurer, state legislator, and instructor in artillery for the New York militia. An early and active member of the Republican Party, Slocum volunteered for service in the spring of 1861 and quickly won appointment as colonel of the 27th New York Volunteer Infantry. He organized and trained his regiment as best he could before leading it south to Virginia. In the opening battle at Bull Run he placed himself at the head of his men and while leading a charge was shot down. When Slocum's thigh wound healed and he had returned to duty, the War Department promoted him to brigade, then division command. His good work at Second Manassas, South Mountain, and Antietam soon won him corps command. He handled his men with high competence at Chancellorsville, though he publicly denounced army commander Joseph Hooker, whose poor judgment, Slocum believed, had cost the Union victory and the lives of many good men. At Gettysburg two months later Slocum played a major role, his name becoming synonymous with the critical fight at Culp's Hill.

Slocum's Twelfth Corps and Howard's Eleventh were sent west in the early fall of 1863 to offset the transfer of James Longstreet's corps from the Army of Northern Virginia. To his dismay, Slocum discovered that they were to be commanded once again by Joseph Hooker. Thereupon Slocum resigned. President Lincoln saved the situation by pocketing the resignation and reassigning Slocum to the District of Vicksburg.

Slocum's and Howard's corps then were consolidated into the Twentieth

Henry Warner Slocum
(U.S. Army Military History Institute, Carlisle, Pennsylvania)

Corps under Hooker, and Howard was assigned command of the Fourth Corps. On the death of James B. McPherson the next summer, Sherman chose Howard—not Hooker—to head the Army of the Tennessee. Hooker lacked "the moral qualities that I want—not those adequate to the command," Sherman explained. Howard's appointment angered Hooker, and he resigned command of the Twentieth Corps, expecting Logan and many of his friends to support him. Sherman stood firm and Logan held his tongue. Sherman "unhesitatingly nominated" Slocum to replace Hooker as Twentieth Corps commander in Howard's Army of the Tennessee.[31]

The Twentieth Corps was the first to enter Atlanta on September 2, 1864, and it was Slocum who wired Washington that day, "General Sherman has taken Atlanta." Sherman promoted Slocum to wing commander for the March to the Sea, and Slocum repaid Sherman's "strong confidence" by proving reliable. His officers and men considered him a "thoroughly accomplished soldier," a "well-chosen leader, brave and cool, faithful and impartial." If he disagreed, as he did occasionally with his friends Sherman and Howard, Slocum would "tell you to your face." He was no gossip. And the "Joe Hooker wars" notwithstanding, Slocum was a team player. Sherman appreciated that.[32]

There was no question about Slocum's sharp tongue, though. He could lash a subordinate, even a private, for inattention to duty and appear quite haughty in the process. Yet when it suited him, he could be as discreet as a defense counsel. Once when questioning a rebel prisoner about Wade Hampton, he listened to the rebel portray Hampton as a dandy, "one of those fellows from West Point." Of course, Slocum knew Hampton had never seen the inside of West Point, but he played the rebel's game, remarking to the effect that "some of the West Pointers did not know enough to straddle a horse."[33]

George W. Nichols of Sherman's staff described Slocum as having a keen sense of order and discipline, and as being proud that he was a New Yorker. "His personal appearance," wrote Nichols, "is prepossessing. Long, wavy brown hair, bushed back behind his ears, sparkling brown eyes, a heavy brown mustache, a height above the medium, and a manner which inspires faith and confidence. . . . He seems to know precisely what he has to do, and to be perfectly sure he can do it. It is very certain that he is one of those rare men who has made few if any mistakes." Critics, such as Maj. Thomas W. Osborn of Howard's staff, noted Slocum's insufferable fixation with dignity. He would not brook undue familiarity. Indeed, he once court-martialed a man who tried. "I have always since Gettysburg had a strong prejudice against him," confessed Osborn. "His peculiarities are unpleasant, and one is not apt to reform his prejudices in favor of an unpleasant man."[34]

Nevertheless, the innovative, energetic, and "quietly competent" Henry Slocum, "in the commanding general's eyes, was 'one of the best soldiers and best men that ever lived.' [Sherman] would not hear a word against him." The Left Wing, almost to the man, agreed. Ole Sloky, they said, knew his business.[35]

Slocum's Left Wing consisted of the Twentieth and the Fourteenth Army Corps.[36] The Twentieth consisted of seasoned troops who had fought in the Shenandoah against Stonewall Jackson and at Antietam, Chancellorsville, and Gettysburg, as well as Lookout Mountain, Missionary Ridge, and the arduous Atlanta Campaign. The Twentieth Army Corps took pride in its emblem, the "bloody five-pointed star," the badge of Slocum's old Twentieth Corps.

They were easterners though, an oddity in a western army. Their brother Fourteenth Army Corps dubbed the Twentieth "kid gloves and paper collars" because of its spick-and-span ways, its proficiency at drill, and its "Potomac airs." It was a "sharp-looking, superbly disciplined body of troops, with excellent fighting skills and a high morale."[37] It did not seem to get along with the other three corps in Sherman's army. Maybe it was because the men were easterners, or better educated, or better dressed. "Jealousy is at the foot of the whole," one soldier asserted dryly. But it was unmistakably serious bias. Already on this march from Savannah a member of the Twentieth had been shot and killed rather than be arrested by a member of the Fourteenth. One wondered if the Twentieth would rush to the assistance of any other corps, particularly the Fourteenth, in the event of a real fight.[38]

Leading the Twentieth Army Corps was Alpheus Starkey Williams, a well-educated, gentlemanly officer, long associated with Henry Slocum. Once a newspaper editor and publisher, the forty-four-year-old Williams was popular with his troops and had been a competent division commander, though probably not aggressive enough for Sherman's taste. Sherman, while characterized and criticized as being cautious in battle himself, preferred risk-taking fighters as subordinates. Williams suited Slocum, though. Williams in later years would smile ironically, realizing that his enduring fame as a Civil War officer resulted not so much as having been the commander of the elite Twentieth, but as having been the general to whom was brought Lee's Special Order 191, found wrapped around three cigars.[39]

The brother corps of the Twentieth was the Fourteenth, a conglomerate outfit that suffered in comparison. The easterners looked askance at the Fourteenth—notorious for its laxity, flaunting "an air of independence hardly consistent with the nicest discipline."[40] No corps in the Federal army, however, had such a breadth of fighting experience. Some troops in the Fourteenth had been at Bull Run and the Seven Days.[41] Men of the 17th New York (those fellows who wore the red turbans)[42] could brag about that. Others had started out in Missouri, fighting at Wilson's Creek, then crossing the Mississippi to build zig-zag trenches and defy rebel sharpshooters around Corinth. Following Perryville and the bloody combat of Murfreesboro, the Fourteenth had served as "the nucleus from which the Army of the Cumberland was reorganized in early 1863."[43] These men, whose corps badge was the acorn, stood obstinately beside George Thomas at Snodgrass Hill during Chickamauga. They were conspicuous for their gallantry at Missionary Ridge and a division of the Fourteenth Army Corps threw themselves with a fury against the Confederates at Kennesaw Mountain. At Jonesboro early that fall they nearly bagged Hardee and his corps. This was George Thomas's prized Fourteenth that he had organized and led at Chickamauga. It bore the spirit of the legendary Dan McCook, the gallant brigade commander Sherman had chosen to accomplish the impossible at Kennesaw. Fighters—the men of this Fourteenth—that was their indisputable reputation, and now they fought under a wild man, Brig. Gen. Jefferson C. Davis.

Strange bedfellows were the volcanic Davis and the imperturbable Williams. But, then, the Left Wing itself was a strange phenomenon. These troops longed for Confederates to fight. Failing that, they were perfectly willing to fight a brother corps, and failing that to fight among themselves, which they did.[44]

It was a great army Sherman commanded—experienced ("more experienced than any other Federal command," maintains Joseph Glatthaar), with high morale and exceptionally strong leadership at the company and regimental levels and in its senior officers as well. Although swamps had rotted their shoes, briars had shredded their uniforms, and pine-knot fires had blackened their faces, their rifles were clean and their cartridge boxes full. They had brushed aside rebels in every engagement since Atlanta. Nothing was going to stop them now. As Cpl. Leander E. Davis of Battery M, 1st New York Light Artillery, put it, the rebels had better get out of the way, "for old Billy Sherman must go through when he starts." "We have the grandest army in the world," echoed Lt. Henry Wright, 6th Iowa, "and the greatest

Military Chieftain at the head of it. Sherman . . . don't know the word impossible. There is nothing he can't do."[45]

Sherman planned to use great care on this last leg of the journey to Goldsboro, at least he said so. He had learned that his old adversary, Joseph E. Johnston, had been reappointed to command.[46] Sherman expected a fight, or said that he did. He wrote home on March 12, "Johnston is restored to the supreme command and will unite the forces hitherto scattered and fight me about Raleigh or Goldsboro."[47] On the same day he notified Alfred Terry: "We must not give time for Jos. Johnston to concentrate at Goldsboro'. We cannot prevent his concentrating at Raleigh, but he shall have no rest . . . every day now is worth a million of dollars. I can whip Jos. Johnston provided he does not catch one of my corps in flank, and I will see that the army marches hence to Goldsboro' in compact form." Sherman told Schofield and Terry that he expected to meet them there on March 20.[48]

Three days later, however, Sherman's actions began to contradict his words. His orders emphasized speed and deception rather than compactness. Sherman directed Slocum with four "light" divisions to march from Fayetteville on the plank road toward Raleigh, almost to Averasboro. At that point they would turn east and proceed via Bentonville toward Goldsboro, crossing the Neuse River at Cox's Bridge. In the event that Johnston attempted to defend Goldsboro, this movement would bring Slocum's wing hard against the Confederate right flank, in position to attack the city from the west. While Slocum's infantry would be maneuvering to form a great infantry screen to the north, Howard, with Logan's Fifteenth Army Corps, would cross the Cape Fear three miles below and take a road south of Slocum's. Logan's four "unencumbered" divisions would march roughly parallel to Slocum and would be within supporting distance of his light column.[49] Howard's route led through Beaman's Crossroads to Everettsville. Thus, the Right Wing would be approaching Goldsboro from the south, prepared to force a crossing of the Neuse and attack any enemy force in the town. With Slocum north of the Neuse advancing from the west, Howard attacking from the south, and Schofield and Terry closing in from the east and southeast, Johnston would find it impossible to defend Goldsboro against Sherman's 90,000 troops.

In the meantime, until this combination could be effected, Sherman intended for Slocum's immense and vulnerable wagon train to follow behind Howard and the unencumbered Fifteenth Army Corps to be protected by

Sherman and his generals. *From left to right:* Oliver O. Howard, John A. Logan, William B. Hazen, William T. Sherman, Jefferson C. Davis, Henry W. Slocum, and Joseph Mower. (U.S. Army Military History Institute, Carlisle, Pennsylvania)

two infantry divisions. The trains of the Right Wing, including Logan's unnecessary wagons, would be escorted by the Seventeenth Corps. This third route, still farther south, followed the Fayetteville–Clinton–Mount Olive–Goldsboro road.

Sherman's army was to be spread widely, dangerously so. But in fairness to Sherman, the wretched state of the roads almost dictated such a course of action if he were to reach Goldsboro expeditiously. Compactness must be sacrificed. The essential ordnance, supply, and headquarters wagons of even one division could churn up a road so badly and so quickly as to make it almost "impassable" for units following.[50]

This was not, however, simply the cross-country movement of the army from Fayetteville to Goldsboro. Sherman also intended, at least on the night of March 14, a deceptive offensive thrust—a raid in force—to confound Johnston by snapping rebel communications north of Smithfield. This sharp punch north would interfere with any attempt by Johnston to rapidly concentrate either at Goldsboro or against Sherman's exposed left flank as he audaciously wheeled to the right toward Goldsboro across

Johnston's front. Kilpatrick's cavalry, reinforced by a single infantry division (to be supplied by Slocum), would be Sherman's instrument. Thus, in effect, Slocum's movement to Bentonville was to establish a staging area for his four light infantry divisions.[51] From that point they could support Kilpatrick's swift hit-and-run attack on the North Carolina Railroad, breaking it between the south side of the Neuse and Eureka, probably near Elevation (where Kilpatrick's cavalry planned to rendezvous), or they could turn east and hurry to Goldsboro.[52]

By nightfall, March 14, both wings were across the Cape Fear. At dawn on the fifteenth they set out "stripped for battle." Kilpatrick's cavalry headed up the bank of the Cape Fear on the plank road for Raleigh. Slocum's light divisions followed. They halted for the night about ten miles out at Kyle's Landing on Silver Run. Three miles beyond this point Kilpatrick began skirmishing with enemy infantry and requested Sherman to send forward a brigade to help him hold the position at Taylor's Hole Creek. Also on March 15 the Right Wing struggled to reach South River. Frank Blair's Seventeenth Corps arrived at its objective late in the afternoon and managed to secure the crossing by sending one division across, driving before it a regiment of Confederate cavalry.

The entire movement that day by both wings had been sluggish. In the morning, as if on cue, the skies clouded over and the rain began to pour. The "roads, already bad enough, became horrible." Rain and mud, not rebels, slowed the march to a crawl. Good news came from the seaboard, however. Schofield had crossed the Neuse and occupied Kinston without opposition on March 14, and Terry had begun his advance from Wilmington to Goldsboro.[53] Things were converging nicely.[54]

Union soldiers passed a miserable night. Benjamin F. Hunter of the 79th Ohio remembered: "It had been raining hard and the whole surface of the wet ground was covered with water. I cut brush and laid my tired limbs and frail body down to pass the night and try to sleep and shook until half-past 4 . . . when the bugles sounded reveille."[55]

During the night of March 15 Sherman learned from Kilpatrick's scouts that Hardee had blocked the road to Averasboro at a narrow piece of swampy land between the Cape Fear and Black Rivers where the road branched off to Goldsboro. Sherman ordered Slocum to have Kilpatrick and the Twentieth Corps drive Hardee beyond Averasboro. The fighting began early. The divisions of Kentucky's William T. Ward and Maine's Nathaniel J. Jackson uncovered Hardee's first line, "turned it handsomely," and drove the routed Confederates back upon a second line which also yielded. At a third line, however, resistance stiffened unexpectedly, and several attacks by Slocum's troops were repulsed. When night fell Hardee still held the ground, and Slocum's troops pulled back, regrouped, and camped for the night.[56]

Another miserable night followed. Strong gusts of wind blew down shelter halves, and the pelting rain continued. But at dawn on the seventeenth came good news—pickets and skirmishers reported Hardee's lines abandoned. The rebels were gone. Kilpatrick set out in pursuit, and his men found them across Black River retreating northeast on the road leading toward Smithfield.[57]

Slocum sent William T. Ward's division (Third) of the Twentieth Corps forward as far as Averasboro itself. There Ward halted, holding the important junction of the roads leading to Raleigh and Smithfield and covering passage of the infantry columns, the trains, and the wounded by interior roads. To deceive Hardee, Ward kept up "a show of pursuit." Slocum hoped that Hardee would interpret this as the advance of a mighty push toward Raleigh. Meanwhile, the remainder of Williams's Twentieth Corps buried the dead and tended the wounded of Averasboro. Although they found and buried over a hundred rebels, the Left Wing itself had suffered about 700 casualties including 477 wounded. The wounded were placed in ambulances and supply wagons and started down an interior road toward Goldsboro. The men suffered terribly, and officers sought to find routes that might minimize the jolting and pitching of the wagons. It was futile. Nearly every mile of road was corduroyed and every circle of a wheel meant eight bumps, if the wagon stayed on the corduroy. "If a wagon drops off . . . , it drops to the hub." "You can hear the wounded groan and yell out going over the rough places. I saw Comrade Nurse several times during the day[.] He said his foot and toes hurt him, his foot was off and it was just the nerves. The wounded had a hard time of it."[58]

While Ward's division, Twentieth Army Corps, pressed Hardee's rear guard through Averasboro and conducted the feint toward Raleigh, the Fourteenth Corps continued to the right or east down the main road that led past Bentonville to Goldsboro. At Black River,[59] Jefferson C. Davis halted his Fourteenth Corps (the advance of the Left Wing) for over three hours while pioneers bridged the swollen stream. Once across Davis proceeded, "wallowing along," until he reached Mingo Creek. There he encamped at dusk on the west bank. March 17 had been another wearisome tramp with only eight miles covered. Furthermore, the number of rebels seen all along the route had increased hourly. They had "disputed every inch of ground."[60]

Nonetheless, it was St. Patrick's Day. The rain had stopped. A drummer boy in the 2d Minnesota might gripe to his diary that the band had played nothing all day but "St. Patrick's Day in the Morning," but spirits in the ranks were soaring despite the mud and slush. General Williams of the Twentieth Corps and his men noticed the first blooming peach trees. It was a good sign. Spring was close by.[61]

Averasboro changed Sherman's thinking. He inferred from Hardee's violent rear guard action that Johnston wanted to buy time to concentrate his scattered troops to defend Raleigh. "The direction of Hardee's retreat strengthened this deduction, as did Sherman's knowledge of Johnston's character" and the faulty intelligence fed him by Kilpatrick. It appeared from the maps that the rebels "had burned the bridges over what was supposed to be the only avenue [from Averasboro] to Bentonville and Smithfield, leading us most naturally to suppose that they had fallen back to Raleigh."[62]

Both Sherman and Johnston were unaware that the 1833 and 1857 (in Sherman's case) North Carolina maps they used "vied with one another in inaccuracy." Moreover, Sherman had lost his chief topographer, Captain John Rziha, who had guided the army through Georgia but who left when it reached Savannah. In Columbia, South Carolina, another dependable Sherman guide, William R. Bergholz, dropped out of the march.[63] The maps did not reveal any route by which Hardee, once he had passed through Averasboro and taken the road to Smithfield, might leave that road and double back to Bentonville.[64]

The deduction that Hardee (and thus Johnston) were abandoning the area south of the Neuse to Sherman seemed confirmed by the trusted Federal scout, Capt. William Duncan, who reported Hardee retreating on Smithfield, "creating the impression that the road to Goldsboro was unobstructed" for the Union columns. Johnston "will call in all minor posts, which embraces [sic] Goldsborough," Sherman wrote Howard. "You may, therefore, move straight for Goldsborough, leaving Slocum the river road." Kilpatrick's strike against Johnston's rail communications also was abandoned. It was unnecessary. Johnston appeared to have made them a gift of Goldsboro.[65]

Sherman eagerly embraced the reasoning that Johnston would stay north

of the Neuse River. He believed that Johnston would content himself collect-
ing his "old Georgia army" and taking up his customary defensive posture,
this time before the North Carolina capital. Now Sherman could open up
his columns, spread them out, utilize more roads—and sprint. The weather
cooperated and supported Sherman's reasoning: skies brightened and
promised greater speed of movement. The wounded accompanying Slocum's wing nevertheless troubled Sherman. He wanted an end to that
unnecessary agony. His able-bodied men, moreover, needed supplies and
rest—soon. He had promised them that. He was within an easy two-day
march of his campaign objective—Goldsboro. Perhaps Schofield might
even be there by now. A glorious conclusion to all his efforts shone only a
short distance away—communication with the sea and home and Grant.
Everything seems to have stoked his confidence. Risk seemed minimal.[66]

James D. Morgan's division (Second), Fourteenth Army Corps, took the
advance for the Left Wing at 5:30 A.M. on Saturday the eighteenth. Federal
foragers repeatedly had to drive annoying rebel cavalry from their front.
Each of these small encounters slowed the march. About six miles out the
Goldsboro road, in the vicinity of Bushy Swamp, foragers engaged a more
formidable body of rebels—a brigade of cavalry supported by a section of
artillery, reportedly Wade Hampton's men. Once the head of Morgan's
column appeared, the foragers broke off the action and took their places in
the infantry lines. Morgan quickly changed column into line of battle and
advanced two brigades.[67] The Confederate cavalry retreated. As Morgan
and Fourteenth Army Corps commander Davis observed the action, Sherman rode up, talked with both officers, watched for a while, then "directed
Morgan to halt his command until the rear could close up." While they
waited, other foragers rode in and reported to their friends in the ranks.
They had found something besides rebel cavalry—"some apple *Jack*." Pvt.
Nelson Purdum, 33d Ohio, penciled in his diary that he received his share
and "got *tight*."[68]

Behind Morgan's command, William P. Carlin's division (First) of the
Fourteenth Corps and the two "light" divisions of the Twentieth Corps
struggled to keep up. The pontoon bridge over Black River had broken
loose, then come apart again; repair consumed two hours. Most of the
infantry waded across, waist deep. Mingo Creek also proved an obstacle,
not to speak of the roads themselves—so cut up that "we were obliged to

corduroy almost the entire distance." With incredible labor the two light divisions (Jackson's and Ward's) of Williams's Twentieth Corps managed to cover twelve miles.[69]

"There were occasional showers of rain," General Carlin recalled, "relieved by a bright spring sunshine." The troops passed small cabins surrounded by women and children. "At or near all these cabins mounted men were seen either watching the troops on the road, passing up toward the head of the column, or working through the woods to get a close view of Sherman's troops. These horsemen were seen almost constantly near our line of march throughout the forenoon of the 18th."[70]

Forget the rebel outriders. Everyone wished to hurry. Goldsboro was within reach—less than a two-day march—just over the horizon. If only the mud would cease its resistance. But the mud fought harder than Hampton— sucking at wagon wheels, swallowing the corduroy. The 82d Illinois, Twentieth Corps, lost two hours that day because the regiment had to pull a wagon from the muck by ropes.[71] Isaac Kittinger, 22d Wisconsin, totally disgusted, complained: "Wet feet all day and all night, Marched 12 miles. All quick-sand, mire holes, poor settlements and tar factorys and yalow pines."[72]

Earlier that afternoon, as the Fourteenth Corps waited for the Twentieth to close up, Sherman, Slocum, Davis, and division commander Carlin stopped at a farmhouse with a wide veranda belonging to a farmer named Cox. While the other generals conferred in front of the house, Carlin took the opportunity to sit on the porch, relax, and "scrape up an acquaintance" with the family. The children, however, were crying, and Mr. Cox and his wife seemed upset. Carlin tried to reassure them that the army would not harm them or their property, but Cox would not be consoled. "That will not save us," the farmer kept repeating. So positive was Cox that Carlin "interpreted it as an intimation that he had knowledge that a battle was to take place near his home."[73]

Carlin's hunch was based on more than Cox's lamentations. Earlier he had received a report from Capt. Charles E. Belknap, who was in charge of brigade foragers. Belknap had told him that local citizens and a wounded rebel he had found at a nearby turpentine mill all stated that the rebels planned to make a stand nearby. Belknap also felt that the stiffening rebel resistance tended to confirm the intelligence.[74]

His suspicions triggered, Carlin approached corps commander Davis and told him of his hunch, which seemed reinforced by Belknap's intelligence. He requested Davis to convey his thoughts to Generals Slocum and Sherman. Davis did so, apparently. But Sherman seemed impatient and brushed aside his subordinates' misgivings. "Oh, no, Jeff, they will not fight us till we get near Smithfield or Raleigh." Then Sherman rode off.[75]

The Left Wing encamped at 4 P.M. on the eighteenth—the Fourteenth Corps spread out at Underwood's farm on the Goldsboro road; the Twentieth Corps, five miles back, camped at Lee's Plantation.

Logan's four light divisions of Howard's Right Wing bivouacked on the "new" Goldsboro road near Alex Benton's, about 11 miles south of Bentonville, "straight across country probably not more than 6–8 miles" from Slocum. Frank Blair, "far back, following some crooked roads," camped about 5 miles from Troublefield's Store. The trains were stretched out between there and Beaman's Cross Roads.[76]

A member of the 6th Iowa, one of Logan's men, noted white oaks at his campsite—a welcome omen—anything to break the monotony of the pine woods. Others in Logan's Fifteenth Corps thought of the morrow. They were in advance and anxious to make good time. John Logan would see to that. The Fifteenth must be first into Goldsboro. It promised to be the "most exciting race in the history of the regiment."[77]

Darkness fell. Yet it was not night. Dense black smoke and fire heralded Sherman's advance. Unlike in South Carolina, the smoke rose from trees, not houses. It was surrealistic, apocalyptic. "The resin pits were on fire, and great columns of black smoke rose high into the air, spreading and mingling together in gray clouds, and suggesting the roof and pillars of a vast temple," recalled an enthralled Capt. Daniel Oakey, 2d Massachusetts:

> All traces of habitation were left behind, as we marched into that grand forest with its beautiful carpet of pine-needles. The straight trunks of the pine-tree shot up to a great height, and then spread out into a green roof, which kept us in perpetual shade. As night came on, we found that the resinous sap in the cavities cut in the trees to receive it, had been lighted by "bummers" in our advance. The effect of these peculiar watch-fires on every side, several feet above the ground, with flames licking their way up the tall trunks, was peculiarly striking and beautiful.[78]

It was in this forbidding semidarkness that Sherman wrote a message to Oliver O. Howard: "Make a break into Goldsborough from the south, and let your scouts strike out for Schofield at Kinston, though I hope to meet him at Goldsborough. Our roads are very bad, but I think the Fourteenth Corps will be at Cox's Bridge to-morrow night, and will aim to strike the railroad to the northwest of Goldsborough."[79]

One of Sherman's weary staff officers, Lt. Col. George W. Nichols, looked about. "The headquarters' camp was pitched . . . in the midst of the soldiers. Artillery, infantry, and cavalry surrounded us upon all sides, and we were lulled to rest by a hundred bugle-calls."[80] Everyone was tired but supremely confident.

2

Glorious Old Joe

SHERMAN CAME ON irresistibly—like Lord Cornwallis—North Carolinians were reminded. The feeling of dread, of terror, may have been comparable to the folk tales of grandparents, but not the speed, the destructive power, the calamitous results. Compared to Sherman's, Cornwallis's invasion during the Revolution was child's play.

Columbia, the capital of South Carolina, fell on February 17; Charleston, the following morning; Wilmington, on the twenty-second. Richmond had looked to Gen. Pierre G. T. Beauregard to coordinate defensive efforts and obstruct Sherman's advance, but Beauregard's dispatches to Richmond offered little hope and indeed seemed to obscure the military situation itself. Nagged by illness and completely overwhelmed by the rush of events,[1] Beauregard would resort to heady 1861 rhetoric: concentrate 35,000 Confederates at Salisbury, North Carolina; fight Sherman there, "crush him, then to concentrate all forces against Grant, and then to march on Washington to dictate a peace."[2]

Eyes shifted nervously in Richmond. There was only one course—something that should have been done long before—the appointment of Robert E. Lee as commander in chief of Confederate armies. It was done. Once he accepted responsibility, Lee turned to President Jefferson Davis and asked that Joseph E. Johnston be retrieved from oblivion. With the greatest reluctance Davis acquiesced.[3] "Mr Davis has every confidence in Genl. Johnston," reported a well-connected Confederate staff officer, "provided he will fight; but he thinks the General will not risk a battle unless he has *all* the chances in his favor."[4]

Nevertheless, in light of Hood's disaster at Nashville, "the return of Johnston to command," according to historian T. R. Hay, "was forced." There was no alternative for Davis.[5] "Assume command of the Army of

Tennessee and all troops in Department of South Carolina, Georgia, and Florida," Lee wired Johnston on February 22. "Concentrate all available forces and drive back Sherman." The controversial Johnston had worked a miracle before—when he gathered fragments of two defeated Confederate armies at Dalton, Georgia, in early 1864, and fashioned them into an effective fighting force that proceeded to frustrate Sherman's heavier numbers and resources for three months. Perhaps he could.

But Johnston had no illusions this time. "It is too late," Johnston responded to Lee, "to expect me to concentrate troops capable of driving back Sherman. The remnant of the Army of Tennessee is much divided. So are other troops." Nevertheless, Johnston accepted Lee's charge, "with no other hope than of contributing to obtain favorable terms of peace; the only one that a rational being could then entertain. For the result of the war was evident to the dullest."[6]

Sherman's strategy by the last week in February 1865 was becoming clearer to the Confederates. He would continue to push through the Carolinas, up into Virginia, and there unite with Grant against Lee. Although uncertain about Sherman's intermediate objective—Charlotte, Raleigh, or Goldsboro—Confederate military and political leaders agreed that he must be stopped somehow. Otherwise the war was lost. Lee doubted that Sherman would move northwest via Charlotte and Greensboro; rather, Lee expected him to turn toward Goldsboro and the coast—to snap the vital Weldon railroad and unite with Schofield. If such were his purpose, Hardee's troops retreating from Charleston might be sandwiched between Sherman and Schofield. Lee urged Johnston to avoid this risk by moving Hardee's men "as rapidly as possible to Fayetteville."[7]

On February 24 Johnston went to Charlotte, assumed command from Beauregard, and immediately held a review. A participant, an officer of the 63d Virginia, wrote his wife happily that the "puny" troops "cheered Gen. Jo. in high stile." This feeling of confidence in Johnston and enthusiasm over his return to command swept through the ranks and the officer corps of the Army of Tennessee. It is difficult to overstate their feelings. They loved the man. He could redeem them. They knew it.[8]

Johnston's primary task, realistically, was to organize and position a blocking force somewhere in upper South Carolina and, if not there, then in lower North Carolina. For manpower he initially had three elements: the remnants of the Army of Tennessee, the Savannah and Charleston garrisons

Joseph Eggleston Johnston
(Library of Congress)

(flushed from their strongholds and now marching north under Hardee), and large cavalry complements under Wade Hampton and Joe Wheeler. Braxton Bragg's North Carolina Department forces, observing the enemy at Wilmington, would be added to Johnston's command on March 6, making a fourth contingent.[9]

Once he combined these major components, Johnston would possess a sizable force, admittedly less than half Sherman's numbers but sufficient to cause mischief, perhaps to wound his adversary seriously. Confederate intelligence believed that Sherman commanded 35,000 infantry escorted by an inefficient cavalry arm, and Johnston seems to have accepted this estimate. If Sherman's army could be caught divided and fought in fractions, certainly before it united with Schofield's, there might be hope of checking, perhaps defeating, even destroying part of his force—an isolated column perhaps. Once this had been accomplished, other positive opportunities would present themselves.[10]

First, however, Johnston had to mass his forces.[11] What remained of the old Army of Tennessee was widely dispersed in small units between Charlotte and Tupelo, Mississippi. They lacked wagons and artillery and rifles. These bits and pieces of a military organization, broken at Franklin and swept away at Nashville, bore little resemblance to an army. Did they lack the will to fight? Most of the infantry had gone home, or had found horses and joined Bedford Forrest, or had scattered to the winds. Mississippi soldiers— entire regiments of them—had been furloughed by Hood after the flight from Tennessee, and the handful willing to return were being reunited slowly at different rendezvous points. Carter L. Stevenson, a seasoned Confederate division commander, lamented Hood's puzzling action: "The failure to extend to the troops of Georgia, Alabama, and South Carolina, when passing their homes, the same indulgences as had been granted to those of Mississippi, gave much dissatisfaction and caused large numbers to leave the ranks en route." As one loyal South Carolina Confederate noted, "in defiance of discipline and all authority, each command as it reached the nearest point to its home, *took* five days leave of absence. In a military sense it was desertion."[12]

But the appointment of Johnston brought hope to these veterans of Shiloh and Resaca. "The army was cheered to the depths of their hearts." " 'The Last Rally' of the dying Confederacy was sounded, for everything and everybody available to concentrate in N. Carolina under 'glorious old Joe,' and what was left of our Army joined in that strenuous move."[13]

As units reassembled, the long march to North Carolina began. The journey of Francis H. Nash, 42d Georgia, Stovall's Brigade, is fairly typical.

The 42d left Tupelo, Mississippi, by rail on January 23 and moved through Okolona to Meridian, then crossed into Alabama. It traveled by boat to Demopolis, then by rail to Selma and next by steamboat to Montgomery. From there flatcars took the troops to Milledgeville, Georgia, then on to Augusta. A day later, February 5, the regiment arrived in Branchville, South Carolina, and took position with other elements of Stephen D. Lee's Corps (commanded by Stevenson) attempting to defend the South Fork of the Edisto River and the approaches to Columbia.[14] When it failed to check Sherman on the Edisto line, Beauregard withdrew Lee's Corps (and the 42d Georgia) into North Carolina. On February 24 in Charlotte, these Army of Tennessee veterans passed in review before General Johnston.[15]

The total number of these fragments, once the Army of Tennessee, bitterly disappointed Johnston: 5,000 men—the size of an 1864 infantry division—was the most optimistic estimate. Two thousand of these troops belonged to Stevenson; 1,000, under A. P. Stewart, were approaching Charlotte from Newberry, South Carolina, by foot; and the remaining 2,000, under Benjamin F. Cheatham, were strung out between Newberry and Augusta. All manner of problems hampered transportation of these troops. The strain on the frail railroad system, weakened by four years of neglect and overuse, caused service to break down. Different gauges of track, particularly at Salisbury, North Carolina, compounded the logistical absurdity. "Whole brigades piled up at the Salisbury bottle neck."[16]

Even if the Army of Tennessee should arrive promptly and intact, Johnston estimated that at least 1,300 soldiers were without arms, not to speak of the crippling lack of artillery, supply wagons, and ambulances. Moreover, many veterans continued to desert en route, drifting away in little bands. "The prospect of marching through S.C. and to N.C. hunting the army and carrying musket and cartridges didn't suit me," one rationalized lamely years later.[17]

While the Army of Tennessee limped to rejoin "glorious old Joe," its other former commander, Braxton Bragg (military adviser and troubleshooter for Jefferson Davis) had rushed from Richmond to the defense of Wilmington. Unfortunately, as in the past, Bragg succeeded chiefly in alienating subordinate commanders and spreading blame. To the dismay of the defenders of Fort Fisher, he failed to come to their relief in January 1865. The fort fell on January 15, thus rendering Wilmington useless as a Confederate seaport. The town was abandoned on February 22. When Schofield's elated and confident Federals shifted their eyes from these coastal objectives inland to Goldsboro, Bragg would turn to Johnston for help.[18]

Braxton Bragg
(courtesy William A. Turner, Even More Confederate Faces Collection)

During the first week in March 1865 Bragg had available near Goldsboro
Robert F. Hoke's veteran division from the Army of Northern Virginia plus
some defenders of Fort Fisher–Wilmington who had managed to escape.
But Bragg and Hoke were confronted by an enemy in heavy force (two
corps) advancing on them from two directions. Moreover, these 20,000
Federals were commanded by the capable John M. Schofield. Goldsboro
threatened to become another Wilmington.

Johnston, though paper-thin in manpower, "loaned out to Bragg" Lee's
Corps (his closest body of infantry) on March 7 and sent Daniel Harvey Hill

along as its commander. Johnston dreamed fondly that with these Army of Tennessee reinforcements Bragg could summarily defeat Schofield's thrusts inland from the sea, then ship the troops back by rail to join Hardee's force and overwhelm one of Sherman's wings. Johnston appears to have had only a dim notion of the forces threatening Goldsboro, and again he would seriously underestimate enemy strength.

Harvey Hill's force moved to Goldsboro by rail quickly and joined Bragg. On March 8 Hoke attacked, routing and capturing large portions of Col. Charles Upham's Brigade. Considerable skirmishing occurred the next day, and on the tenth Hoke undertook another flanking maneuver but was soundly beaten in an attempt to turn Jacob Cox's left. Initial successes achieved by Hoke's Division were squandered, however, when Bragg—perhaps the most distractible of Confederate army commanders—diverted Hill's troops on a "fruitless and wasteful" mission. The result was predictably Braggian—up came more and more Union troops, and following a third day of discouraging fighting, the Confederates retired north of the Neuse River, having lost the Battle at Wise's Forks.[19] Hill—and Lee's Corps—remained with Bragg, but it was an unhappy arrangement, intolerable for Hill personally. He loathed Bragg and simmered over the injustices of Chickamauga in 1863. Privately he wrote Johnston: "I hope that it may be possible & consistent with [the] intents of the service to give me another commander than Genl. Bragg. He has made me the scapegoat once & would do it again."[20]

An odd man was this Harvey Hill. Small and crooked, bookish, he looked like a character from Dickens. Yet he had ability. Indeed, he should have been one of the great heroes of the Confederacy, certainly North Carolina's champion. An 1861 major general, he had been conspicuous in the early fighting in Virginia and had received praise from every quarter. Brave and aggressive, he spoke his mind to anyone, including his superiors. His acid tongue and pen were frightening. Although deeply religious and intelligent and well read beyond his peers, he "time after time defeated his own best interests."[21] No one, however, could question his ability to command troops, especially at the division level. An honorable man and a patriot to the core of his being, nevertheless, Harvey Hill could be a difficult, bad-tempered, carping subordinate.

When Bragg failed at Wise's Forks, Johnston ordered him on March 10 to bring Hoke's and Hill's troops immediately to Smithfield, a town on the North Carolina Railroad equidistant from Raleigh and Goldsboro. But uncertainty nagged Johnston, and on March 11 he countermanded his order, wiring Bragg, "Better remain at Goldsborough till we see Sherman's course from Fayetteville."[22]

Initially Johnston had hoped to assemble his dispersed commands at Fayetteville, North Carolina, "in time to engage one of the enemy columns while crossing the Cape Fear."[23] In anticipation, he had moved his headquarters to that city on March 4. The effort proved futile. Sherman moved too fast—rapidly breaching the Great Pee Dee River defenses, capturing Cheraw, South Carolina, and pushing on, chasing close after Hardee, brushing Hampton and Wheeler aside like tenpins. Then came alarming news of Schofield advancing in force on Kinston and Goldsboro from New Bern and Wilmington, then word of Bragg's failure at Wise's Forks. If Schofield continued on his likely course from the coast and seized Goldsboro, he not only would command that critical rail junction, but also would be above the Cape Fear River, flanking Johnston and jeopardizing his communications with Raleigh and Richmond. Furthermore, any advance west by Schofield from Goldsboro threatened to interpose two Federal corps between Johnston and Raleigh. Thus to fight Sherman at Fayetteville would be madness. Yet to rush east to Goldsboro, combine with Bragg, and attempt to fall upon Schofield also would be folly. By adopting the latter course, Johnston would expose his line of communications (the Goldsboro-Raleigh railroad) and risk having his entire army cut off and pinned against the coast by Sherman's columns advancing from the south. Raleigh would be uncovered and at Sherman's mercy. If Johnston fell back on Raleigh, this would forfeit the opportunity to attack Sherman in detail and would allow Sherman to unite with Schofield, placing an enormous, irresistible force in eastern North Carolina—a force capable of seizing Raleigh at will or of marching up the Weldon railroad to Richmond.

The dilemma confronting Johnston left him little choice. So he backpedaled—apparently returning to the mode of 1864—abandoning Fayetteville with its military treasures and the natural barrier of the Cape Fear. This time, however, Johnston determined to swap distance for time and operational flexibility. He would use the days gained to build up his strength and seek an opportunity to attack Sherman in the vicinity of Smithfield and the Neuse River crossings. My "forces united may impede the march of the Federal army," he wrote Robert E. Lee, "and even find opportunities to strike heavy blows, or at least prevent it from gathering food."[24]

The prospect of continued retreat alarmed Lee, not to speak of Jefferson Davis. From Richmond, Lee urged Johnston to think offensively: "Should you be forced back in this direction both armies would certainly starve. You must judge what the probabilities will be of arresting Sherman by battle. If there is a reasonable probability I would recommend it. A bold and unexpected attack might relieve us."[25]

Late in the afternoon of March 13, Johnston decided. He would fight. First, he would concentrate his army at Smithfield (just north of the Neuse and on the North Carolina Railroad). Once Sherman committed himself— either across Johnston's front toward Goldsboro or by his flank toward Raleigh—Johnston would attack. So for the second time that week, Johnston ordered Bragg with all his infantry to Smithfield. Cavalry would remain behind in the Kinston-Goldsboro area to observe Schofield and obstruct his advance, taking particular care to destroy the bridge across the Neuse River.[26] Johnston also ordered Beauregard (coordinating logistical affairs at Charlotte) to hurry forward the Army of Tennessee. Now all of Johnston's forces would be heading for Smithfield except Hardee's, who would front Sherman, keeping between him and Raleigh.[27]

William J. Hardee, Johnston's most trusted lieutenant, had spent six miserable months since leaving the Army of Tennessee and the presence of General Hood. In vain he had tried to halt Sherman's march across Georgia and the seizure of Savannah. Then stationing himself at Charleston, Hardee shared responsibility with Beauregard for stopping Sherman's advance into and through South Carolina. Again he accomplished little. Ultimately, torn between conflicting orders from Beauregard and President Davis, he evacuated Charleston on the night of February 17.[28]

Knowing that he must organize the Charleston garrison into an active field command, Hardee had divided his troops (including 3,000 heavy artillerists) into three infantry divisions under Major Generals Ambrose R. "Rans" Wright, Lafayette McLaws, and William B. Taliaferro. Taliaferro commanded the James Island force, with brigades under Brig. Gen. Stephen Elliott, Jr., and Colonels Alfred M. Rhett and A. D. Goodwyn. McLaws's Division (larger than any corps in Stewart's Army of Tennessee) consisted of Conner's South Carolina Brigade, a fine but diminished unit of the Army of Northern Virginia, commanded by Brig. Gen. J. D. Kennedy, and four other brigades of doubtful combat value. Wright's Division of Georgia militia and Goodwyn's Brigade of South Carolina militia and cadets would disappear along the road to Cheraw.

It was a strange command, this army of Hardee's—a crazy quilt of veteran and inexperienced units—led by a menagerie of general officers, most of them shelved by the War Department for incapacity, insufferable behavior, or physical inability. To mold it into a cohesive fighting unit would tax the experience and ingenuity of the ablest general. "My troops for the most part," reported Hardee, "had never seen field service, were organized on the march." Even to reach the North Carolina border would be challenge sufficient.[29]

"The men had started on the march," remembered one of Taliaferro's soldiers, "with as much luggage as they could carry; most of them had been for a long time accustomed only to garrison duty, and having little experience in the field soon began to feel the hardships of the march." Soon many fell out of ranks; others "had to be carried in ambulances from sheer inability to walk."[30]

Many of Hardee's men were unarmed, others carried the "old Austrian rifles" that had been discarded by infantry commanders as soon as possible after Bull Run and Belmont.[31] Some troops had not been paid for eight months; some regiments contained companies of "galvanized Rebels" (captured Union troops who had volunteered to serve as Confederates in order to escape prison camp). Hardee on recruiting them euphemistically referred to them as the "Foreign Battalion." They had proved worse than worthless in the defense of Savannah and had mutinied. He had had to execute the ringleaders and send off the rest. He had recommended officially that efforts to enlist these troops be prohibited. In the desperation for manpower in March 1865, however, they were used again in yet another violation of experience.[32]

Hardee originally intended to go to Greensboro, North Carolina, by way of Wilmington in accordance with his orders from Beauregard. When Wilmington fell Hardee's only practicable route was through Cheraw, the terminus of the North Eastern Railroad from Charleston, located less than a dozen miles from the North Carolina border. He could move stores, equipment, surplus rolling stock, and heavy ordnance there by train, which was a great advantage, and already much material had been evacuated to that point.[33] But Cheraw lay on a direct line between Columbia, Fayetteville, and Goldsboro. Already Sherman's Right Wing was dangerously near. The growing stockpile of Confederate war material also made the town a tempting prize. If Sherman veered east toward the coast, toward Goldsboro or Wilmington as it appeared he would do, it promised to be a race between two armies.

Indeed, it became a bizarre race between Hardee's ill-conditioned garrison troops and Sherman's veterans of "the tramp." Hardee managed to win—by the narrowest margin—thanks to miserable weather. Streams became lakes and roads became muck.

Although South Carolina weather befriended Hardee and allowed freight car after freight car of Charleston military and civilian treasure to be dumped at the Cheraw railhead, it made the overland trek all the more difficult for his unseasoned troops. They pulled out of friendly Charleston at night, marched until dawn, and camped the following day at Monck's Corner. Water rose dangerously along and across the line of march; important bridges simply floated away. Wagons stalled, mud sucked at the wheels of the cannon and caissons. "The march was almost unendurable." Troops tossed aside their burdens, even their rifles. "For some miles both sides of the road were strewn with knapsacks, articles of clothing, etc." The men grew disheartened; they lost their faith in Hardee. They began to sneak off at night from their "cheerless camp. . . . All along the line of march large numbers of men were constantly deserting."[34] Hardee's chief of staff, T. Benton Roy, observed on February 20, "Great many desertions from the command on the march from Charleston. Some artillery companies almost disbanded by desertion."[35]

Hardee remained in Cheraw for four days, barely allowing time for his straggling column to close up and cross the Pee Dee. He salvaged what he could of the huge dump of ordnance and supplies, loading as much precious cargo as possible aboard his few wagons. He had received word from Johnston to change his route of march making Fayetteville, not Greensboro, his objective. The prospect of joining Johnston pleased Hardee personally,[36] but he worried about his ability to complete the mission. An attack of typhoid as he was set to leave Charleston had led his surgeon to send him off by train to Cheraw and request that McLaws supervise the evacuation. By the time Hardee returned to active command at Cheraw, he was visibly weakened. He worried over the terrible morale of his shrinking force. How would they fare against Sherman's experienced and confident troops? One of Hardee's men wrote from Cheraw, "the Army has very little confidence in Hardee. . . . The rumors here are *legion*. And as contradictory as possible." Hardee must do something positive, and very soon.[37]

But Sherman gave Hardee no peace. He pressed him so closely that he "had barely time to destroy the bridge [across the Pee Dee] after passing over it."[38] Once beyond the Pee Dee, Hardee took the road north to Rockingham, North Carolina, instead of the direct route to Fayetteville. This cost precious time.

Hardee had made arrangements to march directly to Fayetteville, but he had received an alarming dispatch from Bragg after the fall of Wilmington stating that Schofield was "moving up the west bank of the Cape Fear." This prompted Hardee to order cavalry to destroy key bridges between Cheraw and Fayetteville; meanwhile, he would set his infantry and heavily laden wagon train on the road to Rockingham.[39]

To Hardee's disgust, once his column committed to the Rockingham route, a contradictory dispatch arrived from Bragg stating that the intelligence about Schofield had been wrong. The damage had been done, however, and Hardee received more confusing dispatches. Beauregard ordered him to continue on to Greensboro—then not to Greensboro, but to Fayetteville, as Johnston had requested. Johnston's messages arrived simultaneously: "It is too late to turn to Fayetteville. Take the best route to Raleigh, if you cannot turn to Fayetteville, of which you must judge." Hardee replied to Johnston on March 6, "I hope to reach Fayetteville in 3 or 4 days (not counting today)."[40]

Hardee continued toward Fayetteville with a dissolving army, supposedly to become the bulk and mainstay of Johnston's force. Not only was Hardee losing men hourly from desertion, but also Rans Wright's Georgians had returned home on Feb. 26 under orders from Gov. Joseph E. Brown. The experienced Wright himself was granted leave to attend the session of the Georgia legislature. Next went the cadets and militia of South Carolina (Goodwyn's Brigade—about 1,100 men), following the command of their governor, A. G. Magrath.[41]

As he had promised Johnston, Hardee arrived at Fayetteville on March 9 and immediately made preparations to cross the Cape Fear, which he accomplished on the night of the tenth. Hardee had left Wade Hampton behind to impede the enemy's progress and to defend Fayetteville as long as possible. Meanwhile, he took the infantry up the Fayetteville-Raleigh plank road that led through Averasboro.[42]

At noon on March 11, Johnston provided Hardee with specific instructions. Sherman's alternatives seemed to either unite with Schofield at Goldsboro or move directly on Raleigh: "It is very important, therefore, that your movements conform to Sherman's when he leaves Fayetteville." If Sherman's column heads for Raleigh, Johnston continued, retreat in that direction, and Bragg's troops will be brought to support you; if he turns east toward Goldsboro, abandon the Fayetteville-Raleigh road and your force will be brought to join Bragg (presumably near Goldsboro). "We must endeavor to be prepared for either."[43]

Sherman crossed the Cape Fear on March 14 and pushed toward Raleigh. Hardee divided his cavalry, positioning Hampton "in front of any movement toward Goldsboro" and Wheeler on the Fayetteville-Raleigh road, closely supported by infantry. Hour after hour Sherman shoved Wheeler's pickets back from one position to another. All the while bad weather continued, slowing Sherman's momentum yet creating problems for Hardee's retreating force as well.[44]

Partly to avoid the utter demoralization of his disintegrating command, Hardee on March 15 gave battle at Smith's Mill (Smith's Ferry) on the plank road, about six miles south of Averasboro.[45] The ground Hardee chose to defend, a narrow neck between the Cape Fear and Black Rivers, gave the Confederates advantages of position and tactical surprise. At this fight (which became known as the Battle of Averasboro) Hardee deployed his troops in a unusual manner, placing his less experienced brigades under Rhett and Elliott on the two advanced lines, supported by McLaws's Division and Wheeler's dismounted cavalry on the main line. It was stratagem Daniel Morgan had employed with brilliant success eighty-five years earlier at Cowpens, not many miles away. In fact, it had become a favorite tactic of Hardee's. He had employed it at Missionary Ridge, however, with disastrous results, as orders for the front line to disengage and make the prearranged withdrawal were only partially transmitted. Hardee carefully saw to it that his plan was not botched at Averasboro.[46]

When it discovered resistance in force, Sherman's infantry deployed and by midmorning had flanked and routed Rhett's Brigade, throwing it back upon Taliaferro. Fighting continued stubbornly until Taliaferro, realizing that he was being flanked himself, withdrew to the third and final defense line manned by McLaws's troops. This position was assailed by Sherman's Left Wing but managed to hold throughout the afternoon. Early that evening of March 16, under cover of darkness and heavy rain, Hardee withdrew quietly and skillfully eastward in the direction of Smithfield.[47] He had inflicted some 700 casualties upon Sherman's Left Wing and Kilpatrick's cavalry, but he had lost about 500 troops himself (most of whom were captured when Rhett's Brigade gave way). As he set his army in motion, Hardee sent a dispatch to Johnston requesting that he "send a force to Elevation [located midway on the direct road from Averasboro to Smithfield]. It would insure my forming a junction with you."[48]

Averasboro was a success. Hardee's battle objective had been to determine whether he was being "followed by Sherman's whole army, or a part of it, and what was its destination."[49] In the fight on the sixteenth he discovered that he was pursued by Sherman's Left Wing (two corps of infantry) and Kilpatrick's cavalry. Thus, by making a stand at Averasboro, Hardee had achieved his limited purpose. He would satisfy himself regarding Sherman's destination the following day. Hardee also managed to slow Sherman's advance and limit the mobility of his left column—not only by blocking their path for a day, but also by loading Sherman's ambulances and wagons with nearly 500 wounded.

It is noteworthy as well that Hardee had fought his soft garrison troops, inferior in numbers, against arguably the most experienced troops in the Federal army, repulsing determined attacks throughout the day. The troops began to feel good about themselves. "My troops were much cheered and inspired," wrote Hardee. According to McLaws, "the impression was general that the enemy had been decidedly checked & with considerable loss."[50] Hardee at once issued a field order formally complimenting his men for "their courage and conduct of yesterday, and congratulates them upon giving the enemy the first serious check he has received since leaving Atlanta. This command contended with the Fourteenth Army Corps, most of the Twentieth, Kilpatrick's cavalry command—three times their number."[51]

It is tempting to make more of this small victory. Johnston "hoped" that Hardee's stand might delay Sherman, thereby gaining time for concentration and perhaps an opportunity to attack an isolated fraction of his army, which it did. Johnston also hoped that it might help develop Sherman's intentions, which it did. It was not, however, a calculated objective designed to stretch out the distance between Sherman's two wings and thus provide the opportunity to concentrate and destroy Sherman's Left Wing. Hardee's check at Averasboro did disperse the Federal columns somewhat, and it is probably true that the impressive Confederate stand led Sherman to abandon his plan to cut the North Carolina Railroad west of Smithfield with Kilpatrick and an infantry strike force. Instead, Sherman would move toward Cox's Bridge, his two wings following parallel roads.[52]

Perhaps, as suggested by historians of two Federal regiments, the method and direction of Hardee's retreat from the battlefield toward Smithfield also encouraged Sherman to believe that the road to Goldsboro via Bentonville lay open, thus enhancing Johnston's opportunity for surprise.[53] It can be argued, of course, that Averasboro led to these results favorable to the Confederates, but one should be cautious in attributing such to Hardee's or Johnston's strategic foresight.

All during the night of the sixteenth, Hardee's infantry pulled out of line, marched to Black River, and began crossing. The river was swollen over its banks, which meant that everything and everyone had to use the bridge.[54] It created a terrible traffic jam, a most nervous situation for a disengaging army.

Once across the river, Hardee's Confederates continued in black darkness—slogging down terribly rutted, muddy roads. McLaws, a wily campaigner, tried to avoid every hill, taking side roads whenever he could find them, and thus managed to get ahead of Taliaferro's Division. Hardee and his staff rode by in the darkness. A member of John C. Fiser's Brigade looked up: "He [Hardee] certainly looks dejected and care worn, his uniform badly soiled and riding a poor raw boned horse."[55] How unlike the Hardee of 1864, the elegant beau ideal of the Army of Tennessee.

Lafayette McLaws was no member of the Hardee adoration society. They had served together for almost six months now, sharing the humiliation of Savannah and the abandonment of Charleston. In January McLaws had been charged by Hardee with the defense of the line of the Charleston and Savannah Railroad. Some scoundrel had spread malicious gossip that McLaws had been so drunk that he could not perform his duties on the night the town of Pocotaligo was evacuated and McLaws had to retire from the line of the railroad to the Salkahatchie River. Hardee, to McLaws's dismay, ordered an investigation to "counteract the injustice which has been done to you." He had one of his own staff secure written and verbal testimony from dozens of officers. This affair, and the manner in which Hardee conducted it, humiliated McLaws.[56]

McLaws did not have Hardee's confidence and he knew it. Moreover, he was acutely aware that Hardee had Johnston's ear. Had he not earned better treatment? A member of the illustrious West Point class of 1842, McLaws had served eighteen years in the Old Army, then made a name for himself in the Army of Northern Virginia. He soared from quartermaster, a mere major, in Savannah in May 1861, to major general and division commander in May 1862. His name, familiar enough to the Confederacy at large, would be forever linked with Longstreet's Corps and the great battles of 1862–63. But McLaws had made the terrible mistake of siding with Braxton Bragg in the Chickamauga controversy and thus alienating Longstreet. After the botched Knoxville Campaign in late 1863 and a bitter court-martial, McLaws did not hold field command again until Hardee put him to work in southern Georgia a year later.

McLaws had a good eye for terrain and he could manage troops, but he had the reputation of being too cautious. Veteran division commander though he might be, he did not suit Longstreet or Lee. Apparently he did not suit Hardee either. It is known that Johnston had issued an order, just at the time of Averasboro, regarding reassignment of McLaws and sent it to

Hardee to be implemented. Hardee, on the march to Smithfield, had summoned his subordinate but "thought it best not to mention the order to any one till McLaws arrives."[57]

That morning of March 17, after the last of Hardee's infantry had disappeared down the road to Elevation, Joe Wheeler remained behind as rear guard covering both the road on which Hardee retreated and the Fayetteville-Raleigh road that led through Averasboro itself. He observed Sherman's troops with great care, reporting to Hardee frequently. The enemy took two routes. A large contingent (Ward's division, Twentieth Army Corps, Wheeler discovered) had pushed through Averasboro itself by 9:00 A.M. on the direct road to Raleigh. Harrison's cavalry brigade remained in Ward's front,[58] contesting this advance up the Fayetteville-Raleigh road. Skirmishing continued, but soon Ward's infantry ceased pushing the cavalry. This was unusual; it appeared that Ward's troops might be turning back to Averasboro. In the meantime another mass of Federals (the Fourteenth Corps, according to prisoners) had turned east before they reached Averasboro, then crossed Black River, following the road that led toward Bentonville and eventually to either Smithfield or Goldsboro. Still farther to the east, Hampton reported other Yankees crossing Black River, apparently heading toward Goldsboro.[59] Enclosing the reports of Wheeler and Hampton, Hardee wrote Johnston at 2:50 P.M. from Elevation, stating that he did not believe Sherman intended to advance on Raleigh or to follow him on the road to Smithfield. Information from scouts sent into Federal lines was that Sherman moved toward Goldsboro rather than Raleigh or Smithfield. "If he divides his forces," Hardee continued, "you will have the opportunity to concentrate and whip him."[60]

Meanwhile Hardee's makeshift army, pelted by rain, continued on its gloomy way, arriving in Elevation about noon on March 17. There Hardee halted his men and allowed them to encamp. They were exhausted—the cumulative effect of the Averasboro fight, plodding through the mud all night, and having had "no food save a small slice of raw bacon" for two days. "Our entire march from Charleston. . . . was hard," one soldier remembered, "but the tramp from Averasboro to Elevation was about the worst we had in the whole stretch."[61]

Something was wrong, so Hardee checked his map. It showed Elevation "midway between Averasborough and Smithfield, and at the intersection of the road running between these two places with the road [Wilmington-Raleigh] running from Smith's Ferry to Raleigh."[62] But there was no intersection at Elevation, only the one road leading toward Smithfield! Nevertheless, Johnston had sent him a reassuring dispatch written at nine that morning. It directed Hardee to remain at Elevation "till you ascertain definitely the enemy's movements. Our nearest troops are about nine miles from that point."[63] By the time (about 1:00 P.M.) he received Johnston's message, however, Hardee had decided to move on through the village of Elevation two miles farther north. There, close to a bridge crossing Black River, he found the point where the two roads intersected. Hardee wrote Johnston that he was moving his troops to the junction: "I do not believe the enemy is moving on Raleigh; if so, the [enemy] force which has crossed Black River must come to this intersection, as there is no road east of Black River on which he can move. . . . To-day will develop the purposes of the enemy." Hardee had McLaws reconnoiter and choose a good defensive position in the event that the enemy appeared at the crossroads.[64]

Johnston received Hardee's dispatch of 2:50 P.M., March 17, at 7:00 P.M. in Smithfield. He weighed this intelligence and Hardee's advice, sharply conscious that he lacked absolute knowledge of Sherman's objective, not to speak of conclusive details regarding the routes and positions of enemy units. Prudence insisted that he reorganize this army assembling at Smithfield before giving battle. But Johnston recognized the window of opportunity. Past experience urged him to act—at once! At 9:00 P.M., therefore, he made his decision—it was the time for risk taking, the time for boldness. He would attack Sherman in the act of wheeling east toward Goldsboro. He would fall upon the head of one of the enemy columns with all the power and fury he could muster. Exactly where, exactly when, exactly which column would be determined tomorrow, the eighteenth.[65] From Confederate headquarters accordingly went out a flurry of orders—to A. P. Stewart and the Army of Tennessee, to Robert F. Hoke and the Department of North Carolina troops—"hold your command in readiness to move at dawn to-morrow morning."[66]

While Hardee remained on the Averasboro road southwest of Smithfield, resting his troops and awaiting developments, Johnston attempted to gather the remainder of his army at Smithfield. Cheatham, however, was still at Salisbury, stranded and entangled in the rail yards.[67] As late as March 11, Beauregard reported 65 carloads of infantry, artillery, and wagons awaiting transportation to Salisbury from Chester and 120 loads at Salisbury awaiting shipment.[68]

Johnston, it appears, bore direct responsibility for this logistical catastrophe. Apparently in deference to Bragg, he had allowed him "to operate independently" in regard to troop train movements. The result was a succession of conflicting orders to railroad personnel regarding the use of cars between Raleigh and Kinston. Perhaps of greater importance, Johnston "neglected to instruct the quartermasters at Raleigh" to send trains being held there on to Salisbury. This ineptitude at the highest command level denied—for six days—Cheatham the troop trains he desperately needed to move his corps from Salisbury to Smithfield.[69]

Supposedly with the advantage of interior lines and use of rail, Bragg's Confederates, in an appalling example of squandered resources, had to tramp from Goldsboro to Smithfield. Hill's corps marched eight miles on the thirteenth, encamped, then marched on to and through Smithfield on the fourteenth, bivouacking on the west side of town six miles toward Raleigh. Hoke's troops camped near the bridge over the Neuse.[70]

To give more structure to this mass of manpower converging on Smith-field, Johnston on March 15–16 placed Beauregard in Raleigh with the assignment of acting chief of staff and with the primary responsibility of hurrying forward Cheatham's troops from Salisbury and the rest of Stephen D. Lee's Corps from Charlotte. He gave Bragg command of Smithfield itself and its depot; he assigned Stewart command of the Army of Tennessee.[71] This must have been interesting news for Harvey Hill as his moved from being subordinate to his nemesis Bragg to being subject now to his old West Point classmate, A. P. Stewart.

The Confederates gained heart as they saw their numbers swelling at Smithfield. Nothing, however, stirred the troops—at least veterans of the Army of Tennessee—as much as the presence of Johnston himself. Harvey Hill's troops had not seen him since Atlanta. They cheered him wildly as he rode past. He lifted his hat to his men and spoke to Gen. Daniel H. Reynolds, the veteran Arkansas commander, telling him that he was in excellent health.[72] Johnston paid a visit to Stewart's headquarters, and the young staff officer who conducted him recorded that he found Johnston "surprisingly social, and endeavors to conceal his greatness rather than to impress you with it. I expressed to him the joy the Army of Tennessee manifested, on hearing of his restoration to command. He said that he was equally as much gratified to be with them as they were at his coming, but he feared it 'much too late to make it the same army.' "[73]

3

Playing a Bluff

SHORTLY AFTER 10:00 P.M., March 17, Johnston summoned Lt. Wade Hampton, Jr., to headquarters. He handed him a dispatch to be taken to his father out on the new Goldsboro road. Young Hampton rode for nearly two hours, arriving at midnight at General Hampton's headquarters at or near the two-story frame farmhouse of Willis Cole. The dispatch he handed his father requested more information regarding "the movement and position of the enemy, the number of their columns, their location and distance apart, and distance from Goldsborough." It ended with the key question, ". . . give me your opinion whether it is practicable to reach them from Smithfield on the south side of the river before they reach Goldsborough." Should the Confederates attack or not? The decision would depend on General Hampton.[1]

Hampton responded at 1:45 A.M. He believed Johnston's plan to attack Sherman south of the Neuse "practicable" and suggested that the Confederate strike force be assembled close to Hampton's present location—in the vicinity of "the forks of the Smithfield and Averasboro roads, three miles southwest of Bentonville."[2]

Johnston received Hampton's encouraging dispatch before dawn on Saturday, March 18, and at 6:45 A.M. orders went out to Stewart (camped above Smithfield) and Hardee to move immediately to Bentonville.

Hoke's Division, being the closest major infantry unit, would precede Stewart's Army of Tennessee on the Smithfield-Clinton road. Marching orders for Hoke and his Department of North Carolina Troops came from Bragg, however, rather than from Johnston.[3] Johnston continued to defer to his subordinate, allowing Bragg to function as an independent commander, thus perpetuating an awkward command structure in the face of the enemy.[4] Johnston apparently handled the delicate relationship with Bragg verbally during March 14–19. The only written order from him to Bragg during that period seems to have been one of March 17 relating to the defense of Goldsboro.[5] Johnston had given Bragg command of Smithfield and its depot, and perhaps Johnston allowed this to become rationale for his decorous, if not diffident, behavior. With memories of July 1864 burning in the minds of both men, surely their relations at best must have been coldly formal.[6]

Once commands to set the three infantry columns in motion for Bentonville had been issued, Johnston sent a dispatch to Hampton at 7:40 A.M. telling him that "the scheme" (to attack the enemy south of the Neuse) would be attempted.[7] Hoke's Division had arrived in Smithfield on March 16. It had crossed the Neuse two miles below town and camped near the bridge; on the seventeenth it rested. The division numbered 4,775 effectives, of whom at least 800 were former artillery men now organized as infantry. They were divided into five brigades with Clingman's Brigade, commanded by Col. William S. Devane, the smallest (557). The North Carolina Junior Reserve Brigade, at least 1,000 strong (35 companies organized into 3 regiments and a battalion), was led by Col. John H. Nethercutt. Colquitt's Georgia Brigade, commanded by Col. Charles T. Zachry, was a veteran command of the Army of Northern Virginia, as was William W. Kirkland's North Carolina Brigade. Johnson Hagood's South Carolina Brigade contained experienced infantry, yet a substantial portion of Hagood's troops belonged to defunct coastal artillery units. The 36th Regiment North Carolina Troops (also known as the 2d Regiment North Carolina Artillery) was nothing more than the remnant of Fort Fisher's garrison that had escaped capture, augmented by a number of men from the 1st Battalion North Carolina Heavy Artillery and the 40th Regiment North Carolina Troops (3d Regiment North Carolina Artillery).[8] Also in Hoke's Division was a jackleg artillery regiment commanded by Lt. Col. Joseph B. Starr, numbering over 700.[9]

Twenty-seven-year-old Maj. Gen. Robert F. Hoke had thrilled North Carolina, indeed the Confederate Congress, in the spring of 1864 with his stunningly successful capture of Plymouth. An able regimental and brigade commander earlier in the war, Hoke, once promoted to division command in April 1864, enjoyed the full confidence of President Davis and General Beauregard and was praised by General Lee. Hoke played an important role at Drewry's Bluff and Cold Harbor later in 1864,[10] winning official commendation from Beauregard for his "resolution and judgment" in the former engagement.[11]

The North Carolina team of Robert Hoke and Braxton Bragg, however, disappointed. They failed at Fort Fisher. They lost again at Wise's Forks. Bragg clearly was to blame at Fort Fisher. He interfered in Hoke's attack on the Federal rear. Hoke "vehemently disagreed" with Bragg when he broke off the attack and recalled him to Wilmington.[12] It is less easy to assign responsibility for the missed opportunities during the three-day engagement at Wise's Forks, although it had similarities to the pattern of earlier battles Bragg directed. In any event, the early 1865 efforts to defend Fort Fisher, Wilmington, and Kinston had done little to add luster to the reputations of either Bragg or Hoke.

Hoke's big, important division was his to command according to the Confederate organizational structure, but one may only speculate about the morale of this young, energetic, ambitious, capable major general in mid-March 1865. It appeared that once again he would have to lead his men into battle with Braxton Bragg at his elbow.

Hoke's brigade commander, William W. Kirkland, almost invariably impressed superiors. This North Carolinian had left West Point after three years to become a lieutenant in the Marine Corps. As a regimental and brigade commander in Lee's army, he had proven himself a superb combat officer who knew how to fashion and maintain healthy infantry units. Repeatedly wounded, Kirkland was unfortunately absent at inopportune periods and thus robbed of division command and enduring reputation in the Army of Northern Virginia.[13]

Another brigade commander, Johnson Hagood, promised experienced leadership, although his South Carolinians had been smashed at Globe Tavern in August 1864, suffering high casualties. His 11th, 21st, and 25th South Carolina also had lost about 350 men at Fort Fisher. To partially increase Hagood's sharply diminished numbers, he had been assigned fragments of several North Carolina coastal artillery units. Nevertheless, the heavy combat losses over the past six months and the amalgam of units his brigade represented made the effectiveness of his regiments extremely questionable.

Hoke's troops constituted Johnston's most reliable division. The Juniors presented Hoke's tired veterans a refreshing example of zest and optimism, and March 18 found the division "up before day ready to march." By 9:00 A.M. Hoke's men began their tramp south some fifteen miles down the Smithfield-Clinton road, arriving that afternoon at Bentonville where they camped on wet ground without fires. "It is supposed we are to meet & encounter part of Sherman's army," confided a member of the Juniors to his diary. "God grant us a telling victory, & may He enable us to rid ourselves of this dread incubus."[14]

Meanwhile, Stewart's Army of Tennessee struck its tents and shortly after 8:00 A.M. followed Hoke. The men had cooked three days' rations the day before and were ready for the sixteen-mile march which proved "exhausting," according to Gen. William B. Bate. On the other hand, the clearing weather improved spirits, not to speak of the knowledge that at last the Confederates were marching in force to meet the enemy. Glorious Old Joe would be leading them again—a cheering prospect for these veterans of a thousand broken dreams. "Our army in high spirits and ready to brave the coming storm," wrote a young diarist.[15]

The Army of Tennessee that greeted Johnston in Smithfield was a frightening specter of the army he had known. It numbered a mere 4,500: Stephen D. Lee's Corps under Hill, 2,700 effectives; Stewart's Corps, under William Wing Loring, 900, of which only 459 were armed; and a portion of Cheatham's Corps, under Bate, 900. As Johnston observed, not only were their numbers shockingly small, but also their best officers had been lost at Franklin and Nashville.[16]

Maj. Gen. Edward C. Walthall's Division contained two brigadiers and fewer than 250 men. The 1st Tennessee, which had left for war with 1,250, now numbered 65; the proud 13th Tennessee, once 1,200 strong, "now did well to muster 50."[17] A Tennessee company consisted of a commissioned officer, a noncommissioned officer, and 2 or 3 privates. In the 6th Mississippi, companies numbered about 20 men each, although one had 40. Company K, 1st Alabama, mustered 6 men in a regiment of 100. "The few that arrived in North Carolina were in a state pitiable to behold. There were brigades with less than 100 men, and I recollect that a certain Tennessee regiment was represented by one man." The army lacked its cannon and its wagons. The men had not been paid for months and many were ill. Their uniforms were described by Capt. Thomas B. Hampton, 63d Virginia (Palmer's Brigade): "I have never in life seen such a dirty & filthy set of men[.] something near half of the command has not changed shirts for 4 or 5 months & their pants are in tater[.] well I hope they will get fit out a little better in a short time [.] the Va soldiers that are going home on furlough look like Ball room champions by the side of our officers[.]"[18]

How the Army of Tennessee soldiers would fight was an unknown. Many, even their friends, secretly agreed with Hood that the fight had gone out of them. There was no doubt about their miserable showing at Nashville: most had run away.

As for their present leadership, Maj. Gen. William B. Bate had survived the slaughter of the Tennessee Campaign and brought with him to Bentonville about half of Cheatham's Corps. But Bate was no Frank Cheatham. He would fight and, like Cheatham, was an exceedingly popular commander. Yet Bate's record after Atlanta had been disappointing, if not disturbing. At Bentonville he would lead two brigades of Cleburne's Division, bracketed together under the able Brig. Gen. James Argyle Smith, and his own division under Floridian Daniel L. Kenan.

General Loring, unlike the enthusiastic amateur Bate, had long experience in the Old Army and kept his empty left sleeve pinned to his tunic as a proud reminder of Chapultepec. He had earned promotions to brigadier and major general early in the war and held brigade, division, and corps commands in Virginia, Mississippi, and Georgia. But in spite of opportunity aplenty he badly disappointed his admirers and the Confederate War Department. "Old Blizzards" was profane and bad-tempered and unfortunately given to intrigue, thus winning the enmity of Stonewall Jackson and Robert E. Lee, among others. Loring's men, however, admired his bravery and believed that the old man could "curse a cannon up hill without horses."[19] On March 18, unfortunately for Gen. A. P. Stewart, this veteran combat officer was so ill he could barely sit his horse.

Reaching Bentonville late in the afternoon of March 18, the Army of Tennessee moved through the village and encamped one mile beyond at 5:00 P.M. No fires were allowed. Orders went out "to make no noise in camp—the enemy are near."[20]

Despite the prevailing feeling of harmony and happy urgency that had greeted Johnston's decision to act aggressively, a familiar sense of uneasiness, however slight, began to develop fairly early—even that morning of March 18. The mischief began with a dispatch from Hardee. He had received Johnston's order to march on Bentonville at 8:50 A.M. "It will be promptly obeyed," Hardee responded, "but I am ignorant of the road you designate, and that must first be found."[21]

Johnston's 6:45 A.M. message to Hardee had stated vaguely: "The sheriff of this county represents that there is a road leading from a point two miles this side of Elevation and striking the Averasborough and Goldsborough road a little to the west of Bentonville."[22] According to Johnston's map, the distance from Elevation to Bentonville was twelve miles.[23] Hardee's trusted engineering officer, Maj. John Johnson, had just returned from conferring with members of the commanding general's staff in Smithfield. He had no knowledge of this road and he doubted the reliability of their maps. Nevertheless, Major Johnson and other members of Hardee's staff scouted south down the Averasboro road. At length they found a likely route to the east and laid out, as best they could, a new line of march southeast from the Smithfield-Averasboro road to the Smithfield-Bentonville road.[24]

Was this the sheriff's road? Precious hours seem to have been consumed in the search for the proper turnoff—the only plausible explanation for Hardee's inaction. Hardee had received Johnston's message at 8:50 A.M.; he knew well the importance of a timely start, yet his infantry remained rooted on the Averasboro-Smithfield road. One diarist (Taliaferro's Division) marked the time the soldiers started at "about midday"; another wrote "12 o'clock A.M."[25]

In his dispatch General Johnston had indicated that the sheriff's route would be a shortcut to Bentonville, but initially it required a countermarch, as Hardee was already two miles northeast of Elevation. His headquarters at 7:00 A.M., March 18, were eight miles south of Smithfield, and he remained there until 9:00 A.M., perhaps longer.[26] Taliaferro's Division may have been located even closer to Smithfield than Hardee's headquarters, as one private in Rhett's Battalion of artillery referred to "our bivouac below Smithfield."[27] When his column turned about and prepared for its tramp southwest, Hardee took the precaution of sending a copy of Johnston's order to Gen. Joseph Wheeler, who had been operating under Hardee's close control since appearing on the field at Averasboro on March 16. Hardee asked Wheeler to report directly and frequently and to send duplicate reports to General Johnston as well.[28]

McLaws's Division marched first, followed by Taliaferro's. From the Averasboro-Smithfield road they went down the Wilmington and Raleigh road "to the point where the Fayetteville & Smithfield road crossed it, then turned to left [north] down that road, then cut across the angle to another main road & down that to a certain distance, then camping however before reaching that road near a Mr. Sneed's, a strong Union man." Thus reads the blurry entry in the order book of Lafayette McLaws, a meticulous man by reputation. McLaws even scratched out about one-third of his record for March 18. This entry by McLaws is most unusual and suggests confusion. William A. Johnson, 2d South Carolina, a member of McLaws's Division, stated more simply though with equal opaqueness: "Cut across the country to go to Bentonville. Marched mostly in a settlement road."[29]

Johnston, Hardee, and Major Johnson agreed that Johnston's and Hardee's maps were "very incorrect." Hardee's troops marched fifteen miles that Saturday, "although by the map it appeared shorter." The exact route they used remains a mystery,[30] but there is little doubt that the march proved demanding.

General Thomas M. "Mully" Logan (commanding a brigade in Matthew C. Butler's cavalry division) rode by and observed the struggling infantry. Years later Logan's senior, Wade Hampton, wrote: "Hardee's men, though good soldiers, had been kept so long on garrison duty that the long marches broke down many of them, and half of his command, or perhaps more, fell out of the ranks while going to the scene of the action."[31] Hardee passed by one of his privates soaking his feet in a stream. "He checked his horse and called sternly to me, 'You there, sir! What are you doing straggling from your command? I suppose you are one of those men who behaved so badly at Averysboro.' "[32] The private shook his head, jumped up, and saluted. " 'Excuse me, General, but you are speaking to the wrong man, sir. I have never misbehaved, and never straggled. I am only bathing my feet to prevent them from blistering. There is my company right ahead there, sir, and I always keep up with it.' " Hardee seemed impressed with the man's "injured tone." He returned the salute. " 'I beg your pardon, sir,' " he said, and rode on. "He [Hardee] was a courtly and knightly soldier, and a great favorite with the men."[33]

Hardee halted the head of McLaws's column sometime after dark, one mile short of Sneed's house.[34] Taliaferro's trailing division arrived at the same point "late in the night." Hardee and his staff enjoyed Sneed's "unbounded hospitality," and while there he received a message from Johnston asking him to report immediately where he was encamped and the distance from Bentonville. "Dispatch is important," Johnston wrote. "It is of great consequence that you should be here as early as possible to-morrow morning."[35] Hardee responded at 9:50 P.M. from Sneed's: "This house is five miles from Bentonville. My command is about a mile in rear. I shall start at 4 o'clock, so as to reach Bentonville at an early hour in the morning. I did not reach camp till after dark, but if it be necessary I can start my command at an earlier hour."[36]

While Hardee and his men wandered cross-country to Bentonville, messages from Wheeler and Hampton came into Johnston's headquarters. Each hour it became more certain that Sherman did not intend any advance toward Raleigh and had committed his army to a direct march on parallel roads to Goldsboro. Two Union corps appeared to be on the "lower" Fayetteville-Averasboro-Goldsboro road, about a half day ahead of the Left Wing. Hampton's and Wheeler's reports indicated that the Left Wing of Sherman's army (the one that had fought Hardee at Averasboro) was on the upper Fayetteville-Averasboro-Goldsboro road. Thus, it could be assumed that there was probably "an interval of a day's march between the heads of the two columns [Left and Right Wings]."[37] According to Johnston's map, Sherman's wings should have been about twelve miles apart. The conclusive, activating dispatch was one Hampton forwarded at 10:00 P.M. from General Butler. Butler's scouts had established that the Fifteenth Corps (Right Wing) was approaching Cox's Bridge, and that the infantry advancing up the Averasboro-Goldsboro road was the Fourteenth Corps, followed by the Twentieth Corps.[38]

Johnston's cavalry screen had proven highly effective during March 16–18. It had kept Kilpatrick blindfolded and had promptly brought back intelligence of Federal infantry movements. Hampton and Wheeler not only dominated Kilpatrick—they also excelled when used in close combination with infantry commanders who knew how and when to employ them. Subordinate cavalry commanders—William W. Allen (the New Yorker who led Wheeler's Alabama and Georgia troopers), Mully Logan, the Tennessean George G. Dibrell, William C. P. Breckinridge, and Hampton's trusty M. C. Butler (who had lost his foot at Brandy Station two years before)—all performed with remarkable efficiency and consistency considering the dilapidated state of their commands.[39]

Johnston asked Hampton to hold his position at Willis Cole's, the site Hampton had recommended as an advantageous place to fight. Throughout Saturday, March 18, Hampton managed to hold on, but it proved a challenging task. Union foragers in organized company-sized units assisted by infantry skirmishers had fought with Hampton's cavalry (much of it led by Generals Allen and Dibrell) throughout the morning. By afternoon "I was pressed back by force of numbers," recalled Hampton, "to the crest of a wooded hill which overlooked a very large field that I had selected as a proper place for the battle."[40] There Hampton dismounted his men and put his horse artillery in a commanding though exposed position, far to the right of the Averasboro-Goldsboro road. "I knew if a serious attack was made on me the guns would be lost, but I determined to run this risk." A wag in Hampton's command commented, " 'Old Hampton is playing a bluff game, and if he don't mind Sherman will call him.' " Fortunately, the Yankees did not "call" Hampton, making only "a rather feeble demonstration against us" at sunset. "We were thus left in possession of the ground chosen for the fight."[41]

Johnston arrived in Bentonville on the night of the eighteenth and established his headquarters below the town. Hampton rode in soon from Cole's house and reported on the day's action on the Fayetteville-Averasboro-Goldsboro road. Johnston listened carefully and apparently adopted Hampton's ideas regarding use of terrain and deployment of the army.

Tomorrow Hampton's troopers were to hold their position as long as possible, granting time for the infantry to deploy behind the cavalry screen. Hoke's troops would form across the Averasboro-Goldsboro road as a blocking force and Stewart would position the Army of Tennessee on the right, almost parallel to the road, just within the tree line bordering Cole's great open field. Hardee, the trailing command, would file into the center between Stewart and Hoke. When the infantry had completed its deployment, Hampton was to fall back through Hoke's position and post his troops on the extreme right of the Confederate line. After Hampton passed though, the infantry would attack in echelon from the right, and the vulnerable Federal column that had made contact with Hoke's blocking force would be struck suddenly and violently on its left flank.[42]

It is interesting that although Hampton states that he suggested these dispositions, the plan of battle adopted by Johnston was "virtually identical" to that of the Atlanta Campaign, particularly the aborted attack at Cassville: establish a blocking force—compel the enemy to deploy—lure the enemy to attack—then counterattack with as much force as possible. Oliver O. Howard also saw the plan as a repetition of Johnston's tactics at Fair Oaks in 1862.[43]

Johnston thus hoped to mass and surprise the head of Sherman's Left Wing, defeat it, and destroy its trains. If successful, he then would have a chance against the remainder of Sherman's army, even if it were combined with Schofield's. Perhaps the Confederates might be fortunate enough to attack these additional forces in detail also. No one knew better than Joseph Johnston the trifling odds for ultimate success, but a *hope* for victory existed. That should be enough.

Johnston also knew that "on equal ground the chances would be decidedly against us." This made the idea of ambush at Bentonville not only appealing but also imperative. The site chosen by Hampton lay two to three miles south of Bentonville at the crossroads where the Averasboro-Goldsboro road met the Smithfield-Clinton road, an area in the extreme southeastern corner of Johnston County. The location favored a large attacking force attempting an ambush from a concealed position. Hoke's blocking force would have good fields of fire, particularly to the right front and

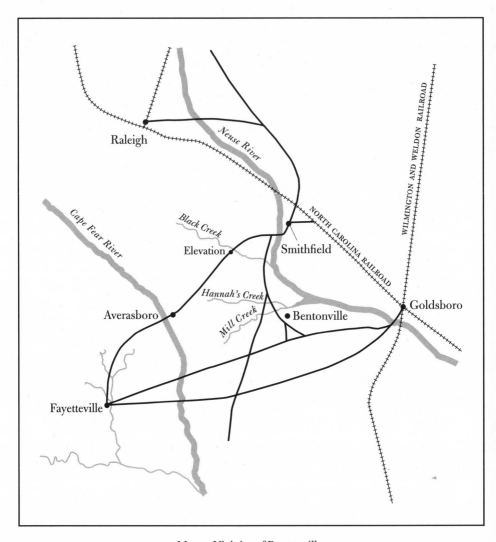

Map 1. Vicinity of Bentonville

directly down the Averasboro-Goldsboro road. This road, which will be referred to as the Goldsboro road, was sometimes called the "old" or upper Goldsboro road, the upper Fayetteville road, or the "old" Fayetteville road. Perhaps most proper would be the Fayetteville-Averasboro-Goldsboro road.

The Goldsboro road bisected the battlefield roughly east to west and would serve as the axis of the battle itself. On the north (upper) side were the fields of Willis Cole. To the west and south, lining these old uncultivated fields were dense thickets of blackjack and terribly tangled forest, cut here and there by streams that flattened out into marshes and swamps. Grasping, razor-sharp vines of briars, which sometimes grew to a thickness of one inch in diameter, acted like reinforcing rods thrust into concrete and stiffened undergrowth in these forests to the degree that they became impenetrable.[44] Bisecting the open land above the road and running roughly north-south perpendicular to it, was a ravine or deeply cut, swampy creek that began in yokelike fashion some 700 yards north of the road. This terrain feature promised protection to defenders and an obstacle to an organized attacking force.

Years later Oliver O. Howard remembered the field "with high ground and good artillery positions near at hand on the west. It was a position substantially at right angles to Henry Slocum's approach. A better position for a sudden descent and attack could not have been selected."[45]

From an overall tactical standpoint it should have been a concern to Johnston that at his back, just beyond Bentonville, was impassable Mill Creek with a single bridge. Furthermore, running into the Confederate flank from the east was, so to speak, a side door—the continuation of the Averasboro-Goldsboro road that led onto Cox's Bridge, the point toward which Sherman's Right Wing was heading. If this force (Howard's Army of the Tennessee) doubled back to assist the Left Wing, that road (the eastern fork of the road from Bentonville that crossed the Goldsboro road) offered an inviting avenue of approach into the Confederate flank and rear. Johnston's plan was to guard the eastern fork with cavalry while he moved down the western fork and hit hard and fast, driving the enemy southwest. If all went well, he could either pull back across Mill Creek and await Sherman behind this barrier like a bristling hedgehog or exploit his defeat of the Left Wing by turning on the Right. Then Sherman might have the Neuse River at *his* back.

Everything was ready. Johnston's troops had concentrated. Perhaps all were not in Bentonville itself, but they were close enough. Johnston had sufficient information about Sherman. So at 11:00 P.M., almost immediately on receipt of Butler's dispatch, Johnston's weary adjutant generals penned a final round of messages. A. P. Stewart was asked to "have your command put quietly under arms at dawn tomorrow." No wagon trains were to go beyond Bentonville itself. Johnston believed that Hardee's 3:00 A.M. start for Bentonville should give him ample time. Johnston then informed Hampton that they would attack the head of Sherman's Left Wing "as soon after dawn to-morrow as possible."[46]

As these warning orders went out from headquarters, veterans rechecked their weapons and tugged their blankets tight against their bodies. They pulled memories of pleasant times like a dancing string of daguerreotypes through their minds. Harvey Hill, like so many, prayed. "God has been very merciful & with me so far," he would tell his daughter. "But I can hardly hope to come through this campaign alive. If I get killed I hope that you children will be a great comfort to your Mother."[47]

4

A Grand Sight to See

HARDEE WAS DETERMINED to reach Bentonville in time for the attack, bringing with him as many men as he could push through the darkness. He would not fail Johnston. About 3:00 A.M., March 19, Taliaferro's troops formed, and soon his lead regiment of South Carolinians was filing down the road past Sneed's house, following in the wake of McLaws's Division.

Lafayette McLaws commanded Hardee's best troops. Conner's South Carolina Brigade (1,100 men) was led by the able and experienced Brig. Gen. John D. Kennedy. The brigade had built an enviable reputation in Virginia, where it was known as Kershaw's Brigade, McLaws's Division, First Corps. These troops were accustomed to McLaws, having served under him in some of the heaviest fighting of the war. Col. George P. Harrison, Jr.'s Brigade (700) was composed of the veteran 5th and 47th Georgia Regiments of the Army of Tennessee and the larger but less experienced 32d Georgia.

McLaws's three other brigades, however, represented combat units of doubtful quality. Col. Washington M. "Wash" Hardy's North Carolina Brigade (329) was led by an officer in whom the men had little faith. Two of his three regiments, properly belonging to Bragg's command, had been gathered up by Hardee in Fayetteville and added to McLaws's Division. Brig. Gen. Albert G. Blanchard's brigade of South Carolina Reserves (340) expected to be ordered home at any time. Blanchard himself was regarded as incompetent. Some counted on Col. John C. Fiser's Georgia Reserve Brigade (700) as additional manpower, but others felt that Fiser's Georgians were looking over their shoulders expecting Governor Brown to call them home also. Fiser, himself, a one-armed veteran of fights from Bull Run through Chickamauga, had come out of retirement to help McLaws defend Savannah. Fiser was brave and dependable.[1]

John C. Fiser
(courtesy V. Poindexter Fiser and Bruce S. Allardice)

The march from the vicinity of Sneed's house to Bentonville was difficult for McLaws's men, not to speak of Taliaferro's cannonless heavy artillery regiments. Many troops "had about two hours sleep and then resumed the march . . . without breakfast." On through the darkness, into the dawn they marched—five miles, perhaps six. They crossed Mill Creek as the sun was climbing up and reached Bentonville about 9:00 A.M.[2] The column halted at the Methodist church, where the men rested and had "such rations as we had: fat bacon and hard tack." The break and the food lifted spirits. The men looked about them, enjoying the bright sunshine. Indeed, it was "a beautiful Sabbath day." Catching sight of Johnston and Bragg, McLaws rode over, dismounted, and greeted them. They "shook hands warmly."[3]

This strong Confederate division remained inactive at the church, "listening to the firing below," and it is assumed that Taliaferro's troops halted with them. Hardee's troops, according to McLaws, could not have moved forward anyway. Stewart's Army of Tennessee filled the road ahead.[4]

McLaws's version of the morning of March 19, particularly the reference to the Army of Tennessee blocking the way, is puzzling, as is Johnston's account itself. Johnston maintained that he waited until Hardee arrived in Bentonville; only then did the rest of the army move "by the left flank, Hoke's division leading, to the ground selected by General Hampton."[5] Johnston must have been mistaken. Too many reliable versions have the Army of Tennessee advancing toward the point of deployment by 8:00 A.M., before Hardee arrived. Indeed, Brig. Gen. George D. Johnston, Walthall's Division, reported that his troops left their camp "shortly after sunrise."[6] It is known that Hoke preceded Stewart, and one of Hoke's men noted that his division moved out of Bentonville at "about 6 A.M." This seems reasonable and coincides with other accounts that have Hoke deploying first and being in position to receive the earliest Federal probe.

McLaws's version can be explained best. He refers to the traffic jam two miles south of the village, on the western fork of the Bentonville road. This road would become the battle line for Hoke's Division. When the Army of Tennessee reached Hoke's right flank, it had to bear off the road to the right (west) on "one narrow road through the thicket."[7] At that turnoff point, no doubt, commands stacked up: troops waited to be guided to their positions while general officers took a look at the ground. It is unlikely that this delay could have interfered with McLaws's progress, however, until the head of his column reached the fork in the Bentonville road behind Hoke's line.[8]

While McLaws made his way to the front, Hoke's Division had left its encampment at Bentonville and marched down the western fork of the Bentonville road toward its position at the intersection with the Goldsboro road.[9] Johnston watched the men of Hoke and Bragg pass, then he saw the Army of Tennessee following. A veteran of the 6th Florida remembered Johnston "sitting on his horse . . . with head uncovered, bowing to the small remnant of the noble army." Stewart's men, of course, cheered Johnston exuberantly.[10]

As Stewart's Army of Tennessee approached this intersection and Hoke's lines, the men heard firing ahead, "and the movements of couriers and aides rushing here and there indicated a battle on hand."[11] Stewart's corps, commanded by Loring, began filing off to the right and taking a position between the Bentonville road and a slight farm road. Harvey Hill, leading Lee's Corps, placed his men on Loring's right; Bate, with four brigades of Cheatham's Corps, later extended the line still farther to the right. But for the moment Bate's troops remained on the Bentonville road waiting for Loring's and Hill's men to deploy.

A Yankee battery opened up from the Goldsboro road when the Army of Tennessee began its deployment. Harvey Hill rode forward to reconnoiter, accompanied by four or five general officers and their staffs—an inviting target. Almost immediately a shell struck the group. Brigade commander Daniel H. Reynolds was hit.[12] His diary entry records the moment with remarkable objectivity: "At 8 A.M. moved out some 2½ miles from town where we were just in the act of going into position in line of battle when I was wounded by a cannon shot." The round "entered my horse's breast & came out under my left leg cutting away my stirrup & breaking my leg just below the knee & tearing off a great part of the calf of the leg." The solid shot continued on its way, killing yet another horse."[13] Reynolds's mount reared up in its death throes. The general pulled his right foot from the stirrup and "threw myself out of the saddle falling on the dead horse, the blood from my Horse's side spurting over me." Fearing that his horse might fall on top of him, Reynolds shouted for help. Fortunately "litter bearers seeing me fall had come running & putting me on a litter carried me a short distance & then put me on an ambulance & carried me to Bentonville. Here had my leg amputated just above the knee."[14] In the latter stages of the war Reynolds had become a darling of the Army of Tennessee.

This was a hard loss for the Army of Tennessee. Without his exemplary initiative and determination during the collapse at Nashville, Cheatham's Corps undoubtedly would have been bagged.[15]

Reynolds had proved an excellent combat officer, and his Arkansas brigade was probably the most reliable in Hill's corps, certainly in Walthall's Division.[16] As Reynolds's brigade faltered, grieving its loss, Edward C. Walthall himself "rode up and said: 'Boys, you have lost your commander, but you shall not suffer for the want of one. I'll command you myself.'" Walthall's statement may have been dramatic and perked up Reynolds's men, but by offering to lead them he limited himself as a subordinate unit commander, thus risking further weakening of the striking power of his tiny division.[17]

Enemy artillery fire had an even greater effect than wounding Reynolds. It compelled the Confederates to be cautious (and slower) in their deployment, forcing them deeper into the woods than they would have chosen. Also, Reynolds's Brigade, which had been forming in Cole's field, was moved to the rear into the woods some 200 yards, as was Quarles's Alabama Brigade (Walthall's Division) under Gen. George D. Johnston. Into their place, on high ground at the northern edge of the field, went Hampton's two horse batteries under Captains William E. Earle and E. Lindsley Halsey (Hart's Battery). Initially, these batteries did not respond to the "hot fire" of the Yankees. Instead they remained in position, gun crews lying behind their pieces, "without the privilege of replying."[18]

Hampton's batteries were almost in the same exposed position where they had been placed on the previous day, a quarter of a mile north of the Goldsboro road, in the corner of Cole's field. This spot (not the Goldsboro road) formed the center of Joseph Johnston's line. Behind Earle and Halsey were Walthall's two brigades. To their immediate right, stacked one behind the other, were the two Mississippi brigades of Loring's Division (now commanded by Col. James Jackson)—Lowry's (Lt. Col. Robert J. Lawrence) and Featherston's (Maj. Martin A. Oatis)—and an Alabama brigade (Scott's) under Capt. John A. Dixon.[19] Walthall's and Loring's Divisions constituted Stewart's Corps, Army of Tennessee (commanded by Loring). To Loring's right, in a double line of brigades, were the three divisions of Stephen D. Lee's Corps (commanded by Harvey Hill)—Hill's own (Col. John G. Coltart), Maj. Gen. Carter L. Stevenson's, and Maj. Gen. Henry D. Clayton's. To the right of Hill were Bate's four brigades, those of Cleburne's Division (Govan and Smith) on the front line and those of Bate's Division (Tyler and Finley) on the back line. Smith's Georgia Brigade, commanded by Capt. J. R. Bonner, formed the extreme right of the Confederate line. All of the troops to the right of Hampton's light guns, therefore, were Stewart's men—Johnston's old Army of Tennessee.[20]

Hoke's Division formed along the eastern edge of Cole's farm with the west fork of the Bentonville road immediately to its rear. Adjacent to Hampton's horse artillery was Hoke's right flank—Lt. Col. Joseph B. Starr's command—13th Battalion, North Carolina Light Artillery, and fragments of two other field artillery battalions.[21] These cannoneers were deployed as infantry with the exception of Capt. George B. Atkins's Battery (two 20-pound Parrott rifles and two 10-pounders). Atkins's guns were placed to the right (north) of the Goldsboro road with a good field of fire southwest down the road itself and directly west across Cole's field. Atkins himself was ill and for some time had suffered from "fearfully bad health," but he was on the field positioning his guns. Immediately to the right of the Goldsboro road, with their left flank extending across it, were John H. Nethercutt's Juniors. Then, as if "prolonging the western fork of the Bentonville road," came Colquitt's Brigade (commanded by Col. Charles T. Zachry) and Johnson Hagood's Brigade. Behind Hoke's first line of battle was Clingman's Brigade (Col. William S. Devane) in back of Zachry and Brig. Gen. William W. Kirkland behind the Juniors. "In front of Hoke it was low, wet pinewoods, interspersed with bay gulls and sluggish drains and having considerable undergrowth."[22]

General Johnston had a great advantage: choice of position. He intended to exploit it. Thus by midmorning, March 19, Johnston had Hoke blocking the Goldsboro road, Stewart making his way slowly through tangled woods to place the Army of Tennessee so as to conform to the northern edge of Cole's farm, and Hardee in the rear, between Bentonville and the fork in the Bentonville road, waiting to deploy his men. In their studies of the Battle of Bentonville, Jay Luvaas and Weymouth T. Jordan, Jr., use appropriately the image of a sickle to describe the dispositions chosen by Johnston on the morning of March 19. Stewart's troops, deployed just inside the woods surrounding Cole's field on the north and northeast, represent the blade, their line "bent back about forty-five degrees before making a long right angle zag to the west." Another Jordan image that conveys Johnston's concept, as well as the deployment of his army, was the hammer and anvil—Stewart's enveloping force illustrating the hammer, Hoke's blocking force the anvil.[23] To crush the Left Wing of Sherman's army, this heavy hammer blow or slice of the sickle required sufficient force. Johnston's infantry and artillery, including those of Hardee, numbered not more than 15,400 soldiers; his cavalry about 4,200.[24] Would that suffice?

Since dawn Confederate cavalry on the Goldsboro road had had their hands full. Longer and stronger Union skirmish lines drove George Dibrell's and Mully Logan's dismounted troops from position to position, from "rail pile" to rail pile. By 9:00 A.M. the Confederate cavalry had retired to the Cole farm and then passed through Hoke's lines.

The Yankees kept coming—straight down the Goldsboro road—directly into the arms of Joe Johnston's ambush. They came fast—too fast—despite the cavalry's efforts to slow them. At midmorning the Yankees struck infantry skirmishers about 300 yards ahead of Johnston's main line. As it went into position, each Confederate brigade had thrown out skirmishers, relieving any remaining cavalry pickets. When a sufficient number of skirmishers had been deployed, their efforts were coordinated on the division level and, in the case of Harvey Hill, on the corps level.

A brisk, deadly firefight soon developed, and the Federals were driven back all along the line. They returned quickly, however, with stronger and longer skirmish lines. Finally Union lines of battle began to come up in support of their skirmishers and the Confederates fell back. This push-and-shove battle of skirmishers, almost a mile in width, lasted from 9:00 A.M. until almost noon and was conducted "with spirit."[25]

When Lee's Corps took its position on line, Bate's Corps had not yet come up, so Harvey Hill instructed the veteran Col. John P. McGuire of the 32d Tennessee to station his regiment as skirmishers in front of Stevenson's and Clayton's Divisions. McGuire also was to extend his troops far enough to the right to screen what would become Bate's front. "Press the skirmish line as close upon the enemy's position" as possible, Hill continued, but do not bring on a general engagement—an enormous assignment for an under-strength regiment.[26]

McGuire did as Hill ordered, covering in effect the extreme right of the deploying Army of Tennessee. Soon the 32d Tennessee came in contact with the enemy and skirmishing began in earnest. "About three-quarters of a mile in our front . . . through the opening in the forest and over the hills and ravines," McGuire observed "what appeared to be heavy bodies of Federal infantry moving rapidly to our right." Once past Hill's right flank, the Yankees changed course and began moving directly toward the Confederate skirmishers. McGuire notified Hill immediately that the approaching column (Buell's Brigade) seemed to be advancing toward the position to be occupied by Bate. Hill sent back word to McGuire to resist as long as possible. Then, as quickly as it had appeared, the blue column disappeared from sight into the forest.[27]

Confederate skirmishing, such as that conducted by McGuire's regiment, represented excellent work, giving the main line of battle sufficient time to deploy—and dig in. By this stage of the war, seasoned infantry when given a moment in the presence of the enemy would "immediately fortify," which meant that "the boys availed themselves of time to cut down small pine limbs, which, to some extent hid them"; others quickly raised "breastworks of rails and logs," and still others "with bayonets dug a little trench, making rifle pits some eight or ten inches high."[28]

With the enemy column bearing down on them, with the arrival of the essential moment for cooperation and enthusiasm at hand, it seems it was then, incredulously, that Harvey Hill and A. P. Stewart, old West Point class-mates,[29] saw fit to squabble—about the necessity of constructing breast-works. Momentarily expecting the order to advance, Stewart believed entrenching to be a waste of time and energy. Corps commander Hill, independent as ever, shook his head doggedly, defiantly, and put his men to digging. Before their works were "half completed," however, a heavy Yankee line of about a thousand men appeared from out of the forest. The blue skirmish line was wide—covering the entire front of Clayton's Division and extending beyond, both left and right. The Yankee line of battle, neverthe-less, was limited—a single line about 400 yards in width. It appeared to be a brigade front, but "they had changed their direction from a perpendicular upon Bate's line and were moving diagonal to our left, and if the direction pursued by them were continued, they would strike Stevenson about the center."[30] As the Yankees closed, McGuire sent runners to Carter Stevenson and Hill, notifying them that they were about to be attacked. Then McGuire and his Tennessee skirmishers retired through Hill's line of battle, taking their place in line beside their comrades in Palmer's Brigade.[31] McGuire himself walked the line. As his men began to dig in, he shouted: "Boys, you remember the 19th and 20th of September, 1863, at Chickamauga? Well, this is the 19th of March, and you may look out for some close work to-day as hot as it was there."[32]

On came the Federals, blindly. They did not know where the Confeder-ates were or their strength. One could tell by observing the alignment of the Federal line of battle advancing at an acute angle to the entrenched and concealed Confederates instead of "square to the front." Thus the enemy left "came within a few yards of Clayton's Division, its right barely came within range of Palmer" (Stevenson's right brigade). The groping Yankees believed that they were attacking the Confederate right flank. Actually they were presenting their own left flank to the enemy.[33]

Almost half of Stovall's 350 men consisted of the 42d Georgia. The Georgians could see the enemy advancing, though their view was partially obscured by pine limbs piled in front of their line. "It was a grand sight to see them moving on us," thought a member of the 42d, "'Old Glory' floating in the breeze so proudly." The skirmish line of Clayton's Division gradually gave way. As the line of battle absorbed the skirmishers, Col. Henry C. Kellogg, commanding Stovall's Brigade, again and again sent word down the line to "Hold your fire. Keep down." The order was carried out "to the letter." Kellogg's men waited until the Federals got within forty paces. Then—"a sheet of fire blazed" into the Yankee flank, although many troops raised their weapons "without seeing any object at which to fire." The enemy line of battle stopped instantly, broke apart, and "ran back in great confusion." Colonel Kellogg showed poise as he directed volley after volley into the Federal ranks. The Confederates smiled; some shouted. It was all so easy this Sunday morning.[34]

A special benefit of the repulse was captured weapons: "The arms secured from the fallen foe immediately in our front equipped an entire regiment of our North Carolina soldiers who had inferior guns." While the men collected rifles, Harvey Hill and his staff rode down the line and complimented the men on their performance, especially Kellogg's Georgians.[35]

On Bate's front another enemy line of battle struck. It too was narrow and thin and seemed to be concentrated against Govan's Arkansas Brigade. Smith's Georgia Brigade, on Govan's right (thus on the extreme right of the entire army), was ordered not to fire but to lie concealed. General Bate rode along Smith's line and spoke to the 63d Georgia: "Why, boys, you lie mighty close. I came very near riding over you without seeing you." The soldiers lay close because there were very few of them. The 63d Georgia itself consisted of about a hundred men, and the four regiments of Smith's Brigade itself were commanded collectively by a captain (J. R. Bonner). Nevertheless, the attack on Govan, was thrown back as handily as the one against Stovall. A. P. Stewart reported to Johnston: "the enemy attacked the right and center of our line at 12:45 P.M. and were easily repulsed. The heaviest attack was made on Stovall's brigade."[36]

Hill's troops had in effect surprised the Federals advancing to locate and turn the Confederate right flank.

This was not the case on Hoke's front, however, in an attack that came somewhat earlier than the one against Stewart. The enemy soldiers opposing Hoke charged carefully, as though they knew that Confederates might be in force and supported by artillery. The swampy underbrush below the Goldsboro road slowed them, breaking their formations, making it extremely difficult to maneuver. Yet the Yankees managed to make their way down both sides of the road, with heavier and heavier lines of skirmishers— then with lines of battle—struggling and slashing through the tangle. They felt for the Confederate left, applying greater and greater pressure. Hoke, receiving word from Hagood that the enemy was moving to the left, decided to strengthen that portion of his line. He ordered Kirkland from reserve to connect with Hagood's left flank and prolong it.

The Federal attacks were now directed almost entirely against General Kirkland. Unfortunately Kirkland had little time to entrench. But this did not seem to matter. Kirkland's men—like beavers—quickly "covered themselves with log and earth obstructions." A young Junior heard all the racket to his left—volleys and countervolleys. Then he watched to his horror as the color-bearer of the 66th Regiment North Carolina Troops waved his flag in the face of the enemy only to be killed by a bullet believed to have been fired from the upper story of the Cole house. Nevertheless, Kirkland and Hagood threw back the determined Federal attack "handsomely."[37]

Despite Kirkland's success, Hoke's superior—Braxton Bragg—was worried. Indeed, "anxious" seems a more appropriate characterization. Bragg knew that Hoke had one more brigade in reserve—Clingman's—but it was positioned at the edge of the Goldsboro road, just behind the juncture of Colquitt's Brigade and the Juniors, the point most likely to attract direct attack. Bragg worried about this center, but he worried more about Hoke's left being turned. That could be disastrous. He simply lacked enough men to cover a front that seemed to extend by the minute. Although each Union attack had been beaten off, another hard push against Kirkland might break the left. What if Federals were to appear beyond Kirkland's flank? Disaster, collapse, and rout were no strangers to Bragg. Doubtless the nightmare of Missionary Ridge returned—Federal troops pouring down the ridge from the left. Therefore Bragg, probably in person, appealed to Joseph E. Johnston, pointing out the danger of the Confederate left being turned and asking that reinforcements be sent immediately to support Kirkland.[38]

This was a critical moment at Bentonville, perhaps *the* critical moment for the Confederates. Johnston conceded to Bragg's alarm and diverted Hardee's largest division—McLaws's—to aid Hoke. Thus, Johnston deprived himself of this important body of troops just at the moment for massive counterattack—just when the initiative passed to the Confederates. Wade Hampton later asserted: "This movement was in my judgment the only mistake committed on our part during the fight, and when the general [Johnston] notified me of the intended change in the plans I advised that we should adhere to the one agreed on." Johnston himself would declare that his action had been "most injudicious." Indeed, six years after Bentonville, in a letter to Hoke, Johnston wrote: "I believe that Genl Bragg's nervousness when you were first attacked at Bentonville, was very injurious—by producing urgent applications for help—which not only made delay, but put a large division out of position. . . . It was a great weakness on my part; not to send him [Bragg] to Raleigh on the 18th."[39]

It thus appears that McLaws's Division received orders either at the Bentonville church or as it moved down the Bentonville road (not, as McLaws implies, as it impatiently waited close to the main battle line behind the deploying Army of Tennessee) to march down to the forks of the Bentonville road, bear left, and "connect with Genl Hoke's left."[40] Hardee, with his engineering officer Maj. John Johnson, preceded McLaws and spent some time reconnoitering on the extreme left, but apparently he was recalled by Johnston and given the assignment of commanding the flank attack to be delivered by the Confederate right. No field orders survive from Hardee to McLaws on March 19, and one must assume that at this juncture McLaws's Division was removed from Hardee's direction, at least until dusk.

The ground to Hoke's left was miserable for offensive operations, or any type of maneuver for that matter—very heavy thickets and underbrush laced with swamps that destroyed the cohesion and precision of lines of battle. McLaws moved behind Hoke's line "with great difficulty. The officers who were sent to guide me to Hoke's left, lost their way every time." Eventually Col. Eli T. Stackhouse's regiment (3d South Carolina Consolidated) did locate Kirkland's left and extended it. McLaws's other troops, however, had become "greatly entangled." It became "impossible . . . to know whether it was friend or foe in our front. Some troops on our right, by mistaking the head of direction, began to face one way, while Kershaw's brigade [now Conner's] was facing another."[41]

A gap developed between Stackhouse's left and the other elements of McLaws's Division. McLaws, determined to avoid more groping and confusion, stretched a thin picket line from Stackhouse's left to the right of Colonel Fiser's Brigade.[42] On Fiser's left, the extreme left of the Confederate army, McLaws placed his best brigade—Conner's—with J. D. Kennedy commanding. Behind Fiser and Kennedy, in a second line in reserve, were the brigades of Harrison and Hardy.[43]

Once his division had ceased thrashing about in the thicket, McLaws set his men to constructing earthworks. Sometime in the early afternoon Bragg told McLaws of Johnston's plan—the flank attack to be conducted by the Army of Tennessee and Taliaferro's Division. McLaws "must be ready to strike a blow if an opportunity offered." Then McLaws, as was his habit as a good soldier, went forward with staff officers and made a personal reconnaissance to his front. He intended to be prepared so that he might hit hard.[44]

About noon Hardee brought up Taliaferro's Division. As it came down the western fork of the Bentonville road behind Hoke's position, the division passed "bloody, rough tables" where regimental surgeons labored. "Amputated legs and arms [were] thrown alongside on the grass. The sight was temporarily depressing, as it foreshadowed what we had to expect."[45] Farther on the troops halted and saw where the Federals had been repulsed, the dead lying on the field. Some of the men stopped and gave water and whiskey to wounded Yankees who lay begging for something to drink. While Taliaferro and his soldiers waited to go in, Hardee talked with Johnston. Johnston ordered him to move Taliaferro's Division into the woods and mass it behind the Army of Tennessee as a reserve. He also directed Hardee to take charge of all troops deploying right of the Bentonville road—Taliaferro (1,500) and the Army of Tennessee (4,500)—and lead them in the attack against the Federal left. Hardee's assault would be followed in echelon by Hoke's (4,500) and McLaws's (3,000). The enemy force before them was estimated at 35,000. Johnston wished for the attack to be launched at 2:15 P.M.

Hardee made his way to the Army of Tennessee and personally spoke to corps commanders Loring, Bate, and Hill, explaining what he wished for each to do. Hill told him, probably without a smile but with obvious irony, that he had awakened that morning feeling ill, "but the battle made me well." Loring, however, was obviously sick, which concerned Hardee.[46] When Hardee spoke to Bate, the latter reported that he had just made a reconnaissance and found the enemy line, "at least his front line, did not extend connectedly at all beyond my right." He urged Hardee to bring up Taliaferro from reserve and place him on the extreme right, beyond Smith's Brigade. From there, Bate felt confident, Taliaferro would crash down on the left flank of the enemy.[47]

Hardee agreed with Bate and, after conferring with Stewart, sent the order to Taliaferro. This would require a delay in the time of attack, so Lt. Col. Bromfield Ridley of Stewart's staff went back to the Army of Tennessee corps commanders—Loring, Bate, and Hill—to notify them that the time of attack had been changed to 2:45 P.M.. Meanwhile brigade and division commanders went up and down the line encouraging their troops, soldiers checked their equipment, and regimental bands played "uplifting" pieces.[48]

Precious time was being lost. Hampton had sent Johnston a dispatch at 12:45 (received at 1:45): "Taliaferro is just going in [deploying to the right of the Bentonville road behind the Army of Tennessee]. I think whatever we do should be done quickly. An advance of the line would break them."[49] The half hour allotted by Hardee for the "detour" of Taliaferro actually had proved insufficient; 2:45 P.M. found the Georgians and South Carolinians struggling slowly through incredible undergrowth while attempting to reach Bate's right flank.[50]

While the Confederates maneuvered and readied themselves for the coming assault, Yankee sharpshooters kept up a deadly fire from the Cole house.[51] The shots from these snipers seemed directed at the Junior Reserves' front and at exposed gunners of Atkins's Battery. Until this time Atkins had been exchanging fire with the Yankee cannon on the Goldsboro road, but now he redirected the fire of two Napoleon twelve-pounders toward the sharpshooters. "A few well-directed shells crashed and exploded into the Cole house, causing Yankees to pour out like rats out of a sinking ship."[52]

To the delight of Capt. E. L. Halsey's gunners, who had been lying on the Cole field enduring the fire of the Yankee battery, Hampton gave permission for them to engage. It had been a costly wait. Two artillerymen had been killed and five wounded.[53] An infantryman passing by later "saw probably a dozen horses dying, dead or wounded where the battery had been. To this day I recall the piteous expressions of two or three of these wounded horses, as they raised their heads in their suffering."[54]

Halsey's and Earle's Batteries opened up at once. The artillery duel grew furious for a time, but then the superiority of the Confederates (three batteries to one) began to tell. The horse artillery found the range: shells struck in and around the Federal gunners. One round passed over the guns and struck an ammunition chest which exploded, creating havoc. The Yankee battery fell silent and limbered up, either to abandon the field or to move to a different position. The Confederate infantrymen, though, knew the time was close at hand when they could rush those guns. They also longed to clean out any snipers remaining in the wreckage of the Cole house.[55]

All the Amusement We Want

"A MORE BEAUTIFUL MORNING I never saw," thought Pvt. W. C. Johnson, Company F, 89th Ohio. It seemed impossible to disagree. Sunday, March 19, was warm and cloudless. Birds appeared everywhere, singing good-bye to the rain and the cold. Peach trees burst into bloom; fields looked green again.[1] Musicians, inspired by the loveliness, awoke the camp of the Federal Fourteenth Army Corps by "playing 'Old Hundred,'[2] a grand old anthem, which never sounded to me [Maj. George W. Nichols] more sweetly solemn."[3]

While his men indulged themselves with the joys of morning, division commander William Passmore Carlin opened his field chest. "So thoroughly convinced there would be a battle that day, I dressed for the occasion, putting on my best uniform of a Brigadier General in order if killed, wounded or captured, my rank would be known."[4]

The thirty-five-year-old Carlin, a West Pointer and division commander, took great pride in being a professional soldier. He tried his best to act and look like one. He had won his appointment to the Academy through competitive examination, not political preferment, and had served diligently under the most respected officers during the 1850s—William S. Harney, Edwin V. Sumner, and Sidney Johnston. When war broke out in 1861, he took command of the 38th Illinois and saw his first action in Missouri. His aggressive but dependable work so impressed John C. Frémont that Carlin was soon named commander of the District of Southeast Missouri.

Carlin proceeded east of the Mississippi in 1862 and won distinction as a brigade commander at Perryville in October 1862, when he went to the rescue of Phil Sheridan's division and led his brigade in a thrilling, audacious assault that punctured the rebel line. At Murfreesboro two months later, he proved himself a steady combat leader, repulsing attack after attack by Confederates who hit him from all sides. During this critical phase of Murfreesboro, the Union center held firm, Carlin's "pipe-smoking calm contrasting favorably with [Jefferson C.] Davis."[5] At Chickamauga, however, things turned out differently. Again commanding a brigade under Davis, Carlin was driven from the field. He blamed Davis. The two men had never gotten along, and twice before Chickamauga Carlin had sought to have Davis removed from command. George H. Thomas in the fall of 1863 transferred his two quarreling subordinates to the Fourteenth Corps but separated them, placing Carlin (with eight regiments rather than the four he led at Chickamauga) in the division of Richard W. Johnson. Carlin fought very well at Missionary Ridge and continued his good work in the Atlanta Campaign.

Davis and Carlin were thrown together again in August 1864, when Davis assumed command of the Fourteenth Corps and Carlin took over the division of the disabled Johnson (no favorite of Sherman's) within that corps. The two adversaries seemed to have worked together fairly well for the past six months, especially at the Battle of Jonesboro.[6]

As Carlin's men prepared to move out that beautiful Sunday morning, they heard shots in the distance down the road. But this was nothing unusual. They assumed that the noise must be foragers driving Joe Wheeler's cavalry. The "bummers," as was their custom, were out early. Awakened at 3:00 A.M., they had fed their horses and made their coffee, then at 4:00 formed on the Goldsboro road, "tired, sore, cross and ugly, but every one in his place." They rode forward about two miles and, just as it "began to grow light," surprised a rebel picket post—a "few men huddled about a small fire at the side of the road, ragged gray blankets wrapped about their shoulders." The rebels ran off and the foraging party continued to advance, down a hill and into a wide swamp with deep water. When they emerged it "had become quite light," and almost immediately they encountered a rebel picket line. The enemy fired a few hasty shots and fell back.[7]

The foragers spurred their horses in pursuit, "when, to our surprise, we came in full sight of a line of earthworks, not more than forty rods away."[8] The commander of the forager's advance guard, Maj. Charles E. Belknap, reported, "as far as I could see to the right and the left the dirt from thousands of shovels was flying in the air." He saw men throw away their shovels and grab their weapons; he heard rebel officers shout commands. Belknap prudently withdrew into the swamp and sent back "one of my best

William Passmore Carlin
(Illinois State Historical Library)

men" to inform Carlin of the formidable rebel position. It might be Johnston's army ahead, he was to tell the general. Then the foragers spread out,
and a lively firefight developed.[9]

Many bummers soon abandoned the skirmishing, however, and fell back
toward camp. It seemed that day that the usual division foragers "had been
accompanied by a considerable body of stragglers and camp followers,

mostly officers' servants, all intent to forage in search of food, and so eager that they kept well up to the front." But they wanted no part of such a fight as this.[10]

Belknap's courier, meanwhile, never reached Carlin.[11]

At 7:00 A.M. Carlin's lead brigade under Brig. Gen. Harrison Hobart stepped out, quickly passed the camp of Brig. Gen. James Dada Morgan's division, and headed down the Goldsboro road. Morgan would follow at 8:00. Carlin's two other brigades then marched past Morgan's camp "in the usual column of fours," "with colors flying and bands playing the national airs. It was a splendid scene," observed one of Morgan's officers. "All felt gay and joyous under the influence of the mild spring weather, with the prospect of very soon being at the end of our journey." Shortly after he cleared Morgan's camp, Carlin threw out skirmishers to his front and on his flanks. He had already taken the precaution of putting wagons and pack mules at the rear of the division.[12]

After an hour, about three miles out from his camp at Underwood's, Carlin came up on the foragers engaged with the enemy. They "for once had got hold of something they could not get away with." Two companies of the 94th Ohio, Hobart's lead regiment, were on the skirmish line in front of the brigade. They passed through the foragers' ragged line, and almost immediately "a cannon ball came whistling among the trees and heavy lines of rebel skirmishers opened up in front." We "saw that business of a serious nature was on hand." Hobart quickly reinforced the 94th with the two other regiments constituting Briant's wing of his brigade.[13]

It was common practice for brigades to divide into wings, and not uncommon for regiments to do the same, thus providing far greater flexibility of movement. Hobart's advanced wing was under Lt. Col. Cyrus E. Briant, 88th Indiana, but Hobart himself retained operational control. Following in close support was Fitch's wing, commanded by Lt. Col. Michael H. Fitch, 21st Wisconsin. Briant "attacked the enemy and drove him very rapidly." Hobart, directing the two wings, cautiously halted Fitch, then ordered him to push forward again, the delay allowing Briant to advance out of sight. All the while Carlin with his two other brigades followed close behind, marching steadily down the Goldsboro road. Although there were more Confederates than usual and their resistance seemed organized and determined, Briant's wing appeared to be handling them expeditiously.[14]

Back at the Fourteenth Corps camp, Sherman, Slocum, and Davis sat on their horses in a group, chatting with their heads cocked toward the sound of the firing. Davis reminded Sherman of Carlin's premonition. Perhaps Carlin had come upon the enemy in force. Sherman "listened attentively a moment or two," then he "replied, in his usual brisk, nervous, and positive way, 'No, Jeff; there is nothing there but [George C.] Dibrell's cavalry. Brush them out of the way. Good-morning. I'll meet you tomorrow morning at Cox's Bridge.'" Sherman then told Slocum that "he believed Hardee had fallen back to Raleigh, and that I could easily reach the Neuse on the following day." Sherman seemed impatient to leave the Left Wing, apparently focused on crossing the Neuse, getting to Goldsboro. And so he rode off to the east to join Howard, "confident that Johnston and his infantry were forty miles away."[15]

Of course, Sherman wanted to believe that only light opposition lay ahead obstructing Slocum's path to Goldsboro. It fit his plans; it fit Johnston's pattern of perpetual withdrawal. Judson Kilpatrick had encouraged Sherman's line of reasoning. Federal cavalry dispatches, even on the morning of March 19, confirmed that Johnston was concentrating near Raleigh. One could tell, Kilpatrick concluded, by the number of rebel pickets on the Raleigh and Smithfield roads. Besides, Lt. William M. Potter of Kilpatrick's staff had come in from behind Confederate lines reporting that every preparation was being made to confront Sherman about ten miles east of Raleigh.[16]

So Sherman rode off, and Slocum and Davis started to the front, moving past Morgan's marching column. Wing commander Slocum arrived first. He found the head of Carlin's division about three miles out, beyond the line of foragers, deployed to the right of the Goldsboro road in two lines or wings. It was about 10:00 A.M. Hobart's front line (Briant's wing—33d Ohio, 94th Ohio, and 88th Indiana) had two companies from each regiment thrown forward as skirmishers. Slocum, who "assumed general control," approved Carlin's dispositions and instructed his aggressive brigade division commander to press forward.[17]

Soon after passing the Morris house on the left of the road,[18] Briant's wing struck infantry skirmishers fighting from behind rail barricades. Briant's extended skirmish line, closely supported by a line of battle, nevertheless continued to drive ahead, the enemy falling back steadily through the woods and undergrowth. Hobart's men tended to drift north in pursuit. Briant's wing, under Hobart's immediate supervision, crossed the Goldsboro road at a forty-five-degree angle and continued its attack northwest into a great open field. But Fitch's wing, under orders from Carlin, halted and took position with its left flank on the road itself at a point "where the Goldsboro road, which for some distance ran almost north, turned east." Slocum and Carlin, on the road close behind Hobart's divided brigade, noticed that "the woods were more open on the left hand, and a dim road led off in a north-easterly direction." Slocum directed Carlin to send Buell's brigade (Second) down this country road feeling for the enemy right flank, in effect a reconnaissance-in-force. So "our brig. (2nd) about faced and marched back to a road that led to the left."[19]

George Pearson Buell, the cousin of Don Carlos Buell and formerly colonel of the 58th Indiana, had performed poorly as an infantry brigade commander at Chickamauga (his troops had bolted). In contrast, in his next assignment—command of the Army of the Cumberland's Pioneer brigade—he excelled. Indeed, as a result of his dependability and originality in late 1863, he had been brought to Sherman's attention by Maj. Gen. William F. Smith. In the March to the Sea, Buell performed well as commander of the pontoon train and won not only Sherman's confidence but also promotion to brevet brigadier general.

As Buell's column marched off to the west, two of Slocum's staff officers observed Briant and Carlin fighting with the rebel infantry skirmishers, and it was evident that much greater care was being taken. This seemed to be no ordinary "brush the enemy from the road" affair. Maj. William G. Tracy and Lt. Joseph B. Foraker, both mounted with their orderlies beside them, watched attentively as Hobart and Briant halted their men on the edge of a field and regrouped. Then cautiously the two-company-per-regiment skirmish lines advanced into the open. It was an old field, a quarter mile wide, on the left of the Goldsboro road. When the skirmishers were about halfway across, Briant gave the order to charge the pine woods directly to their front. The skirmishers rushed to the edge of the wood line, the main bodies of the three regiments following in close support.

The Confederates opened fire from the woods with a great racket, but it turned out to be a line of outposts protected by rifle pits or barricades, "each far enough back in the woods not to be seen." It was a bad time for mounted staff officers to be in the middle of an open field, "in the midst of which we were sorry to find ourselves," Lieutenant Foraker recalled. "I remember we hardly knew what to do—we could do no good by going on and none by remaining. To be killed under such circumstances. . . . While we hesitated a spent ball struck Tracy on the leg." Although not serious, it was a painful wound, and Foraker sent Tracy to the rear with his orderly and then remounted and rode forward to see the results of Hobart's attack. Already the rebels had been driven from their works, "back through the woods and out of sight."[20]

Foraker found a group of soldiers standing around a seriously wounded Confederate. They were trying to help the man, but "to everything said to him he answered by reaching about him for sticks, pebbles or anything he could get hold of and viciously throwing them at his would-be good Samaritans." A squad with prisoners came by, and Foraker learned from them that Johnston was in front with his entire army. Foraker immediately remounted and rushed back to Slocum.[21]

Things were going well despite what the rebel prisoners said. By 11:00 A.M. Hobart with his advance wing of three regiments had pushed the rebel skirmishers almost a mile, past a white two-story house (Cole's) standing on the edge of yet another large field on the left of the Goldsboro road. Briant's wing entered the open ground and made its way halfway across. Suddenly, from the woods on the edge of the field about 200 yards away, the enemy opened a heavy fire of musketry and artillery. Hobart's thin front line staggered, halted, then quickly "abandoned" the field. Many of the men sought shelter behind Cole's house and outbuildings, but rebel "shells and cannon Balls soon began to knock these Buildings to pieces." So Hobart led his wing back into a pine thicket that covered a ravine running almost parallel with the Goldsboro road. There in front of the ravine Hobart began to throw up light works. Men worked with a fury. "Bullets were whistling all around us and cutting the limbs on Every side."[22] Hobart's new line would run almost at right angles to the Goldsboro road.

The other wing of Hobart's First Brigade—Fitch's—was immediately to the right of the road. Beyond Fitch, Carlin placed his Third Brigade, commanded by Lt. Col. David Miles.[23] Carlin did this as a precaution, having learned that enemy units of undetermined size were moving about to his front and right, "demonstrating against my right flank." To further strengthen his position and to silence that deadly rebel battery, Carlin brought up a battery (Scovel's) himself, placing it just left of the road facing Cole's house, about 350 yards ahead. Hobart's three regiments immediately to the right of the road under Fitch would provide the necessary infantry support for the battery. Miles and Fitch also began to throw up temporary works.[24]

Lt. Palmer F. Scovel, who commanded these four guns (Battery C, 1st Illinois Light Artillery), immediately unlimbered and engaged the rebels beyond Cole's house. Scovel's gunners scored a number of hits on the enemy battery itself and on another battery that had appeared to the northeast, across Cole's open field. Indeed, it proved a gunner's paradise, for targets abounded. Scovel would fire at the enemy batteries alternately, then he would shift his fire and direct shells into clumps of enemy horsemen, then shift again, firing into the piles of fresh earth dimly visible at the edge of the woods. In the course of three hours (10:00 A.M.–1:00 P.M.) Battery C expended some 300 rounds, an unusually heavy rate of fire.[25]

Hobart, even with the vigorous support of Scovel, obviously lacked the strength to drive the rebels from their position in the woods ahead. It would have to be a division effort. So Carlin, apparently with Slocum's approval, sent a staff officer to stop Buell and bring him back to the pine thicket that Hobart occupied with Briant's wing. At this point corps commander Davis arrived at the front. "Attack vigorously and push on," he told Carlin, believing that Buell ("a favorite of Davis"), if he moved forward promptly, would fall upon the right flank of the force blocking their path. It looked like a splendid tactical opportunity. Only affairs above the road must wait until Buell retraced his steps and linked with Hobart's left.[26]

As though determined not to be outdone in aggressiveness by his corps commander, Carlin ordered Miles, as well as Briant's three regiments left of the road, to attack simultaneously on the right.[27] Committing the entire division (except Fitch's wing beside the road in support of the guns) would "multiply [their] chances of success."[28]

Harrison Hobart's men received the order to charge with a smile. "Nothing but cavalry in our front" was the word. "We on the front line knew better,"[29] especially the men of Buell's brigade. When he received the order to break off his reconnaissance and connect with Hobart's left, Buell marched "through a tangle of scrub oak breaking cover into a large field on the far side of which were enemy behind earthworks, passing obliquely across this field into the edge of a pine woods beyond."[30] Hobart was still not in view, but Buell's movement was in "plain sight of the enemy." A private in the 13th Michigan, a member of Buell's flanking party, reported: "Our Brig was sent to the left calculating to flank them but thair [sic] line was to long[.] we fooled around untill about noon and then we was ordered to charge the Rebel works." Another of Buell's men was less charitable. "Some thought there might be at least 2,000 of them [rebels] there but Jeff Davis laughed at the *largness* [sic] of the estimate & ordered Gen Carlin to charge with a Brigade [.]"[31]

And thus it was that Carlin's division—supervised by Carlin, Davis, and Slocum—attacked Johnston's deploying army head-on. Of course, these Federals did not know that Johnston's army lurked in the woods ahead.

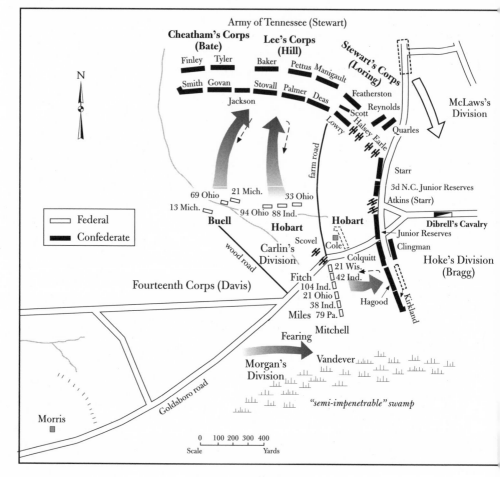

Map 2. Carlin's Attack

Their mission was to determine what did lay ahead, brush aside any enemy they encountered, then push on. After all, Sherman was in a hurry.

David Miles's brigade struck first.[32] His troops made their way "through a dense thicket and swamp and charged again and again, with no chance of carrying the works in consequence of the impenetrable thicket and the depth of the swamp." It was a determined effort, one in which Miles's brigade behaved "very handsomely." Yet, although the physical obstacles provided splendid cover, Miles's troops lost heavily when they dashed themselves against Hoke's partially constructed breastworks. Their casualties included the commander of the 38th Indiana, Capt. James H. Low. Proof positive of the impact of Miles's vigorous assaults was Braxton Bragg's call for reinforcements.[33]

As Miles battered himself against the face of a strong rebel division, Buell's brigade was sent in by direct order of corps commander Jefferson C. Davis. Buell's men would attack Stewart's Army of Tennessee. From the few prisoners already picked up, Davis believed that to his front lay "only a division of cavalry with a few pieces of artillery obstructing our march." "Looking across an open field on the left, Davis saw that there were troops in line but could not judge as to their number," so he ordered Buell forward to develop their strength and hopefully strike their flank. In accordance with Davis's orders, Buell deployed with the 21st Michigan in advance (some 230 men), supported by the 69th Ohio and 13th Michigan (300 men). The second line was to pass through the first line once the rebel position had been reached. Carlin was with the 21st Michigan and went up and down the line speaking "words of encouragement."[34]

Buell's three regiments advanced about 400 yards, driving rebel skirmishers before them. Instead of striking the rebel flank, however, they found that they were advancing obliquely toward the waiting enemy, exposing more of their own flank with each pace. Suddenly they received a destructive volley from the concealed and entrenched enemy: "The Rebs held there [sic] fire until we were within 3 rods of the works when they opened fire from all sides & gave us an awful volly [sic]. we went for them with a yell & got within 5 paces of their works." The first line was stopped, bloodied and disorganized. Through them charged the 13th Michigan into the hail of bullets, advancing into the woods and close to the enemy line. It was here that Maj. Willard G. Eaton, leading the 13th Michigan, was killed. "He was thought a good deal of in the Regt." The 13th, "seeing [Eaton] fall, gave way, and was followed by the remainder of the line under heavy fire from the enemy." Buell's broken regiments fell back across the field into the pine thicket and threw up temporary works on the edge of the ravine.[35]

Now it was Hobart's time. A beloved leader, Harrison Carroll Hobart was quick witted, well educated, and good company. A leader of the Democratic Party in Wisconsin, he had played a prominent role in the state house of representatives. "He is the father of the Homestead Law, which has been adopted by so many states," reported his friend, Union brigadier John Beatty. Captured at Chickamauga, Hobart and others had escaped from Libby prison in Richmond on the night of February 9, 1864, by digging a tunnel. He immediately returned to his regiment and had led it throughout the Atlanta Campaign.[36]

Hobart cheered his three regiments forward about 1:00 P.M. against "the Enemies works which was about an half mile from ours partially hid from us by the woods which lay between." When within 300 yards of the enemy breastworks, they were met with a terrific fire, including enfilade fire from a rebel battery close enough to use canister. The whole line "was shattered." In the 88th Indiana a sergeant was left in command of one company, a corporal in charge of another. Company I's commander was gone; Company C "had lost both color sergeants as well as the company commander. Not an officer from the right to the flag, but Capt. Ferd F. Boltz of Co. F who assumed command of the right wing of the regiment." For the second time that day Hobart's men abandoned that awful field.[37]

Carlin's 1:00 P.M. attack had failed. Or had it? No one could question the vigor, indeed the enthusiasm, with which his three brigades hurled themselves against a concealed enemy of undetermined strength. Yet the rebel positions remained intact—not even dented. It was a disjointed, poorly coordinated effort, one might argue. Nevertheless, these assaults by Miles, Buell, and Hobart had gained three important advantages, two of which were unknown to Carlin, Davis, or Slocum at the time. They had upset the Confederate tactical timetable, they had caused a reactive deployment of Confederate troops, and, perhaps most important, they had purchased, albeit at a high price, information about Confederate strength.

Three Confederate privates were brought to Carlin as he supervised the placement of Buell's and Hobart's brigades in a defensive posture. Actually, they were former Federal soldiers who had joined the enemy to escape prison, "Galvanized Rebels." Carlin's attack had given them an opportunity to desert. One man seemed particularly well informed and told Carlin that it was Johnston's army out there. "He said at that moment the Confederate generals were riding among their troops making speeches and explaining to them their plans to destroy the left wing of Sherman's army, and then turn on the right wing and destroy that."[38] Carlin was so impressed with the man and his information that he dismounted and gave the man his horse, Rosey (named in honor of Maj. Gen. William S. Rosecrans), and "detailed my only staff officer present," Maj. James E. Edmunds, "to take him to Davis and Slocum." He sent this message with them: "I attacked the enemy with Buell's brigade and half of Hobart's, but failed to drive the enemy. The same result attended the attack on the right by Miles' brigade. The enemy is strong in men and artillery." Carlin then told them what his unusual prisoner, a New Yorker, had related—that "Hardee, Hoke, Lee's corps, and a great deal of artillery are in our front. I shall hold my present position until further orders from you. . . . My loss is considerable, but not definitely known."[39]

Carlin's "prisoner" and his dispatch reached Slocum on the Goldsboro road as he hurried forward two of Morgan's brigades to Miles's right, under orders to "press the enemy closely and force him to develop his position and strength." Slocum and Davis were talking when Col. H. G. Litchfield of Davis's staff rode up from Morgan's position on the right. To Slocum's inquiry as to the situation on Morgan's and Carlin's front, Litchfield replied: " 'Well, General, I find a great deal more than Dibrell's cavalry; I find infantry entrenched along our whole front, and enough of them to give us all the amusement we want for the rest of the day.' "[40]

Slocum now turned aside and confronted the rebel deserter—"an emaciated, sickly appearing young man about twenty-two or twenty-three years of age, dressed in the Confederate gray." The prisoner explained about his past service in the Union army and the fact that he had been a resident of Syracuse, New York, before the war. Slocum paid closer attention, for he too had lived in Syracuse and was familiar with the unit in which the man had enlisted. Yet he was skeptical: the man could be a double deserter. However, "While I was talking with him one of my aides, Major William G. Tracy, rode up and at once recognized the deserter as an old acquaintance whom he had known at Syracuse before the war." His credibility established, the deserter proceeded to tell Slocum and Tracy about the force immediately ahead, and how he had seen Johnston himself at the front. He estimated the rebel force at 40,000.[41]

It was a decisive moment. Slocum reversed himself on the spot and sent his staff spinning. The lead brigade of the Twentieth Corps, Brig. Gen. James S. Robinson's (Nathaniel J. Jackson's division), just arriving on the field about 2:00 P.M., was pushed straight down the road to support Lt. Samuel D. Webb's 19th Indiana Battery.[42] About 2:30 the Second Brigade of Jackson's division under Col. William Hawley arrived, accompanied by Twentieth Corps commander Alpheus S. Williams. Slocum had Williams send Hawley immediately about a quarter of a mile to the left to anchor that flank and to provide deep support for Buell. To Robinson's dismay, orders came (probably from Williams) to pluck out two of his regiments (his reserve line) and send them to support Hawley on the left.[43]

Slocum next countermanded an order he had given Williams less than a half hour before. Instead of positioning the remainder of his corps on Morgan's right "with a view of turning the left of the enemy's position," Williams was to send off all his wagons on the interior road taken by Logan's Fifteenth Corps and "bring forward with the least possible delay every regiment of his command" and take a defensive position "on Morgan's left

Williams and his generals. *From left to right:* James L. Selfridge, Alpheus S. Williams, James S. Robinson, and William Hawley. (U.S. Army Military History Institute, Carlisle, Pennsylvania)

resting his left flank on a ravine." Kilpatrick's cavalry would be massed on Williams's left and rear.[44]

Capt. William Ludlow, Slocum's engineering officer, was sent forward to Carlin, suggesting that he should fall back behind a little creek or ravine in his rear and construct breastworks. Carlin, however, decided against it, "being confident of my ability to hold my position until the troops in rear should come up." Besides, Carlin reasoned, to pull back across the creek would mean displacing the division hospital that had just been established on its banks. Instead, he urged Buell to rush the fortification of his left flank. He seemed certain that his division could hold.[45]

Carlin was not alone. Not everyone agreed with Slocum's assessment. Kilpatrick urged Slocum "to make a bold dash." Capt. William W. Moseley of Slocum's staff spoke for others when he suggested: "you ought to have the advance division charge and drive them out of the way; that it could not be possible that there was much force ahead of us, and that if we waited for the others to come up we would lose a whole day, and if it should turn out that there was nothing to justify such caution it would look bad for the left wing."[46] Such reasoning was grounded in experience, it seemed. After all, had not all their campaigning since Atlanta demonstrated conclusively that a division would suffice to overcome any roadblock? Slocum splashed ice water on their zeal. "'I can afford to be charged with being dilatory or over-cautious,'" replied their leader, who seemed to have been inoculated with caution, "but I cannot afford the responsibility of another Ball's Bluff affair.'"[47]

As of 3:00 P.M., March 19, the wary Slocum's position stood as a semi-circle with the Goldsboro road as its axis: on the extreme left, Hawley's brigade was fortifying, but well to Buell's left and rear without a connection even of pickets; Scovel's battery, without infantry support, was also to Buell's rear;[48] Buell's brigade (three battered regiments) was rapidly entrenching on a slight ridge about 300 yards in advance of a ravine or swamp; Briant's wing of Hobart's brigade held a position following the line of the ravine, which resulted in its right being thrown well forward and thus dangerously exposed. Across a wide gap of several hundred yards to the right and rear was Robinson's reduced brigade supporting Webb's battery, which stood on the Goldsboro road. Next was Fitch's wing (three regiments of Hobart's brigade), with its left on the Goldsboro road; then Miles's brigade; then Morgan's division, digging in as fast as possible, with John Grant Mitchell's brigade connected to Miles's right and William Vandever's brigade tight against Mitchell's right.[49] Vandever's own right ended in the relative security of a "semi-impenetrable" swamp. Behind Mitchell was Fearing's reserve brigade. Robinson also believed himself to be in reserve, but unknown to him, there was no friendly force to his immediate front. Furthermore, any Federal unit to his left was out of sight.[50]

It was a precarious front that Slocum presented: disconnected, erratically aligned, unevenly manned—full of risk. Yet, the veteran New York general knew that all he needed was a little time. He had about 12,000 experienced

David Miles
(U.S. Army Military History Institute, Carlisle, Pennsylvania)

troops taking defensive positions, with an equal number on the way. The right was strong—Morgan's front was quite narrow, with a brigade in reserve. Moreover, Morgan had been fortifying since his arrival on the field.[51] A fault line existed in the center, however, where Webb's battery was positioned—with Robinson facing north and Hobart west, totally separated, out

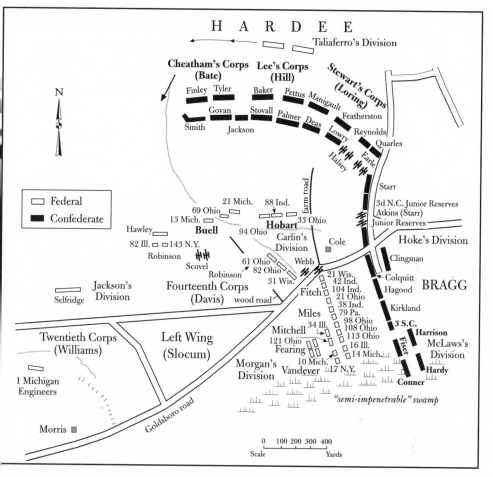

Map 3. 2:30 P.M., March 19

of supporting distance. Then there was Buell on the left flank. Although he had refused his left regiment somewhat, Buell's observant infantrymen could see enemy activity well beyond their left flank. These two left brigades of Carlin's were stretched thin along a wide front and had their flanks exposed. Their only hope if attacked was the cover offered by the ravine at their back and the Twentieth Corps reinforcements rushing down the Goldsboro road.

To buy additional time for the Twentieth to come up, perhaps to tempt the enemy to sit back and await another attack, Fourteenth Corps commander Davis sent an order to Carlin to have Buell make a "strong demonstration against the enemy line." Whatever its tactical merits, division commander Carlin set aside this order from corps commander Davis. "I thought best to employ what time and force I had in strengthening my position," Carlin explained.[52]

It was about 2:30 P.M. when Slocum summoned Lieutenant Foraker and handed the young officer this dispatch:

> General Sherman, or General Logan:
>
> I have met [the enemy] in strong force on the road from Bentonville to Cox's Bridge. It is reported by prisoners that Johnston and Hardee are here. I think a portion of the Right Wing should be brought forward at once.[53]

"Ride well to the right so as to keep clear of the enemy's left flank," Slocum cautioned Foraker. And *"don't spare horse-flesh."*[54]

6

The Battle of "Acorn Run"

ABOUT 2:30 P.M. on March 19 Lt. Marcus W. Bates, an acting company commander in Buell's brigade, observed rebel skirmishers advancing "far out on our left in an open field."[1] Division commander William P. Carlin saw them also. Already as a precautionary move Carlin had stationed two companies of Michigan skirmishers "over half a mile to the left" of Buell's position at the ravine. He answered this new development by removing Buell's reserve regiment, the tiny 69th Ohio (less than a hundred effectives), to support his absurdly extended left.[2]

The crisis on Carlin's far left was compounded, about 3:00 P.M., by an enemy frontal attack: hundreds of rebel skirmishers appeared, closely followed by what appeared to be hordes of infantry "swarming over their works. As far as we could see on both right and left, they were coming in unbroken lines with that old yell we had learned to know so well."[3] Fighting behind half-completed works, Buell's two remaining regiments, the 13th and 21st Michigan, braced themselves. Then, displaying exemplary fire discipline, they loaded, aimed, and shot deliberately. The rebels to their immediate front, at least those in the first assault line, halted and wavered, stunned by Buell's volleys. The paper-thin Michigan line of battle could be proud—we "gave them fits."[4]

Division commander Carlin, now without a mount or a single staff officer, won the admiration of George Buell during the repulse, for "doing all any one man could do to encourage the men, not only with words, but by exposing his own person."[5] Carlin, resplendent in his best dress uniform, walked calmly down the line from left to right, watching intently and proudly as the Confederates were beaten back. "We all liked our old Div. Comd.," said Lt. Charles S. Brown. "He was as cool a man in a fight as I ever saw. he was right beside of me in the mess (on the right of the 21st Michigan)."[6]

George Pearson Buell
(U.S. Army Military History Institute, Carlisle, Pennsylvania)

There at the end of Buell's line (in the flank company of the 21st), Carlin spotted a private who seemed nervous. Visible directly to their front was a line of Confederates, apparently regrouping for another charge or waiting for a second line to pass through. Clumps of rebels, meanwhile, were inching up.[7] Carlin looked closer. "I noticed particularly three soldiers among the trees directly in front of the man and myself. Thinking it would steady his nerves, I took his gun from his hand and fired it at the group of men just mentioned, who were not over twenty yards from us."[8] After he had fired Carlin lowered the rifle and calmly handed it back to the private. It was then the two men looked about and were astonished: "there was not another Union soldier of his brigade or any other command in sight."[9]

What had happened? Had Buell's entire brigade vanished?—and so soon after dramatically repulsing the Confederates? Buell later explained: the enemy had attacked a second time and "the line immediately on my right [Hobart's] as far as I could see gave way . . . so that my brigade which still stood was almost entirely cut off. In this condition, with both flanks turned, and no reserve, I concluded that to remain there longer was to sacrifice my brigade. Hence I gave the order to fall back."[10]

Had he done so without orders? without notifying his division commander? "At first," Buell continued, "I waited for him [Carlin] to order, but seeing that too much delay would cause our certain capture, and there being no time for consultation, I ordered the retreat. Half a minute's delay, and General Carlin, myself, and most of my brigade would have been captured."[11] One of Buell's officers, Lt. C. S. Brown, 21st Michigan, agreed: "It was the best thing we ever did for falling back we met a line of Rebs marching straight for our rear & in 15 minutes more we would have been between two lines of the buggers."[12]

Carlin was outraged, understandably. Buell had not been "driven back." He had vamoosed "without order or authority."[13] The division line, although attenuated, could have been held if only Buell had held his ground. Thus played Carlin's fanciful line of reason, of justification. Without question Buell was guilty of insubordination by withdrawing without securing permission from his commanding officer or at least informing him. But the desperate situation (rebels crashing down upon his left flank and left rear, not to speak of those heavy lines threatening his front) demanded immediate action by the brigade commander. For Buell to have maintained his position would have been foolhardy, irresponsible in the extreme.[14] Doubtless Buell's action saved hundreds of Union troops from capture or worse, thereby denying the Confederates a more substantial success.

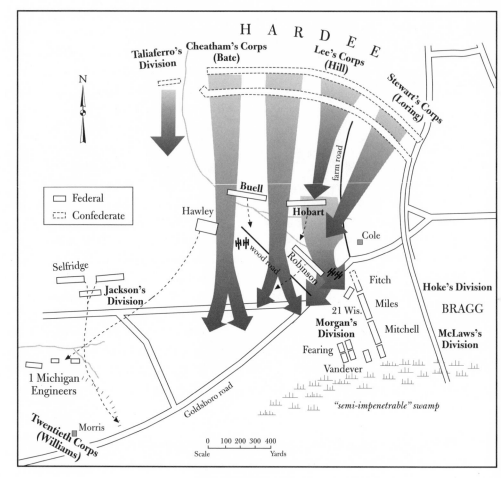

Map 4. Johnston Attacks

Briant's wing of Hobart's brigade thus found itself to be a salient thrust forward like the paw of some great angry cat. Buell was gone, leaving Briant's left flank wide open. Then, multiplying danger upon danger, there seemed to be no Union troops between Briant's right (33d Ohio) and the Goldsboro road, a distance "of at least" six regimental fronts. And now suddenly, from the right rear, the isolated 33d heard "scattering fire," "bullets whistling over our heads." Capt. Joseph Hinson, commanding the regiment, saw Federal skirmishers behind him, but they were shooting into his men. "Be careful," he shouted out angrily, "or we [will] retaliate."[15]

At that moment, however, Hinson's attention was jerked back to the front. Advancing from the woods beyond came a heavy body of rebels, three to six lines deep. Both Hobart and Carlin went among Briant's three regiments to steady them while Hinson reassured his company commanders that his regiment "could hold our front against any force that might be brought against us." The troops themselves probably had more faith in their breast-works. Already "our shoulders when standing erect in the ditch were about on a level with the ground in front." This was fine, indeed ideal, for defending against a frontal attack. But what about the flanks? What about their cartridge boxes? Many soldiers had been firing since midmorning. The sixty rounds they had been issued were running low.[16]

On came the Confederates. Briant watched the fire from the 94th Ohio approvingly; the 88th Indiana fired by file, blazing away textbook fashion. All the while Hinson directed careful volleys by the 33d Ohio, giving the rebels "the best we had in store, but it made no difference." Twice Hinson told his men to cease firing so "that the men might be kept cool." But the enemy advanced relentlessly. "There was neither halt nor pause, only when they came within 50 or 60 yards they began firing, but still advancing."[17] The rebel lines "extended into the field and beyond my right." A member of the 88th Indiana, dismayed at the determination of the rebels and the sheer weight of their numbers, knew then, despite any action the regiment might take, that "our situation was truly awful."[18] The 33d Ohio abandoned its works when the rebels charged to within ten yards of its right. The men pulled back, trying their best to maintain a semblance of a line of battle.

Hinson held his troops there in the woods. Although the order of his regiment was unraveling before his eyes, Captain Hinson refused to abandon the position altogether without notifying Briant. Neither Briant nor Hobart, nor any of their staff officers, were in sight, so Hinson ran down the line to the left until he found Briant with the 88th Indiana. "I can't hold my line," he told the wing commander. Then Hinson turned around to return to his men, and at that moment he saw the right of his 33d Ohio "break to the rear, and I was thankful for that much time gained."[19]

Hit from the right, left, and front, virtually surrounded, Briant's wing buckled. Every man for himself. Hinson would comment later with icy realism, "the officers and men did nobly by saving themselves."[20]

What had happened to Robinson's brigade of the Twentieth Corps? James S. Robinson—Carlin's support, his center, the link between the two wings of Hobart's brigade—where was he?

Robinson had come up shortly before 3:00 P.M.,[21] as directed. He passed through the lines of William Hawley's brigade to take a forward position perpendicular to the Goldsboro road, just behind a shallow ravine. These dispositions put his five regiments some 200 yards in the rear of Webb's battery and about the same distance behind a conjectural north-south line connecting Briant's right and Fitch's left. Robinson knew that he was to fill the gap in Carlin's line and support Webb. But he also knew that he lacked sufficient manpower—it was a two-brigade assignment. As if that were not enough, corps commander Williams proceeded to send off Hawley's brigade to guard Carlin's left flank and rear. Then he stripped Robinson of his second line, sending those two regiments to strengthen Hawley. This reduced Robinson to three regiments and made his assignment virtually impossible.[22]

"I was so d—d mad," Robinson wrote a month later, "over the position in which my Brigade was placed that I felt like pitching into the whole fraternity of commanding generals. In fact I told Slocum the next time 3 Regiments of my Brigade were sent to the front[,] 3 to the rear, I would go with the latter."[23]

So Robinson felt no compulsion to move up and extend Fitch's line north of the road. Besides, if he had, it would have meant occupying a terribly exposed position near Cole's house—one from which Hobart's troops (Briant's wing) had been driven two hours earlier. Also it seems that Robinson believed that some of Carlin's troops, a skirmish line at least, lay between him and the enemy. Therefore, he decided to establish himself behind the ravine. Being the veteran combat commander that he was,[24] Robinson doubtless appreciated the defensive advantages of this retired position. To his front lay the ravine "and beyond an open field, containing on its farther side a group of buildings [Cole's house]. In my rear was a dense pine forest, along the outer edge of which my line extended."[25] While his men built barricades, Robinson kept searching for Carlin's skirmishers, hoping that they would pop up somewhere ahead. Otherwise, that open space at which he stared represented an invitation for a rebel attack.[26]

Using rails from Cole's fences and chopping trees furiously (they had no entrenching tools—only hatchets that day), Robinson's men quickly constructed a "respectable shelter." As they labored, however, word came of a rebel skirmish line advancing "apparently to obtain the buildings in the field" and "the elevated ground extending to the left and covering my position."[27] Robinson countered by pushing forward a strong skirmish line. Lt. George Lyman, 31st Wisconsin, led this line and succeeded in reaching Cole's house before the enemy. It soon became apparent that the Confederates were attacking in great strength. They flung Lyman's skirmishers aside like kindling, inflicting many casualties including Lyman himself, whom they wounded and captured.

The survivors fled back to their parent regiment. Once his skirmishers were safe within his lines, Robinson gave orders for the brigade to open fire. It was a short, unequal fight. "In a few minutes it became apparent that the troops on my left [Briant's wing] were being driven back in great disorder. This permitted the enemy to come directly in upon my left flank and rear, and left me no alternative but to withdraw my regiments or have them captured. . . . To have remained . . . would have been madness."[28]

So this towering giant, James S. Robinson, humiliated and angry, retreated about one-quarter of a mile into the woods along the Goldsboro road, close to the original position of Hawley's brigade. Carlin, still attempting to cling to his position with a handful of Hobart's men, watched Robinson go. Then "I saw the Confederate flag waving over the wooden breastworks, and a line of Confederate troops holding the works tenaciously."[29]

Unfortunately, when Robinson's brigade broke to the rear, it also uncovered the battery it had been sent to support—Webb's 19th Indiana Independent Light Artillery. The 19th had suffered already that afternoon from rebel cannon fire, having lost two men, several horses, and an ammunition chest. Battery commander 1st Lt. Samuel D. Webb had limbered up one section and moved it some 400 yards north of the Goldsboro road, seeking cover and a more favorable angle of fire. But rebel infantry charging through the gap between Briant's right and Robinson succeeded in cutting off this section (two guns) and mortally wounded Webb. The demoralized Indiana gunners abandoned their pieces. A private in Company B, 31st Wisconsin Infantry, however, determined to do what he could. His regiment had left the battery to its fate, but Peter Anderson would not. He found a team of six horses, hitched them to a piece, and "entirely unassisted, drove the team out with his ramrod and saved the gun." For his heroic action, Private Anderson would receive the Congressional Medal of Honor.[30]

Col. Alexander C. McClurg, Slocum's chief of staff, riding to the front along the Goldsboro road, met the surviving section of the 19th Indiana Battery stampeding down the road. Lt. Clinton Keeler cried out to the startled colonel, "For Heaven's sake, don't go down there! The lieutenant commanding my battery and most of the men and horses are killed."[31]

Everything above (or north) of the Goldsboro road had been swept away. But Lt. Col. Michael H. Fitch could not see what was happening, being south of the road and on lower ground. He had put his trust in the 19th Indiana guns and Briant's wing. Besides, Fitch was more concerned with his own right. He had already switched the only regiment (104th Illinois) he had north of the Goldsboro road to his right flank. This move left the 21st

Wisconsin abutting the road in close support of the battery. From time to time a staff officer (from corps or Left Wing headquarters) would ride up from the rear, stop on the road, and ask the company commander of the left company, 21st Wisconsin: " 'Why don't you move on, there is nothing but cavalry there.' But just then, an artillery shot or a few minnie balls would whistle about his horse, and he [the staff officer] would go to the rear."[32]

Carlin had ordered Fitch to hold his position on the road, support the battery, and push forward skirmishers aggressively.[33] Fitch fulfilled these responsibilities with confidence. The furious artillery duel to his left was unsettling, but for a long time, like the cocky staff officers, Fitch dismissed it as nothing more than an obstinate enemy battery supported by dismounted cavalry. He felt much better about his right flank when David Miles's brigade came up and went into position beyond the 104th, although Fitch lacked visual contact with Miles because of a swamp separating their units.

Everything seemed to be going well until almost 4:00 P.M. Then Fitch's skirmishers were driven in, falling back through the heavy blackjack. Even more troubling, "tremendous firing and cheering broke out over where the other wing had made its charge in the forenoon." Then came calamitous reports from the left companies of the 21st Wisconsin: Briant's troops "were all gone," and strong rebel columns were passing to the left and rear.[34]

Fitch raced to the road to see for himself. The 19th Indiana Battery was gone; one unmanned gun remained, looking "very lonely." Two hundred yards north of the road was a Confederate line of battle bearing down at a right angle on his flank. "It stretched to our rear farther than I could see through the timber. I could not help admiring for the moment, their fine soldierly bearing." Fitch knew full well that the presence of this large body of rebel troops meant that Briant's wing, and probably the left of Carlin's division, must have collapsed.[35]

Determined not to give ground, Fitch took immediate action. He placed the 21st Wisconsin parallel to the Goldsboro road and "sent them forward" to attack the advancing enemy. He also ordered infantry privates to man the abandoned piece and turn it toward the enemy. These two acts "checked the enemy slightly," giving time for the 42d Indiana and 104th Illinois to change front, bending back parallel to the Goldsboro road to oppose the Confederate advance. But while making these dispositions, Fitch discovered to his dismay that enemy fire against his old front (facing east) enfiladed his new position. Caught in this cross fire, attacked simultaneously from two sides, Fitch abandoned his position. He retreated south to the right of his original line into and across a large swamp.[36]

The 42d Indiana and 104th Illinois, not under Fitch's eye, seem to have reacted independently, seeking their own routes to safety. Almost the entire command would fall into the net of Brig. Generals John G. Mitchell and James Dada Morgan. These two leaders, with Fitch's assistance, regrouped many of the troops and used them as a stopgap (unfortified) extension of Mitchell's left flank now bent at a sharp angle parallel to the Goldsboro road.[37]

When Fitch's wing of Hobart's brigade gave up its position on the Goldsboro road and retreated into the swamp, it uncovered the left flank of Miles's brigade. Miles's troops had fought hard earlier in the day, charging enemy works to the east repeatedly, then had fallen back to a line parallel to and south of Fitch's. There they remained, exposed and dreading the worst. "No one, at the time we took our position, knew just where the enemy was," recalled a member of the 21st Ohio. Sometime after 3:00 P.M. Miles's three regiments found out: "Bullets from our rear, bullets from our left flank, and a few from our front, were too much for even veterans. Every man in the regiment knew somebody had blundered." Now they felt trapped. Capt. J. L. Keller could "remember no time, when gloom and discouragement settled so thick and fast upon us."[38]

Displaying initiative and energy, David Miles extracted his brigade. He fell back south, then changed front and counterattacked. The Confederates, undaunted, soon closed in again, this time primarily from the west (almost to the rear of Miles's original position). Outflanked, Miles retreated, then once more turned and made a stand only to be outflanked again. In the last of these desperate running fights, Miles himself was wounded and brigade command passed to Lt. Col. Arnold McMahan, 21st Ohio, an unusually able officer.[39]

Carlin's division was smashed. His three brigades, plus that of Robinson, had been driven from their positions; Webb's Indiana battery was gone. Colonel McClurg on the Goldsboro road observed "rebel regiments in full view, stretching in fields to the left as far as the eye could reach, advancing rapidly. Everything seemed hopeless on our center and left." Almost a mile behind Buell's position, Hawley's and James L. Selfridge's brigades (Robinson's sister units from Jackson's division, Twentieth Corps) were rapidly building barricades and digging trenches to defend the Union left flank. They had heard the heavy firing to their right but kept at their work. "Just as we had got a few rails piled up, the whole *14th corps* broke pannick stricken, throwing away guns, knapsacks & everything and all running like a flock of sheeps."[40] One officer "saw a great many men and officers coming out of the woods in greatest confusion and disorder. It looked to me like a stampede."[41] The panic "brought back vividly to our minds a similar scene at the Battle of Chancellorsville," thought a member of Hawley's brigade. Brave leaders in broken units attempted to stop the flight. "A Color Sergeant of one Regiment stuck his colors in the ground and drawing his sword called upon the men to rally around him and not give up the field, but the crowd surged past him and he grasped his colors and went to the rear with them."[42] Lt. Charles S. Brown, 21st Michigan, one of those who fled, put it candidly: "We however showed to the Rebs as well as our side some of the best running ever did."[43]

Among the casualties of the rebel attack and the panic that followed was the Fourteenth Corps hospital. Placed on the bank of a creek above the Goldsboro road, it "had to be taken down in a hurry. The wounded were thrown in ambulanses [sic]." Drivers grew frantic waiting for their loads. One demoralized driver jumped from the wagon seat "to cut the traces and fly." The situation was saved by a surgeon, Dr. John Avery, who drew his revolver and pressed it against the driver's head, convincing him to return to his seat and wait until the patients were safely loaded. A member of the 13th Michigan would later point out defensively and opaquely that although Buell's brigade "retreated in confusion," it "left no wounded except those on the field."[44]

Briant's wing of Hobart's brigade, being more advanced and clinging to its position longer, found retreat more hazardous than had Buell's regiments. Men of the 33d Ohio left their works, ran back into the ravine, climbed out of that "ugly swale" under fire, and quickly encountered a field full of rebels. Startled, they turned this way, then that, looking for a way around their enemy. How could they escape? Those attempting to cut across the corner of the field did so "under a perfect shower of bullets." Ninety percent of their casualties "occurred during this foot-race of a few minutes duration."[45] "My mess mate," declared one of Hobart's privates, "had the coffee pot shot off of his back and thirty two Bullets [sic] holes shot through his dog tent." Another private wrote thankfully, "I did not know but every moment would be my last and put an End to all my fond hopes of Ever seeing home and friends again in this world."[46]

"If any disgrace is attached to the confusion in which they retired," declared conscience-stricken Capt. Joe Hinson, "it rests altogether with me in not assuming the responsibility and taking them from a position which I saw they could not hold but would be driven from in a very short time."[47]

Harrison C. Hobart
(U.S. Army Military History Institute, Carlisle, Pennsylvania)

Division commander Carlin shared the plight of his men. He found himself alone—"not an officer, man, or horse at my disposal." But there was a "compact line of Confederates not 30 yards from me." Would he surrender or run? "I decided to walk deliberately to the rear," said Carlin. He did so, as calmly as on parade, for about 100 yards toward the ravine, "during which time not a shot was fired at me." He scrambled across the ravine, up the far side, and "then for the first time the enemy seemed to notice me. A sharp fusillade was opened on me by the line in my rear. . . . Bullets . . . came in sheets. The ground was torn up around and under my feet."[48]

Again Carlin thought of surrender but decided to dash for some thick bushes. To his delight, he found almost a dozen young Federals hiding there. "Can't we do something to stop those rebels," one private asked. "We have been picking off color-bearers and officers for some time." Ever the division commander, Carlin organized his makeshift squad, having them "fall into line & tried a 'Chinese system of noise.'" That is, he shouted commands as if to a regiment, a commendable improvisation but futile. Bullets whizzed into the bushes, answering his parade ground voice. Carlin and his "heroic little squad" parted company hurriedly. A little later Lieutenant Brown caught sight of him as the general splashed through a swamp. "Carlin got down & I saw two boys use him as a stepping stone to cross dry shod."[49]

Carlin, his fine uniform bespattered, his wind gone, and his legs wobbly, finally arrived at the Goldsboro road. Unfortunately, he found it full of rebels "advancing as steadily and calmly as if regiments on review." In front was an officer wearing red trim about his collar and cuffs, and beside him was an orderly or bugler "who carried an old-fashioned horse-pistol which was levelled at me."[50] As inconspicuously as possible, Carlin backed away toward some dense undergrowth. Miraculously the man did not fire. Determined to remain concealed, Carlin continued on his way, parallel to the road, struggling through briars and switches. Then he came upon two artillery horses. They were tied to a tree but with a knot that defied Carlin's best efforts. Close to exhaustion now, surrounded by rebels, and confounded by the knot, Carlin gave it up. Once again he blended into the wilderness. Eventually (not long before dark) he found the lines of the Twentieth Corps and was saved.[51]

Thus ended the battle of "Acorn Run," as Twentieth Corps wags were wont to call it.[52] Their sarcasm is unfair. One division of the Fourteenth Corps, which proudly wore the acorn as its badge, had been overrun and had fled the field, but not Davis's Fourteenth Corps itself. Acorn Run was Carlin's fight, Carlin's disaster. So Gen. James S. Robinson believed, as did most of Sherman's officers. And as a result, Carlin would be relieved of division command. It is doubtful that Jefferson C. Davis raised a word of protest. Apparently Slocum went along. Carlin's "incompetency," according to Robinson, had led to the near-rout of his brigade and the unnecessary loss of good men. "Carlin exposed his flank, and permitted the enemy [to] mass on his left flank and in his rear. Of course they doubled him up and the result was that I had to change position, and form a new line under a terrible fire, with Carlin's division in route breaking through my Regiment."[53]

Robinson had not done so well himself. He seems to have stumbled into his position, failed to connect with, or even notify, friendly units of his presence, and taken a position that suited him, hardly closing the gap between Hobart's wings. His fight from behind hurriedly erected barricades appears to have been halfhearted. Seemingly out of pique at having three regiments taken from him, Robinson left the 19th Indiana Battery to its fate, exposed Fitch's left flank, and deprived Carlin of essential support.

It is difficult to fault Buell, Hobart, Briant, or Fitch. They appear to have done as well as circumstances permitted, with the Army of Tennessee and Taliaferro's Division washing over them like waves over sand castles. Miles performed very well: the importance of his service was recognized a few hours later.

Carlin himself fought bravely but impetuously. The act of depriving himself of his horse and his last staff officer to send back intelligence to Davis says much. By doing so, of course, he lost the ability to communicate with (and control) Fitch, Robinson, and Buell. He gave up the initiative. After hurling his three brigades against the strong Confederate lines, Carlin needed to organize a defense. Here he failed badly. He prepared to meet the enemy's attack with Buell's left and Briant's right flanks unprotected. Dismounted, he could hardly look to the great gap that separated Briant and Fitch. Of course, his division had been deployed "without reference to any such force" as would confront it. The idea of falling back and organizing a defensive position in the vicinity of Robinson apparently did not occur to him. Was not his mission, after all, to break up this rebel obstruction and drive it off? It was delaying the march to Goldsboro.[54]

In this conviction Carlin mirrored the attitudes and tactics of Sherman's army throughout the Savannah and Carolinas Campaigns: come upon the enemy—deploy—attack. Be aggressive, extremely aggressive. With the exception of Joseph A. Mower, there was not a more daring division commander in the army than William P. Carlin. And at Carlin's shoulder that day stood Jefferson C. Davis, Sherman's favorite corps commander—a fighter who bowed to no man in audacity. Davis was close to Carlin, at least until Carlin took position at the ravine and launched his attacks with Briant and Buell. Granted, Davis and Carlin probably did not know that an enemy army stood before them. Yet, if anyone should be faulted for having a division deploy and attack an enemy army, it should be corps commander Davis—or Slocum, for that matter.

Indeed, it was an overconfident, impatient Union army—from the commanding general himself to the crack-of-dawn forager that stumbled into Johnston's trap. As a result, a fine division was wrecked. Many men were killed, wounded, and captured by this headlong crash into the unknown, this Battle of Acorn Run.

Was it futile? Carlin later argued that his division had sacrificed itself and thus saved the Left Wing from defeat. He had occupied Johnston for at least six hours. There is merit to such an argument. Furthermore, Carlin's vigorous attacks along a wide front upset Johnston's timing and brought about the redeployment (and weakening) of the Confederate enveloping force. Perhaps it was worth the cost after all.

We'll Whip 'Em Yet!

WHEREAS William Passmore Carlin, in the eyes of privates and generals alike, would become the goat of Bentonville, James Dada Morgan would become its hero. Morgan had chosen a good position, had he not? He had dug in and was ready when the rebels attacked. Morgan had foresight; Morgan had resilience. There was nothing reckless about him.

One of the oldest division commanders in the Union army, James Dada Morgan was fifty-four, an unusually advanced age for a field commander. A Boston Yankee and the son of a sea captain, Morgan had quit school at nine, worked as an apprentice in a cooper's shop, then at sixteen went to sea himself. Thirty days out, however, the crew mutinied, burned the ship, and then drifted in small boats for weeks before finally making landfall on the South American coast. When young Morgan returned to Boston, he abandoned the life of the sea and went to work in a fish store. At twenty-four he moved to Illinois and established a cooper shop in Quincy. Soon he turned to the confectionery business, then tried his hand at paving levees. Finally he discovered pork packing, an enterprise that, over twenty-five years, made him rich.[1]

From his youth Morgan had been a citizen-soldier, a militiaman, and it seemed natural that he organize the Quincy Riflemen. A tough, wiry little man, James Morgan seems to have sought action and excitement, first in a campaign against the Mormons, then as captain of volunteers in Mexico where he won brevet promotion for gallantry. When war came in 1861, Morgan quickly became colonel of the 10th Illinois. To his dismay he and his regiment narrowly missed Belmont, the opening engagement for the Mississippi Valley. On the day of the battle an observer found him upriver in Cairo, Illinois, listening to the distant sounds of fighting. "Tears coursed down his cheeks," reported his companion. Morgan "exclaimed with disgust and grief, 'They are in the fight and we are carpet soldiers.' "[2]

During his four years in the Union army Morgan "never was absent from duty for a day. He never asked for a furlough." Although he was dependable and thorough, some criticized him for following orders too literally, and some carped that Morgan in his uniform "looks more like a wagon-master than a General." He endeared himself to his men, however, by sharing their life, "sleeping under a fly tent on a lawn while his staff spent the night in a fine house in town." Pragmatic, outspoken, with a highly developed moral sense, Morgan would argue with Sherman about the impending charge at Kennesaw, yet himself champion the practice of "assaulting the enemy with unloaded guns." He also would go on record deploring the excesses of foragers. "These men are a disgrace to the name of soldier and the country," he maintained.[3]

Despite his independent ways, Morgan seemed to work well with superiors. Sherman and George H. Thomas praised him and depended on him. He also held the respect of the mercurial Jefferson C. Davis. They had worked well together in the Atlanta Campaign. Morgan did his job; it seemed that Morgan had nothing to prove.[4]

On the morning of March 19, Morgan had come up the Goldsboro road following Carlin's winding column. When Carlin deployed to clean out rebel resistance, Morgan kept the proper interval behind, not hurrying, just deliberately awaiting developments. As the skirmishing intensified, Davis and Slocum both began to worry about enemy activity on Carlin's right, so Davis sent a courier riding back to the head of Morgan's column. He found Capt. Tolan Jones, who was leading the 113th Illinois, Mitchell's brigade: "General Davis instructs that you come forward as rapidly as possible without fatiguing the men." Jones pushed forward at the double-quick accompanied by brigade commander Brig. Gen. John Grant Mitchell. After about twenty minutes, the 113th passed Davis, "looking anxious and peering in the direction of the contending forces."[5]

When Morgan himself came up, Davis ordered him to deploy his division to the right of Miles's brigade (Carlin's division) and to advance a skirmish line. An officer in Buell's brigade caught sight of Morgan's men as they filed into position. "Just as we passed the underbrush Morgan's men were swinging into line with all the precision of a dress parade. Morgan always went into battle in that way."[6]

Mitchell's brigade, at the advance of Morgan's division, turned off obliquely to the right (south) of the Goldsboro road. It passed through one

James Dada Morgan
(U.S. Army Military History Institute, Carlisle, Pennsylvania)

swamp, then another. Finally, after thrashing about in this quagmire, all the while pressing back enemy skirmishers, Mitchell came abreast of David Miles's line. Miles, who already had met stiff Confederate resistance and yet managed to develop the enemy's position, was busy constructing log breast-works. Mitchell did likewise, "our main line having closed well up with the skirmishers, and the enemy position having been ascertained."[7] He placed his brigade on Miles's right, although the brigades were out of sight of each other, separated by yet another swamp. Mitchell formed his troops in two lines—three Ohio regiments in front, supported by two Illinois regiments. To his right and right front was Lt. Col. Maris R. Vernon's 78th Illinois, deployed as skirmishers.

While Mitchell consolidated his position, Morgan took precautions. Previously (when he discovered that Carlin had become engaged), Morgan had sent a staff officer to Davis requesting that Vandever's brigade (back with the wagons at the rear of the corps) be rushed to him. William Vandever received the summons at noon and immediately set out to join the division. Morgan also ordered his Third Brigade, Benjamin Fearing's, to support Mitchell, placing Fearing to Mitchell's right and rear massed in columns of regiments, with one regiment thrown forward to stiffen Vernon's skirmish line. Reflecting the concern of Davis and Slocum about the Federal right flank, Morgan also directed Fearing to conduct a reconnaissance beyond the extreme right. This was done promptly, and nothing—no roads or enemy force—was found within a mile of the right. This discovery eased Morgan's mind greatly.[8]

Meanwhile, firing increased on Morgan's left as Carlin committed his division to probing attacks. Vandever came up about 1:30 P.M., his men having made a rapid march from the campsite of the night before. Morgan happily greeted Vandever and sent him to the extreme right, beyond Mitchell and in front of Fearing, with the order to anchor his own right upon "an almost impassable swamp." Because of the low, marshy ground, Morgan did not direct his battery to the right of the Goldsboro road, but positioned it on high ground to the left commanding an open area. Thus Morgan's division front consisted of Mitchell and Vandever deployed in two lines with skirmishers thrown forward. Behind them was Fearing, no longer in a column of regiments, but also deployed in two lines, giving Morgan, the right of Davis's Fourteenth Corps, defense in depth—four distinct lines of troops.[9]

Morgan's men required little urging to dig in. They could hear the volume of fire increasing north of the road, and they knew that rebels in force were to the east, to their front. They hurried to gather "logs and anything that could be got hold of for turning bullets"—pine trees, stumps, limbs. A fascinated Union surgeon observed:

> It was surprising to see the rapidity with which men will intrench themselves under fire—a few rails piled up in a twinkling, then dirt thrown upon them with numberless tools, bayonets, frying pans, bits of board, bare hands, anything to move dirt and it is not long before a protecting mound rises sufficiently to cover men lying behind it and as the digging proceeds, the ditch deepens fast as the mound rises until in an almost incredible space of time an intrenchment has been thrown up sufficient to protect from cannon shot as well as rifle balls.[10]

All the while, Morgan's troops cut timber in front of the line to give them-selves fields of fire and deprive the enemy of cover. Camp hatchets and axes flew "as if life and death depended on it." Tree limbs were trimmed to arms' length and sharpened with their tops toward the enemy. Such makeshift abatis would slow an assaulting line of battle. "After forty minutes we were nearly ready," recalled one of Morgan's men. It was "just long enough to construct decent works." Others estimated that this fortunate lull lasted one hour or more.[11]

Now one could see rebel soldiers to the front, in the thick undergrowth, just barely discernible. Skirmishers would appear, then melt back into the woods; then more skirmishers were noticed behind trees, partially con-cealed among the bushes. Finally, one could observe the shadow of a line of battle. On they came, these rebels, from the east against Mitchell's front. Every man dropped to his knees in two ranks and waited until the Confeder-ates came closer. Their line of battle was becoming distinct now.

Mitchell suddenly shouted, "Fire!" A volley roared from the Union line, "the men in the rear rank loading the guns and those in the front rank firing. Mike Huddleston, my [F. M. McAdams's] rear rank man, shouted in my ear after we had been engaged some time: 'My God, Mack, these guns of ours are getting too hot; we had better rest.'" But the fight went on until the rebel line of battle gave up and faded back into the dark forest. Nevertheless, their attacks seemed to lack their characteristic resoluteness and fury. "During the remainder of the day," reported Capt. Peter F. Walker, commanding the 34th Illinois (Mitchell's brigade), "the enemy did not make any regular and persistent attack on our front; they sometimes advanced in considerable force, but were easily driven back."[12]

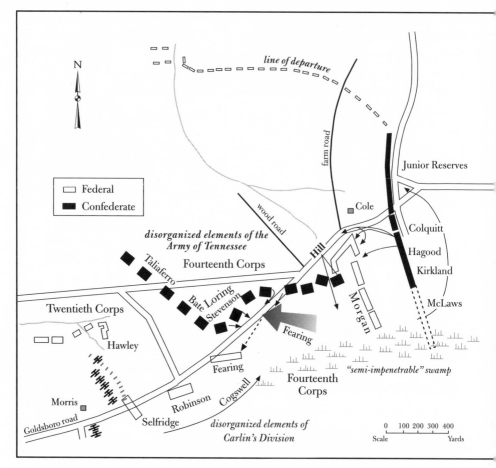

N

line of departure

farm road

Junior Reserves

Federal
Confederate

wood road

Cole

Colquitt

Hagood

Kirkland

disorganized elements of the Army of Tennessee

Fourteenth Corps

Hill

Taliaferro

Bate Loring

Stevenson

Morgan

McLaws

Twentieth Corps

Fearing

Hawley

Fearing

"semi-impenetrable" swamp

Morris

Robinson

Cogswell

Fourteenth Corps

0   100 200 300 400
Scale   Yards

Goldsboro road

Selfridge

disorganized elements of Carlin's Division

Map 5. Fearing's Counterattack

Trouble would come, however, from the left—above the road—from Carlin's front. As the afternoon wore on, the firing from that sector became heavier and heavier, closer and closer. Corps commander Davis had sent a staff officer (Lt. Col. Henry G. Litchfield) to alert Morgan's reserve brigade (Fearing's) to be "in readiness to march in any direction." It was not long before Davis himself rode up, "plunging through the swamp on his fiery white mare." " 'Where is that brigade, Litchfield?' " Davis asked. " 'Here it is, sir, ready to march,' "[13] and Litchfield pointed to Fearing's men. They were formed compactly in columns of regiments waiting patiently in ranks between the breastworks of their first line and Mitchell's second line.

Davis told Morgan on the spot "that the center and left had been broken, and that the enemy had gained the rear and was moving toward the trains."[14] Forget his earlier order (to relieve Miles and join in the general attack against the Confederates), said Davis. Everything had changed.

Now, although aware that a powerful force opposed him, and that it was quite likely that his entire corps might be swept from the field, Davis still wanted to hit back. That was the way he thought, the way he fought. He believed that he saw a chance—strike the vulnerable left flank of the Confederates sweeping irresistibly down the northern side of the Goldsboro road, arrogantly or unwittingly bypassing, ignoring Morgan's division. So Davis shouted to Fearing, " 'Advance upon their flank, Fearing! Deploy as you go! Strike them wherever you find them! Give them the best you've got, and we'll whip them yet!' "[15]

So changing front to the left, Fearing's men deployed into a line of battle as they advanced. With their lengthening front of blue running almost parallel with the Goldsboro road itself, they lunged forward into an unknown jumble of trees to find and attack the rebels. The members of the brigade caught the spirit of Davis as they passed the rear of Mitchell's left regiment. They shouted for the world to hear, " 'Hurrah for old Jeff! We'll whip 'em yet!' " And they passed out of sight into the dark woods.[16]

With the entire Union left collapsing, with his reserve brigade (Fearing's) removed, Morgan prepared to confront the enemy with his two remaining brigades. He ordered Mitchell to bring up his second line of two regiments and use them to extend his first line to the left. "My whole division was drawn out into a single line, and the question now was could we hold it."[17]

Mitchell had anticipated Morgan's command. He had directed the left regiment of his rear line, the 34th Illinois, to change front and to face left (north). The left regiment of the front line, the 98th Ohio, refused its left almost at a ninety-degree angle and linked its left flank with the 34th's right. To aid Mitchell, Morgan also ordered the second line of Vandever's brigade to slide left, thus becoming the division reserve.[18]

John G. Mitchell had been in tight places before—at Chickamauga's Horseshoe Ridge where the fighting had been desperate, at Kennesaw Mountain where he launched a stubborn, futile assault to save Dan McCook, and at Buzzard's Roost Gap where only a loosely slung pair of binoculars saved his life. The genial twenty-six-year-old Mitchell, one of the Union's youngest civilian generals, had left Thomas immediately after the Battle of Nashville and rushed east to rejoin Sherman. This was the same young man whose uncle had written to Mitchell's father when Mitchell enlisted as a private in June 1861. "I fondly hope that your son will in no way disgrace the stock," Mitchell's uncle declared, "but lend lustre to the name and family."[19]

As Mitchell formed his brigade into a great right angle, into his lines fled a panic-stricken mob, "a perfect mass of stragglers." "Whole regiments, came rolling back upon us in dismay, telling us we were flanked and would soon be surrounded."[20] These were Carlin's demoralized troops, and the enter-prising Mitchell halted as many as he could and tried to put them into line beside the 34th Illinois. He had some success with three of Hobart's regi-ments, still recognizable as Michael Fitch's wing. Fitch, a conscientious and cooperative soldier, had brought most of his men south across a swamp into Mitchell's and Morgan's lines.[21] Mitchell told Fitch to link his command to the left of the 34th Illinois and prolong it. "Never did men work more ea-gerly to place between themselves and rebel bullets a work for protection."[22]

To further strengthen this crazy-quilt left flank, Mitchell brought up his last regiment, the 121st Ohio, placing it on the left of Fitch.[23] This gave Mitchell's brigade a fortified position: two sides of a square—three regi-ments on the east side, five on the north. "All of this was done in a swamp covered with water and thickly overgrown with underwood and brambles as well as larger trees, and under a continual fire, which was growing hotter every minute." The swamp, at least on the left flank, appeared to be an ally, shielding the defensive line.[24]

Mitchell quickly found himself besieged on both sides, with "the most vigorous attack at the angle formed" at the juncture of the 34th and 98th Illinois. "It is my opinion," declared one of Mitchell's officers, "that had the 34th Illinois and 98th Ohio become panic-stricken or been compelled to leave their works the brigade and I doubt not the division, would have been driven back."[25] Although the Confederates attacking at this point had "en-filading fire down both of my lines," Mitchell's men, fighting with extraordi-nary bravery and coolness, managed to repulse them *except* for a break-through that occurred left of the 34th Illinois. Fortunately for Mitchell, the key sector—the angle itself—was commanded by a veteran officer, former commander of Mitchell's brigade, Lt. Col. John S. Pearce, 98th Ohio, although Pearce himself would be wounded in this struggle at the angle.[26]

Maj. Aaron B. Robinson, commanding the 121st Ohio and positioned on the extreme left of Mitchell's line which was bent back and almost faced south, had become anxious about his own left. It was completely unsupported. Reports came to him of Confederates within 200 yards moving parallel to his position. He could not be sure of what he saw himself. The woods were burning. Smoke was everywhere. The dusty, faded Federal uniforms were so similar to those of the rebels, many of whom were dressed in blue. Robinson ordered his men to lie down and hold their fire. Meanwhile, he sent Lt. James Ball with six men to reconnoiter.[27] Ball had hardly left when Robinson spotted a Confederate battle flag. He ordered his men to open fire, and for about fifteen minutes they fought obstinately, holding off the attacking rebels. Meanwhile, the fire to Robinson's right—the sector held by Fitch—"became a perfect tempest." "Here the firing was terrific," reported Fitch, "and on our part very effective, as I saw the next day in riding over the field. I thought the Confederate dead on the battle-fields of Perryville and Stone's River, whom I saw, were numerous, but they were not equal to those in front of this position. We lost many, but logs saved us."[28]

Perhaps one might credit logs for "saving" the right and center, but the left of Mitchell's defense line buckled under assault. Later Mitchell would explain charitably that the enemy was repulsed "except by the two [sic] regiments of the First Division [Carlin's], who, having inferior protection, were compelled to retire." Fitch, on the other hand, placed the blame squarely on Maj. John H. Widmer, 104th Illinois, who was aligned next to Robinson's 121st Ohio. Widmer, worried about his low ammunition supply and the rebels moving to Robinson's left and rear, openly pulled his men out of line "for the second time" that day. When Widmer bolted, Fitch's other two regiments broke to the rear themselves. Robinson's 121st Ohio, their comrades to the right having fled and Confederates closing in on their left and rear, had little choice but to abandon their position also. So the 121st fell back, apparently in considerable disorder.[29] With Robinson gone, Mitchell's left—the line that he had so carefully constructed from bits and pieces of different commands—was smashed. All that remained was the gallant 34th Illinois fighting for its life at the angle.[30]

Rebel troops crashed through the opening resulting from the flight of Fitch's wing. Fortunately for Mitchell, the ferocity of the Confederate thrust had been "broken when the charges on the front were checked," and the troops that penetrated into Morgan's rear, according to Union observers, numbered less than a brigade. Nevertheless, Mitchell was surrounded. Indeed, it appeared that Morgan's entire division would be encircled. The 34th Illinois and the 98th Ohio now "had to hastily mount over our works"

John Grant Mitchell
(Rutherford B. Hayes Presidential Center)

and turn about, "changing front to rear." "The boys bounced the works and fought them in rear, front and flank." Then, "recrossing our works again we met foe in our original front." "The great fear was that the ammunition would become exhausted, and every captured rebel was made to shell out that remaining in his box, to be fired at his own friends."[31]

Attack after attack smashed into Morgan's beleaguered position, rapidly reshaping itself from an elongated *T* into a rectangle. Most agree that there were six distinct, organized assaults against this veritable "hornet's nest." When his left broke apart and Harvey Hill's rebels penetrated to the rear of his front line, Mitchell ordered his troops who remained in their positions facing east toward the Confederates to about-face and open fire. This surprised the enveloping enemy and drove it back in confusion. Mitchell's men reversed their lines repeatedly during the late afternoon as the Confederates in the rear or in the front edged closer once again. After the sixth attack, many of Mitchell's men were down to only two cartridges. Mitchell sent word to fix bayonets and prepare to charge. "Some Jump the Works and Hand to Hand Fight with the Rebs. Many of the Rebs are Dressed in Our Blue Clothes which Deceive us." Who was friend? Who was foe? The "ragged condition and unmilitary clothes" of both sides made identification almost impossible. Attacked on three sides, the troops compelled to switch continuously from one side of their works to the other, Mitchell's brigade "stood like a rock."[32]

Five days later Pvt. William C. Robinson wrote his father: "All agree in saying it was the hottest place we were ever in. The rebels had us completely surrounded and nothing but the most obstinate resistance saved the entire division from capture."[33] The enemy suffered frightfully. "The dead were on both sides of our works. . . . Bloody garments and bloody men strewed the ground." The 98th Ohio, besieged in that awful angle, "killed more of the enemy than that regiment reported for duty the morning of the battle."[34] "Many of the trees had numbers of 'ramrods' sticking out of them, showing that our men, upon reloading did not take time to remove them from their guns." Some trees were "almost completely filled with bullets."[35]

Mitchell's brigade itself lost heavily. "The aggregate loss is 160, only 8 of whom are missing . . . very large, when our position, fighting behind works is considered."[36] Pvt. John M. Branum, 98th Ohio, was hit by a minié ball and killed. His captain and college classmate wrote, "I loved him as a brother." The next morning they placed Branum "with full suit on" in a grave beside a corporal from his company. "We built a vault of logs, and on the bottom we laid pine boughs, covering it all over smooth, then a blanket, and we laid the bodies on that, then put two blankets over them, and building up the vault closed it in at the top. We buried them the best we could."[37]

In the rear, on high ground near the Morris house, Jefferson C. Davis was frantic. The tatters of Carlin's division were streaming past. What about Morgan? "If Morgan's troops can stand this, all is right; if not the day is lost. . . . They must fight it out."[38] Colonel McClurg, standing beside Davis, believed that the noise ahead on the right (Morgan's position) was so "continuous and remorseless . . . it seemed more than the men could bear. . . . Soldiers in the command who have passed through scores of battles will tell you they never saw anything like the fighting at Bentonville."[39]

Morgan's First Brigade, his right flank, was commanded by forty-seven-year-old William Vandever, a former Iowa lawyer and politician, whose war record had been hardly distinguished. He was an adequate leader of men like Robinson, no doubt, but could Vandever handle troops coolly, skillfully, in a crisis? As the firing intensified to his left, Vandever used every moment to strengthen his log fortifications and dig in deeper. His troops were compact, which was an advantage: two lines, 120 yards apart—the front consisted of the 16th Illinois and the 14th Michigan. The back line, the 10th Michigan and the 17th New York, began the action directly behind the front line but was displaced left twice, so that in effect it became a reserve for both Vandever and Mitchell, occupying entrenchments formerly held by the 34th and 121st Illinois. Screening Vandever's left front was an extended regimental skirmish line—Vernon's 78th Illinois, Mitchell's brigade. Vandever's own 60th Illinois guarded the right front and right flank. The ground in every direction from Vandever's position was very swampy.

Earlier the 78th Illinois had succeeded in driving back the rebel skirmishers upon their main line, and it quickly became apparent to Maris Vernon, commander of the 78th, that the Confederates were in great strength and ready to assume the offensive, probably with the intent of attacking Mitchell's right flank. So Vernon ordered his reserve wing to be thrown out to the right flank, where, once in position, it opened fire on the enemy. Soon the rebels, in two lines of battle, advanced directly on the 78th from the east without attempting the anticipated flanking movement. Vernon reacted by pulling back his wing and having it fortify as a reserve line. The rebels broke

William Vandever
(U.S. Army Military History Institute, Carlisle, Pennsylvania)

through Vernon's first line of skirmishers without much difficulty but were sent reeling by a volley from the concealed second line. But the enemy regrouped and advanced again in even greater strength.[40] The 78th, its ammunition almost exhausted, formed itself in a single line of battle, fired one last volley, and, under cover of its smoke, fell back upon the main line.

"All at once our skirmish line came bounding over our works, telling us to be ready." It was about 4:15 P.M.[41] Vernon's skirmishers had fought an outstanding delaying action.

Vandever allowed the Confederates to approach within thirty paces of his works, then "a deadly and destructive fire was poured into them, which drove them back in confusion." The enemy regrouped and returned to the attack, but once again Vandever met it with a terrific fire, "which was continued for about twelve minutes." The rebels again fell back, disorganized and with heavy losses. This time the defenders climbed over their works and counterattacked—Morgan-style—with fixed bayonets. The right of Vandever's line (14th Michigan) charged the retreating rebels, creating havoc. Aiding the 14th materially were two companies of the 60th Illinois that had been cut off when Vandever's skirmish line had been driven in. The fight was furious. Down went the color-bearer and color guard of the 14th Michigan. At the critical moment Pvt. Henry E. Plant seized the flag and waved it high with a shout, inspiring his comrades to even greater efforts. Soon after, when the regiment retired in triumph back to its lines, it brought with it 32 rebel officers and 200 soldiers; proudest of all, the 14th Michigan had captured the colors of the 40th Regiment North Carolina Troops (Hagood's brigade).[42]

Twenty-two-year-old Pvt. George W. Clute, Company I, 14th Michigan, captured the rebel colors. "In the midst of the struggle I saw a Confederate flag and made a rush for it. It was in the hands of their lieutenant." Both the rebel officer and Clute "were out of ammunition. Nothing but a trial of strength could determine which one of us was entitled to those colors. We had a desperate fight, but I proved to be the stronger and dragged color-bearer and flag along for over 100 feet before he let go of the staff and ran back to his lines."[43]

Promising to offset this good fortune came another Confederate attack, this time from Vandever's left—from Mitchell's direction. Mitchell's brigade was fighting for its life, virtually surrounded and hidden from Vandever's men. "The woods on our left were on fire, and the smoke was so thick we could see but indistinctly."[44] When Mitchell's left broke and he reshaped his defenses into a thin, defiant rectangle, many Confederates pressed on behind his position toward Vandever, "flanking us" and capturing pockets of Mitchell's men as they passed. Vandever's second line, which bore the brunt of this assault, changed front twice.[45] The commander of the 17th New York,

Capt. Alexander S. Marshall, "quickly wheeled his regiment" to face north and fought off the attacks "in the most gallant manner." A member of the beleaguered 98th Ohio credited the 17th New York, "those fellows that wore the red turbans," with saving them.[46]

But Marshall's front was narrow—only a regimental front. To Marshall's left (now from the west) came still another Confederate column. "Covered by the underbrush they swept stealthily to our rear" and crashed into the old second line occupied by Vernon and his 78th Illinois skirmishers. The enemy charged and drove Vernon out of the works. These indistinct lines of Confederates also approached very close to the left of the 17th New York, then "summoned us" to surrender, offering "to parole us on the field." Marshall conferred with Capt. William H. Dunphy (commanding the 10th Michigan) and "concluded we would charge with the bayonet."[47] Fortunately, as the two regiments launched their counterattack, they saw to their left the rest of Vandever's brigade simultaneously charging from their trenches.[48]

Vandever had been astonished by what he saw. To his rear the 78th Illinois had been driven from its works and in its stead came rebels— hundreds of them. Flushed with victory, the enemy had mounted fortifications originally occupied by the 10th Michigan and there planted three battle flags. Now the rebels began cheering, calling upon Vandever to surrender. Vandever calmly, and in the manner employed by Mitchell scarcely fifteen minutes earlier, ordered his men to face about and defend their works in reverse. "Just at this moment the Fourteenth Michigan and the Sixtieth Illinois returned from repelling the charge of the enemy." Back over their works Vandever's troops charged, straight into the rebel ranks. Simultaneously the 17th New York, now on the rebel left flank itself, opened up enfilade fire and charged, led by Color Sgt. C. S. Crist, who would earn his commission that day. Struck from two sides the Confederates scattered. Over 150 rebels were captured along with the flag of the 54th Virginia (Palmer's Brigade, Army of Tennessee).[49]

While Mitchell and Vandever fought for their lives, Morgan's Third Brigade, Benjamin Dana Fearing commanding, dutifully marched toward the Goldsboro road, "wading through numerous swamps, over bushes, vines, and briers."[50] Morgan had given him somewhat different, certainly less dramatic, orders than Davis. March left to the road, Morgan had said, then place your lines beyond it and parallel to it. Soon after he set out, Fearing began to encounter stragglers from Carlin's command. He continued on blindly, nevertheless, fighting his way forward now, pushing rebel skirmishers before him, until he was thirty yards from the road. There, above (north of) the road, he established his skirmish line. "Heavily engaged all the time," Fearing deployed his four regiments on line below the road.[51]

Fearing found himself truly isolated, with fighting all about—to his front, his right front, his right flank (especially), and his right rear. Could he maintain his line, his battlefield presence? It was in his blood, surely. This twenty-seven-year-old descendant of Israel Putnam was a veteran of Shiloh, Chickamauga, and the Atlanta Campaign. Up until now Fearing had been a highly dependable citizen-soldier, certainly a favorite of General Sherman. Had not Sherman entrusted him with Dan McCook's brigade?[52]

Fearing sized up his situation. He had no contact with Morgan's left, and his own left company commander reported a break—a separation of at least 250 yards from any Twentieth Corps units. So Fearing extended a thin line of skirmishers until he touched the first Twentieth Corps unit, then "moved my main line as far to the right as I deemed practicable."[53] He had no time to dig in, however.

As Fearing was making his dispositions, the enemy attacked his center and right, "driving our skirmishers into the main line." Fearing held his own for about fifteen minutes, repelling one rebel column. But enemy soldiers continued to appear—on the Goldsboro road with heavy blocks of them moving to his right. Subordinates first reported that they were friendly troops. At least they wore blue uniforms. "Hold your fire," Fearing commanded. Then he saw, and his men saw, their mistake—Confederates in mass marching to their right and rear. Fearing reacted to this threat by refusing his right to conform with the enemy line of advance, then opened fire. But it was in vain. Rebels attacked him "vigorously in front, and at the same time the flanking column having straightened up its lines came pressing down upon my right flank with crushing force."[54] A Confederate division "was within 20 yards of the right of my regiment," reported Lieutenant Colonel Fahnestock, 86th Illinois. "Bullets flew like nails among the pine trees." Being struck "squarely on the right flank," Fearing's line was "doubled up and thrown into confusion." Back his men went, about 500 yards, some running without a glance over their backs, some stopping, trying to make a stand, then retreating to another position, selling ground as slowly and as dearly as they could. But for the most part, at least on the right, it became a "most terrible stampede." We were "at their mercy."[55]

At this critical moment a minié ball struck Fearing. It tore off his thumb,

Benjamin Dana Fearing
(U.S. Army Military History Institute, Carlisle, Pennsylvania)

his forefinger, and the lower portion of his right hand. Despite the agony, the young commander worked to rally his command, finally succeeding in re-forming them at "the edge of an open field." His left, fortunately, had time to withdraw in a somewhat orderly manner and went into position anchoring his new line (only two regiments) facing east, at right angles to the Golds-boro road. Fearing's new left flank rested just north of the road itself. Nothing, however, would deliver Fearing's battered brigade more than the

Confederates themselves—who, "having suffered severely did not, or could not, follow up with his broken and straggling ranks the seeming advantage gained."[56]

While this line was being established, Fearing, suffering greatly from pain and loss of blood, turned the brigade command over to Lt. Col. James W. Langley, 125th Illinois. Langley sent staff officers scurrying to collect the shattered 52d Ohio and 86th Illinois. Form them on the right of the 22d Indiana and 125th Illinois, he ordered. Langley then moved the entire line, each man carrying a rail in his hand, forward about 75 yards and began to construct works at that point. No sooner had they begun erecting barricades and entrenching than Robinson's brigade of the Twentieth Corps appeared, took position on Langley's left, "and began construction of a refused line."[57] Stragglers and small broken units, many of them Carlin's men, rapidly came up—from the woods, from the rear, from the swamps—filling empty spaces and strengthening the entire line. Even Davis's escort and a train guard fragment took their place in line. But the works were not yet "strong enough to protect men lying down" when rebel skirmishers appeared and "lively firing" started all over again.[58]

A minor command crisis occurred at this juncture. One of Slocum's staff rode up and asked Langley to throw back the entire line about 75 yards. "This direction I could not obey," said Langley, "even if the point selected by him had been more advisable, for the main line of the enemy at this moment vigorously assaulted my works and were handsomely repulsed." "I determined to strengthen and hold it." On came the rebels, attack after attack. They would break out of "the woods in perfect line and yelling like demons." Langley held them off again and again. It was easier each time.[59] Credit Fearing's and Langley's sturdy defenders, of course, but also acknowledge the splendid efforts of Robinson's brigade. Robinson himself, flag in hand, had rallied his men and set them in place beside Langley. Now, as Confederates battered themselves against Langley's flimsy works, Robinson's men "fired by battalion into his [the enemy's] right flank."[60] A member of Ward's division, coming up from the rear breathless, observed one of these Confederate attacks from high ground behind the Federal artillery:

We halted there, and just below us was a *grand sight*.

. . . At the bottom of a gentle slope in an old field, the Yankee boys were lying down behind a very slight breastwork that looked like it had been thrown up in a hurry. Beyond them, the Rebels were just coming out of the woods for a charge. They came at a walk with bayonets fixed, while their officers rode along in their front, waving their swords and cheering on the men. . . .

The Rebs came at a walk until thirty or forty rods from our boys. Then their officers went to the rear and their bugles called "Charge!" . . . The Rebs lowered their guns to the position "charge," and started for our lines with a yell.

Our boys continued lying down. They remained as quiet as logs until the Rebs got so near that it seemed as if they would be run over. Suddenly, when the Rebs could not have been more than ten rods away, our bugles sounded "Rise up, Fire!"

We could see the smoke leap from our guns almost into the faces of the Rebs. They fired so fast that the smoke hid the Rebs from us.[61]

Truly it was a "grand sight." Grim-faced midwesterners, shoulder-to-shoulder with their comrades from the East Coast, hurled back repeated, furious rebel assaults, a half dozen of them. One had to admire the determination of the rebels, too. They kept coming out of those woods, again and again. But it was futile; it was slaughter.

Solid Union infantry destroyed these attacks, but they were aided in devastating fashion by sixteen well-served Federal cannon. Perched on high ground, on both sides of the Goldsboro road, a few hundred yards to the rear (west) of Robinson and Langley, they enfiladed the Confederate assaults and fired with splendid effect. To the utter delight of the beleaguered Federal infantry, behind these guns could be seen line upon line of fresh blue troops waiting to be thrown into the fight.

After driving most of the Fourteenth Corps back nearly a mile, the attacking enemy, instead of enjoying the pleasures of a mopping-up action, now confronted a mighty, carefully prepared, Union position, bristling with Napoleons and three-inch rifles.

All the while the Confederates fought Morgan, wing commander Henry W. Slocum had continued to rush forward troops and build a fortress on high ground in the vicinity of the Morris house. Perhaps Johnston could be defeated by Davis and his Fourteenth Corps. If so, well and good. Slocum believed this initially, it appears. Prudence born of costly combat experience, however, as well as his innate sense of caution, dictated that he anticipate adversity and provide a backup plan. So Slocum let Davis tend to the fighting while he proceeded with two parallel courses of action.

First, he fed troops into the front lines to strengthen the Fourteenth Corps. Thus when Nathaniel J. Jackson's division, Twentieth Corps, came up, Slocum immediately committed two of his brigades—William Hawley's to support Carlin's left and James S. Robinson's to fill the gap in Carlin's division.

Second, while awaiting developments to his front, Slocum established a strong point almost a mile behind Carlin's advanced position. Here he placed his headquarters and the Left Wing staging area. So, as the firing ahead increased in intensity, he had his engineers busy staking out and clearing a magnificent artillery position, utilizing the advantages of the high ground near the Morris house. There the pieces could be massed, not in battalion but regimental strength (six batteries).

When the 3:00 P.M. Confederate tornado struck and berserk teamsters— the army's predictable messengers of doom—came tearing down the Goldsboro road, Slocum realized the seriousness of the situation: he must meet and blunt an enemy advance, apparently in overwhelming numbers. Assisted by corps commander Alpheus Williams, Slocum hurried to provide the Left Wing with defense in depth, all the while hoping that the rebel onslaught would weaken, if not exhaust itself, in assaults on Carlin and Morgan. In any event he would be waiting for them at the Morris house, a battle site of his choosing. There he would lay his own ambush.

Williams pulled Hawley's Second Brigade back from his detached and exposed position behind Carlin. He positioned him several hundred yards left of the Goldsboro road, protecting the main line against a flank attack. Here Hawley rapidly constructed breastworks above a ravine. Until more troops came up (or back), Hawley would be the left of Slocum's new position. Four hundred yards to Hawley's right was Robinson, facing northwest, below and generally parallel to the Goldsboro road, his right resting in heavy woods. Skirmishers linked his line with that of Langley.[62] No Federal troops connected Robinson and Hawley, it was true, but several hundred yards behind this gap, athwart the Goldsboro road, was James L. Selfridge's brigade (Jackson's division).[63] Behind Selfridge were the guns.

While Slocum defined this basic defensive structure, he and Williams sent staff officers flying far to the rear to rush forward every possible man in the Left Wing. " 'Hurry up, boys, the Johnnies have got the First driven into a trap and are giving them Hell,' " he would shout as he rode along the column. "We knew what the next word would be, of course, and every man tightened his belt for a run. The courier had hardly passed us when our brigade bugle sounded: 'Attention. Forward March, Double Quick!'" At the double-quick, then the run, they raced forward as fast as they could go. Almost eight miles they ran "without a halt." "That is, some did. Some played out and fell down and were run over by the rest."[64]

As the weary brigades of William T. Ward's division came up, Slocum and Williams sent them left, extending Hawley's line and securing the left flank. Soon Slocum's entire line bent slowly in that direction (west), beyond Hawley, following the contours of the terrain. The 1st Michigan Engineers, Sherman's crack troubleshooters, manned the extreme left of the infantry line. Beyond was Kilpatrick's cavalry, dismounted, massed, waiting.[65]

Thus Slocum's first concern—to block the Goldsboro road with a powerful position—had been met by stationing Selfridge across it and gathering division batteries at that point; the second concern—to prevent the strong point from being turned—had been met by developing an extended and fortified left flank.

Slocum's plan succeeded beautifully. When the Confederates, elated but dead tired, spilled out of the woods and advanced in measured pace against Langley's and Robinson's infantry, six Union batteries blasted them, tearing gaping holes in their formations and demoralizing the assault force. If they continued down the road to attack the artillery concentration, they received flank fire from Robinson's infantry below the road; if they attacked south against the infantry, those terrible guns on high ground enfiladed their formations.

When the rebels struck, the Twentieth Corps guns—Batteries I and M, 1st New York Light, and Battery C, 1st Ohio Light—were up and well placed. Maj. John A. Reynolds directed their fire with frightening efficiency. Alongside Reynolds's batteries were Jefferson C. Davis's guns, commanded by Maj. Charles Houghtaling—Battery I, 2d Illinois Light; Battery C, 1st Illinois Light; and the one remaining gun of the 19th Indiana Light. An awestruck Union infantryman watched: "There were 8 full batteries going for them as best they knew how & they would average 2 shots a minute to the gun[.] as the Rebs charged on the batteries they began to fill up the guns with boxes of Cartridges which was too much for Mr. Reb[.]" A member of the 3d Wisconsin agreed: "Williams ordered the guns doubleshotted. The gunners came to the regiments and begged for bullets which they wrapped in rags and put into their guns on top of the canister."[66]

Surely the concentration and execution of Slocum's artillery was fundamental to Union victory on March 19. But it was only one of a series of decisions, of measures, taken by Slocum, Davis, Morgan, and leaders on the brigade and regimental level, any of which might have been indispensable.

Yet there remains the story of William Cogswell, 2d Massachusetts, commander of the Third Brigade, Ward's division, Twentieth Corps. Some consider Cogswell's role the most important of all.

Another of Sherman's bevy of twenty-seven-year-old leaders, Cogswell was born in Massachusetts and received a privileged education at Phillips Andover Academy and Dartmouth College. A longing for adventure—an effort to escape the predictable life—took him to sea, like James Dada Morgan, but just for a short time. Returning home, he entered Harvard Law School, was graduated, and then started a practice in Salem. In the spring of 1861 he abandoned all for the Union, and his military career became a success story. Able and intelligent, this volunteer officer rose steadily in rank, becoming a brevet brigadier in December 1864. The following month Sherman gave Cogswell brigade command. "It may not be improper here to state," said Cogswell, "that on the 16th of January I came to this brigade a stranger, and commenced the campaign with them the next morning."[67]

Cogswell's men had marched all night, Saturday, March 18, reaching camp at 5:00 A.M. on Sunday. Wearily they took up the march again at eight, monotonously plodding behind the trains that they had been instructed to protect. It was hardly a glamorous assignment in the closing scene of their campaign through the Carolinas. At 11:30 A.M., however, came Slocum's order to hasten to the front. They set out "at the double-quick a good deal of the way."[68] Often they would have to leave the road because it was clogged with artillery and wagons, rushing forward, tearing back. Nevertheless, they hurried alongside the Goldsboro road through woods, through fields, and finally reached the battlefield about 3:00 P.M.

As Cogswell came up past the Harper house, he was met by Lt. Col. Charles W. Asmussen of Williams's staff. Move your brigade to the right of the road and forward, directed Asmussen. Report to Major General Davis. He needs you to plug a hole between Carlin and Morgan. Asmussen assured Cogswell that he would inform division commander Ward that corps commander Williams himself had plucked the brigade from the column.[69]

Half a mile ahead, well behind John G. Mitchell's line, a curious incident had occurred. Division commander Carlin, desperate to reenter the fight,

Ward and his generals. *From left to right:* Benjamin Harrison, William T. Ward, Daniel Dustin, and William Cogswell.
(U.S. Army Military History Institute, Carlisle, Pennsylvania)

groped through the woods searching for David Miles's brigade, hoping that Miles still held his position. Carlin was mounted now and had a trusty staff officer beside him. He could not find Miles, but he found Confederates! Unknowingly he rode smack through a Confederate skirmish line. "They paid no attention to me, standing at 'order arms' with eyes to the front."[70] Carlin, his heart pumping for the twentieth time that day, turned his horse Rosey about and calmly rode back through their lines.

There in the deep woods, where the ground was dark even at midday, who should Carlin next encounter but his nemesis, Jefferson C. Davis. Davis was riding straight into the rebels. Carlin told him to stop. Davis, undoubtedly made perverse by even the sight of Carlin, looked ahead, saw the troops to which Carlin referred, and "in his emphatic way said: 'No, —, they are not.' Then after advancing a few steps, Davis said: 'Yes, they are, —.'" The two generals skedaddled.[71]

It was Davis who instantly recognized not only the danger to Morgan's division, but also an opportunity to blindside the Confederates. He rushed back for help. He found Williams, Williams sent Asmussen, Asmussen discovered Cogswell, and Cogswell answered the summons.

Cogswell advanced on the lower side of the Goldsboro road, exercising great caution. Who knew what lay ahead in this no-man's-land? As Carlin had observed,[72] "while in that wood, it seemed to me that one was as liable to be killed by his friends as by the enemy." Do not "fire till ordered to do so," Cogswell directed. He and his troops pushed ahead, parallel to the Goldsboro road, behind Langley's line, on past Langley's right. Then they met General Davis, who pointed out to Cogswell the line of march he should take. Forward they went, Cogswell and his men, alone now, deeper into the wilderness, "through thick bushes and in water nearly up to their waists," through heavy pine, in front of which was a "thick mass of undergrowth."[73]

In a matter of minutes Cogswell's right struck two advancing Confederate lines. The enemy was groping for the rear of Morgan's line, its attention focused to the east. Thus both sides were surprised; both recoiled and attempted to re-form.[74]

The momentum, however, was with Cogswell. He regrouped, throwing back his right slightly. Out went his skirmishers while he placed four regiments on line with each flank supported by one regiment in column. Then, led by skirmishers, his men attacked the rebels and drove them "through dense swamps." The enemy columns splintered, and a group was cut off and surrendered. It proved to be a part of Joseph B. Palmer's Brigade, and Captain Blasland, 33d Massachusetts, received the colors of the 26th Tennessee.[75] Cogswell pressed on, driving the enemy back toward the Goldsboro road with his big, strong brigade. More importantly, and perhaps unknowingly, his counterattack totally disrupted the rebel movement in the rear of Morgan's position. Assaulted from the left, the right, and the rear, the Confederates retreated from behind Morgan's position and now tried to re-form in order to confront what seemed to be a continuous Union line running from Vandever to Mitchell to Cogswell to Langley to Robinson. Cogswell's portion of that line ran straight through the middle of a swamp.[76]

Cogswell's timely and powerful attack, after "coming on the field with tired troops," had saved Morgan, restored the Union line, and broken the

Confederate attack. The initiative passed. It was a remarkable, if not decisive, performance.

Slocum recognized this. Always quick to give credit, he himself would tell Cogswell's brigade—"we had saved the day."[77]

Cogswell and Morgan opened communications, connected their lines, and together at sundown withstood a "storm of bullets." "So terrible and withering was this fire of small arms, that, had our battalions stood up, they must have been utterly annihilated. And thus, on until darkness set in, the air was thick with hissing bullets." They remained "hotly engaged," knee-deep in swamp water, until 8:30 P.M., when night mercifully intervened.[78]

8

If the Lord Will Only See Me Safe Through

SHORTLY AFTER 3:00 P.M. the Army of Tennessee began emptying from the woods bordering Willis Cole's field.[1] The North Carolina Juniors had box seats. From their position close to the Goldsboro road, at right angles to the lines of their comrades, "it looked like a picture and at our distance was truly beautiful." Nearly the entire Army of Tennessee was visible, "with colors flying, and with line of battle in such perfect order as to enable us to distinguish the several general officers."[2] Then the Juniors heard the rebel yell echo against the opposing tree line. The attackers looked invincible; they sounded invincible. It was all thrilling.

Col. Charles W. Broadfoot, 1st North Carolina Junior Reserves, looked more carefully: "But it was a painful sight to see how close their battle flags were together, regiments being scarcely larger than companies and a division not much larger than a regiment should be."[3] Close at hand, to Broadfoot's right, Walthall's Division swung into the open—a pitiful column of 250 men. Indeed, A. P. Stewart's entire corps numbered less than 800.[4]

Hardee had Stewart arrange the Army of Tennessee in two lines. The attack would be in echelon, beginning with William B. Bate (Cheatham's Corps) on the right, then Daniel H. Hill (Lee's Corps), then William W. Loring (Stewart's Corps). The three corps would guide on Joseph B. Palmer's Brigade, Stevenson's Division, the center of Lee's Corps and thus the center of the army.

As carefully aligned as possible, the Confederates stepped out "as if on parade." For the first 300 yards they marched at quick time, Cleburne's Division under James Argyle Smith leading the way. Smith's own brigade (led by Capt. J. R. Bonner) was to have formed the extreme right, but Bonner's Georgians tangled themselves in their own abatis and were slow coming on line. Smith decided not to wait. He pushed forward with his remaining brigade (Govan's). These Arkansas troops had been Hardee's Brigade, then Cleburne's, and eventually the pride of the western army. Today they were commanded by the veteran Lt. Col. Peter V. "Pea Vine" Green. He commanded a shadow, however—eleven decimated regiments consolidated into three small ones.[5]

Hardee now ordered the double-quick, and Bate's Corps pressed forward through an "old field dotted with second growth pines," stepping over bodies of Buell's men killed in the noon assault.[6] As they approached the Federals concealed in the woods, the enemy opened fire. Their first volley staggered the Confederates. Pea Vine Green's men halted and Bonner's sought cover in the woods, closing to the left tight against Green. Their ranks mixed. Some men hid behind trees; others found protection in a ditch. A private in the 63d Georgia, Smith's Brigade, would report:

> The "zips" of the minies get thicker and thicker and the line partially demoralized by the heavy fire suddenly halts. Frank Stone is carrying the colors (Cleburne's division flag—a blue field with white circle in the center) and he and I jump for the same pine. It is only six inches thick and will cover neither of us fully, but we divide its protective capacity fairly. Fifteen or twenty feet to my left there is an exclamation of pain and as I turn to look Jim Beasley clasps his hand to his face as the blood spurts from his cheek.
>
> My cartridge box has been drawn to the front of my body for convenience in loading as well as for protection and as I look to the front again a ball strikes it, and strikes so hard that it forces from me an involuntary grunt. Frank hears it and turns to me quickly, "Are you hurt?" I said I believed not and proceed to investigate. The ball passing through the leather and tin had struck the leaden end of a cartridge and being in that way deflected had passed out the right side of the box instead of through my body.[7]

By drifting left into the woods, Smith had exposed the right flank of his division. Because Taliaferro was not up (he was still floundering through the wilderness behind the Confederate line of deployment),[8] Bate called up the second line of the corps, his own division under Col. Daniel L. Kenan, sending it to the right of Smith. It was early in the battle but a critical moment for the Confederates. Bate had committed his second line; his left (Smith's Division) apparently had been checked, at least it was no longer advancing. Did the pain of Franklin, the memories of failed assaults at Atlanta and Jonesboro, inhibit the Army of Tennessee? Did fear rule them? Was Hood right, after all?

It was at this point that the Army of Tennessee's "Old Reliable" presented himself. General Hardee rode to the front of his troops, the men who had followed him at Shiloh and Murfreesboro. In sight of hundreds, "in full view of the enemy," he boldly led his mount up to the ditch where men were hiding and jumped it, waving his troops forward. For many of these men it was the first time they had seen Hardee since October 1864, and the very sight of him excited them. They raised a cheer, rose out of the ditch, and renewed the charge.[9]

To the right of Hardee another inspirational figure appeared. He was in Bate's old division:

> The gallant color-bearer of the First Florida . . . is making his way alone towards the breastworks at half speed, with his flag held aloft, fifty yards in front of the halted ranks. Inspired by his example or recovering from the temporary panic, the line moves forward again, and the enemy desert their breastworks and make for the rear at a double-quick. Leaping the entrenchments, a hatchet, frying pan and Enfield rifle lie right in my path. Sticking the pan and hatchet in my belt, I drop my Austrian gun and seizing the Enfield I see across the ravine a group of the enemy running up the hill. Aiming at the center of the squad I sent one of their own balls after them.[10]

The enemy abandoned its first line, dropped back to its second, and then, after a momentary stand, was quickly flushed out. Across the ravine the Yankees fled. The attack of the Confederate right under Bate had been successful.

Lee's Corps, led by Harvey Hill, formed the middle of the Army of Tennessee. Hill's three divisions were in two lines, 300 yards apart, with Joseph B. Palmer's Brigade, Stevenson's Division, in the center of the front line as "the directing column." As they were forming, the men caught sight of General Johnston, the first time they had seen him since Atlanta. They cheered loudly and "off went every hat."[11] Then the command "moved steadily forward about 400 yards in common time, preserving its alignment almost as if on parade, although for a part of that distance under considerable fire."[12]

When they closed to within 200 yards, Hill's men charged and the enemy, after a volley, fled. Two Georgia brigades in Henry D. Clayton's Division crashed into the Union first line, breaking it. Then they halted. Clayton's second line, an Alabama brigade under Brig. Gen. Alpheus Baker, passed through the Georgians in pursuit. The brigade chased the Federals to the Goldsboro road, and when it came upon the road, there "was not a Yank to be seen." There was plunder aplenty, however. Pvt. Frank Lee found a silk dress, daguerreotypes, and a small bag of silver. Pvt. Ben Watson, one of Baker's men, "picked up a frying pan and stuck the handle under my belt as a sort of shield."[13] Prisoners also fell into their hands, and these were sent to the rear under guard. Col. Osceola Kyle, commanding Jackson's Georgia Brigade, Clayton's Division, was particularly elated. He just had been ex-changed from prison (two years at Johnson's Island) and longed for the sight of fleeing Yankees. Kyle's men rejoiced as well, not only because of routing the Yankees, but also at being able to fight in a command other than Bate's. Their old commander, Brig. Gen. Henry R. Jackson, had been captured in the Nashville debacle, and both he and they had blamed Bate for their continuing misfortunes. It was a relief to fight under Henry Clayton and Harvey Hill.[14]

The movements of Hill and Loring seem to have been controlled by A. P. Stewart, at least in this initial attack. Loring had two divisions, his own Mississippi division, commanded by Col. James Jackson, and Edward C. Walthall's Arkansas/Alabama division. Walthall's two brigades formed the extreme left of the Army of Tennessee. His division represented an interest-ing marriage of brigades—Reynolds's Arkansans (now commanded by Col. Henry G. Bunn)[15] and Quarles's Alabamians (commanded by Brig. Gen. George D. Johnston). The two brigades did not get along. The Arkansans distrusted the Alabamians because of incidents prior to and during the Battle of Nashville. With their commander shot from his horse in the open-ing round, Reynolds's troops worried if Johnston's men would do their part when the fighting got tough. They counted on Walthall to deliver them—from the Federals and from the Alabama excuse makers.

In the past Walthall had accomplished miracles. His men knew this. The army knew it. Had not he and Bedford Forrest held at bay, for a week, the heavy and aggressive Union cavalry of James H. Wilson, not to speak of George Thomas's advanced infantry, thereby allowing Hood's broken army to withdraw from Tennessee to safety?[16]

Not only had Walthall lost Reynolds, his most experienced brigade com-mander, but also he had different and perhaps more difficult orders than the other division commanders. Walthall was the connecting link between the Army of Tennessee and the troops of the Department of North Carolina. He was to guide right on Jackson's men (Loring's Division), all the while attempting to maintain an "obtuse angle" with the North Carolina troops on his left. In advancing by echelon, if Jackson's and Hoke's lines began to converge, thus squeezing his front, Walthall was to give way and fold his command as a second line behind Jackson.[17]

When Loring advanced with Loring's (commanded by Jackson) and Walthall's Divisions, he placed a strong skirmish line across his front, and these aggressive troops drove the enemy skirmishers back upon their breastworks. These hasty fieldworks in turn were "easily carried," and about two hundred Federals were captured. Walthall continued his attack, almost due south now, aiming his advance at two Union fieldpieces that kept up a constant fire. The enemy abandoned these guns, however, and Walthall passed on "till density of undergrowth and rapid pursuit so deranged my line that it became necessary to rectify it before proceeding."[18] At this point Gen. Joseph Johnston rode up, congratulated Loring and Walthall, and shouted so that Reynolds's Brigade might hear: " 'It has been reported to me that the Army of Tennessee was demoralized; if that be true I had rather command demoralized troops, because they fight better.' "[19] A North Carolina artilleryman who observed the charge agreed. He noted in his journal that "the charge of Walthall's Division was the most splendid thing I ever witnessed."[20]

As the Army of Tennessee penetrated the Union fieldworks and drove the Federals back upon the Goldsboro road, it became obvious that the army must be reorganized. Units had become mixed, confused, orders were "being issued by different commanders," and a number of men had stopped to plunder. Before halting, some of Hill's corps (Palmer's Brigade certainly) had crossed the Goldsboro road itself and driven Fitch's command (Hobart's brigade) back into the swamps. Hardee, however, recalled these troops to the northern side of the road. There he had the Army of Tennessee re-form.[21]

Thus the initial phase of the Confederate attack ended. An elated Johnston rode up to Hardee: "General I congratulate you on your success, or rather on doing what you always do."[22] The right wing had accomplished its mission. Three Union positions (those of Buell, Hobart, and Robinson) had been assaulted and carried without high loss. Yankee resistance north of the road had been blown away.

In considering this attack by the Army of Tennessee on Carlin's division, one should bear in mind the numbers engaged, especially on the Confederate side. There is a tendency to think of unit strength in 1861–64 terms. Under that assumption Bate's Corps attacked Buell's brigade and thus should have made short work of it. Actually Bate attacked with over 2,000 troops (60 percent of the Army of Tennessee). Buell defended with about 800, thus badly outnumbered but perhaps not overwhelmingly so. Indeed, Carlin's division itself numbered conservatively about 4,000 (including Robinson's three regiments); Davis's reinforced Fourteenth Corps (2+ divisions), about 8,500.[23]

The Army of Tennessee had captured three guns and several hundred prisoners. Hill's and Loring's Corps had done very well. Bate's Corps performed less well. His flank division had blundered and become entangled. It had taken extraordinary measures by Hardee himself and a brave Florida color-bearer to get Bate's stalled attack going.

While Hardee's men straightened their lines and regained their breaths, Johnston might have concerned himself with two negative aspects of the attack. Taliaferro's Division had contributed nothing. Perhaps this had been Hardee's fault. In any event, Taliaferro was out of position initially and not a factor in the defeat of Carlin. Taliaferro also would have been unavailable for Hardee's second push down the Goldsboro road. Of greater moment, certainly, was the lack of participation by Bragg and Hoke. Loring's attack, it seems, had cut across Bragg's right, the front of the North Carolina reserves—in effect screening them and transforming them (and Starr's artillerymen) into observers. One must not blame Loring. Bragg's right should have moved forward once Loring advanced. What was Bragg doing?

For some reason Bragg's and Hoke's troops remained as onlookers. Johnston's orders were clear: attack in echelon from the right and advance "simultaneously" with Walthall.[24] Johnson Hagood, one of Hoke's brigade commanders, placed the blame on Hardee. "In swinging out, Hardee had lost connection with the left wing."[25] The paucity of Confederate reports handicaps attempts to assess responsibility for the disjointed Confederate attack. At the hinge point in the Confederate line was Brig. Gen. George D. Johnston, commanding the Alabama brigade, Walthall's Division, Loring's Corps.[26] In his Bentonville report Johnston says nothing about the units to his left. His fellow brigade commander, Colonel Bunn, simply reported that he "was ordered to advance simultaneously with General Hoke, on our left. . . . With Brigadier General Johnston I advanced, obliquing to the right through the open field, directing my right to General Loring's left. General Hoke not moving simultaneously, I continued to occupy the line to the left of General Loring."[27]

Walthall, who controlled the movements of George Johnston and Bunn, emphasizes that he was directed by either Loring or Stewart (his reference is unclear) that he "in advancing should guide right, unless, however, the commands on my right [Loring's Division] and left [Starr's mixed bag of North and South Carolina artillerymen] should so converge in advancing as to cover the ground in my front, and in that event he [Loring or Stewart] directed me by moving to the right to put my troops in support of Loring's [Division—Col. James Jackson, commanding]."[28] According to this report, Walthall fixed his attention to his right and concentrated on maintaining the connection with Loring's Division (Jackson).[29] Bragg made no Bentonville report; neither did Hoke nor any of Hoke's subordinates.

In seeking an explanation in the face of such fragmentary evidence, one should keep in mind that when military units are "guiding right," responsibility for maintaining connection belongs to the left unit. Also, one should consider the letter of Joseph Johnston to Hoke five years after Bentonville: "In the afternoon too, I thought that he [Bragg] did not execute my instructions for the attack—nor subsequent ones."[30]

In any event, the sickle's blade parted company with its handle. About 4:30 P.M., when the Army of Tennessee was regrouping on the northern side of the Goldsboro road, Hagood reports that Bragg ordered Hoke to advance two brigades and regain the connection with Hardee. So Col. Charles T. Zachry (commanding Colquitt's Brigade) and Hagood advanced. Zachry's right regiment had the good fortune to find the enemy flank, and Zachry, a veteran commander, quickly had his flank regiment "sweeping down to the left to clear the front of Colquitt's [Zachry's] left."[31] But then Bragg, "who had not been on the field and had heard of Hoke's movement through some aide or courier," ordered Hoke to make an immediate direct attack to his front, not waiting for the flank attack to mature.[32]

So Zachry and Hagood advanced straight ahead over difficult ground. Zachry struck first, probably Miles's left. He drove the Federals from their works and then, aided by Colonel Taylor's regiment of Hagood's Brigade, struck against Mitchell's refused line. Capt. Jonnathan D. Cowart, Company C, 6th Georgia, personally led the last charge. As was his habit, he carried his hat in his left hand and his sword in his right. This veteran of the Army of Northern Virginia, previously badly wounded at Sharpsburg, leaped over the Yankee works only to be shot through the heart. His company and regiment were hurled back. It had been a great effort by Zachry. One soldier wrote, "I don't think I ever saw them more valiant." All were well aware, he believed, that the war's end was near. They were determined to make this last effort their best.[33]

Col. John D. Taylor commanded 267 men. These were inexperienced soldiers, called "Red Infantry" because of the traditional artillery red facings, chevrons, and trim of their uniforms.[34] At Bentonville on March 19 they advanced through the woods and swamps and soon reached the enemy line. In a moment the colonel, who was leading the charge, found himself atop the Federal breastworks. Yankee resistance, however, quickly stiffened. A soldier not more than twenty paces away from Colonel Taylor shot him down. Other Confederates began to fall. Taylor's line was struck by enfilade fire. Then the Yankees counterattacked. Taylor's command crumbled and fled to the rear. Lt. John A. Gilchrist, who brought them back, counted only 115 men. Every officer except two had been killed, wounded, or captured. This bloody repulse of Hagood's center sent his entire brigade reeling.[35]

Hagood's center had hit the Mitchell-Vandever line head-on and probably penetrated the interval separating the two Union brigades. Maj. William A. Holland, 40th Regiment North Carolina Troops (3d Regiment North Carolina Heavy Artillery), commanded the center. He, like Taylor, led raw troops—long on enthusiasm, short on experience—more of Joseph Johnston's Red Infantry. Holland's men moved forward from their breastworks through the swamp into a thicket, taking casualties as they advanced. Then they charged. But in sight of the enemy breastworks, suddenly "they were halted and dressed to the right, under heavy fire."[36] To compound this tactical absurdity it seems as though Holland or Hagood had already stripped these troops of their skirmisher curtain, sending the column to the left while the skirmishers veered to the right. Then, when close to the Federal breastworks—when most vulnerable—their commander halted them and ordered them to re-form, thus casting away any hope of success. The result predictably was devastating—Yankee volleys tore holes in their ranks. Holland's Red Infantry, "badly cut up," fell back in disarray, some companies having lost all of their officers, the 40th having lost its colors. Among the mortally wounded was Lt. Col. Edward Mallett, commander of the 61st Regiment North Carolina Troops.[37]

Hoke thus met with a costly repulse on Morgan's lines. The attack was late and seems to have been delivered piecemeal. Hagood's left regiment (a consolidated unit of South Carolina state troops) does not appear to have been as heavily engaged as Taylor's and Holland's troops.

Of greater consequence, Starr's Artillery, the Juniors, and Clingman's Brigade seem to have taken little, if any, part in Hoke's attack. The role of Kirkland's Brigade also raises questions. Although battered at the Battle of Wise's Forks ten days before, these men were generally regarded as Hoke's best troops. Kirkland on March 19 suffered considerably fewer casualties than Zachry and Hagood. Indeed, Kirkland's losses may have resulted from Miles's late morning and early afternoon attacks; there is no mention by Hagood or other sources about Kirkland or his troops in the charge. Zachry's Georgians, who pressed their attack, suffered the worst: 33 killed, 163 wounded, and 18 missing.[38]

Johnson Hagood lays the responsibility for Hoke's defeat on Bragg's decision to launch a frontal attack: "The loss in our division at least would have been inconsiderable and our success eminent had it not been for Bragg's undertaking to give a tactical order upon a field that he had not seen."[39] Harvey Hill, quoting Hoke, backs Hagood's interpretation.[40]

What should be said of McLaws's performance? His big division formed Bragg's left. With almost as many men as the Army of Tennessee itself (3,500 effectives, 4,000 present),[41] his role was crucial. McLaws reports that his men dug in on Hoke's left while he went forward and reconnoitered. "Not long afterwards I was notified by Genl Bragg that Stewart had turned the enemy's left and was driving him towards my position. I moved the 32nd Georgia forward with a section of Artillery and advanced a line of skirmishers in a direction towards the sound of the firing."[42] That was all. Other orders reached him before his skirmishers "had gotten well into line," so McLaws pulled back and prepared to march his troops back to the right, beyond the Goldsboro road.[43]

While Bragg suffered a bloody nose smacking into Yankee works with frontal assaults, Hardee launched a second general attack on the right. There appears to have been no coordination between them. The timing of Hardee's renewed effort is impossible to determine with certainty, but it appears to have come after Hoke's repulse.

Bate apparently continued parallel to the Goldsboro road to a point about half a mile southwest of the Fitch-Miles-Morgan line. Being on the extreme right of the Army of Tennessee, Bate then swung to attack the enemy across the Goldsboro road, probably colliding with Fearing's brigade and portions of Robinson's brigade. These Federals repulsed him handily and some (Fearing's skirmishers) continued their advance, crossing to the northern side of the Goldsboro road, jabbing into Bate's left flank.[44] Bate, startled by Fearing's counterattack, appealed to Hill for assistance. Hill detached Clayton's Division and sent it "obliquely across the road" to meet this threat to Bate's left. As Clayton's three brigades swung right and south, his left brigade (Baker's) became entangled with Palmer's Brigade of Stevenson's Division (cut through its center). At the time Palmer's Brigade, the spearhead of the initial attack of the Army of Tennessee, had continued its advance with "impetuosity" well across the Goldsboro road.[45] Palmer was in the act of retiring north of the road and going into reserve when Baker broke his brigade into two wings.

It was at this point that Hill came up. Intent on continuing the attack across the road against the enemy position behind the swamp, Hill (without notifying division commander Stevenson) ordered the right wing of Palmer's Brigade (under Palmer's immediate command) to extend Baker's right and to "attack the enemy again." So Palmer, who thought his brigade was going into reserve, found himself detached from Stevenson and once again advancing south (300 yards) of the Goldsboro road on the right of Baker's Brigade—in effect becoming part of a makeshift strike force composed (right to left) of the brigades of Palmer and Baker plus Coltart's Division, all directly under Hill's command.[46]

Palmer found no organized enemy units to his front, but he and Baker did see that they had flanked the Yankees to their left—"two lines of breastworks running rather perpendicular to [the Goldsboro] road." Displaying commendable initiative, Palmer reasoned that

> it was wholly unsafe to move farther forward or pass this force on my left, and, indeed, on discovering these works and their singular direction I came to the conclusion that to carry them was in part the objective point of my movement. I therefore wheeled to the left, assaulted and carried the first line and part of the second line, the balance manifesting a disposition to surrender by throwing down their guns, etc.[47]

Thus the Palmer-Baker-Coltart command, about 1,300 strong, struck hard into the left and rear of Morgan's line, buckling Mitchell's newly formed left flank. Lt. Col. John C. Carter, 24th Alabama (consolidated), commanding Manigault's Brigade, Coltart's Division, reported to Hill that his brigade had secured the Federal line "opposite the swamp."[48] The attacking force was startlingly weak in numbers, however, and their assault, although successful, had been delivered piecemeal. "Our line was so scattered," reported one of Baker's men, "that we struck the enemy in disconnected groups." By swinging left and joining in the attack, Palmer (the right of Hill's ad hoc force) unfortunately had opened the door into the right and rear of Hill's small command.[49]

To Hill's right existed a huge hole in the Confederate line. Hill believed that Bate was there, but Bate had been bounced north of the road by Fearing. When Bate (for the second time that day) called for assistance to protect his flank, Hill had sent two brigades of Clayton's Division (Kellogg's and Kyle's).[50] Carter Stevenson, receiving a direct appeal from Bate himself, also responded, dispatching his second line (Edmund W. Pettus's Brigade) to strengthen and extend the left of Bate's Corps. As if this were not sufficient, Loring's Corps, temporarily in reserve, marched down the northern side of the road and went into position to the left and rear of Pettus.

Henry Clayton's two Georgia brigades—Kyle's and Kellogg's—counterattacked effectively and repeatedly on Bate's left, hammering Fearing's brigade until it broke and retreated to the protection of Robinson's line and Slocum's waiting batteries.[51]

Thus about 5:00 P.M. the Confederates waged three distinct battles. Bragg attacked Morgan's left and front and was thrown back; Hill broke Morgan's extreme left flank position behind the swamp and turned to assault Mitchell's brigade in the rear; and Bate, supported by Stevenson and Loring, fought off Fearing's flank attack and continued to press down the Goldsboro road toward the Federals' Twentieth Corps position.

Obviously command confusion existed. Hardee appears to have been intent on massing the Army of Tennessee, at least Bate's Corps, and pressing down the Goldsboro road, continuing to collapse the Federal right. Hardee must have known that Taliaferro was close at hand to support Bate on the right. Furthermore, Hardee had sent orders to McLaws to hurry from the extreme left and join in the pursuit. Hill, on the other hand, faced his corps parallel to the Goldsboro road and prepared to attack what remained of the Federal force south of the road. He had every reason to believe that this would be a cooperative movement, the enemy being struck from above by Hoke's strong division simultaneously. Loring's small corps would be kept as Hardee's reserve, ready to support either Bate or Hill.

The concept had merit, no doubt. Hill and Bragg should have been able to destroy Morgan. Hardee should have been able to vigorously pursue the fleeing enemy, overcoming temporary lines of resistance as he came upon them. Four developments, however, fouled the Confederate plan. Bragg's attack was poorly executed; Fearing appeared from nowhere and threatened Bate's flank, causing Bate to call upon Hill for help, thus weakening Hill's assault; William Cogswell attacked unexpectedly and blindsided Hill; and, finally, McLaws's heavy division, the reserve of Johnston's army, was frittered away.

The two Union counterattacks proved devastating. Harvey Hill, elated over turning Morgan's left, threw all his available troops into the attack against Mitchell's rear. He personally rode to the front of Palmer's wing and urged the Tennesseans to make a determined attack.[52] Alongside Palmer (to his left) were Baker's Alabama regiments.

Brig. Gen. Alpheus Baker of Eufaula, Alabama, was an emotional leader; his men considered him "very eccentric and superstitious." As his troops were marching forward in quick time, Baker reportedly saw a big rabbit streaking on a line that would cross their path. Baker believed that if the rabbit were "to cross him he would have been killed and his brigade decimated." So Baker "struck spurs to his horse and dashed ahead of the rabbit, and then ordered his brigade to charge, which it did."[53] Baker's Brigade closed to within fifty yards of Mitchell's second line. "The blue jackets," a member of the 42d Alabama remembered, "began to wave hats and handkerchiefs over their works, so it was natural for us to suppose they were wanting to surrender, for we knew full well that we were in behind them; therefore, we rose up and told them to come over, and they in turn told us to come over, and thus we found there was a misunderstanding, so each line dropped back into a comparatively safe position."[54]

The men looked at Alpheus Baker. He had "turned up the cuff of his left coat-sleeve—wrong side out—and felt no danger." Yet apparently it was not Baker but a color-bearer named James Flinn from Mobile who then seized the initiative. Flinn proposed to the men of two Alabama regiments (all mixed together) that they attack. He would lead them and plant his flag on the Yankees' works if they would follow him:[55]

It seems that this was promised him, therefore, he deliberately stepped out with his flag into that open space and got some three or four paces forward with only about two others with him; almost at once he was felled with a bullet from the line so near in front. The other two men jumped back behind the log breastworks, while one of the two, or another man, jumped out and brought in the flag without being touched by a ball.[56]

Baker's disordered line began to waver. An Alabama private looked to his rear "through the big pine timber." He saw "Yanks—the woods looked blue with them—but they were standing still and not firing a gun, which they could not do without endangering the line we had just left in front of us."[57]

Capt. George W. F. Harper, commanding the 58th Regiment North Carolina Troops (Palmer's Brigade), could barely see through the smoke that saturated the woods. Suddenly Palmer appeared. " 'Which is the right of your Regiment?' " he asked. A strange question, Harper thought, as the 58th faced the rear of the enemy position. "Countermarch your regiment," Palmer directed peremptorily. Puzzled, Harper reminded the general that "the Regiment was already facing the enemy, who was close at hand." " 'Yes, I know,' " Palmer said, " 'but I want you to look after these fellows over here,' " pointing over his shoulder to our rear and right."[58]

Harper accordingly faced his regiment about, aligned it, and ordered his men to lie down for protection. "Gen. Palmer in the meanwhile [remained] quietly seated on his horse apparently unconscious that anything unusual was going on, although musket balls were flying pretty thick." Palmer was hit, however—not seriously, but a flesh wound, "his sixth battle wound." His horse was killed, as was a staff officer (Capt. Gideon H. Lowe) at Palmer's side.[59] Meanwhile, the 42d Alabama, Baker's Brigade,

> found ourselves (in military parlance) in a hollow square, the enemy on four sides of us in heavy timber, and each one close by at that! In this position at the very close of the day, we lost, I feel reasonably sure, about a third of our men in killed and prisoners, mostly prisoners. Our men who got out of there were either those who hid themselves in the thick gallberry [sic] bushes until after dark or those fleet of foot. I was in the latter class, and I am not ashamed to own up to such on that particular occasion.[60]

Thus Harvey Hill's troops, who had broken Morgan's left and pushed into his rear, were struck from three sides by Federal counterattacks. Cogswell's Federal brigade, six regiments strong, made short work of them. Baker broke and fled, as did Palmer and Col. John Coltart's Alabama division (Harry T. Toulmin's and John C. Carter's Brigades).[61]

The tables were turned completely. Many Confederates surrendered on the spot; many fled into the swamps and thickets to hide. "A Michigan outfit" (the 14th) captured men of the 40th Alabama (Baker's Brigade). The Yankees "gave us credit for fighting them as hard as they were ever fought and some told me it was the first time their line was ever broken. Some

Joseph Benjamin Palmer
(courtesy Tennessee State Library and Archives)

thought we had whiskey to incite us on. Quite a compliment." Baker's Brigade was smashed, its loss "frightful." For the 40th Alabama, 21 were killed or wounded out of 32 participants.[62]

Some escaped, however. A squad-size group with regimental color sergeant A. A. Meyers, 10th South Carolina, lay in the swamp until the middle of the night. Meyers tore the flag from the staff, "took down his pants, tied it around his leg," then he and his comrades groped their way into Confederate lines before morning.[63]

Others, mostly Palmer's men, found themselves one moment occupying enemy works, the next, cut off, Yankees all about.[64] A private in the 32d Tennessee dashed into a swamp and hid behind a thick pine. "Not a living soul did I see." Then he heard a voice and saw Col. Anderson Searcy, veteran commander of the 45th Tennessee, step from behind another tree, "and I never in my life was so glad to see any one."[65] Others began to appear, until there were about seventy soldiers.[66] Searcy organized them, then had the men toss away their cartridge boxes and rifles "to keep the Yanks from getting them." "Boys," said Searcy, "let's get back here a little bit on dry land," so they moved deeper into the swamp where they discovered here and there solitary Yankees hiding under logs or behind bushes. They eventually captured twelve of the enemy including a captain who surrendered his sword to Searcy. They hid deep in the swamp until dark, then set out, prisoners and all, doing their best to avoid the enemy. A severely wounded lieutenant of the 3d Tennessee kept up as long as he could, supported by two of his comrades. Knowing that he would eventually jeopardize everyone's escape, he asked to be left behind, so Searcy found a dry spot and propped him up against a tree.[67]

The band of men continued on, carefully picking their way through thickets and wading swamps. East they marched—to the rear and right flank of the Union army, all the while "literally surrounded" by Yankees. They passed an enemy battery, filed "noiselessly" through a "bivouac of infantry resting on their arms," and walked "more boldly" through an ordnance train park. About midnight they stopped, "not knowing where we were going," and concealed themselves again in a swamp, searching desperately for a dry place. There they hid the remainder of that night and the next day and night, listening to Federals talking and riding by. To their dismay they discovered that their concealed position was still close to the Goldsboro road! Down that road the following day would come column after column of Howard's Right Wing.

On Monday night Searcy and his men set out again, making as wide a detour as possible around the Federals. They continued east until free of the enemy, then they swung south for several days, then west, then north, making in effect a great "square" and arriving at Raleigh nine days later. Food had been scarce all the way. Searcy's column proved more adept at capturing Yankees than securing food—only one pig (25 pounds) and twelve ears of corn. "I never suffered so much from hunger as I did those eight days we were trying to get through the Yankee lines."[68] In Raleigh they turned over their prisoners, then "took the cars" to Smithfield where they reported back to their regiments. Proudly they returned the precious colors of four Tennessee regiments that they had carefully carried with them. They found themselves the toast of the Army of Tennessee. Ecstatic division commander Maj. Gen. John C. Brown went so far as to compare Searcy's feat to "Napoleon crossing the Alps."[69]

Cogswell's troops had smashed Hill's attack and now they threatened to advance to, perhaps across, the Goldsboro road, breaking into the rear of the Army of Tennessee. Harvey Hill and Brig. Gen. Edmund W. Pettus, perhaps more than any other individuals, should be credited with preventing this, at least with closing the wide rip in the Confederate line caused by wrecking Palmer's right wing and Baker's Brigade. Pettus and his Alabama brigade, as ordered by division commander Carter Stevenson, had started to Bate's relief. As Pettus came up he heard to his left—across the Goldsboro road—"firing increasing and approaching my line."[70] He also saw Confederate stragglers (Hill's men) fleeing toward him. He wheeled about, faced his brigade east, crossed the road and advanced, driving enemy skirmishers before him. At this point Harvey Hill rode up and told Pettus of Cogswell's counterattack. "Halt and prepare to meet the charge," Hill ordered.[71] In accordance with Hill's instructions, Pettus took up a defensive position. He had his men lie down.

"It was then about sunset," Pettus reported, "and from the smoke of the guns and the burning woods it was difficult to see objects at a distance." Hill agreed. It was not only dim but also chaotic. Confederate regiments, brigades, and divisions were mixed and milling about; high-ranking officers rode from this group to that issuing orders. Men became disoriented, angry. Hill observed that "after nightfall, when natural darkness was much increased by the smoke of battle and from thousands of smoldering pine stumps and logs, it [the confusion] was greater than I ever witnessed before."[72] The enemy came on, nevertheless, and drove in Pettus's skirmishers, "following them with a shout." Pettus opened fire when the enemy closed in, and after exchanging a few volleys the Federals to his front retreated. Pettus, much relieved, threw out skirmishers once again. All in all it was a remarkable effort by Pettus's Brigade, displaying "more than its usual steadiness."[73] It repulsed at least double its numbers. Pettus himself, however, received a painful flesh wound, and his nephew and aide-de-camp, Lt. E. W. Pettus, was killed.

Carter Stevenson praised Pettus. Unlike Palmer, who had impulsively launched an attack across the Goldsboro road and thus had taken himself from his division commander's control, Pettus "had executed my orders to the letter, and in spite of all obstacles had kept his command thoroughly in hand, well aligned, and ready to move in any direction." Pettus defended his position so effectively that his support—the left wing of Palmer's Brigade, which had been left behind—had not been committed. When Palmer and the remnant of his right wing returned from the unfortunate attack against Morgan, Stevenson instructed him to re-form the entire brigade in the rear of Pettus as a reserve.[74]

Harvey Hill commended Pettus as well but quickly added that Pettus had been aided significantly by the timely arrival of Loring's Corps, especially Walthall's tiny division. Walthall's and Loring's Divisions (together constituting Loring's Corps), when they spotted Hill's retreating men and heard the heavy firing, crossed the Goldsboro road, linked with Pettus's left flank, then swung into line facing left (south), almost parallel to the Goldsboro road. Small but welcome support also came from Col. Harry T. Toulmin and about fifty of Brig. Gen. Zachariah C. Deas's Brigade (Coltart's Division) who arrived and hooked onto Walthall's left, providing flank protection. Loring (900 men) was attacked twice by Cogswell, but each attack was beaten off. Reynolds's Arkansas Brigade (Walthall's Division) lost its commander for the second time that day as Colonel Bunn was wounded and left the field. Lt. Col. Morton G. Galloway, 1st Arkansas Mounted Rifles (dismounted), assumed command.[75]

It was at this point, when Cogswell pressed hard against Pettus and Loring, that McLaws's brigades began coming up. McLaws had moved with reasonable speed since receiving Hardee's summons. When he reached an open field near the Cole house, he met Generals Johnston, Bragg, and Stewart. "A brisk cannonade was going on just above. The shells from the enemy bursting over the field we were in."[76] McLaws initially had his troops take cover,

Daniel Harvey Hill
(National Archives)

then the rifle fire ahead (probably the Clayton-Fearing fighting) subsided. "The opinion was that the attack was over and orders were given to collect arms, but immediately the musketry recommenced with great fury, and I was ordered to send two Brigades toward the firing."[77]

While McLaws dillydallied near the Cole house, interpreting sounds he heard and having his men gather shiny Yankee rifles, Bate and Taliaferro launched heavy attacks against the Federals' rapidly hardening Twentieth Army Corps position north of the Morris house and extending east along the Goldsboro road to the positions of Robinson and Fearing. Every minute the Confederates delayed the Union line grew stronger. Fresh units kept coming up from the rear, officers rushed to reorganize Carlin's battered division and put them into line—if not as regiments, then as clusters of individuals. Three batteries found advantageous positions above the road, and another took its place below the road, emplaced so as to fire directly down the front of Robinson's and Fearing's troops.

Within sight of the Yankees' feverish activity, Bate deployed his two divisions. Thirty-eight-year-old William Brimage Bate wanted to make the best of this opportunity—being on the offensive again. He knew that the Federals were strongly positioned to his front, and for an hour he had listened to shells and solid shot sail over the heads of his troops. Taliaferro was up, however, and Bate knew McLaws was on his way. Perhaps one more attack . . .

Most of Bate's men still believed in him. Certainly they loved this battle-scarred Mexican war veteran with his shiny black beard. He had remained faithfully with the Army of Tennessee since the beginning, and this Sunday afternoon he rode up and down the lines, crutches strapped to his saddle, exhorting his men to do their best. Many thought it fitting that this charge—perhaps their last—was to be made by his division and Cleburne's.

Bate led them forward once, perhaps twice, but the charges were futile, pitiful parodies of Chickamauga and Atlanta assaults—"their single line was too weak, from casualties and exhaustion."[78] The fire into which they advanced was appalling—bullets flew everywhere, shot and shell showered the open field and tore the forest to splinters. In the Oglethorpe Grays, 63d Georgia (Cleburne's Division), only nineteen troops took part in the charge. One was killed, three were wounded, and "thirteen others bear on their bodies, clothing or equipment marks of the enemy's fire, some of them in three or four places."[79]

Soon after they began their charge, a ball struck Pvt. John Miller, "passing directly through his body." The line pressed on "and John lies down under the pines to die":

Lafayette McLaws
(National Archives)

A Federal battery opens on us and the color-bearer of Olmstead's 1st
Ga. regiment is knocked six or eight feet and disemboweled by a solid
shot as it ploughs through the ranks. As the litter-bearers are carrying
off another wounded man from the same regiment he begs piteously
for his haversack. . . . They are under fire and refuse to halt. One of the

Oglethorpes, in pity for the poor fellow, leaves the protection of his log and running up the line secures the haversack, takes it to him, then hastens back.[80]

As they fell back from their final charge, the Oglethorpes found their comrade John Miller's body and beside it a "naked arm taken off at the elbow by a cannon ball."[81] They placed Miller and the arm on a blanket and carried them to the rear to bury in the woods.

Bate's own division fell back with Cleburne's. The division carried with it its leader, Col. Daniel L. Kenan, veteran commander of the Florida brigade, whose leg was shredded and would be amputated. Brigade commander William H. Wilkinson (Tyler's Brigade), a young man who had served closely with Bate for four years, had been killed while attacking. Bate's men talked of Wilkinson and Kenan, but especially of the "conspicuous bravery" of the color-bearer of the 1st Florida in the last charge.[82]

Conspicuous bravery was commonplace. These attacks of the Army of Tennessee were doomed. The well-served Yankee batteries had a turkey shoot. Their infantry grew more confident by the minute, and they seemed to be taking steadier aim.

General Hardee, who was here and there, doing his best to form an effective assault force, put Taliaferro's two brigades on line with Bate and ordered him to attack. There must be a weakness in the enemy line, Hardee reasoned. Somewhere.

Brig. Gen. Steven Elliott, Jr., who had been badly wounded at the Battle of the Crater, moved out in front of his brigade and examined its formation. No sooner was it formed in the field than bullets started whizzing by, a few striking into his ranks. At "Forward!" these South Carolina and Georgia cannoneers advanced at the "double-quick, steadily, and in good order." Elliott's men were conspicuous for the regularity of their uniforms and the bold red stripe down their trouser leg designating them as artillerymen. They raised the rebel yell, "an intensely nervous description; every man for himself yelling 'Yai, Yai, Yi, Yai, Yi!' They were simply fierce shrieks made from each man's throat individually."[83]

Elliott's Red Infantry continued at the double-quick. Then Yankee fieldpieces began to tear patches of men from the lines. Eyes filled with sand "dashed up by grape which struck around." Men wiped their eyes, "keeping them closed as much as I could." Closer they advanced, then were "met with rapid volleys of grape and canister, besides a heavy rifle-fire."[84] Many of Elliott's men continued on until they were fifty yards from the enemy's lines, then "they suddenly wavered, halted." Panic seized them and they fled to the rear, breaking through what remained of Col. Alfred Rhett's Brigade, Taliaferro's second line. A private described Taliaferro's charge:

We [Taliaferro's Division] were formed in double line under the trees . . . until General Elliott had gone out in front with his field glasses. . . . As soon as he returned to us, we heard his voice in loud tones: 'Forward'. . . . In approaching their artillery, about half of our regiment on the right had come into the open, in a field where there was nothing to conceal or protect them. Our men fell rapidly, killed and wounded, until soon forced to withdraw from the old field. The enemy's guns, cannon and rifles, were immediately turned upon our left wing, and soon, under what seemed a tremendous concentrated fire upon us, orders were given to 'fall back' to a reformed line in the woods in our rear.[85]

Elliott rallied his men and led them forward again—as many as would follow. In this attempt Elliott himself was wounded in the leg. Once again they retired. Elliott's officers now tried to gather men for still another charge, but the brigade was demoralized. A hundred troops from the 2d South Carolina Heavy Artillery went back into the field, but, unnerved, they fired on their own men. Then they broke again. "They were useless for the remainder of the day."[86]

While Elliott attacked, Taliaferro directed his reserve line (Rhett's Brigade—Col. William Butler commanding) "to lie down and lower their colors." All the officers knelt except Taliaferro and two others. While they measured the interval separating them from Elliott and prepared to step out into the open, a "raging leaden hailstorm of grape and canister literally barked the trees, cutting off the limbs as if cut by hand." A sergeant maintained that there was no place "in the battle of Gettysburg as hot as that place."[87]

Maj. A. Burnet Rhett, commander of Taliaferro's field artillery (there were no guns in this advanced position, however), calmly rode in front of some of Colonel Butler's men (Alfred Rhett's Brigade) preparing to charge as Red Infantry. "Men," Rhett addressed them, "France has just recognized the Confederacy."[88] The soldiers broke into cheers. There always would be a straw of hope. But one private turned to his comrades standing beside him and said, " 'Well, boys, one out of every three of us will drop to-day, I wonder who it will be?' " Butler's men then advanced through "very thick blackjack oak woods full of briars and then double-quicked."[89] When they

William Booth Taliaferro
(National Archives)

struck a worm-rail fence on the edge of an old field, an officer called them back. There had been a mistake: Taliaferro's Division had not gone far enough to the right. So they re-formed their lines, moved 200 yards to the right, and "halted just on the inside edge of dense woods, and concealed by the brush, and I could see on the other edge of the field, about 300 yards distant, twelve pieces of artillery glistening in the sun, and behind them a dense mass of blue infantry. . . . One man said, 'If the Lord will only see me safe through this job, I'll register an oath never to vote for secession again as long as I live.' "[90]

William Butler's men advanced, but only halfway to the Yankee position. They began to take casualties and saw before their eyes the disintegration and destruction of Elliott's line. They stopped, milling about in confusion, "then broke and went back in a clear panic."[91] "Our small Brigade . . . was cut to pieces." That night, exhausted from marching all day and from the assaults on the Federal line, they pulled blankets over their heads and slept "philosophically indifferent to the shells that were tearing through the trees, bursting over their heads and occasionally causing casualties."[92]

Bate and Taliaferro had failed. Perhaps others might succeed—perhaps McLaws's brigades. Hardee ordered them to try.

Lafayette McLaws watched them go. "The sun was declining rapidly," McLaws noticed, "and the smoke settled heavy & dense over the country. A fog also came on, which added to the smoke, made it impossible to see but a very short distance. The firing was very rapid and continuous for some time after my brigades went forward, but gradually ceased as the darkness increased." This was a strangely detached observation from a veteran division commander who stationed himself in the rear.[93]

Kennedy's troops (Conner's Brigade—Kershaw's old unit, now led by Brig. Gen. John D. Kennedy) set out first from the Cole house, obliquing to the left past Harrison. The brigade "passed Gen. Jos. Johnston, sitting on a log by the side of the road. We cheered him." Then Col. Benton Roy, Hardee's chief of staff, guided Kennedy and his regiments forward. The young Virginia staff officer rode alongside their column "gallantly inspiriting the men."[94] When Kennedy reached the Goldsboro road (his left across the road, his center on it), Harvey Hill appeared and took charge. Hook onto Walthall's left, Hill ordered. Kennedy stumbled forward ("It was impossible to see ten yards ahead"), attempting to comply with Hill's command. One regiment managed to find Walthall's left and connect, but the rest of this fine brigade fronted on a line "I took to be Walthall's." According to Walthall himself, Kennedy ended up on the right, not the left; there his troops remained relatively inactive. Their presence, however, did cause Jackson's Mississippi division of Loring's Corps, which had been on Walthall's right and whose ammunition was exhausted, to retire. Kennedy considered mak-

William Brimage Bate
(Courtesy Tennessee State Library and Archives)

ing an advance (a charge by the center), "but the dense smoke, approach of night, and uncertainties of my left flank (no one being on it) made me desist."[95] Kennedy apparently was unaware that Walthall was on his left. Indeed, it seems that both Kennedy and Walthall (certainly Kennedy) were confused. Walthall believed that Kennedy (all but one regiment) was on his right; Kennedy thought that he was on Walthall's left.[96]

This comedy of misposition ended when Hardee sent for Kennedy again and directed him to pull out of line and move to the front and right. Kennedy did as ordered, but his withdrawal alarmed Walthall. Jackson was gone; now his right stood "entirely open, the nearest troops to my right, understood to be Pettus' brigade, being several hundred yards distant." Walthall filled the gap by deploying both his brigades (Johnston and Bunn) as skirmishers. Fortunately the Federals did not probe this thin sector, and when night came Walthall still held his position.[97]

Kennedy appears to have been shifted farther right beyond Pettus, probably behind Colonel Toulmin, who had his "Alabama troops lying down to let us pass over them. They fell back after we passed them."[98] From this place on Bate's left, Kennedy advanced toward the Robinson-Fearing fortified position across the Goldsboro road: "While we were heavily engaged, orders were passed along the line to left oblique. We left obliqued. Another Gettysburg maneuver. Just wanted to show Sherman's ranks that we could make any kind of a maneuver right under the muzzle of their guns . . . nothing like war when you get used to it."[99]

Kennedy's brigade quickly found itself "between two fires (front and rear)." Its color-bearer, William A. Johnson, Company D, 2d South Carolina, felt "like a target." The brigade accomplished nothing.[100]

McLaws's second brigade, Col. George P. Harrison, Jr.'s Georgians, also passed through Bate's lines and "halted a few paces in its front." Then it advanced for a short distance. Minié balls flew thickly. Four Federal batteries completely dominated the approaches into the Twentieth Corps position. Harrison's troops halted, dropped to their stomachs, then withdrew.[101] Harrison's aide, twenty-year-old Gratz Cohen, a member of the Jefferson Society at the University of Virginia and already a poet and novelist, rode up. He delivered a message to Harrison. As he did he was shot through the head.[102]

Fiser's little brigade of Georgians went forward with Harrison through the lines of the Army of Tennessee. "The roar of battle and rattle of musketry rent the sky, making a noise inconceivable in its magnitude": "when we commenced the charge up a hill in the weeds upon which was the main line, we were ordered to lie down. I took it for granted that if the enemies lines were broken upon our left, that we were then to charge them in our immediate front, to complete the victory. But the lines were not broken."[103]

The Georgians using the cover of the woods approached close to the enemy line, then began their charge up a slope. The Yankee artillery was waiting for them, however, and opened a fire deadly "enough to quail the stoutest heart." The Confederates dropped to the ground, "a storm of shell streamed from five to twenty feet above us all, bursting far in our rear. If any one of us had stood upright I think he would have been torn to pieces." Even Col. Richard A. Wayne, "who usually refused to bend his head at the whistling of a ball or the bursting of a shell, lay down as we did, close upon our mother earth."[104] The Harrison-Fiser assault against the Twentieth Corps position thus sputtered and came to a halt.

McLaws's fourth brigade belonged to Col. Washington M. Hardy. Hardy advanced late and far left of where he was supposed to have gone. He commanded 329 men—the 50th Regiment North Carolina Troops, the 77th Regiment North Carolina Senior Reserves, and the 10th Battalion North Carolina Light Artillery—a brigade of "dubious fighting qualities."[105] Inexperienced and blinded by the ubiquitous smoke, the brigade shoved forward, almost directly south, across the Goldsboro road.

After advancing several hundred yards, apparently without skirmishers deployed to his front and flanks, Hardy ordered his men to halt. Where were they? He prepared to attack nevertheless, but first he must notify adjacent friendly units. So he sent out staff officers to the left and right. Unknown to Hardy, there was no Confederate unit on either his right (where he believed Kennedy to be) or his left. Indeed, "twenty paces" to his left were the lines of John G. Mitchell's 113th Ohio.[106]

Several conflicting accounts describe what happened next. Union vedettes fired into Hardy's men, and one of Hardy's lieutenants, Lt. John Blaylock, Company C, 77th Regiment North Carolina Senior Reserves, investigated to "see if they were our own men who fired into us." When Blaylock ventured up close and shouted "What regiment?" two Yankee vedettes yanked him over their breastworks. Capt. Tolan Jones, 113th Ohio, immediately sent Blaylock to General Mitchell, who was preparing to bed down. The well-dressed young Confederate said to Mitchell, " 'Colonel Hardee [sic] presents his compliments to you, and asks that you will apprise your line that he is forming in your front to charge the Yankee lines on your left.' "[107] Mitchell "sprang to his feet" and asked Blaylock to repeat what he

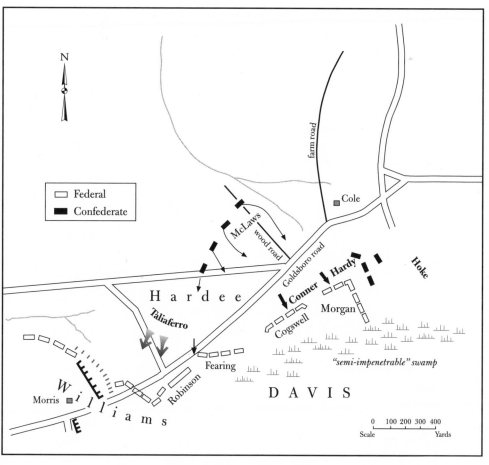

Map 6. Hardee's Night Attacks

had said. Then calmly Mitchell asked him the most disarming question possible, " 'have you had anything to eat? Orderly, take this young gentleman to the rear and give him something.' "[108]

Mitchell drew in his pickets and told his men to hold their fire until they heard the "tap of a drum." That would be the signal for all to fire. The plan worked to perfection. Hardy's troops moved closer until Mitchell's men could hear them talking and their feet rustling in the leaves. Then came "one loud tap on a bass drum." Mitchell's men fired, taking care to aim low. Mitchell said later, " 'I never expect to hear again such a volume of mingled cries, groans, screams, and curses.' "[109]

Wash Hardy's North Carolinians were caught, trapped. It was "too hot to either advance or retreat, being exposed to a destructive cross-fire." After receiving "a terrible volley," Hardy prudently ordered his men to lie down. The troops hugged the ground, protecting themselves as best they could.[110]

Col. George W. Wortham, commander of the 50th Regiment North Carolina Troops, "showed the white feather." He fled to the rear "to report the disaster." When he came across a brigade courier bringing up a message for Hardy, Wortham sadly told him that it was no use. "When Col. Hardy fell from his horse," Wortham recounted, he [Wortham] had "dismounted and raised Col. H's head from the ground, he found the blood running from his mouth, and in that position he expired." So had Major Gardiner, Lieutenant Edmondson, Lieutenant Gillett, and other officers.[111] A calamity had befallen McLaws's North Carolina brigade.

In truth, it had been a stinging repulse. The next morning Mitchell's men found a line of rifles and knapsacks "almost as straight as if laid out for Sunday morning inspection." "There we lost," a Confederate reported, "about 51 men in about half a minute," including Colonel Hardy wounded. The command, however, had not been annihilated. Poor Wortham—the next morning Wash Hardy reappeared, shaken and bloody but very much alive, and accompanied by subordinates whom Wortham reported as having seen dead on the field.[112]

The fighting was over. The bloody Sunday had ended.

McLaws's troops retreated deep into the tree line, through Bate's lines. There they attempted to re-form and dig in. They waited while the darkness grew even deeper and smoke settled to the bases of tree trunks. Some men put fingers in their ears, trying to shut out "the groans and cries of the wounded just in our front." Many simply wandered off. McLaws took preventative action. He stationed Fiser's Brigade behind his position, stretched out like a great net, "to stop all men coming to the rear, and tell them where to form."[113] Stretcher bearers worked hard, gathering the wounded and undertaking the awful task of carrying them back to primitive field hospitals. The Confederates unfortunately had no ambulances. "It is now well in the night," a Tennessean observed, "and I spent several hours more bringing our wounded men on my horse, which was the hardest night service I ever did since the war commenced. At times I had to wade through mud and water nearly knee deep, walking and leading my horse with a wounded man on him."[114]

About midnight, General Johnston ordered the army to withdraw to the positions from which they had attacked that morning. McLaws would occupy the extreme right flank, extending Taliaferro's early afternoon position to the northwest. Johnston then wired Lee of victory at Bentonville, telling him of an enemy routed and driven back a mile, three guns captured, and a Federal counterattack "resisted without difficulty." Johnston continued proudly, "Troops of the Tennessee army have fully disproved slanders that have been published against them."[115]

Meanwhile, many of Joe Johnston's weary troops began their tramp to the rear—a retrograde movement conducted in the face of the enemy—with the skill characteristic of a Johnston army of June 1864. Dozens, however, slipped off into Union lines and surrendered. They told their captors they wanted "to come in now they are whipped."[116]

No, thousands of others thought to themselves. The Yanks did the running. Tomorrow Ole Joe will whip them again. After all, they could look up through the pines and see a beautiful moon. There was no rain to torment them tonight. It seemed warmer. Perhaps they could get some food. It had been so long.

9

This Afflicted and Troublesome Day

WHILE THE LEFT WING FOUGHT for its life, Slocum's eighteen-year-old staff officer, Lt. Joseph B. Foraker, rode to find Sherman. The Left Wing commander's words kept ringing in his ears: "Keep clear of the enemy. *Don't spare horse-flesh!*"[1]

Foraker found the road congested with soldiers and wagons and cut to pieces by preceding infantry and artillery. His horse slipped on the corduroy, occasionally catching a hoof between the rough logs. But the young staff officer pushed on, digging spurs into the sides of the animal. Finally, about nightfall, he found Sherman at Howard's headquarters.

"You burst upon us in a grove of pines," Sherman remembered, "with a message from Slocum, saying that he needed to be reinforced. I recall your figure, sir, splashed with mud, your spurs that were red, your splendid horse, hard-ridden and panting, and how you sat erect; and I shall not forget the soldier that you looked and were."[2]

Sherman grabbed the message Foraker carried, "tore it open, read it, and called out 'John Logan! Where is Logan?'" Logan was lounging on a blanket about twenty yards away. He "jumped up and started toward us."[3]

"We all gather in a circle around the Aid-de-camp," recalled Howard's chief of staff, Lt. Col. William E. Strong, "and listen attentively as he [Foraker] recounts the particulars of the battle":

> The Commander-in-Chief [Sherman] would have made a good subject for "Punch" or "Vanity Fair." Every officer present was nearly bursting with laughter at his ludicrous appearance. He had been lying down in Genl. Howard's tent and hearing the inquiry for him, and being of course anxious to hear the news of the fight rushed out to the camp fire without stopping to put on his clothes. He stood in a bed of

ashes up to his ankles, chewing impatiently the stump of a cigar, with his hands clasped behind him and with nothing on but a red flannel undershirt and pair of drawers.[4]

Every man in the Right Wing had been hearing heavy firing to their left and rear, in the direction of Slocum's column. All day they had heard it. Nevertheless, "we took it for granted it was a cavalry fight and kept on our march." Sherman's plan was to have Slocum's Left Wing reach Cox's Bridge that night and cross the Neuse on March 20. As late as 5:00 P.M. Sherman dismissed the thought that the Left Wing might have encountered John-ston's army. He wrote John M. Schofield at that time: Slocum "thinks it is the main army of the enemy. I can hardly suppose the enemy will attempt to fight us this side the Neuse."[5] Not allowing itself to be distracted, the Right Wing continued toward Cox's Bridge, the direct route from Fayetteville over the Neuse to Goldsboro. In effect, however, each mile it advanced widened the distance between the wings. As a precautionary measure Howard had sent word back down the line that if Slocum needed help, "he might call upon General Hazen," the trailing division of Logan's Fifteenth Corps. Somewhat later, probably early afternoon, Howard sent his artillery chief, Maj. Thomas W. Osborn, to Slocum "with instructions that Slocum could call on the Fifteenth for all the troops he might wish."[6]

Osborn had ridden back about two miles when he encountered Sherman, who stopped him, saying that "he had just heard from General Slocum, and he had a fight with Debrill's [sic] division of cavalry, whipped them, that all was right now, and that I should leave the troops as they were and make no changes in the present disposition."[7] Soon another Slocum staff officer rode up with more encouraging news. He told Osborn that the rebels opposing the Left Wing "are retreating toward Cox's Bridge" and that Slocum "asked that the right wing should push down and cut them off." Convinced by now, Major Osborn decided that his duty lay not in conferring with Slocum, as Howard had directed, but in hurrying the head of the Fifteenth Corps along the new Goldsboro road,[8] toward Cox's Bridge—the blocking point—the place where Sherman intended to unite the Fifteenth and the Left Wing. Thus Osborn abandoned his mission and turned back.[9]

Osborn's vacillation mirrored the dilemma of Sherman and the Right Wing. Their true course, they must have thought, was to continue ahead as rapidly as possible, cross the Neuse, and reach Goldsboro. Slocum's tangle with rebel cavalry must not be magnified or allowed to divert their efforts. After all, look at what they had accomplished in the past five months. If

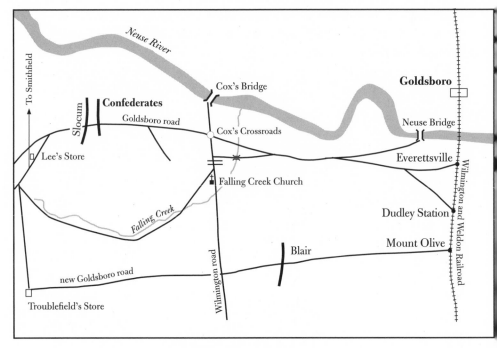

Map 7. Vicinity of Falling Creek

they had permitted caution, timidity, to rule them, they would never have reached Savannah.

Ten miles south of John Logan's line of march, on the new Goldsboro road, Frank Blair's Seventeenth Corps labored east on roads from Trouble-field's Store toward Mount Olive (two divisions) and Everettsville (Mower's division).[10] This tended to scatter the Seventeenth, but it saved the fragile roads and thus expedited movement.[11]

As the afternoon of the nineteenth wore on, the Right Wing (particularly Logan's Fifteenth Corps) heard heavier cannonading and musketry. This was troubling—the sound identifiable to veterans as "the peculiar sound of a pitched battle."[12] "It was like the rumbling of thunder low down in the sky." Men looked at each other. "All shook their heads and . . . General Howard hardly knew what to do," reported William Strong. "We were all satisfied that the artillery fire we heard indicated heavy battle, but we could not of course tell which army was acting on the offensive, neither could we tell whether or not our army was needed."[13]

John Logan, however, remained focused. He meant to reach and secure the crossroads midway between Falling Creek Church and Cox's Bridge— the same spot Major Osborn believed so vital. This was the intersection between the "old" and the "new," or "upper" and "lower," Goldsboro roads, the juncture of Slocum's route and his own. There "the sign-board indicated '12 miles to Goldsboro, via State Bridge and 13 miles via Cox's Bridge.' "[14]

Confederate cavalry appeared near the crossroads in midafternoon. This could not be tolerated. Nothing must jeopardize Federal possession of the crossroads. So Lieutenant Colonel Strong, Howard's trusted staff officer, raced ahead with the 10th Iowa to drive off the enemy. They pushed the rebels back toward the Neuse (Cox's Bridge) without great difficulty. Logan wanted even more security for the crucial crossroads, however, so he hurried Clark Wever's brigade of John E. Smith's division to the spot. Smith's division was the advance of Logan's Fifteenth Corps, which "was strung out upon the road for fifteen miles." The ordnance and supply trains were stalled in the mire and quicksand all the way from Lee's Store to Falling Creek Church.[15] Logan was anxious, almost obsessive, to seize the crossroads, thereby ensuring linkage with Slocum. Furthermore, Logan believed that massing troops there would block the only line of retreat of the enemy engaged with Slocum. But this assumption was based on the false report that Slocum "had secured the last road to Smithfield."[16] Following Wever were Charles R. Woods's and John M. Corse's divisions. Thus, virtually the entire Fifteenth Corps intended to encamp at the crossroads that night. Logan also ordered that his men throw up entrenchments when they arrived.[17]

Sherman and Howard pondered these developments, and while they discussed measures to be taken, Howard glanced at Osborn, "a good deal disappointed in my not having gone to General Slocum." Sherman, to Osborn's dismay, had failed to inform Howard that he had countermanded Howard's order to Osborn. Major Osborn cared greatly for Howard's good opinion, but he was prudent and held his tongue. Finally Sherman spoke up, absolving Osborn. "I felt a good deal relieved," Osborn recorded in his journal.[18]

Foraker's news, however, had changed everything. Johnston had ambushed the Left Wing. Slocum must be helped immediately: Goldsboro must wait. Sherman sent Lieutenant Foraker back to Slocum with this message: "General: Call up Geary and Baird, leaving a brigade to each train. All of the Right Wing will move at moonrise toward Bentonville. Fortify and hold your position to the last, certain that all the army is coming to you as fast as possible."[19]

Once he had sent Foraker on his way, Sherman ordered William B. Hazen's division to Slocum's assistance. Hazen's was the trailing division in Logan's column, thus the closest unit to the Left Wing. Hazen was to set out immediately and march through the night. This would require backtracking over the same road "the column moved out on to-day, by way of Blackman Lee's Store, and go into position as General Slocum may direct."[20] Howard, as ordered by Sherman, also instructed Blair to close up the Seventeenth Corps, mass his trains, and leave them behind under the guard of one brigade. Then, beginning his march at 3:00 A.M., Blair was to reach Logan's corps and follow it toward Bentonville. The Fifteenth Corps (except Hazen's division) would "move one brigade with a section of artillery and drive the enemy across Cox's Bridge and get possession of the same or force the enemy to destroy it," thus clearing the crossroads beyond Falling Creek Church. Logan would then "immediately" march west from the junction on the "old" Goldsboro road (the "river road") toward Bentonville. This would bring the Right Wing into the rear of Johnston's position.[21]

As Sunday night wore on, Sherman received good tidings from Schofield and Alfred H. Terry. Schofield had captured Kinston and would reach Goldsboro on March 21; Terry had arrived at Faison's Depot. Sherman ordered Schofield to seize Goldsboro, then prepare "to cross Little River in the direction of Smithfield." Terry was to advance from Faison's to Cox's Bridge, where he would lay a pontoon bridge and establish a crossing.[22]

More couriers arrived from Slocum. The news got better by the hour. About 1:00 A.M. Sherman learned (probably from Lt. Col. Charles W. Asmussen, assistant inspector general on Alpheus S. Williams's staff) that Slocum had not only held his own at Bentonville, but he also had dealt Johnston a sharp, bloody repulse.[23]

Sherman's attitude changed. At 2:00 A.M. on the twentieth he sent the following message to Slocum via Asmussen: "The whole army is moving to your assistance as rapidly as possible. Upon its approach he [Sherman] wishes you to be prepared to assume the offensive against the enemy."[24] Now Sherman began to fret that a battered Johnston might disengage and retire to Smithfield undisturbed.[25] So he followed his 2:00 A.M. order with an even more aggressive command to Slocum at 4:00 A.M.: "be ready to attack the enemy the moment you see signs of let go; follow him as far as Mill Creek, and take position covering the movement of your trains on the direct Goldsborough road."[26]

At daylight, as he prepared to leave Falling Creek Church, Sherman wrote Terry and Schofield that he was "now turning Right Wing on Bentonville." He directed Terry to move to Mount Olive Station and communicate with Schofield, "who ought to be at Goldsborough to-night, and then feel up for me on the south of the Neuse, toward Bentonville. . . . By to-night I will know if Joe Johnston intends to fight me in force. . . . Until you know the result, you and General Schofield should work up to my support, south of the Neuse."[27]

While Sherman grew more confident and seriously considered offensive strikes, Hazen's division slogged along through the night, going (it believed) to the rescue of Slocum's men. Thirty-four-year-old William Babcock Hazen was the man for the job. Time and time again he had proven himself in every significant action since Shiloh. A brave professional soldier, Hazen had the absolute trust of Sherman and Howard, and in their minds he helped offset any amateurish tendencies in the Fifteenth Corps on the part of John Logan.

Hazen's division had been patient all morning of March 19, waiting at Lee's Store for hours while other units passed toward Goldsboro. At last it fell in line behind the Fourth Division (John M. Corse's) and began its march, having to corduroy roads much of the way. Late in the afternoon the troops halted temporarily at Pleasant Union, then continued on toward Cox's Bridge, arriving at King's Plantation (a distance of about seven miles) about midnight. "We had no more than got our beds made down, when we received orders to fall in again."[28] Back they went over the road on which they had come. "Marched all night never sleeping abit[,] marched till the sun one hour high." "This was tough, to go without sleep and without food, and march too, was indeed hard."[29] Back they went, past Blackman Lee's Store, and on to the upper Goldsboro road, then north toward Bentonville. In all Hazen's men marched about 8 miles during the afternoon of the nineteenth and about 14 miles that night. They reached Slocum's headquarters at the Harper house at daylight (6:30 A.M.). "I have never been so fatigued," complained one private, a veteran of many long, hurried tramps.[30]

Hazen's men spread out near the Harper house. "We remained there 4 hours & slept in the hot sun. Of course we all got up with a headache and our Brig was marched two miles to the right and then three miles across a swamp filled with cypress & pine so thick the pack mules could not get through." No one seemed to care that it was a fine, "very warm" day, almost summerlike.[31]

Slocum wanted Hazen on Morgan's right, deep in the woods and swamps. This would strengthen and lengthen his right flank. Furthermore, it would locate Hazen's Fifteenth Corps division at the point where Slocum expected to connect with the Right Wing. Hazen moved out at noon, massed his division behind Morgan, then sent two regiments around Morgan's right, aggressively "feeling" for the Confederate left. When the leading elements of the Fifteenth Corps came up the Goldsboro road in midafternoon, Hazen linked with the First Division, Fifteenth Corps (Charles R. Woods's), then moved forward—driving rebel skirmishers until he developed the enemy main line. At that point he established a strong skirmish line and entrenched, Morgan on his left, Woods on his right. Morgan would report that this reoriented his division line "from a northeast to nearly a northwest front."[32]

On the morning of March 20 Slocum had two objectives. The first was to consolidate his position and recharge the Left Wing with its old cockiness. As he wrote Twentieth Corps commander Alpheus S. Williams, Sherman "wishes the troops informed" that the "entire army is moving to our assistance. . . . He [Sherman] directs that cartridge-boxes be filled, all stragglers and foragers collected together, and everything done to make the command as effective as possible." Second, in accordance with Sherman's 4:00 A.M. dispatch, Slocum decided to push hard all along the front to determine the enemy's position and to exploit any opportunities that might present themselves. Thus Slocum had sent Hazen to the extreme right to probe for the Confederate left flank. Similar directives were to sent to division commanders Baird and Morgan of the Fourteenth Corps and to the Twentieth Corps. Carlin's division, however, was conspicuously exempted.[33]

At dawn two brigades of John W. Geary's division, Twentieth Corps, came up from the wagon train park. Slocum posted Geary beside Hazen in reserve on Harper's farm. One of Geary's brigades, Ario Pardee's, massed far to the left behind Kilpatrick's cavalry, where it remained throughout the day. When two brigades of Absalom Baird's division, Fourteenth Corps, came up late in the morning, Slocum ordered them to pass through the line (Carlin's brigades of Miles and Buell). From that point Baird would deploy heavy skirmish lines and make a reconnaissance-in-force. The remainder of the Fourteenth Corps artillery (5th Wisconsin Light) would accompany Baird in order to offer direct fire support.[34] Slocum also called up Capt. Thomas S. Sloan's Pennsylvania battery of the Twentieth Corps and positioned it with the artillery concentrated along the high ground in front of the Morris house.[35]

Slocum had faith in Baird. He was Jefferson C. Davis's best division commander and a professional soldier, experienced and savvy, who had distinguished himself repeatedly in the Army of the Potomac as well as in the Army of the Cumberland.[36]

Then there was Carlin. He had his troops in hand once again—an organized division, hungry for action, or so Carlin believed.[37] Slocum had Harrison Hobart's brigade (Carlin's division) relieve Cogswell and Fearing's brigades on the line and tie on to Morgan's left, facing the Goldsboro road. Fearing's brigade returned to its reserve position behind Morgan; Cogswell went to the extreme left flank about a mile west and entrenched beside William T. Ward's other two brigades. Jackson's division, Twentieth Corps, remained to protect the center and left of Slocum's primary defensive position, above and to the west of the Morris house. As the sun rose higher, Slocum's breastworks rapidly became impressive—traverses built to guard against flanking fire, trenches deepened and strengthened, reserve lines dug, abatis "extended well in front of the works," and timber cleared, even in the ravines, to give better fields of fire.[38]

Meanwhile, despite all the attention turned to the fighting units advancing to meet the enemy, an undramatic but important scene played out to the rear, beyond the Harper house. Slocum started his trains (less a minimum number of indispensable ordnance and supply wagons) toward Kinston, thus anticipating an order that Sherman would give him at 8:00 P.M.[39]

Before Baird had come up and advanced through the Fourteenth Corps line, Federal soldiers had begun to go forward singly or in small units. Motivated by humanitarian concerns, curiosity, or greed, they searched the ground in front of the main line. They found the usual debris of battle, but mostly dead and wounded rebels. Union soldiers had looked the other way during the night, allowing the enemy to carry off its wounded, so those they discovered on the morning of March 20 were either badly wounded or wanting to be captured. Lt. Col. Allen L. Fahnestock, one of Fearing's officers, supervised a party gathering muskets and burying twenty-six Confederate dead: "Found a dead boy laying close by a dead officer, supposed it was his father. We could only dig the depth of a spade and the water would fill up the ditch. We laid them side by side and covered them the best we could. I found many wounded and one man, A Virginian, Capt. John Hall. Made him some coffee and dressed his wound."[40]

Slocum's men also discovered some of their own wounded whom they rushed to ambulances in the rear. Later that Monday, about dusk, a Pennsylvania soldier crawled into the lines. He had been shot in the leg on the nineteenth and captured. A rebel surgeon had amputated "his leg above the ankle." When his captors contracted their lines at midday, they evacuated the field hospital, abandoning the Pennsylvanian and half a dozen others. Those strong enough attempted to crawl back to friendly lines, but at least two Federals were "killed by skirmisher firing."[41]

Jefferson C. Davis's Fourteenth Corps took the offensive early in the afternoon. At 7:50 A.M. Slocum had told Davis to "move forward your skirmish line along the whole line and support it, but without bringing on a general engagement." Davis implemented this order enthusiastically, apparently employing only Baird and Morgan.[42]

After he cleared Carlin's fieldworks, Absalom Baird accompanied by Davis began a methodical advance behind clouds of skirmishers. They covered the bloody ground over which the Confederates had charged, finding "a lot of wounded"—Confederate and their own. "I passed 3 of the 20th Corp [*sic*] that was wounded and one that was dead. I gave them some water. One said he was dying. I could see death approaching on him," reported one of Baird's Missouri privates.[43]

Remaining left of the Goldsboro road, Baird's troops pushed ahead more than half a mile, almost to Cole's house. They drove in rebel pickets, then skirmishers. The division advanced from field to field, thicket to thicket, fighting dozens of miniature battles. It was dangerous work, this skirmishing. A private would shoot, and it seemed like the same instant, one would hear the bang of a rebel rifle, and the man who had just shot would be hit.

Nevertheless, Baird's troops captured the first line of enemy skirmisher pits and soon found themselves pressing hard against the rebel works, within easy rifle range. There they halted. Baird himself was well forward observing. Davis was also up, encouraging his men as they fought. He and his staff sought vantage points from which they might train their field glasses on the Confederate works. Occasionally batteries on both sides "threw some shell," but the artillery had little effect, most projectiles sailing "over our heads" or crashing about in treetops.[44]

Things went badly for the Wisconsin battery that Baird had brought along. One section "lost all their horses in the fight today and was left on the field between the lines and we could not get them away nor the Johnies could not get them. Several efforts was made by both sides to get them and after dark we pulled them off. The wheels was literally shot to pieces by musket balls."[45] This deadly skirmishing along Baird's front went on until dark. Then Baird drew back, passed through Carlin's lines once again, and went into reserve. "They call this battle-ground 'Bentonville,'" one of

Baird's privates wrote disgustedly in his journal, "I have not seen any town or even a good place far on as it seems to be all swamp here."[46]

Word spread through the ranks, however: tomorrow morning they would be going back over the same ground. Slocum was going to make a bayonet charge against those rebel works. "After hearing this news, we were a sober, silent party. For it is desperate work to charge the enemy's lines over open fields, where, if we should fail, there would be slight hope of escape from death or imprisonment. We all went to bed early—silent and thoughtful."[47]

A melancholy Illinois private attempted to describe his innermost thoughts as he "sat by the fire, waiting for the time when the work should commence. I almost longed for the time to come that the work might be finished and off my mind. This thinking of a battle so long before it is to take place, and knowing it must be fought, almost makes a coward of the thinker."[48]

To the left of these sober volunteers of Absalom Baird, things had gone pretty well. Jackson's division, Twentieth Corps, advanced its skirmish line at 2:00 P.M. alongside Baird's. The men continued forward until they developed enemy breastworks with abatis in front. Then corps commander Alpheus Williams had Jackson pull back, establish his skirmish lines, and entrench. Two brigades of Ward's division on the extreme left met little opposition and ventured about two miles forward toward Mill Creek Bridge. They eventually uncovered "a strong line of rebel works . . . extending to the creek." Having done so they withdrew, covered by Kilpatrick's cavalry on their left, to a line about 600 yards in front of the main line. There Col. Daniel Dustin's brigade, Ward's division, Twentieth Corps, dug in.[49]

On the right of Slocum's line (Morgan's sector) things went less well. John G. Mitchell pushed forward his pickets early. Skirmishing continued until about noon, when resistance softened and it was discovered that the Confederates had evacuated their works. Mitchell immediately pushed forward his brigade en masse and found "a new line, full of 'Johnnies,' west of and parallel to the Goldsboro road."[50] When Mitchell's brigade occupied the old rebel line, it was hit by rebel artillery fire. The Confederates had emplaced guns so as to "rake the works they left." Mitchell's easy prize suddenly became a "pretty warm place," relieved only when the battery accompanying Baird's advance challenged the enemy artillery and distracted its attention from the infantry. Rebel sharpshooting, however, took its toll; among the wounded was one of Mitchell's staff, Lt. Orlando M. Scott, 121st Ohio.[51]

Mitchell felt comfortable with Baird on his left, but when Baird withdrew it seemed to surprise not only Mitchell but Morgan as well. The move was believed to be the result of "some mismanagement," at least according to Lt. Col. James W. Langley, commanding Fearing's brigade. The left of the division was open! Morgan ordered Langley to bring up two of his regiments and extend them across the Goldsboro road. Still there was no connection with friendly units. Thus Morgan's division spent a second consecutive night feeling very much exposed and open to attack.[52]

This breakdown was partially remedied on the morning of the twenty-first, when Morgan deployed Langley's entire brigade to his left. But Langley was strung out in a single line with no reserve, about "one-third of a mile in advance" of Carlin, and "with no connection on my left." Slocum came up to personally inspect and gave orders for a Twentieth Corps division to fill in immediately.[53]

Morgan's right caused him equal worry on March 20. Vandever's troops, Sunday's heroes, caused the trouble. That morning, when he discovered the rebel works to his front unoccupied, Vandever ordered the 16th Illinois and 14th Michigan (under the command of Lt. Col. George W. Grummond, 14th Michigan) to seize them. These were the two regiments that had achieved spectacular success on the day before, capturing hundreds of prisoners and two battle flags. Grummond charged the empty Confederate works and seized them so easily that he decided the enemy must be in retreat and vulnerable. Therefore he continued to press forward, unsupported. As the commander of the 16th Illinois reported, Grummond pursued "without throwing out any skirmishers or stopping to reform our line." On they went "for nearly half a mile," racing across the Goldsboro road.[54]

There the two regiments came upon a new line. Grummond could see rebel battery positions within those works but he was not deterred. He determined to capture them and immediately ordered the regiments to attack. As they charged they were met with a terrible fire. Some of Grummond's men bravely rushed to the base of the enemy works. But their heroism was futile. The two regiments, totally outmatched, were quickly thrown back with heavy losses.[55]

Undaunted by Grummond's foolhardy adventure, Morgan advanced the remainder of Vandever's brigade to the enemy's deserted works that Grummond had captured and occupied. Once the Fifteenth Corps arrived, Morgan pressed forward again, this time in heavy force across the Goldsboro road. That evening he entrenched close to the new Confederate line.[56]

By the evening of March 20, therefore, Slocum occupied most of the ground the Confederates had abandoned, in effect regaining all the terrain lost during the fight on the nineteenth, as well as the area that Hoke had seized on the first day. Slocum had established a strong line that now extended from the vicinity of Cole's house northeast to, and including, the crossroads from which the enemy had attacked on Sunday. On the twentieth Slocum's line faced northwest, away from the Goldsboro road which he now controlled. He had entrenched this line and run it up close against the Confederate defenses. Moreover, he had made a solid connection with Howard's Right Wing on his right. All in all, despite Grummond's misadventure and the existence of a gap between Morgan and Carlin, Slocum had had a good day.

His men tended to agree. Granted, these swamps and thickets were not the rest camps of Goldsboro, but it was good to be winning. One of Slocum's fellow New Yorkers wrote: "Weather very warm and so ended this afflicted and troublesome day."[57]

Reveille had sounded for the Seventeenth Corps on Monday at 1:00 A.M. The soldiers formed quickly and began the march for Falling Creek Church, a distance of about five miles.[58] They arrived at the church promptly at daybreak. The men "prepared a coffee-lunch, and took a brief rest." They also built fires to dry their clothes. That early morning march had required wading five creeks, "knee deep," then crossing Falling Creek, "waist deep." So they sat or napped as they waited for Logan's Fifteenth Corps to pass ahead and clear the road. Frank Blair and many of his senior officers were invited to have breakfast with General Sherman. As they ate and relaxed, Sherman's staff briefed them on Slocum's fight on Sunday and explained that their corps was to follow the Fifteenth Corps from Cox's Bridge crossroads down the river road into the rear of Johnston's army, a distance of about eight miles. When they confronted Johnston's lines, they were to deploy to the right of the Fifteenth Corps. At 9:00 A.M., when all of Logan's regiments had passed, Blair's men fell into ranks and resumed their tramp, keeping a close interval between the two corps. Thus Howard's Right Wing now moved as one continuous powerful column.[59]

Logan's men had begun their march before Blair arrived. Their first order of business was to clear the Cox's Bridge crossroads by driving the rebels across the Neuse. Howard, at the head of this massive column, "threw a brigade and a battery toward Cox's Bridge." Clark Wever, who had been stationed at the crossroads since the afternoon of the nineteenth, itched for the assignment and carried it out in splendid fashion. His troops quickly and skillfully flanked the weak Confederate force and drove it back to the Neuse and across to the northern side. Thereupon the Confederates themselves set fire to Cox's Bridge, partially destroying it. Wever's men raced after them and "completed its destruction."[60] Then they returned to their post at the crossroads. All was accomplished in an hour—by 7:45 A.M.—with light losses. Wever and his brigade remained at the crossroads as a guard for the Fifteenth Corps train, then moved forward with the wagons at 6:00 P.M.[61]

With the crossroads secure, Logan led his Fifteenth Corps down the new Goldsboro road and turned left (west) down the old Goldsboro-Fayetteville road. Bvt. Maj. Gen. Charles R. Woods's division led the way, closely followed by Bvt. Maj. Gen. John M. Corse's and Bvt. Maj. Gen. John E. Smith's divisions. Very soon they encountered rebel cavalry "that resisted as stubbornly as cavalry is able to do."[62] From time to time the column would stop "to give time for skirmishers to drive the enemy from a swamp or dense thicket." Nevertheless, Woods's reinforced skirmish line pushed the rebels steadily. "The firing was brisk and the boys were hot for the sport."[63] The Confederate cavalrymen usually made stands at rail barricades, but Col. Robert F. Catterson's brigade, Woods's division, alternating fresh regiments to the head of the column would engage them in a firefight, and if that were not sufficient to knock them back, Catterson would flank them. Particularly good at this work were the men of the 46th Ohio with "their 7 shooters" who rotated assignments with the 97th and 100th Indiana and the 6th Iowa. "General Sherman personally directed Colonel Catterson . . . to drive the enemy as fast as the men could travel."[64]

It was exhausting work for Catterson's troops. They flushed the dismounted rebel cavalry out of six "well constructed barricades without great difficulty or loss." Particularly annoying, however, was a little three pounder the rebels would unlimber and fire from masked positions. Then they would limber up and gallop off. Eventually, Catterson's men captured it. Theodore F. Upson, 100th Indiana, told how:

> We were perhaps 80 rods away. Some of our boys had been firing at the men with the gun, but could not seem to have much effect. Then Capt Pratt called me to try it with my Henry rifle.[65] I got as close as I dared, for they were firing at us with their small arms too. By that time they had the gun limbered up and were starting away with it, but I was close enough now so I could see them good. The rider was on the rear mule. I pulled up my rifle, thinking I would shoot him which I could easily

have done as his whole body showed plainly above the mule. Just as I was going to fire something seemed to say to me: 'Don't kill the man; kill the mule,' so I dropped my rifle a little and shot the off mule just behind the fore leg.[66] He went down and that delayed them so much that we got the gun.[67]

Once the rebels retaliated. They charged as the 6th Iowa was retiring, having exhausted its ammunition, and as the 46th Ohio was moving up to take its place. Suddenly mounted rebels appeared, having turned their left flank and "gained their rear." Four companies of the 100th Indiana had been advancing alongside the 6th Iowa, and these men had not been relieved but remained at the front engaged with the rebels behind the barricade. Fortunately at the time the enemy struck, Ruel M. Johnson, colonel of the 100th Indiana, was following in close support with the remainder of his regiment. Johnson "saw cavalry coming out of woods." He faced his rear wing toward the Confederate horsemen and fired a volley that checked their charge. But the front wing of the 100th, commanded by Capt. John W. Headington, still found itself fighting rebels in front, flank, and rear. Some of his company commanders urged Headington to cut his way out and allow the wing to retreat back to the column, but Headington decided to hold his position. Meanwhile, Ruel Johnson attacked the flanking party again with the other wing of the 100th Indiana aided by the rapid-firing 46th Ohio. This effort scattered the rebels and they pulled back. Johnson's "quick action," Upson believed, "no doubt saved not only us but the Generals[68] from capture."[69]

Thus the advance continued steadily, mile after mile. Finally "we were relieved," Private Upson reported, "and stopped to rest for we had been pushing the Johnnys hard for over 4 miles. While resting the little gun we captured was brought back where we were and Capt Pratt told Col Johnson how we got it. The Colonel thanked me before all the boys and I felt pretty good. I am glad I shot the mule instead of the man."[70]

Howard's Right Wing continued irresistibly down the Goldsboro road, nearer and nearer to Bentonville. Sherman himself appeared here and there in the great column. Occasionally he would signal one of the batteries to unlimber a gun and fire a round "to inform Slocum we were moving to his support."[71] About 11:00 A.M. Catterson's lead regiment struck Confederate infantry. The rebels "had a position at the forks where the right-hand road leads to Bentonville and the straight-forward road on toward Averasborough," a point called Flowers' Crossroads.[72] So far it had been a movement with a minimum of delay and tiring troop deployments. Catterson, Woods, Logan, Howard, and Sherman excelled in efficiently massing the Right Wing and bringing it expeditiously to the field of battle. Frank Blair's corps, starting out at 1:00 A.M. rather than at 3:00 A.M. as ordered, typified the spirit and determination of Sherman's army—formidable and eager for the fight.[73]

General Woods assigned Col. George A. Stone's Iowa brigade the task of clearing the Confederate roadblock and fighting through to Slocum. Stone came up on Catterson's left and deployed. The enemy looked to be in brigade strength "as their line assumed length on both their flanks." But Stone's troops, assisted vigorously by Lt. Col. Edward N. Upton's 46th Ohio (Catterson's brigade), charged with a great shout and drove the rebels from their high rail barricade back toward their main line. If one looked carefully, rebel defenses could be seen in the distance—to the right or north, across the Goldsboro road—menacing earthworks featuring here and there what appeared to be artillery redoubts.[74]

Stone's 25th Iowa planted its colors in the Goldsboro road, the road the brigade had been assigned to clear. Three regiments of Stone's brigade now wheeled right, parallel to the road, away from Slocum's flank and into the heaviest concentration of Confederates. Resistance by rebel skirmishers became furious. For a while it looked quite serious, "very much as if we would have a general engagement."[75] A private in the 4th Minnesota commented that "our boys are charging but don't drive the rebs much. They are fighting very stubbornly." The men felt much better when they noticed General Sherman himself standing at the right of the 4th Minnesota observing the skirmishing.[76]

Colonel Stone was having a hard fight with exceedingly stubborn rebel skirmishers, but he was soon happily surprised. About 3:00 P.M. two of Hazen's regiments, the 6th Missouri and 30th Ohio, suddenly appeared and fell in alongside Stone and his Iowa boys. This combined force under Stone's leadership made a "handsome charge," driving enemy skirmishers out of their rifle pits, across a swamp, and back to their breastworks. Once the Confederates retired, Stone's and Catterson's troops immediately began erecting barricades and "going underground." They had developed the habit of bringing their defenses with them—portable barricades. "Almost in the twinkling of an eye, some rail fences were transferred, and transformed into a barricade."[77] About 4:00 P.M. Logan had Woods and Corse shoved forward again, this time placing their main line "on a ridge opposite" the Confederate works. Methodically, after placing heavy skirmish lines to the front, the main body "advanced 300 yards taking the rails with them."[78]

Before this final general advance, Lt. John Ackerman, 46th Ohio, had seen his opportunity. With rebel sharpshooters and pickets all about, he entered "no man's land" by himself, crawling 100 yards in front of the Federal line. There he found a soldier belonging to the 33d Ohio, one of Harrison Hobart's men, who had been shot through both legs Sunday afternoon and who had laid there in the swamp for twenty-four hours. Ackerman lifted him onto his back and carried him back.[79] All was well. Sherman possessed the crossroads leading to Averasboro and Smithfield. Junction with the Left Wing had been effected.[80]

Once Logan had occupied the ridgeline, Howard immediately deployed the Right Wing beside Morgan's division, Fourteenth Corps. To Morgan's right were Logan's four divisions, left to right: Hazen, Woods, and Corse in front, with John E. Smith in reserve. The Fifteenth Corps line extended along the northern side of the Goldsboro road until it met Bvt. Maj. Gen. Giles A. Smith's division of the Seventeenth Corps. Blair's line then bent east toward Mill Creek with Brig. Gen. Manning F. Force's division in the center and Maj. Gen. Joseph A. Mower's on the extreme right. These two divisions fronting along the Goldsboro road actually refused the Union line sharply east, so much so that in effect they seemed to be in reserve. Thus, about 4:30 P.M., Howard had four divisions on line (Hazen, Woods, Corse, and G. A. Smith) and three in reserve (J. E. Smith, Force, and Mower).[81] As an act of sound coordination, Howard had one of his staff pass behind Hazen's lines through Morgan's division and seek out Slocum. This officer in the course of their conversation inquired of the general how the battle of the day before had ended. Slocum, in his laconic manner, replied, " 'We whipped them.' "[82]

The Confederates may have been "whipped," but there they were—to the northwest on a hill or ridge "with a small creek and swamp between us." Logan reported that the rebel right covered the Goldsboro road, the left was "refused along the face of Mill Creek. No artillery was developed to our front." To Sherman, Johnston's position seemed a "bastion, its salient" pointed to the juncture between Slocum and Howard. Confederate parapets, according to Sherman, extended "from the road well down to Mill Creek."[83]

As Howard extended and fortified his lines and sealed the joint with Slocum's command, "musketry fire on the skirmish line was vigorously kept up, intermingled with heavy cannonading from both lines, which often reminded us of the old times before Atlanta."[84] Skirmishing and sorties (two rebel and one Federal) continued all night long, but these fights amounted to nothing except dozens of more dead and wounded. "At short intervals scare demonstrations were started, when the skirmishers on both sides would pour in volley after volley and the Union shouts were answered with defiant Confederate yells, making the night horrid, a bedlam of noise and battle." By midnight Sherman's lines had been reshaped, his units distributed to his satisfaction, and the army "firmly intrenched." Now Sherman told Howard that he could have Clark Wever bring up the trains.[85]

Sherman readied himself for next day. The two armies faced each other along the Goldsboro road that night. Johnston had his line astride the two branches of the Bentonville road, and his artillery covered the Goldsboro road. His left was "broken back" and prolonged toward Mill Creek, as was Sherman's right. Sherman did not believe that Johnston would "invite battle." He had failed to overcome Slocum's wing by himself; why should he attempt to fight two wings? "I don't want to fight now or here," Sherman wrote Terry at 9:00 P.M., "and therefore won't object to his [Johnston's] drawing off to-night toward Smithfield, as he should. . . . If Johnston insists on fighting us here I may call you up."[86]

In any event, Sherman looked to his wounded, whom he had moved by ambulances toward Goldsboro. He told Slocum: "I would rather avoid a general battle if possible. . . . Dispose your troops so that we have our back toward Faison's and Goldsborough . . . feel the enemy at several points tonight, and, if he retreats, try and get some prisoners."[87]

It is evident that Sherman simply intended to confront Johnston with overpowering strength, all the while masking the roads to Goldsboro over which his wounded men and empty trains were moving (and could easily return if desired). He stated this repeatedly in his communications and reports. As long as Sherman held the upper Goldsboro road, Johnston offered no threat south of the Neuse. Time worked for Sherman. He could remain on this side of the Neuse indefinitely, facing Johnston. Schofield's imminent occupation of Goldsboro,[88] however, would threaten Smithfield "and the rear of Johnston's army now in my front."[89] B. H. Liddell-Hart put it conclusively: Sherman's object was defensive, "not to bring on a battle in this blind and sodden country but to frighten Johnston back, so that he could slip safely into Goldsboro and reprovision himself as a preliminary to a fresh spring upon Johnston from that secure base."[90]

If Joe Johnston would only slip away in the night . . .

10

A Regular Indian Fight

ABOUT MIDNIGHT, March 19, Johnston disengaged the Army of Tennessee and Hardee's two divisions from their exposed positions. It was dangerous, delicate work.

As they began retiring, brave men would dash back to the field over which they had charged just hours before with such high hopes. Their mission this time was to rescue as many wounded as they could. Their foes, chopping and digging only a hundred yards to their front, intentionally ignored them in a display of that curious courtesy that sometimes character-ized Civil War enemies. Yet many wounded were left behind. About mid-night, when Taliaferro's men fell in and withdrew, they could not shut out the "pitiable groans and cries" of the wounded comrades they had aban-doned. It was hideous.[1]

Back they trudged, north of the Cole house, where "we had first started." That Sunday morning, so bright with promise, must have seemed so long ago. Now they dug in once again, much deeper this time, and by dawn their wide gashes in the earth were becoming substantial, "and what was of more consequence to most of us, [we] obtained a scant meal; the first food we had had since the night of the 18th."[2]

Pity the wounded, not only those left behind suffering untended on the field or screaming unheard in the thickets, but also those who had survived the first phase of being transported to the rear. Lt. Col. John D. Taylor, who had lost his arm Sunday afternoon in Johnson Hagood's abortive charge, found himself at Bentonville's "country church in which there was not a pew to be found." He lay on the hard floor in agony until "Capt. Sweetman, Yankee born, but of spirit and purpose of the South, managed to get me a cot."[3] Wounded who could walk were started on their way to Smithfield. Others remained at or near the church in Bentonville awaiting transportation. There were so many. The Army of Tennessee alone counted 624 soldiers already collected. Then there were the numerous wounded Yankees who had fallen into Confederate hands.

Care of Confederate casualties proved an enormous problem, baffling and infuriating. Reports of the suffering of these men and loud complaints of neglect and improper treatment soon reached Johnston. He responded by directing Bragg "to send a medical officer of experience in the field to Smithfield, to take charge." But the receiving station at Smithfield should be temporary—ship the wounded to Raleigh by train "as fast as possible." Furthermore, Johnston wanted Bragg himself at Smithfield to bring order and system to the Confederate rear. He armed Bragg with authority to make any necessary changes to relieve the situation and to secure necessary rail transportation.[4] This, of course, disposed of Bragg as a field officer. Indeed, it would place him in a semi-independent position where he should excel—terrifying logistical functionaries and incompetents. Regardless of this unexpected advantage, the nightmare of collection and removal of the wounded and burial of the dead became Johnston's rationale for remaining in Sherman's front for two nights. As late as 7:20 A.M. on Tuesday morning, he wired Robert E. Lee, "we are remaining here to cover the removal of our wounded to the railroad at Smithfield."[5]

Characteristically, Johnston also hoped that Sherman might attack. The Confederates had the advantages of terrain and interior lines, and by midmorning on Monday Johnston believed that he would have his troops behind formidable works.[6] His chief engineers, Col. John J. Clarke and Maj. John Johnson, and others had been busy selecting good defensive positions, and their reconnaissance work would continue throughout March 20. Hardee, however, seemed most concerned about a threat to the Confederate extreme right flank, an attack that might bypass the defensive works now being constructed. About dawn Hardee had received word from Wade Hampton of an enemy advance east along Overshot road leading across a tributary of Mill Creek and past a mill up to the higher ground or plateau on which stood the Confederate positions and Bentonville itself.[7] To pinch off this approach (picketed by Wheeler's cavalry), Blanchard's Brigade of reserves from McLaws's Division, supported by an artillery section, was posted on high ground behind "the mill race and mill pond."[8]

In the early hours of March 20, Johnston's intent was for Hardee to have McLaws occupy the right (Blanchard being detached to guard the extreme right), Taliaferro on McLaws's left, the Army of Tennessee in the center, and Hoke on the left. Additional units as they arrived from Smithfield could fill in between Hoke's left and Mill Creek or wherever needed. Thus the army would be facing southwest in a great defensive perimeter stretching from Overshot road on the right to Mill Creek on the left.

Johnston's "bastion" rapidly took shape. The army "worked very hard and completed good entrenchments with logs, and an abatis of brush, a few yards in front of the line. About one hundred yards in front of our main line were rifle pits; they represented our skirmish lines, and were capable of holding four men each, twenty steps apart." Rifled cannon (ten- and twenty-pounder Parrotts) "were placed in the centre of the field while the Napoleons were on the left."[9]

The danger point, contrary to Hardee's concern, proved to be not the right but the left. Apparently it all began at 3:00 A.M. when McLaws's trusted scout, Sgt. T. M. Paysinger, went to McLaws's tent and reported that "the enemy were moving on our left."[10] McLaws, of course, relayed the intelligence to his superior, Hardee, but Hardee

> had been notified by General Hampton that the enemy were marching on my right, and I was sent with my command on the right. I then told General Hardee that I was apprehensive that there was a mistake, that I was so certain that our left would be attacked and not the right, I would not fortify it, but wait for the order to return to the left. We had not been on the right an hour before General Hardee came himself in great haste, calling for my command to hurry to the left, and we did get back just in time to check the enemy.[11]

Paysinger's announcement coincided with other cavalry reports received during the afternoon and evening of March 19. The Fifteenth Corps, and perhaps additional units, were advancing toward Cox's Bridge on the lower Goldsboro road. Johnston, after consultation with Hardee and Hampton (who now minimized the threat to the right), decided that it was highly probable that Sherman was proceeding in force down the Goldsboro road from Cox's Bridge toward Flowers' Crossroads. Perhaps he had one corps, perhaps more. This menace could not be ignored.[12]

Thus everything changed. Instead of preparing for a general Federal attack up the Goldsboro road from the southwest, Johnston had to shift his thinking. He must strengthen his left flank and rear—immediately. Johnston responded by sending Wheeler out to Flowers' Crossroads and beyond— up the Goldsboro road toward Cox's Bridge. He also pulled McLaws's Division (all brigades except Blanchard's) to the left. Later that morning, as McLaws approached and prepared to connect with Hoke, Hampton stopped McLaws, wanting two brigades sent to defend Flowers' Crossroads itself. Hardee became involved at this point and again conferred with Johnston and Hampton. The generals decided to post Harrison's Brigade (McLaws's Division) on Hoke's left and form a second line, somewhat refused, extending from behind Harrison and Hoke "to the swamp on the left."[13]

Confederate cavalry operating east of Bentonville belonged to Hampton's command and was considered reliable. Unfortunately, its able division commander, Matthew C. Butler, had become ill on the nineteenth. This proved an untimely loss of experienced leadership, but Johnston immediately replaced Butler—not with Mully Logan, but with the higher-ranking Brig. Gen. Evander McIvor Law, a distinguished infantry brigade and division commander from the Army of Northern Virginia. Law, like his friend Lafayette McLaws, had incurred the disfavor of James Longstreet and at the moment was without a command, serving as a staff officer for Johnston.

Law took charge of the brigades of Mully Logan, who led Butler's old brigade, and Young (Col. Gilbert J. Wright).[14] This cavalry division, according to Col. J. Fred Waring of the Jeff Davis Legion, had resisted Howard's advance on the lower Goldsboro road on the afternoon of the nineteenth and the next morning. Early on the twentieth, however, Law and Waring still did not know in which direction the Federals might advance—perhaps north over the Neuse toward Goldsboro, perhaps west into Johnston's rear. Johnston had given orders that Cox's Bridge be destroyed if necessary to prevent a major Federal force from crossing the Neuse, and this was done. That seemed to eliminate one option.[15]

Everything became clear by midmorning. The Federals in massive force had turned west at Cox's Crossroads, marching down the old Goldsboro road. Law reported this alarming news to Johnston at 9:50 A.M. The enemy "infantry and artillery is advancing rapidly from the direction of Cox's Bridge. He is now about two miles from Flower's [*sic*] House. A few regiments of infantry would check his advance, I think, very materially. Our cavalry is too weak to accomplish much."[16]

Johnston knew that he was fortunate to have already moved McLaws to the left that morning. For at the time of crisis (11:00 A.M. on March 20), as Howard closed in, McLaws had arrived and was deploying on high ground north of Flowers' Crossroads. His men "threw up heavy works out of logs and light wood knots, then covering them with dirt. We then placed on top of the works a line of head logs, believing that the pine timber was too heavy for the enemy to use artillery."[17]

Of equal importance had been the shifting of Wheeler to the left. Joe Wheeler knew that he must buy time for Johnston to position McLaws and redeploy Hoke. Therefore, when he reached Flowers' Crossroads, he continued his advance up the Goldsboro road until he met the van of Howard's column. Wheeler dismounted part of his command astride the road as a blocking force, then he led several regiments wide around the flank of the leading Yankee brigade, charged into its rear, and caused confusion. In this attack Wheeler displayed personal leadership and gallantry, narrowly escaping death as his horse was killed beneath him. But this cavalry counterattack checked the Federal advance only momentarily. Wheeler's flank attack was tossed back and the force at the barricade quickly dislodged. Wheeler then retired to Flowers' Crossroads and deployed his men behind another barricade.[18] From there he wrote Johnston at 11:05 A.M. that the Federals "are engaging us very warmly": "General: I have formed a dismounted line here very near Flower's house, and can hold the enemy in check till we are flanked out of it. The line is a very short one, however. I have sent General Law back to Bentonville, with instructions to scout all roads running eastwardly from that point."[19]

News of Howard's advance had caused Johnston to swing back his left (Hoke) 120 degrees. He posted the North Carolina division about a half-mile northwest of the Goldsboro road—on defensible high ground behind yet another tributary of Mill Creek, fronting Flowers' Crossroads. There Hoke rapidly entrenched. On his left was Harrison's Georgia brigade, McLaws's Division. McLaws's three other brigades formed a second line to the rear of Hoke and Harrison. When Wheeler fell back from Flowers' Crossroads, he took a position extending the Hoke-McLaws line to Mill Creek.[20]

An encouraging aspect during all this rushing to-and-fro by the Confederates was the arrival of reinforcements. Three brigades came up during the afternoon of the twentieth: Lowry's and Granbury's of Cleburne's Division and Cumming's Brigade of Stevenson's Division. Johnston halted the latter unit and stationed it at his headquarters as a general reserve. Meanwhile, Frank Cheatham with a large part of Brown's Division would reach Smithfield about 5:00 P.M. and bivouac.[21] Hampton provided more encouragement. He investigated the threat to the Confederate right that worried Hardee so much and reported it to be only "a small foraging party." Hampton assured Hardee that he personally would look to the security of the right flank, now weakened by the removal of McLaws, and had ordered cavalry to that point.[22]

Skirmishing took place all along the line throughout Monday, the twentieth. The heaviest fighting occurred on the left as Hoke pulled back in response to Howard's arrival. On the opposite face of the Confederate thimble-shaped line, the Army of Tennessee and Taliaferro's Division fought skirmish actions, primarily against the Twentieth Corps and Absalom Baird's division of the Fourteenth Corps. Although they enjoyed prepared positions, these Confederates were apprehensive. They knew that the enemy was strong and increasing in strength. The loss of McLaws's big division had resulted in the right being stretched so thin that men "had to be deployed singly about four feet apart."[23] Then, too, the Army of Tennessee had lost a veteran commander—General Loring had become ill and turned over the corps to Walthall. All this was disquieting.[24]

Equally worrisome was the retirement of Hoke's Division. This fashioned the left units of the Army of Tennessee into a salient. Harvey Hill believed their position vulnerable and wanted the troops stationed there pulled back. A. P. Stewart disagreed, however, so the troops remained.[25] Atkins's battery of Parrott rifles supported the Army of Tennessee and was emplaced in the salient. Monday afternoon, when Kirkland's Brigade in Hoke's sector was assaulted, these guns in the salient (under Harvey Hill's direction) would provide effective enfilade fire. Then they in turn would be engaged by the batteries that Baird brought up close to the front. But Atkins's guns "didn't reply." Baird's cannon soon fell silent.[26]

As the day wore on, Stewart's skirmishers retired before Baird's, then advanced themselves, then retired, then advanced. These mini-battles, involving squad to brigade strength, went on all afternoon but subsided that night as Baird withdrew and pressure eased against the Confederate center and right flank.[27]

The most conspicuous engagement on Monday occurred on the Confederate left, Hoke's line. It happened just at that vulnerable moment as Hoke withdrew to his new position facing Flowers' Crossroads. To cover the division's displacement Hoke had ordered Kirkland to deploy his brigade as skirmishers. Kirkland was to hold his position as long as practicable, then slowly retire to the newly established main line and take his place in the center.

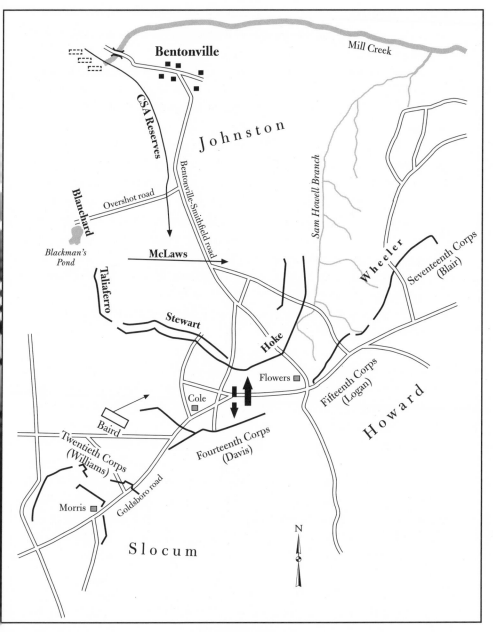

Map 8. March 20

The Union army (Vandever's brigade) began probing Kirkland's front early in the morning but was kept at bay long enough for Hoke to establish his new position. Although pressed closely, Kirkland brought his troops back in orderly fashion and put them into line. Then the Yankees struck. Without time to prepare breastworks, Kirkland ordered his men to lie down and load. The brigade, partially concealed, waited until the Federals came up close. The silence was excruciating. At least it seemed so to Kirkland's immediate neighbors, the North Carolina Junior Reserves. Company A, 17th Regiment North Carolina Troops, Kirkland's extreme right, touched the left of the Juniors' position. These youths had an excellent view, and they watched Kirkland's veterans of Cold Harbor intently, focusing their attention on Company A's commander, Capt. William Biggs: "Biggs made his men stand up in two ranks and wait for the word, then fired 'by rank', giving commands: 'Rear rank, ready, aim, fire! Load! and then 'Front rank,' etc. The volleys were all distinct amid the rattle of 'firing by file' all along the line."[28]

The volley was highly effective. Kirkland's officers knew well that firing "by rank" (second row of troops fire, then first, then second, etc.) had great shock effect as contrasted with the customary fire "by file" (two soldiers firing simultaneously—a soldier and man immediately behind him fired together, then the next two men, usually from the right of the line to the left). The latter mode of firing was generally favored because it offered the advantage of sustained fire.

After a second volley the Yankee charge collapsed. "Their ranks were mowed down like wheat before the scythe and the attack repulsed with great loss." The enfilade fire of Atkins's battery added to the devastation. When the enemy fled, Kirkland immediately advanced his skirmish line and had the remainder of the brigade begin constructing earthworks. Kirkland's sharp little victory pleased Johnston, of course. He turned to Hardee and commented, "I am glad of it. I would rather they attack Kirkland than any one else."[29]

The North Carolina Junior Reserves, doubtless emboldened by Kirkland's steadiness, also fought well. Maj. Walter Clark, eighteen years old, commanded the brigade skirmish line that afternoon. He saw the dead and wounded of Vandever's brigade as he went out 200 yards and positioned his men. "It was in a good wood for skirmishing," he wrote his mother a week later, "with little or no undergrowth. We had a regular Indian fight of it behind trees. They charged my line twice but were both times driven back. That night the whole skirmish line kept up an almost continuous firing as they expected our Army to leave. That together with the scamps trying to creep up on us in the dark kept us up all night."[30]

It was a solid performance by Hoke's Division, offsetting its lackluster effort the previous afternoon. Col. John H. Nethercutt's Juniors handled themselves commendably, as did Kirkland and his brigade. Perhaps most impressive about Hoke's work that afternoon was changing front in the face of the enemy. In the hands of a less skillful commander, this could have led to disaster.[31]

The skirmishing on the Confederate left, especially in Hoke's front, continued all afternoon and into the evening. McLaws's troops also came under considerable pressure. The 1st Georgia Regulars (Fiser's Brigade) found themselves in a vulnerable position on the far left, "both flanks unprotected." When the pickets in front of them withdrew and balls began whizzing through the trees, they became keenly aware of "the total inadequacy of our force."[32]

The 1st Georgia numbered only seventy-five troops, and twenty of these were advanced as skirmishers while the others entrenched. Lt. A. H. "Gus" Rutherford, commander of the skirmishers, went to his "mess-mate and friend," Lt. John P. Fort, "and handed me two articles to care for, as he did not expect to return. These two articles were a daguerreotype and a meerschaum pipe. I knew that he valued his pipe above all his other possessions (he was an inveterate smoker), but I had no idea that he possessed such a treasure as this photograph." Fiser's men continued to entrench feverishly, and as he dug Fort considered several possibilities in the coming fight. Finally he turned to "a soldier of my company, a large, red headed man named Gilham. 'Gilham, if anything happens to me put your hand in my right hand pants pocket and take from it what you find there, they belong to Lieutenant Rutherford, give them to him.'" Gilham answered, " 'Lieutenant, I will, and if I fall, tell my old lady, who lives at Stone Mountain, Georgia, that I died fighting like a man.' "[33] Fortunately for the 1st Georgia, Rutherford's men put up a show of strength and discouraged the enemy from advancing farther; thus Rutherford was able to reclaim his treasures.[34]

It also helped to have a strong defensive position. By nightfall Johnston's army had entrenched and appeared to possess an "unassailable" position. One could point to the left entrenched "behind a swampy ravine with rifle pits lining its edge" or to the right where the Army of Tennessee's "powerful defensive positions with elaborate traverse lines extended over a mile to the west."[35] Sherman certainly regarded Johnston's position cautiously; Oliver O. Howard openly admired it. "Johnston chose well," wrote Howard.

Robert Frederick Hoke
(U.S. Army Military History Institute, Carlisle, Pennsylvania)

"It was a kind of bridge-head with bended line, having Bentonville behind it, covering the crossing of Mill Creek, and thus holding the Smithfield road." It also commanded the Goldsboro road. With his "wings broken back to protect his flanks," Johnston had a compact position with easy movement from flank to flank, front to rear. It was a defensive commander's dream—or so it seemed.[36]

Actually the appearance of great strength was deceiving: Johnston held a dangerous position. He and his army were in a trap. Faulty intelligence reports led Johnston to believe that Sherman had only 44,000 troops. Based on that figure, Johnston was outnumbered three to one.[37] The odds were probably greater. Furthermore, considering the reliability and experience of the opposing armies, the odds leaped in Sherman's favor. Interior lines were an advantage, but Johnston faced the possibility of his lines, thinly manned and thrown back at an acute angle, being forced at some point. Once they were punctured, the attacking force could quickly reach the rear of the reverse side. With pressure being exerted all along the defensive "parapets," on both wings, a breakthrough, even if met with a prompt counterattack, probably would be disastrous.[38]

Moreover, the Confederate left was wide open. Beyond Hoke's Division and Harrison's Brigade were McLaws's three other brigades on a refused line. Then, to conform to the widening front of the Federals, the fragile Confederate front continued to extend, manned only by dismounted cavalrymen who disappeared into "an ugly fen,[39] seventy or eighty yards wide" guarding rain-swollen Mill Creek which was virtually impassable.[40]

"Our line was a very weak one and our position was extremely perilous," wrote Wade Hampton years later. "Our flanks rested on no natural defenses, and behind us was a deep and rapid stream over which there was but one bridge. . . . Our left flank—far overlapped by the enemy—was held along a small stream which flowed into Mill Creek, and this was held only by cavalry videttes stationed at long intervals apart."[41]

Johnston knew the weaknesses of his "bastion" as well as Hampton. He maintained that he had wanted to withdraw north of Mill Creek at the first opportunity. The large number of wounded had encumbered him Sunday night, so he stayed and fortified. Late Monday afternoon, however, he planned to pull out and so notified his subordinates.[42] But he did not. It is not known why. Sherman certainly expected him to retreat and had made his plans accordingly. Something changed Johnston's mind. Perhaps, as his report states, the strength of his position encouraged the hope of a frontal assault by Sherman. But this expectation of a costly Federal attack seems somewhat disingenuous. Perhaps, as he said, transporting the wounded to safety continued to govern the army's actions.

In a curious note, almost peevish in tone, A. P. Stewart wrote Johnston at 6:00 P.M.: "If we are to retire to-night would it not be well for me to withdraw the artillery on my line at an early hour and give timely notice, so that every one can be prepared?" This message seems to suggest that subordinate commanders would be caught off guard and unprepared and appears to advise that the retreat should be postponed. No one knew the risks of remaining better than Johnston, surely. It was odd for a general whose name was synonymous with cautiousness.[43]

In any event, Johnston recklessly, one might argue, decided to remain one more day.

11

Shoulder-to-Shoulder and Then Back-to-Back

SHERMAN WAS DISAPPOINTED. The clear, pleasant night had raised his hopes, but it began to cloud over by midmorning and Tuesday steadily turned murky gray. Before noon came drizzle, then a heavy shower, then more rain. It would rain all afternoon, "sometimes in fierce torrents." Even worse, it promised to continue. A frustrated Sherman complained to Alfred H. Terry, "After raining six weeks it is apparently set in for another six weeks." Once again the roads would be spoiled and the troops made miserable.[1]

Joe Johnston also had let him down. As Sherman explained to Schofield on the morning of March 21: "I thought Johnston, having failed, as he attempted to crush one of my wings, finding he had not succeeded but that I was present with my whole force, would withdraw, but he has not, and I must fight him here. He is twenty miles from Smithfield with a bad road to his rear, but his position is in the swamps, difficult of approach, and I don't like to assail his parapets, which are of the old kind."[2]

In preparation for this battle he did not want, Sherman issued a field order directing Howard and Slocum to send all nonessential wagons to Kinston for supplies. Camp equipage would be stored in wing depots to be established south of the Neuse along the Wilmington and Goldsboro Railroad. Slocum furthermore would shift his operational train (essential wagons) to the far right of the army, stationing them on the Goldsboro road behind Howard. Slocum's pontoon train also would be transferred to Cox's Bridge so that Terry might use it to cross to the northern side of the Neuse. Howard's pontoon train would proceed farther east to a point between his new depot and Goldsboro. Schofield (approaching Goldsboro) would place a third pontoon bridge across the Neuse in the vicinity of Jerico (for the convenience of Howard's and Slocum's wagon trains moving to and from Kinston). Schofield, once he had secured Goldsboro with a division, would advance without delay to meet Terry at Millard (immediately north of Cox's Bridge and about twelve miles west of Goldsboro). There Schofield and Terry would combine to make up a lean, highly mobile strike force of 25,000 to maneuver in close coordination with Sherman against Johnston.[3]

Sherman thus expected Tuesday, March 21, to be used ridding the army of its encumbrances, all the while consolidating and tightening the lines around Johnston's bridgehead, particularly on the east side (Howard's). In effect, this meant that the army would be repositioning itself, adopting generally a north-south line, facing west, away from the Goldsboro road and the Neuse crossings.[4] If Johnston were to attempt anything offensively, Sherman's staff believed that it would be an attack on the Right Wing.[5]

While Howard and Slocum adjusted their lines, Schofield and Terry were to employ Tuesday positioning themselves advantageously across the Neuse, shielding Goldsboro yet poised with their strike force to dash toward Smithfield and thus cut off Johnston. Sherman intended, however, *not to fight* if Johnston withdrew across Mill Creek. He stated this explicitly in a dispatch to Schofield at 11:30 A.M., March 21: "but the moment Johnston gives ground I propose to fall back on Goldsborough and await the completion of our railroad and re-equipment of my army. I will probably post you at Kinston, General Terry about Faison's, and this army at Goldsborough."[6]

To implement his design and to give himself further options, Sherman's first step was to tend to his wounded—get them out of harm's way and settled in Goldsboro. But to do this required hundreds of wagons. So Henry Slocum set about emptying as many as possible. He distributed precious rations, replacing boxes of hardtack and tins of coffee with wounded members of the Fourteenth and Twentieth Corps. Slocum's great hospital train set out at noon swinging wide behind the Right Wing. About seven hundred wounded were transferred in this efficient manner. Howard's train of empty supply and ordnance wagons got under way about the same time under strict instructions to yield to Slocum's ambulances.[7]

March 21 saw continuous skirmishing along Slocum's front. Word went through the ranks that they had the rebs "penned in here. . . . We are looking for a charge by them on our line."[8] Slocum alerted Jefferson C. Davis to hold the Fourteenth Corps in readiness: "a general engagement this afternoon is not improbable." Davis's corps was tired and jumpy. Men had "slept with one eye open last night—therefore very sleepy this morning. . . . Lay down with head against the works ready to fall into line of battle at a moment's warning."[9] They missed their tents and rubber raincoats and mess gear, all of which they lost in Sunday's debacle, but they gave thanks for being alive as they pondered the graves of the unfortunates. There was a "great contrast" between those of their army and those of the enemy—three Connecticut soldiers buried "with good order and headboards up, theirs [rebels] with mud thrown on carelessly." One soldier examined the trees about him: "Counted 7 shots in one small tree the size of my wrist—all below the height of my head."[10]

Tuesday morning Morgan's division threw out heavy skirmish formations to protect troops establishing fortifications along a more advantageous and advanced line. Some of the skirmish companies (John Mitchell's men) took advantage of the Cole house, halfway between the picket lines, and posted sharpshooters there.[11] This provided an excellent field of fire, and they concentrated on rebel battery positions. "A few of our boys," reported Mitchell, "from the second story windows, annoyed the rebels by shooting down in their works, killing many artillery horses. This it seems they could not bear."[12] The Confederates reacted quickly. Out stormed a heavy skirmish line (Mitchell contends that it was a line of battle), supported by artillery, driving Mitchell's men from Willis Cole's house. Then the rebels burned it.[13]

The scrap at Cole's house concerned Davis more than the Confederates realized. Not far behind this point lay a vulnerable gap in the Fourteenth Corps line, "a ticklish place." The left flank of Langley's (Fearing's) brigade, Morgan's division, "stuck [out] at the enemy like a sore thumb."[14] There was still no connection between Morgan and Carlin. When the rebels advanced past Cole's house, they drove Langley's skirmishers back to his main line and exposed this weak point. If they had veered right in sufficient force, they would have flanked Morgan and once again lodged themselves between the two divisions. But happily for Davis, the Confederates retired after burning Cole's house and making the strong show of force.

Davis was glad to see the rebels go. To patch his line he ordered Morgan to withdraw Langley yet somehow establish a connection with Carlin. Slocum, Davis advised Morgan, would not release any unit from the Twentieth Corps to plug the hole. "Be vigilant," Davis cautioned.[15]

Rebel deserters continued to drift into Slocum's lines. Some had been taken prisoner in the skirmishing, some simply seized the opportunities presented by the confusion of battle and did not return to their units. One of Bate's men, an "intelligent" fellow, gave Slocum accurate information on the

Confederate dispositions—which corps were positioned on which flanks and so forth. Another deserter casually sauntered in, stating that he just "wanted to find out what the chopping was for."[16]

All the while the rain continued, becoming heavier as the afternoon progressed. Clothing became sodden; dirt turned into unworkable mud; breastworks oozed away, sliding into newly dug trenches.

Alpheus Williams's Twentieth Corps remained quiet until about noon on the twenty-first, when Nathaniel Jackson's division ventured forth along the Goldsboro road to a point close to where Robinson's brigade originally had fought on March 19. As they moved up over Sunday's battlefield, a private reflected:

> I saw fifteen unburied Confederate soldiers lying where they had fallen. It was not a pleasant sight to me, even though these men had been our enemies. I thought when I saw them, of the sorrow and grief there would be in fifteen homes somewhere; and for what had these young lives been sacrificed? I hoped if I survived the war never to witness or take part in another. There should be some way to settle political differences without slaughtering human beings.[17]

Jackson held this advanced position for about an hour and even began constructing substantial works. Then suddenly (probably on orders from Slocum) the division withdrew from the line at the double-quick. Twice heavy rebel skirmish lines advanced, broke through Jackson's abandoned position, and engaged his skirmishers. Jackson's skirmish line was reinforced, however, and the rebels were beaten off.[18]

One of Baird's men watched these attacks against Jackson, especially one conducted by Taliaferro's Red Infantry. To him the rebel maneuvers seemed amateurish, characterized more by enthusiasm than technique:

> A Rebel Regiment of heavy artillery from Charleston who had never been in battle before and who sent out from their fortifications fought desperately and their ranks will tell the tale tonight. They were dressed better than the Rebs are generally and was a "crack" regiment. They are wiser tonight than before as regards fighting. From the number to be seen lying around with their "toes turned up" (as our boys say) there can't be many left. The color bearer set his Flag on our works but it remained there and he was riddled with bullets. We expected orders to charge their works all day but it was better for us to let them do the charging.[19]

The situation was different on Sherman's right Tuesday morning. Howard's wing was active and aggressive, far more so than Slocum's. Howard himself was everywhere—it was dangerous even to ride with him. One of his staff officers, Lt. Col. William E. Strong, lamented:

> I have been riding with Genl. Howard for five hours, backwards and forwards, along our skirmish line, exposed to a deadly fire. I thought both of us would be killed. I never hesitated yet to go where my duty called me, or where ordered, but I do object most seriously to being made a target for the enemy to practice on. Captain Howard once said at "Ezra Chapel,"[20] that "riding in battle with a man who is always prepared to die is not as pleasant as one might think." I entirely agree with Captain Howard.[21]

Riding with General Howard evidently presented a wealth of anecdotal opportunities. Lt. Col. Andrew Hickenlooper recorded an incident occurring as he rode beside General Howard on the twenty-first. They passed "an ammunition wagon whose lead-mules had become tangled up in their harness. [The teamster] was addressing them in terms more forceable than polite, when, notwithstanding other much more important matters demanding his attention, General Howard rode to the irate teamster, and yelled out, "Hold on, hold on there my man." Thus, even in the midst of the Battle of Bentonville, Oliver O. Howard, in a manner reminiscent of Rosecrans, would allow himself to be diverted and seemingly was willing to risk a ridiculous situation. So wing commander confronted teamster. " 'Suppose,' " continued Howard, " 'just as some of those vile oaths are issuing from your lips one of these passing cannon balls should take your head off?' "[22]

The teamster, unimpressed and having ultimate concerns and priorities of his own, responded without a blink: " 'Well General it would just be my God d—d luck. Get out of there you God d—d b—h.' " Once again he raised his whip and applied the lash, ignoring the major general. Howard surrendered on the spot and rode on, remarking "sadly" to Hickenlooper "that he was afraid that man was beyond redemption."

Careful reconnaissance by Howard and his engineers consumed most of the morning. Then out went strong skirmish lines, "pressed well forward." "Annoy [the enemy] as much as possible," Howard ordered Blair and Logan. In the meantime hundreds of Right Wing wagons set out for Kinston. Bring back, Howard directed, "hard bread, sugar, coffee, boots."[23]

At daylight on the twenty-first Logan's Fifteenth Corps sent out skirmish lines that immediately became engaged with determined Confederates.

About 10:00 A.M. the divisions of Corse and Woods pushed forward in strength and established a new, more defensible line about 200 yards northwest, "thrown forward at an angle of 35 degrees." C. R. Woods occupied the center of the Fifteenth Corps line with Corse on his right, Hazen on his left. Hazen deployed two brigades forward, connecting his skirmish line firmly with Woods on the northwestern side of the Goldsboro road. The resulting position, however, had Hazen's left—the extreme left of Howard's wing— "several hundred yards in advance of the troops on the left [Morgan's], the Fourteenth Corps." As a precaution Hazen massed his Third Brigade in reserve behind his exposed flank. He did so in lieu of extending a flimsy skirmish line across the 500 yards separating his left from Morgan's right. Logan also brought artillery forward. Although it was difficult to move guns through the forest and the mud, one of his division commanders, John M. Corse, succeeded in emplacing the four pieces of the 1st Missouri (Battery H) in close support and Charles R. Woods established a section of the 12th Wisconsin Light Battery near the center of his line.[24]

While skirmishers kept the Confederates occupied, the Fifteenth Corps rapidly entrenched its advanced line. Spades and new axes came up from the rear and were shared carefully like precious jewels. Within each regiment a company was allowed ten minutes' use of the tools, then they were passed down the line. When not digging, the troops hacked away underbrush in front of their works with hatchets and heavy knives and fashioned a "pile of rubbish" which they covered with dirt. Meanwhile, a steady and heavy fire was "kept up by both sides until noon . . . across a deep and miry swamp in our front." Shielding Frederick J. Hurlbut's brigade, Corse's division, was the 7th Illinois, a regiment renowned for its ability in skirmishing. The men were "as usual having lots of fun with their sixteen shooters."[25]

Fortifying in the presence of the enemy was not fun, the 7th Illinois notwithstanding. Pvt. Robert B. Hoadley, 26th Iowa, Woods's division, wrote: "was engaged nearly half a day, raining hard all the time. We had to build works under the Johneys fire, it was not very pleasant work, raining & Bullets flying, one about as hard as the other, only the rain would not hurt & the bullets would. My company ('C') lost 2 men badly wounded. That looks small, but when you come to see how few men we have, it is like taking a Brother out of a family."[26]

Between 2:00 and 3:00 P.M., once his new alignment had been established and fortified satisfactorily, Howard ordered a general advance tight against the Confederate main line. For the Fifteenth Corps this meant crossing the swamp and driving the rebels out of rifle pits into their breastworks.

The enemy resisted stubbornly. When Catterson's men of Woods's division captured advanced rebel rifle pits on the western side of the swamp, the Confederates tried repeatedly to regain them and succeeded in recapturing some. At several points along Woods's front reinforced groups of his skirmishers dug in "not more than 50 yards from the enemy lines and were held under heavy volley firing from the enemy in his main works." It reminded the men of hot, deadly days besieging Atlanta, the skirmishing of Woods's division "almost amounting to a battle."[27] Capture rifle pits, reverse them, then fight off counterattacking rebels who "repeatedly" leaped over their main line in daring assaults. "At three different times the rebels followed their volleys by an assault" on the Federal skirmishers. "Their men swarmed over the works," related brigade commander Col. George A. Stone of Woods's division, "and charged gallantly, but I had re-enforced the line till I had nearly a line of battle, and our incessant firing prevented them from charging as a perfect organization and every charge was repulsed."[28]

The Federals' line would be reinforced and they in turn would counterattack, retaking sections of rifle pits that had been lost. Counterattacks by both sides would succeed, then fail, then succeed. There was "one unceasing roll of musketry." "The rebels came out of their works twice to retake the pits," one of Woods's men recalled. The first time "our regt had to fall back, . . . but we all rallied in a minute and made the johnnies fairly fly back." The next time "our left brigade again broke, but our men held their pits." A fresh regiment, the 26th Illinois, arrived at the perfect moment and counterattacked, going "after them with a fierce yell. You should have seen the Rebs run. It did me a *power* of good. . . . I think this has been as exciting and lively a P.M. as ever I saw."[29]

Regardless of local successes, it was extremely dangerous for the Union troops manning captured rebel rifle pits. Their unseen enemy could mass behind their breastworks and spring out upon them in sudden, vicious attacks. Up so close to the main Confederate works and under "murderous fire," Corse's troops could no longer maintain their positions. So they retreated back across the swamp, blaming one of Woods's brigades for having withdrawn first and exposing their flank. Actually, it is remarkable that they were able to maintain these lodgements as long as they did.[30]

Two elements helped Logan's troops who attacked the enemy works across the swamp—sharpshooters and artillery. The sharpshooters did excellent work, keeping the rebels pinned down, making it possible for Logan's infantry to refashion and reverse the shallow rifle pits they had captured under the very noses of the rebels.[31] Corse and Woods also enjoyed close fire support from the batteries they had brought up and emplaced. Four pieces (Capt. Charles M. Callahan's Battery H, 1st Missouri Light) supported Corse. They "opened with great fury and effect on the enemy pits and fortified lines." William Zickerick's 12th Wisconsin Light (supporting Woods) "briskly engaged the enemy with but little cover; expended 222 rounds of ammunition. . . . Too much cannot be said of the conduct of this battery on this occasion," reported Logan's chief of artillery, Lt. Col. William H. Ross. "Within 100 yards of the main line of the enemy, with rude covering, they fought with brilliant success, the enemy's works and dead demarking the fire of this battery."[32] Ross's sentiments were echoed by Bvt. Maj. Gen. William F. Barry, Sherman's chief of artillery, who praised the steady handling and precise fire of all the batteries of the Fifteenth Corps, materially assisting "in advancing our own lines, in repelling the enemy's assaults, and in inflicting heavy loss upon him."[33]

Frank Blair had only one division, led by Giles A. Smith, of his Seventeenth Corps in close contact with the enemy Tuesday morning. Similar to Logan's divisions, Smith advanced a heavy skirmish line and "a furious fire broke out from both lines." The rebels soon retreated, however, and Smith continued to press until by midmorning the enemy had retired "over half a mile across a deep ravine running north and south, and with a swampy ground in its wide basin and thick underbrush and young timber covering its whole surface." Smith placed his skirmishers along the eastern edge of the ravine, carefully connecting with Corse's division on his left. Then he began to construct his main line 150 yards behind the ravine.[34] Not long after Smith secured his position, Force's division came up on his right and established a parallel position. Once it was fortified, Smith wedged his skirmish line over the swamp and up close to the rebel breastworks. When they had crossed the ravine and captured rifle pits, the skirmishers of Force's and Smith's divisions had to withstand counterattacks similar to those that greeted Logan's troops.[35]

While the Seventeenth Corps moved on line with the Fifteenth, Sherman reevaluated his situation, apparently without consulting Howard or Slocum. He sent his trusted chief engineer, Col. Orlando M. Poe, to inform Slocum of his intentions shortly after noon on Tuesday. Sherman wanted Slocum to withdraw and move to Howard's left and rear on Wednesday morning, March 22. "The best mode of drawing from your left to the right," instructed Sherman, "is to let the cavalry relieve by a thin skirmish line the skirmishers of the left corps [Williams] till it has gained its new position, when it, too, can withdraw. So instruct General Kilpatrick."[36] Slocum, promptly implementing his commander's design, alerted Davis that Williams would pull out the Twentieth Corps first, which would place the Fourteenth on the left and rear of the army. Although Sherman did not state his plans explicitly, it appears that he did not intend to employ Slocum as a covering force for Howard's subsequent withdrawal, but rather to move the Left Wing on toward Cox's Bridge and either cross the Neuse to Goldsboro or take a "position across Falling Creek, where our communication with a base of supply would be satisfactory." The Right Wing would follow, screened by Kilpatrick's cavalry.[37]

Everything seemed so orderly on Tuesday afternoon—so Shermanlike—until 4:00 P.M., that is. Then division commander Joseph A. Mower, Sherman's great favorite, the general he wanted with him, the man he considered "the boldest young soldier we have,"[38] surprised his patron and startled Joe Johnston. Boldness would turn Tuesday's careful, methodical sparring match topsy-turvy. Mower went for a knockout.

It all began that morning as Frank Blair brought up Force's and Mower's divisions on the right of Giles A. Smith, thus extending the line of the Right Wing along the same swampy ravine toward Mill Creek. Manning Force went into position and began to fortify on the eastern bank of the ravine.

By 8:00 A.M. Joseph Mower had plunged into the wilderness with his men, intending to come up on Smith's right. Frank Blair and his staff intercepted Mower and directed him to his new position "along a small swamp-flanked creek, tributary to Mill Creek," where he would be "facing almost due west."[39]

" 'I suppose, General,' Mower said finally, 'after I get into position, there will be no objection to my making a little reconnaissance.' 'None at all,' Blair replied."

Mower, however, advanced with two brigades along a road that he found turned northwest crossing "Sam Howell" Branch, another tributary of Mill Creek. There was no bridge at the crossing but an easy ford. Thinking this a dangerous avenue of approach into the right and rear of the Right Wing, Mower decided to defend it. So he ordered five companies of his 18th Missouri to dig in on the northern side of Sam Howell Branch. Then, according to his instructions, he began deploying his two brigades along the eastern side of a "wide marsh," occupying a strong, easily defensible position, although not connected to Force's right.

Once the division had settled in, "the rain slackened sufficiently to encourage Mower to start the reconnaissance he had been aching to try all day." Throwing out skirmishers well forward, he advanced on a two-brigade front across the swamp. " 'In we went. In our front the marsh was so deep and such a tangle of vines that all the mounted officers were speedily on foot, and the entrenching tools thrown away.' "[40] Soon Mower's right brigade, commanded by the English-born publisher-soldier, John W. Fuller, floundered badly (his troops up to their "arm-pits") in the swamp. Fuller's plight forced Mower to halt Col. John Tillson's brigade for almost an hour. Tillson struggled to maintain contact with Force's left flank, adding company after company, stretching this line beyond reason, in an attempt to compensate for the difficult nature of the terrain. Meanwhile, Mower's audacious skirmishers, strung out wide across the swamp, continued advancing, pushing rebels before them. Confederate resistance stiffened, however, on the far edge of still another swamp. Mower's skirmishers encountered rebel artillery fire from high ground. When Fuller had passed the bog that ensnared him and came on line with Tillson, Mower ordered both to advance at the double-quick. Together they splashed out of the swamp, then charged up the slope toward the annoying cannon. Mower's "wildly cheering lines" easily carried a string of rifle pits and captured a caisson abandoned by the fleeing Confederates. They also took prisoners.[41]

When he reached the top of the rise Mower ordered Tillson and Fuller to halt and regroup, but his skirmishers, advancing almost at a trot, kept shoving the rebels back. It all seemed so simple—maintain the initiative, keep the enemy off balance. Strike hard and fast. Keep the pressure up. The leading skirmishers now came upon log structures. In one they found a hospital and "wounded men of the Fourteenth Corps" with whom they talked. In another they discovered Johnston's headquarters. "Over the door of the old log house . . . was nailed the general headquarters sign."[42]

As Mower prepared to push on with his brigade lines of battle, Tillson relayed disturbing news. He had lost all contact with General Force's division. "Being convinced that I had obliqued to the right in moving through the swamp," reported Mower, "I immediately gave the command to move by the left flank, and proceeded myself to the left to see to the execution of the order."[43] As Tillson's brigade turned about to "oblique to the left in a southwest direction," back tumbled skirmishers from the left and center. Close on their heels Mower saw two lines of gray infantry. Quickly he ordered up a regiment from Fuller's brigade—only to receive the alarming report that Fuller himself was under attack on his right flank and in front, "the heavy firing where I was preventing my hearing the firing on the right."

Mower reacted by throwing back his left and occupying "the reverse side of the rifle pits, which had been held by the enemy."[44] Fuller was ordered to disengage, pass behind Tillson, and form on his left. Mower also brought up his reserve regiment, the 25th Wisconsin of the Second Brigade, and threw it into the opening between him and Force's division.[45] "In this manner I connected with the right of the main line."[46]

Other Union accounts treat Mower's predicament somewhat differently. It seems that Tillson's two left regiments "recoiled" when attacked by Confederate cavalry, "threatening to unhinge the Third Brigade's (Tillson's) line." These were Wheeler's men, supported by two lines of infantry who "made our men scamper." Meanwhile, Fuller was thrown back; the "entire line had to retreat down the hill" back into the swamp. Tillson's 32d Wisconsin and Fuller's 39th Ohio, however, "standing shoulder-to-shoulder and then back-to-back, proved solid pivots" on which Mower could rally his two broken brigades. Tillson himself credited Maj. William H. Crenshaw, 25th Indiana, for "seizing and planting the colors," which "prevented, I think, the center . . . from breaking."[47] But by about 4:45 P.M. Mower seems to have reorganized his troops. Subordinates pleaded with him to counterattack. The rebel lines looked so thin. Their assaults had lost momentum.

Mower knew the folly of that course. Alone on the flank of Sherman's army, separated from the Right Wing by treacherous and blind swamps, he realized that he might not be supported in time. But to be the prisoner of caution made him totally frustrated, like an infuriated lion. "Glaring at Hampton's 'roystering, cheering, and defiant' troopers, Mower shook his fist in the air, raised himself high in the stirrups . . . and yelled: 'God, man, wouldn't you like to wade in there with a saber.' "[48]

Mower had startled Johnston by suddenly appearing with two brigades on his left flank, puncturing the flimsy screen of cavalry guarding that flank. Mower's skirmishers, unknown to their commander, had penetrated dangerously close to the Confederate spinal column, the Smithfield-Bentonville road. They presented themselves in the very field where Johnston's headquarters were located—almost within sight (musket range) of the single bridge across Mill Creek! The desperately imperiled Johnston, of course, struck back at Mower with every reserve within reach. The Federal skirmishers were overwhelmed, astonished at the ferocity of the counterattacks, mostly by pistol-wielding horsemen. The skirmishers fled the open ground, then Mower abandoned the high ground he had won, and the division found

Mower's charge against the Confederate left. From a sketch by Joseph Becker.
(National Archives)

itself ingloriously back in the swamp. The risky escapade had cost Mower about two hundred men—mostly troops captured from Tillson's brigade.[49]

By 5:30 P.M. the threat to Mower was over and the front stabilized. Oliver O. Howard's thoughts turned to the offense. Now was the time for a powerful counterattack. Already he had ordered the entire Seventeenth Corps to Mower's assistance, so it was properly positioned and ready. Resume your attack, Howard told Mower; Blair will be in support. Logan was to cooperate by attacking the rifle pits to his front.[50] Mower eagerly pushed Fuller's brigade back to the top of the hill. There the troops halted and resupplied themselves with ammunition, preparing to advance once again. "All this was done and well done; but just as Mower was again confidently leading a connected column against the same Confederate flank with better prospects of a complete success . . . General Sherman called him back . . . and also withdrew Blair's entire command."[51]

Sherman countermanded Howard, issuing a direct order to once again "bring Fuller back down the hill and put him in the gap between" Tillson and Force.[52] Concentrate on establishing a firm connection with Manning Force's division, Mower was told. "I think I made a mistake there," Sherman reflected later, "and should rapidly have followed Mower's lead with the whole of the Right Wing, which would have brought on a general battle, and it could not have resulted otherwise than successfully to us."[53]

According to Howard, Sherman's "final action created much feeling at the time, and some severity of criticism." Sherman explained his action afterward: "One reason he gave was that Mower was apt to be too rash and he thought he was acting of his own motion; another that he had over estimated Johnston's force; and still another, that there had been bloodshed enough, and that Johnston would surely retreat northward and leave him to go on and complete his connections and establish his new base of supplies. None of these reasons fully satisfied our officers at the time."[54] These explanations certainly did not satisfy Howard, who had "call[ed] Blair to account" for failing to carry out his order. Blair responded, "The withdrawal is by Sherman's order." Howard remained unhappy about the botched opportunity.[55]

It appears that Sherman vacillated in midafternoon, changing his mind at least once. At 3:00 P.M. he must have known that Mower's bold envelopment was under way, for at that time he had sent the following dispatch to Kilpatrick: "I think General Mower got around the flank toward Mill Creek, threatening the enemy's line of retreat. Look out, and in case of a general battle hold your cavalry massed and dash at infantry toward the Mill Creek bridge on the road from Bentonville to Smithfield."[56] Additionally, Sherman alerted Slocum about the crisis on the right. Send a brigade of infantry supported with a section of artillery, Sherman directed, around the Confederate right. Threaten Mill Creek bridge from the west; that should put pressure on Joe Johnston. "Make it two brigades if you prefer," Slocum told corps commander Alpheus Williams. "Kilpatrick will cooperate."[57]

In response to Sherman's order, Alpheus Williams moved forward portions of Ward's and Jackson's divisions (two brigades each). They advanced cautiously, with heavy lines of skirmishers preceding the main bodies. As the leading elements of Jackson's division neared the lines of the Army of Tennessee, the order was countermanded. Ward and Jackson broke off their reconnaissance-in-force and withdrew before any serious fighting developed. Williams evidently regarded this Twentieth Corps effort as inconsequential for he neglected to mention it in his official report. Slocum simply stated that the "enemy was forced into his works." Davis's Fourteenth Corps was not involved; Kilpatrick apparently remained in position as well. In effect, Williams, like Logan and Blair, had made a demonstration "in favor of Mower."[58]

Although Mower pulled back, the rest of the Right Wing remained heavily engaged in "quite a noisy battle." Logan's divisions under twenty-nine-year-old John M. Corse (the "hero of Allatoona") and C. R. Woods again sent waves of skirmishers across the ravine. They forced the stubborn Confederates out of their isolated rifle pits or simply overran them. Back to their lines fled the rebels. In support of the infantry Howard's two forward batteries blasted away, ripping Confederate breastworks. Logan's men carried their attacks to the rim of the enemy fortifications, but there they stalled and the men retired back to the old Confederate skirmish line, which they worked feverishly to reverse. The rebels, of course, could not tolerate Logan's men remaining so dangerously close. "Repeatedly the Rebels dash out of their works, making frantic attempts to retake the rifle pits . . . , but they are as often driven back."[59] The rebel sorties, which appear to have struck primarily in Logan's sector, were thrown back repeatedly with heavy losses. It was simply a bloody repetition of the early afternoon fighting, some thought, but this time Woods's division and part of Corse's captured and held the rebel rifle pits, thus exerting enormous pressure on the left flank of the enemy main line.[60]

Giles A. Smith's division also made a strong demonstration "to create a diversion in favor of Mower." Closely supported by a line of battle, Smith's skirmishers, like Logan's, drove past the rebel rifle pits to the base of their works. Some soldiers "actually fell on the parapet." Fortunately one of the wounded (left for dead in the attack) turned up a few days later, "a modern Lazarus." "He wore a large patch near his nose, and a bandage around his head, a rifle ball having passed through his cheek, making its exit behind the opposite ear."[61]

Particularly punished in the attacks by Smith's division was William W. Belknap's predominately Iowa brigade, volunteers and conscripts alike: "In the charge one poor fellow, a drafted man (for which class the veteran volunteers manifested a supercilious contempt), bent over the ground as the line came well under fire. 'You—'connie' (conscript), come on and fight!' yelled an officer. 'Wait till I tie my shoe, and you'll see how a 'connie' will fight!' was the answer. He finished tying his shoe, for that is what he was really doing, regained his position, and fell dead on the enemy's works."[62]

Darkness fell but the fighting did not stop. Each brigade of the six Right Wing divisions on line put about half of its men in advanced works, and with the rebels almost in pistol range, skirmishing continued all night. "Several times, at the least sign, real or imaginary, of an advance or charge, the firing broke out in a perfect fury, sending a storm of bullets, ball and shells into the opposite line and as often bring everyone in the front to his position in the line of battle." Impatiently waiting for dawn men stood or sat in the water-filled ditches, not daring to sleep, unable to stop nodding off.[63]

Howard's guns added to the misery of the night. "Firing at intervals of fifteen minutes to each gun was kept up during the night." Rebel sharp-shooters would instantly respond, firing at the bright blasts. Nevertheless, the Federal tactic of "fire then immediately get cover" thwarted the Confederates' deadly volleys. Harass them, keep them awake, that was the idea. Do not let the firing stop. "Our cannoneers," wrote Howard, "continued to fire their projectiles from time to time during the whole night, lodging them as they believed, somewhere within Johnston's camps."[64]

So the dark hours passed with bullets flying, shells bursting, and tree branches crashing to earth. It also "rained in torrents," cold March rain, all night long. It was impossible to keep dry—"The ground is covered with several inches of water." Worst of all was the creek bottom—the swamp where many of Howard's weary soldiers hunched down in their precious mud holes, guarding them with their lives. Would the rain never end?[65]

Sherman must have smiled to himself, nevertheless. All in all, Tuesday, March 21, had been a very good day.

12

Nip and Tuck

JOHNSTON HAD TAKEN the precaution of pulling back his guns (Atkins's ten pounders) from the salient during the late afternoon of Monday, March 20. He allowed the gunners and drivers to rest past midnight, then sent them back into their mud redoubts before daylight. Tuesday's dawn brought flat gray light instead of sunshine—the kind of morning dullness rifle marksmen appreciate. It augured death for gunners. Just as they poked the noses of their pieces into embrasures, Yankee sharpshooters opened fire. Pvt. John H. Curtis, was hit almost immediately.[1] Then the sharpshooters, those relentless enemies of cannoneers, raised their sights and took aim at the faithful battery horses standing patiently in the rear. Several animals were wounded or killed before the remainder were led deep into the woods.[2]

Atkins's gunners spent a miserable morning hunkered down behind their parapets, hiding from the sharpshooters. From time to time they glanced up at the unsympathetic sky, which threatened, then burst into rain before noon. Other than the sharpshooters' "annoyance," the Yankees remained curiously inactive along Stewart's and Taliaferro's front. On the left, to the contrary, Sherman's men had pressed hard since dawn against Hoke and McLaws. Why was the right "unmolested?" Johnston wondered. Adding to his suspicions came worrisome news of activity on the extreme right. A. P. Stewart, at 10:25 A.M., had received reports of Federal attempts to turn Taliaferro's flank.[3] The information seemed not only puzzling but also contradictory. To ascertain, to confirm the intelligence, Johnston ordered the entire right (the Army of Tennessee plus Taliaferro's Division) to advance a strong skirmish line. Enemy resistance proved light and hesitant so the Confederate skirmishers probed deeper. In Hill's sector they drove back the Yankees steadily and soon recaptured Willis Cole's house, flushing sharpshooters from their nest in the top story. Then they burned the house and the outbuildings as well "to prevent their further use by the Yankee sharpshooters."[4]

Johnston sifted the intelligence received from this reconnaissance-in-force by Stewart and Taliaferro, trying to make sense of it. The threat to the right flank (beyond Taliaferro) appeared to be a feint, so he discounted it. Sherman, Johnston concluded, ostensibly "had drawn back his left and entrenched it, as if to cover a march toward Goldsborough."[5] This would be well and good. If the enemy abandoned the battlefield and crossed the Neuse, Johnston did not fear an immediate thrust west toward Smithfield from the force in Goldsboro or, indeed, from Sherman himself once north of the Neuse.[6] Yet, if this passiveness on Johnston's right represented the beginning of a Yankee withdrawal toward Goldsboro, how could one explain the pressure, the "very brisk firing," on the left—against McLaws and Hoke? It sounded too serious for a diversion—a cover operation. In any event, the Union army appeared during early Tuesday afternoon to be aligning itself in a giant *S* with the upper bulge, the lines nearest Johnston, puffed out just west of Goldsboro road—along the eastern edge of the ravine.

As the afternoon of the twenty-first wore on, however, the upper portion of this bulge seemed to be swelling northward toward Mill Creek in an echelon or lapping fashion. McLaws had sent word through Hardee. The situation seemed so threatening that McLaws had brought up Washington Hardy's Brigade and put it on line, to Fiser's left. Even this response proved insufficient, so McLaws took a couple of regiments from Gen. John D. Kennedy (in reserve behind Harrison and Hoke) and placed them beyond Hardy.[7] These units connected loosely with Joe Wheeler's dismounted cavalry, thus giving the left the look if not the feel of coherence.

It still was not enough, evidently. Even after strengthening his line with these dispositions, McLaws continued to hear firing farther left, so he rode over to investigate, accompanied by Maj. Samuel L. Black of Hardee's staff. Interrogating cavalry pickets as they went, the two officers discovered that Wheeler now occupied a road that "started about a quarter mile from town [&] ran around into the Goldsboro road. . . . Seeing at a glance the importance of the position [I] returned & reported the result of my observation to Genl Hardee at Genl. Johnston's headquarters."[8] This apparent vulnerability of the left flank, combined with the evident withdrawal of the enemy facing Stewart, caused Johnston to order Hardee to switch Taliaferro's Division from the right to the left. This would place Hardee's corps (McLaws and Taliaferro) and Hoke's Division on the left, leaving only Stewart's Army of Tennessee on the right.

Stewart's position was dangerously thin. Bate's corps, which now had become the extreme right of the army, extended its lines to cover the wide space left by Taliaferro's withdrawal. Bate replaced Taliaferro's Division (which was larger than Bate's corps) with Tyler's Brigade (which numbered about 100). The new arrangement stretched the main line of Bate's corps "three to five feet apart in single rank . . . I kept Taliaferro's pickets on post; will retain them. There is no cavalry on my right that I can find, and I made search. The enemy can come in there with impunity."[9]

Regardless of how well founded was Bate's nervousness about the frailty of the Confederate right, the opposite flank still appeared more threatened, more vulnerable. By midafternoon, all along the Confederate left, Federals had crashed across the swamp into the rifle pits of Hoke and McLaws. Their strong, bold skirmish lines hit hard. "The yankee skirmishers charged up nearly to our breastworks."[10] Sometimes they were beaten off. Once, at least, Fiser required the assistance of a North Carolina "militia" unit.[11] But sometimes repulse required counterattack. A member of the 1st Georgia Regulars reported one of these charges made by Fiser's Brigade:

> Our skirmish line was then ordered forward to retake our rifle pits. As the boys mounted our works and advanced, a private in Company C lagged behind his comrades and finally got behind a tree and stayed. Col. [Richard A.] Wayne ordered 1st sergeant of his company to shoot him, but he begged the colonel to excuse him. Col. Wayne told the sergeant to hand him his rifle, which he did. Col. Wayne placed the gun to his shoulder and called to the fellow behind the tree to advance, which he did in double-quick time.[12]

Fiser's Georgians recaptured their rifle pits, then to their astonishment received fire from Yankee fieldpieces. How could the enemy have advanced its cannon through all the mud and water and forest tangle? Fiser's rifle pits were struck by solid shot. "The first one grazed one of our head logs. Almost in a twinkling of an eye every log was on the ground and the shelling was kept up for some time."[13]

Punch and counterpunch—thus went the fighting on the left throughout Tuesday afternoon. The rain continued and grew even heavier. The attacks against the rifle pits of Fiser and Hardy showed that the Federals were extending their line rapidly and in force all along the ravine toward Mill Creek in a great whipping fashion.[14] The need for Taliaferro's support was obvious.[15]

Until Taliaferro arrived, however, cavalry must hold the unfortified portion of the left flank—the area between McLaws's left and Mill Creek. Cavalry commander Wade Hampton had divided the responsibility between Evander M. Law and Joe Wheeler. Law (with two small brigades from the Army of Northern Virginia) was thrown well forward between Mill Creek and Goldsboro road scouting and picketing, in effect wrapping around the right flank of Blair's Seventeenth Corps. Law's brigades—Butler's (Mully Logan) and Young's (Col. Gilbert J. "Gib" Wright)—were supported by one three-pounder from Earle's horse battery. To fill in between Law's advanced position and McLaws's line, Hampton had summoned Wheeler back to the left at 6:45 A.M.[16] Bring "all of your available men," Hampton directed. It appears that Wheeler originally took position on the opposite side of the ravine in advance of McLaws's refused line.[17] Then, as McLaws came on line and deployed behind the swamp, Wheeler released and concentrated on establishing a semblance of a line from McLaws's left to Mill Creek, a distance Wheeler estimated as about 1,200 yards.

Wheeler assigned William W. Allen's Georgia-Alabama cavalry division the right sector of this line and Col. Henry M. Ashby's Tennessee cavalry division the left. The troopers dismounted and dug in. The "breastworks" they created might temporarily give the appearance of fortifications and thus deceive, but to think they could withstand infantry skirmishers was fatuous. No one knew better than Wheeler. His cavalry could delay, perhaps "string out," an enemy infantry envelopment. It could not stop the envelopment. Nevertheless, to provide flexibility, depth, and some counterstrike capability, Wheeler kept a portion of his command mounted in the rear (two of Col. Baxter Smith's regiments—the 8th Texas Cavalry and the 4th Tennessee Cavalry of Ashby's division).[18]

Not long after 1:30 P.M. a wide advancing line of Federals on the extreme left drove off Mully Logan's and Gib Wright's cavalry skirmishers and vedettes.[19] Law's cavalry gave way rapidly, and Law himself rode to the rear to report the deteriorating situation to Hampton. Hampton, who was busy hunting a force to be sent out on the extreme right of the army (near Blackman's Pond), told Law to call on Wheeler for help. Wheeler, however, had his hands full. He "refused to extend his line to the left, claiming that it was thin enough."[20]

Unable to procure reinforcements, Law galloped back to his command and found Capt. William E. Earle with one gun firing point-blank at the approaching enemy. He was unsupported, Mully Logan's South Carolina cavalry having "stampeded" to the rear. Law, "seeing the line of Federal infantry, said, 'Capt. Earle, get your gun out of here.'" Earle limbered up and escaped but had to leave his caisson behind.[21]

On came the Yankees. They broke out of the swamp, up onto the high ground where Earle had positioned his piece, over through the pine and blackjack into a scattering of fields adjacent to the Smithfield-Bentonville road and the village of Bentonville itself. In one of these open areas the skirmishers in blue discovered the Confederate field hospital, abandoned except for helpless, immobile patients. Nearby some Yankees even poked their heads into the John Benton log house (Johnston's headquarters)![22] They were in sight of the Devil's Racetrack,[23] and, if they had looked very carefully down the road and through the woods, they might have seen the bridge across Mill Creek.[24] These patches of Federal skirmishers, of course, threatened Johnston and his men with disaster. If supported, they would command the Confederates' line of communications, their "only line of retreat." Col. Benton Roy, Hardee's chief of staff, recorded in his diary that the enemy (two divisions, he believed) "broke thro' Cavalry picket line on Extreme left & penetrated to the church—into the town & within two hundred yds of bridge."[25]

A Confederate private underlined the importance of the bridge. It "spans a deep creek which runs close to the little town of Bentonville, and owing to the recent rains is very much swollen, and not fordable any where; therefore it is very important for us to hold the bridge."[26]

This final crisis in the life of the Army of Tennessee was to be resolved by desperate counterattack. When he learned that his left flank had been turned, Johnston entrusted Hardee with the urgent mission. Drive back the enemy. Give the army time to repair the breakthrough. Taliaferro's Division was on its way. Hardee had to buy time. He must reverse the battle's tempo.

Fortunately Wade Hampton was already on the spot. Preoccupied with stationing a cavalry force on the extreme right, Hampton had brushed aside Evander Law's alarm. But when he saw with his own eyes Federals penetrating toward the field hospital, Hampton stationed himself on the Smithfield road and set to work feverishly organizing a hasty defense. He found a section of Capt. H. M. Stuart's battery already limbered up, so he hurried it forward and put it in position along the road, facing southeast.[27] In the emergency Hampton's staff and even Evander Law became crews serving these two pieces. Hampton also sent a staff officer to bring up the nearest infantry—Cumming's Brigade, which was being held in reserve 400 yards behind Hoke.[28]

Hampton's aide happily encountered Cumming's Brigade already in column marching in double-quick time north on the Smithfield road toward the bridge. At its head was Lt. Col. Benton Roy. Passing General Johnston as it hurried down the road, "The brigade cheered [Johnston] lustily, but he motioned with his hand for them to cease, and lifting his hat . . . said, 'Don't cheer me, boys. I should cheer you.' "[29] It was a pitifully short column, however—only two hundred troops.[30] A battered combat unit, these Georgians had lost their old commander, Alfred Cumming, disabled by wounds, at Jonesboro. Three months later, led by Col. Robert J. Henderson, 42d Georgia, they had met disaster at Nashville when half of the brigade had been captured. By the time it arrived in North Carolina, Cumming's Brigade was a shadow of itself.

The men were fortunate, nevertheless, in having Henderson as their new commander. An observant Confederate noted that Henderson "was remarkably expert in managing his command on the field of battle. . . . In short, he was a superb soldier, of splendid appearance, and a magnificent horseman."[31]

Assigned to guard a trainload of precious artillery near Smithfield, Cumming's Brigade had missed the fight on Sunday and marched down the following day. Although it belonged to Stevenson's Division, which was on line with the Army of Tennessee, Johnston had stationed the Georgia brigade in reserve on the left. Once he received the assignment to halt the Yankee breakthrough, Hardee looked about for the nearest infantry. No one knew better than he that only infantry could restore the breach in the line. Immediately he sent Roy to bring up Colonel Henderson. "Genl. H seized this Brigade," Roy recorded in his diary, and formed them into two lines on both sides of the Bentonville-Smithfield road. From this point Henderson (who had been reconnoitering while Roy brought up the brigade) led the men toward the enemy, angling right as he observed the Federal skirmishers "drawing off" toward high ground.[32]

Hardee also sent staff officers to bring over Joseph B. Palmer's and Alpheus Baker's Brigades, the reserves for A. P. Stewart's right. Of more immediate help were Wheeler's reserves—two regiments of Col. Baxter Smith's brigade, the 4th Tennessee Cavalry and 8th Texas Cavalry. Hardee commandeered them as well. Joe Wheeler himself had anticipated that they would be required on the far left, so he had alerted them and brought them back to the Bentonville-Smithfield road. There Hardee's staff officer, Lt. Col. D. G. White, found them mounted and "standing in column."[33]

White ordered the cavalrymen down the road to the left. As Baxter Smith brought them toward Bentonville "at a gallop in columns of four," one of his men noted: "The field hospital of General Johnston's army was close by, and as the command passed down the road, we could see men escaping from the hospital and a general scattering of men, evidencing that something of a stirring nature was happening. We found General Hardee standing in the road about half a mile . . . from where we started. . . . There was some artillery immediately in our rear that fired over our heads." Hardee ordered the cavalry "into line along the road." The 8th Texas (Terry's Texas Rangers) deployed on the left facing southeast; Baxter Smith's own 4th Tennessee deployed on the Rangers' right.[34]

What followed was a magnificent, audacious counterattack, conducted by only a handful of troops but fortuitously coordinated and splendidly led. From the left came Wade Hampton and Col. Gib Wright leading about 300 dismounted Georgia troopers at the dead run. Wright, leader of Cobb's legion, the cavalry commander who had almost captured Kilpatrick in the daring attack at Monroe's Crossroads, was a former infantryman himself. Possessed of "bulldog courage," Gib Wright was the perfect man for the moment.[35] He and Hampton quickly formed "a new line at right angles to the old," then "struck the [right] of the enemy (as they emerged from the swamp), squarely,"[36] creating panic among the surprised Federal skirmishers. From the Confederate right (the Yankees had penetrated well beyond the left flank of Wheeler's cavalry skirmish line) came Wheeler with Hagan's Alabama brigade, also dismounted. These 500 cavalrymen were led by their division commander William W. Allen, a Princetonian planter-turned-soldier, and Hardee's staff officer, D. G. White. They charged through partially cleared woods and maintained a reasonably tight formation. Allen's assault on foot was aided substantially by "timely enfilade" fire from the 10th Confederate Cavalry of Col. Robert H. Anderson's Brigade. Other cavalrymen seem to have joined in—fragments of regiments and brigades, officers and men on an individual basis, some mounted, some on foot. Henry Ashby, for instance, gathered together a block of men, apparently mostly Tennesseans, and threw them into the charge. Riding beside Ashby was his old Knoxville friend, Col. Richard M. Saffell, former commander of the 26th Tennessee Infantry, now a supernumerary. Saffell would be killed in this attack against the Yankee left along with Lt. Col. Abijah F. Boggess, Saffell's former second in command.[37] This menagerie of mounted and dismounted

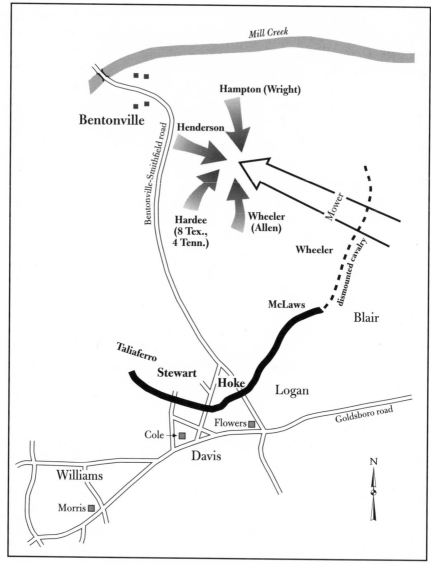

Map 9. Mower Punctures Johnston's Left

horsemen, led by Wheeler, Allen, and Ashby,[38] smashed through the Union skirmish line "with such dare-devil ferocity as to throw it into great confusion" and took about fifty prisoners.[39]

Meanwhile, from the center came Henderson's two lines of infantry in line of battle driving the Federal skirmishers before them. The Georgians charged at the double-quick. The enemy skirmish lines scattered and fell back on their regiments "that had just begun to entrench on the crest of a slope." The first Yankee line of battle buckled, then the second. The Federals fled over half a mile, back to a second position "in open piney woods. . . . They began to pepper away. . . . We halted 80 yards away and all that could got behind trees."[40] By the time Henderson neared this line at the edge of the swamp, the Federals had regrouped and "began to close in on us from both sides." In the meantime the Confederate cavalry charging on both sides of the infantry had fallen back. Colonel Henderson found himself almost isolated, his left flank in air, his right "lapped" by an advancing line of the enemy that extended "as far as could be seen."[41] Prudently Henderson retreated at once and hastily, his right regiment becoming "somewhat scattered." The Yankees broke off their pursuit, fortunately, allowing Henderson to re-form some 400 yards back. Hardee spotted him there, complimented him and the brigade on their splendid charge, then ordered them to entrench on the right of Taliaferro, who had just come up.

Men rushed to congratulate Colonel Henderson, the forty-two-year-old Georgia farmer–flour miller turned combat leader. His infantry, they said, had saved the army. Division commander Carter Stevenson reported, "No encomium that I can pass . . . will be so expressive a recognition of its gallant behavior as the simple statement that it received upon the field the thanks and compliments of General Johnston."[42] Old Joe lifted his hat in salute and praised the tiny brigade publicly. It thrilled the men. As they cheered the commanding general, one Georgia private thought to himself, "we would have charged Old Nick himself if Joe Johnston had ordered us to."[43]

While Henderson struck the face of the Union advance, Wheeler's reserve cavalry regiments hit its left. Baxter Smith led his old 4th Tennessee. Following Hardee's direction, Smith's troopers left the Smithfield road, passed "over and down the slope of a hill," and "came into view of a line of enemy skirmishers extending half a mile across the field." The Yankees opened fire but were clearly startled, "and as we rode in among them, using our 'navies,' we scattered them and forced them back to their main line, a distance of several hundred yards."[44] As he approached the enemy line of battle, Smith dismounted his regiment, ordering horses to the rear. The troopers resumed their advance, throwing down a fence and once again engaging the Federal infantry's skirmish line. At this point they received orders from Wheeler to retire to the main line. The courier who brought this order to Baxter Smith was killed just as he delivered it. As they fell back, Smith encountered General Hardee returning from a similar assault. Hardee complimented Smith for the "success of his gallant charge."[45]

Hardee himself had remained with the 8th Texas. He saw Baxter Smith and his men formed and ready to make the charge, so he rode over to the mounted Texans and asked, " 'Who commands this regiment?' " Capt. John F. "Doc" Matthews replied that he did. Matthews, "a smooth-faced boy" promoted "by the bullets of the enemy," had been in command only two days for on Sunday, March 19, Maj. William R. Jarmon, the last of a dozen commanders of the Rangers, had been wounded. Lt. Col. Gustave Cook had been disabled earlier at Bentonville. Of course, this was no surprise. Cook had been hit so many times that the Rangers dubbed him "their Yankee lead mine."[46] Such had been the fate of this ill-starred regiment since the combat death of its original colonel, Benjamin F. Terry, in December 1861; 1,170 men had shrunk to 80.

A new recruit had transferred in. "Scarcely sixteen," Willie Hardee, the only son of the general, had run away from school in Marietta, Georgia, a year earlier, "wrought upon by a generous military enthusiasm, and captivated by the renoun [sic] of Terry's Rangers." His father naturally found out and "took him on his staff," wrote Benton Roy. Willie "won his spurs at Resaca where he had a horse killed under him and did a soldier's duty throughout the campaign."[47] Willie had become everyone's favorite. Even the general's reticent, task-oriented engineering officer, Lt. Col. William D. Pickett, a veteran staff officer with the reputation of being slow to compliment, confessed, "I was much attached to him, as were all who knew him." When his father assumed command of the Department of South Carolina, Georgia, and Florida, Willie went along but found staff life in Charleston tame. He enlisted in Stuart's South Carolina light artillery battery, fought with that unit in the defense of the Salkehatchie line and at Averasboro, and accompanied the guns to Bentonville. On Tuesday, March 21, Stuart's battery came on line with McLaws's infantry, replacing the 8th Texas. Willie saw his chance, walked over, and presented himself once again for enlistment in Terry's Texas Rangers.[48] "The soldiers of the Regiment, proud of the boy's preference for it, urged him to join them." But Captain Ferg Kyle of Company D (who had reported the underage Willie previously) dutifully sent word to the general. This time, however, Hardee relented. "Swear him into service in your company," he told Kyle, "as nothing else will satisfy."[49]

In an odd circumstance of history Willie thus joined the outfit preparing to charge the skirmishers of Mower's division, Seventeenth Corps, Oliver O. Howard's Right Wing. Howard, a close friend of the Hardee family at West Point before the war, had been Willie's personal tutor and had grown fond of the boy.

William Joseph Hardee
(National Archives)

The Rangers were relaxing in reserve when General Wheeler himself rode up. "He seemed a little excited. 'Captain,'" he shouted to Doc Matthews, "'mount your men, go as fast as you can and charge whatever you find at the bridge.'"[50] The young Texas cavalry leader and his men knew full well that a Yankee breakthrough at Mill Creek Bridge could spell disaster for the army. Matthews quickly had his troopers in their saddles, and, accompanied by a Hardee staff officer, they set out pell-mell down the Smithfield road toward the village. "Within about half a mile of the bridge we passed a small brigade of infantry [Cumming's] 'double quicking' in the same direction. We saluted each other with a cheer as we passed, for all felt that it was a critical time in the battle."[51]

They came upon General Hardee, who was observing from some high ground. "We had a good view of the enemy across an open field about 500 yards distant." The column closed up, and Hardee ordered Captain Matthews to have the Rangers face to the right in line, then directed the Rangers to charge the advancing enemy. "It looked like the old regiment was this time surely going to its grave. . . . Matthews gave the order, 'Charge right in front,' and with that wonderful rebel yell we charged."[52]

An irresistible impulse seems to have overcome Hardee himself. Perhaps it was the presence of Willie—they tipped their hats to each other as Willie went into line. Perhaps it was the rush of old 2d Dragoon memories—the spontaneous dash at the stone bridge, Puente de Moreno. The forty-nine-year-old Confederate lieutenant general's fighting blood was up, and he attacked like a reckless eighteen-year-old. The Rangers rode directly toward the enemy. They "dashed by us at breakneck speed," a member of Cumming's Brigade related, "right into the line of infantry." They "broke through the line of skirmishers," reported Wheeler, "without breaking their impetus and pushed on, striking the main line almost the same moment with Allen's gallant Alabamians, which threw the entire force of the enemy in a most rapid and disorderly retreat." Having exhausted our carbines, "We rode them down and emptied our pistols at close range." The shock effect demoralized the Federals. "They fell back in confusion, the Rangers immediately withdrawing with quite a number of prisoners, bringing out their dead and wounded" and empty saddles.[53]

Among the casualties in Terry's Texas Rangers was Willie Hardee. He "was shot through the chest—a dangerous wound." "Held in his saddle by a Ranger who sat behind him," Willie was brought to the rear. Meanwhile his father, unaware of Willie's wound, rode back with Wade Hampton. Hardee's face was "bright with the light of battle," Hampton related. "He turned to me and exclaimed: 'That was Nip and Tuck, and for a time I thought Tuck had it.' " As he entered the Confederate lines Hardee saw Willie. He dismounted, went over to his wounded son, kissed him, and directed that he be placed in an ambulance and taken to the rear. Then the general "remounted and proceeded to give orders respecting the disposition of the troops."[54]

There were no Confederate ambulances, however, so Willie was placed in a wagon. He survived a tortuous wagon ride to Smithfield that night, then a train carried him on through Raleigh to Hillsborough. There, nursed by his stepmother and sisters, Willie lingered two days at Ayrmont, the home of his first cousin Susannah Hardee Kirkland, wife of William W. Kirkland, former W. J. Hardee staff officer and now one of Hoke's brigade commanders. Private Hardee died on March 24 and was buried "after the military funeral he would have wanted, in the churchyard of St. Matthew's Episcopal Church, Hillsborough, North Carolina."[55] Benton Roy, using stoic language his commander would have felt appropriate, noted in his diary on the twenty-fourth: "Genl H went to Hillsboro to be present at the funeral of his son."[56]

The Confederate cavalry commanders Wheeler, Hampton, Allen, and Hardee had bought precious time with their heady victory. "In as brilliant a charge as the war furnished,"[57] they, with the support of Cumming's infantry, had stopped and thrown back two veteran brigades of Sherman's boldest division. But it was no time to rest. Expecting a heavy attack at any moment, the Confederates immediately set to work extending fieldworks to Mill Creek, using, in the instance of Cumming's and Strahl's Brigades, picks and shovels dropped by the Yankees who had been caught in the act of entrenching.[58] Strahl's Brigade, commanded by Col. Carrick W. Heiskell, represented the first of Brown's Division of Cheatham's Corps arriving from Smithfield—a most welcome sight.[59]

Although six brigades from Cheatham's Corps had arrived or were arriving from Smithfield,[60] Johnston singlemindedly continued to brace his left with almost every man he had. Quite rightly did he anticipate what should have been Sherman's next move. Into line went Taliaferro's Division as well as the three reserve brigades of Hill's corps: Henderson, Palmer, and Baker. Believing that he was still too weak on the left, Johnston stripped Stewart's right of Bate's corps and Loring's old corps now commanded by Walthall. This left only Harvey Hill on the right commanding three greatly diminished divisions. Johnston also pulled out Hagood's Brigade from Hoke's line, filling the gap with Clingman's Brigade, which had occupied a second line. Thus Johnston had changed front entirely. His army now faced east holding a line from Cole's house on the right to Mill Creek on the left. It had no reserves. Actually tactical logic left him no choice.[61]

And the Yankees did attack again—before dark, all along the line—from Hill's salient to beyond the limits of McLaws's position. Some of the troops had time to dig in; others did not. Baker's Brigade, which had been so roughly handled by William Cogswell on Sunday afternoon, came on line beside McLaws "on a bald pine ridge. We had to lie down behind stumps, trees, logs, etc., but many of us had no protection from the fire of sharp-shooters for an hour or more till dark, losing a few of our number, while we had orders to hold our fire unless we were pressed by an advance." Hoke's Division, to Baker's right, had a desperate fight as well. Clingman's Brigade under Col. William S. Devane managed to repel attacks by the Fifteenth Corps but suffered casualties including Devane himself wounded.[62]

On McLaws's front the enemy captured a line of rifle pits about "a hundred yards wide," which put them perilously close to the main line of breastworks.[63] McLaws ordered that the rifle pits "be retaken at all hazards," so one-armed John C. Fiser directed that four men be selected from each company. They would constitute the brigade counterstroke force and make the foray from the breastworks to the pits: "About this time I heard Col. Wayne [1st Georgia Regulars] cry out, 'Where is Fort?' I knew my time had come. I was commanded to lead the charge to retake the pits. Handed my overcoat and blanket to Sgt. Duke and asked him to care for them, and standing on our entrenchments, sword in hand, I commanded the detail 'forward.' The men rose and charged."[64]

Lt. John Porter Fort led Fiser's storming party of about one hundred men through their own abatis. They moved slowly, cautiously. Once past this obstacle, Fort formed his troops into line. Then they charged down the slope "with a spirited yell." The Yankees occupying the rifle pits fired one volley at Fort's Georgians. Then they fled. Fort's men retook the pits with the loss of about four men and killed about the same number of Federals. Immediately they set to work reversing the rifle pits so that they faced east once again. The enemy did not attack through the swamp a second time but attempted "to dislodge us by shelling, but we refused to abandon them." "Shooting from our pits and skirmishing with the enemy continued until late at night. It is astonishing how few were killed by this wild shooting in the dark; the flash of guns and the bursting of shells were incessant. . . . A shell burst in the pit in which I was standing with the men, covered us with a column of sand, without injury to any of us."[65]

As the night wore on it became even more dangerous in the pits. To their rear, men in the breastworks became jumpy; they were apt to fire at anything forward of the main line—anything that moved. An officer on Hoke's line reported: "The enemy's line of battle was within three hundred yards of our works, where they threw up breastworks & continued heavy demonstrations against us. No fires were allowed at night. It rained nearly all day & night. My feet were soaking wet & my overcoat saturated. I lay on the wet ground with nothing over me & got a few moments of hurried sleep."[66]

Obviously the Confederates were in a precarious position; they were badly outnumbered, with a single route of retreat within reach of a determined enemy attack. This is why Johnston gambled by stripping troops from his right. An even greater gamble would have been to have maintained his right flank. He must protect the Bentonville-Smithfield road. In an important respect this risk taking worked to Johnston's advantage, for it positioned the army favorably for withdrawal. According to McLaws, Johnston had determined by midafternoon to "fall back that night on the road to Raleigh." The removal of the wounded had been "very slow," indeed maddeningly slow. "We had no ambulances," explained Johnston, "and very few wagons." That is why withdrawal was delayed from March 20 to 21. Before midnight on Tuesday, the twenty-first, however, all the wounded "that could bear transportation had been removed." It was time to go.[67]

Soon after dark all the artillery was removed and tugged through Bentonville "over roads in which we plunged almost kneedeep at every step."[68] Although a great hindrance, the torrents of rain actually benefited the process of disengaging from the enemy—muffled sounds discouraged Yankee probing. First out and over the bridge was the artillery, then the infantry began pulling back by echelon at 2:00 A.M. beginning with those positioned closest to Mill Creek. Hoke would pull out last, although pickets would man the breastworks until 3:00 A.M. "to impress the enemy" that Johnston still held his position. Under cover of chilling rain and extreme darkness the army crept out of the trenches back to the Smithfield road, then sludged through Bentonville and across Mill Creek. The road was incredibly bad— "fearful abysses of mud." Until they reached the bridge it was an extremely nervous movement. The Yankees might discover their absence and lunge forward at any moment, ripping apart the fragile picket line. Meanwhile, enemy shells kept screaming over the abandoned breastworks, hitting and exploding near the Smithfield road "at intervals of only a few seconds, it was kept up until dawn, and I suppose was intended to prevent our crossing. The line of fire was from ten to twenty steps to the right of the road. It was dark and the range not exact, and it did but little damage."[69]

At last Hoke pulled out of line, then the infantry pickets—all except some men of Rhett's Brigade, Taliaferro's Division. They did not get the word and the brigade's entire picket line was captured, as was a group of Hoke's men, victims of conflicting orders in the darkness. "The night was a wild one. The pine-forest had taken fire, and at frequent intervals the crash of burning, falling trees mingled with . . . the occasional boom of cannon. Slowly the defeated army filed along the road lighted by tens of thousands of blazing torches."[70]

The last of the infantry did not clear the bridge over flooded Mill Creek until after sunrise. This put great pressure on Wheeler's cavalrymen who covered the rear. Many had remained in the infantry breastworks protracting the show of force, then they mounted and gradually withdrew. The Federals, however, began to press and before daylight advanced a skirmish line. Finally the enemy came on "with great vigor," reported Wheeler, "making it necessary to dismount most of my men and fight with considerable warmth." Wheeler expected to gain his breath once across Mill Creek. To his dismay he found that the infantry assigned to destroy the bridge across Mill Creek had failed to do so. Wheeler had men remove the flooring and toss it into the creek, but he knew that expedient would stop the enemy only momentarily.[71]

Meanwhile, Johnston's infantry marched on and by midmorning had crossed Hannah's Creek about two miles north of Mill Creek. Once across, Johnston had McLaws form into line and establish a defensive position. Near the creek bank itself Johnston masked a section of artillery. He halted the remainder of the army in column well down the Smithfield road out of range. There he allowed the troops to rest and eat. While McLaws's infantry dug in, Hampton supervised the burning of the bridge.

It was not long before Wheeler appeared at Hannah's Creek, closely followed by determined Yankee infantry skirmishers. Wheeler's men forded the river and lined the opposite bank. The enemy skirmishers formed into column and attempted to charge across the burning bridge. They were met with heavy fire, particularly from the concealed guns. It was a sharp, resolute Union thrust. Three color-bearers fell just short of Wheeler's line. The Federals evidently realized that they required more manpower to force a crossing, so they withdrew. Soon after, to the Confederates' joy, the Yankees pulled back to Mill Creek and destroyed the wagon bridge at Bentonville. Wheeler kept an eye on them.[72]

At noon on March 22 the weary Confederate infantrymen were roused from their sleep and took up their tramp again. The rain had stopped, but a high wind had come up making it a "dusty Disagreeable day, smokey," "the air filled with fine sand." Compounding the misery of retreat, Hardee, tired and heartsick, had taken the wrong road with Taliaferro's troops. In mid-afternoon he wrote Johnston about the road "which I have been working on and pulling wagons through all the morning. . . . The wagons on this road must go forward, as they can't be turned back." On they went, though, on two separate roads until the entire army had crossed Black Creek about nightfall. Once across, Johnston gave orders for the troops to rest at an old campsite used during the concentration at Smithfield the previous week. They dropped in their tracks, exhausted. The next morning Harvey Hill wrote: "I then had a bed for the first time in three nights & I was so tired that I had hardly strength to pull off my coat. I have slept a good deal & feel better than I have for several months."[73]

On March 23 a weary and discouraged Johnston wired Robert E. Lee: "Sherman's course cannot be hindered by the small force I have. I can do no more than annoy him. I respectfully suggest that it is no longer a question whether you leave present position; you have only to decide where to meet Sherman. I will be near him."[74]

13

Sherman's Star

For Col. Robert F. Catterson, March 22 was a milestone—his thirtieth birthday. The rain had stopped, as if in recognition. Perhaps dawn would bring a fine day, perhaps the rebs would crack, perhaps there would be just one more attack. Catterson, impatient as any Irishman, wanted to settle things with the Johnnies.[1] He had given up his medical practice to enter the army and whip rebels; he wanted to be done with the job and get on with his life.

Catterson's brigade had not slept Tuesday night. Rain pounded the trench line, dissolving the carefully packed dirt. The men seemed to be sinking in muck. So they pounded the enemy in retaliation, the brigade firing some 17,000 cartridges during the night. Before dawn Catterson's patrols were out and cautiously advancing toward the rebel rifle pits "to feel of the enemy." Meeting no opposition they sent back word to Catterson, who relayed the news up the line. Push on aggressively, division commander Charles R. Woods directed. Catterson reinforced his skirmish line and advanced with a rush. His men cleared the enemy rifle pits without opposition, regrouped, spread out, then rushed the main fortifications. They were empty too. Woods immediately reported this news to Maj. Gen. John A. Logan, who ordered the division to continue toward Bentonville itself; Catterson's brigade would lead.[2]

Once his brigade had passed through the enemy abatis and muddy fieldworks, Catterson advanced quickly to the Bentonville-Smithfield road. There he redeployed: a skirmish line composed of two companies of the 26th Illinois acted as point, fanning out along both sides of the road. Behind them came the remainder of the regiment on an even wider front, then in column came the other six regiments of Catterson's big brigade. The rebel cavalry to their front gave way after token resistance. The pugnacious 26th

Illinois pressed on—up the road past Johnston's headquarters and the log building that had served as the Confederate hospital, on past the village itself, down to the creek bank. There it found the bridge over Mill Creek in flames. Some of Catterson's men ran forward just in time to toss flaming barrels of rosin off the bridge into Mill Creek. This quick action saved the bridge. The entire brigade then crossed the creek and boldly struck out along the Smithfield road toward Hannah's Creek, "driving our opponents in wild confusion."[3] Rebel cavalry attempted to contest its advance, but it clearly was only a delaying action: the Confederate infantry was in rapid retreat.

The brigade covered the two miles to Hannah's Creek without difficulty by midmorning. There it discovered rebel cavalry dismounted and in a strong position lining the bank. Once again the rebels had fired the bridge. And once again Catterson immediately launched a determined assault. Although they suffered casualties, Catterson's troops seized the bridge, extinguished the fire, and prepared to cross Hannah's Creek in force.

No sooner had they captured the bridge, however, than Gen. Charles R. Woods, who had halted his other brigades at Bentonville, ordered Catterson back to the southern side of Mill Creek. Return immediately, Woods directed his aggressive brigade commander, and take up a defensive position controlling the Mill Creek bridge.[4]

Although Catterson had captured Bentonville and had driven the Confederate rear guard across Hannah's Creek, another party had won an even more audacious victory that morning. The signal detachment from Logan's corps—Lt. William H. Sherfy and two privates—had moved out early "to establish a station of observation." The three men passed through abandoned Confederate lines and soon approached Mill Creek. They suddenly encountered rebel cavalry. Startled, Sherfy and his men looked about and found themselves unsupported. Nevertheless, when the enemy seemed hesitant to attack, Sherfy boldly took matters into his own hands. He rode up and told the rebel commander that he and his troops had been cut off. "Escape was impossible and at the same time I demanded their surrender." Thereupon the Confederates (five officers and seventy-five enlisted men) gave up and stacked arms. The fight seemed to have gone out of the rebels. Sherfy and his two men marched their long line of prisoners back to camp themselves.[5]

By midmorning Charles R. Woods's division had occupied Bentonville in force.[6] The troops looked about. The Confederate field hospital held some seriously wounded Confederates who had been left behind as well as about forty Federals. It was a gruesome scene at the hospital, "where was strewn around their operating tables, . . . many legs and arms which had been amputated, and a large number of bodies of men who had died from wounds while waiting attention." A number of dead Confederates were found along the road and in the woods. "Saw 2 rebels that had been burned by fire till cooked, horrible sight. There were six dead rebs to one union man." Just off the road, the Federals noticed a "large number of little mounds freshly thrown up." Woods's men, joined by parties from Mower's division and even some of Slocum's men, searched for unburied Federal dead. They found a few. Most of these had been robbed and stripped of their clothes. Lt. John Nilson, 25th Indiana, to his horror, discovered "3 or 4 of our men who had been beaten to Death. One of them had his head split open by an ax & one of his feet cut off." Jesse L. Dozer, 26th Ohio, confirmed what Nilson saw.[7]

Back on the battlefield, between Slocum's and A. P. Stewart's lines, a wandering detail from Absalom Baird's division found "many dead men unburied and lots of wounded Rebels one of which we took out of a pond of water and gave him a drink. He was wounded in the head and was delirious, but the water revived him and I enquired his name and he told me Francis White of the 4th Georgia and that his home was near Pond Spring. Then he seemed to think we were Johnies and said 'boys if I could kill one more Yankee I would die happy' and we left him."[8]

From a distance Bentonville itself seemed ablaze. Actually it was Mill Creek! In their eagerness to save the wagon bridge, Catterson's men had pushed off barrels of flaming rosin into the creek. But the rosin continued to burn in the water. Someone else had ignited a great pile of rosin at a factory on the creek bank—perhaps Catterson's men, perhaps rebels. The intense heat of the blaze on the bank and in the creek itself "caused the burning and melted rosin to flow down into the creek, until the bed of the stream was filled with the burning mass for several hundred yards," creating a "phenomenal spectacle."[9]

The poor trees—blasted and broken—had been disfigured terribly with "numbers of 'ramrods' sticking out of them." Pine and oak thickets, which had been on fire for three days, suddenly began blazing furiously, fanned by the high wind. Soon heavy smoke covered the battlefield, filling nostrils and choking throats. This ubiquitous smoke, coupled with the ceaseless, gusty wind, made what would have been a beautiful Wednesday into yet another misery to be endured.[10]

Nothing—not the bitter, insistent smoke, nor the grisly exhibits at Bentonville, nor Joe Johnston himself—could divert Sherman. The army continued its march to Goldsboro. As previously planned, the Left Wing led the way. Sherman wrote Howard: "Let Slocum have the roads today, and to-morrow move at your leisure to your new position [north of] Goldsborough. . . . I promise that no pains or efforts on my part shall be spared to supply your command in the most thorough manner before calling on them for new efforts."[11] Thus Howard spent the day removing the Union wounded and burying the dead while Slocum's Left Wing filed off to the east behind his position toward Goldsboro.[12]

Early that morning, when he learned that Johnston had evacuated and Woods's division was in pursuit, Sherman sent orders to Howard to halt his advance on the southern bank of Mill Creek. The order arrived too late, however—Catterson had already crossed and begun his push toward Hannah's Creek. So Catterson had to be recalled. Sherman wanted Howard to occupy Bentonville, control the bridge, and picket Mill Creek in order "to cover operations in the rear." One brigade (Catterson's) would suffice.[13]

Good news poured into Sherman's headquarters all morning: Johnston was gone, apparently in full retreat to Smithfield; Terry had secured Cox's Bridge, establishing a strong bridgehead across the Neuse; and Schofield had captured Goldsboro. "The three armies were in actual connection, and the great object of the campaign accomplished." After a ride to the battlefield and a cursory look around, Sherman went to Slocum's headquarters. There on the Goldsboro road, close to the Harper house, he stopped to watch troops of the Left Wing being put into column for their march to Goldsboro. A group of elated general officers surrounded Sherman—wing commanders Slocum and Howard and corps commanders Blair, Logan, Williams, and Davis—"a happy lot of men." They all congratulated their commander. He "thanked them and gave compliments in return." Then either Blair or Logan said that the March through Georgia and the Carolinas Campaign "would make him so popular that people would make him the next president." Sherman responded "curtly" that he had "no ambition to ever hold any political office and that he would never be candidate for president, and as for popularity, that was an uncertain factor."[14]

While the generals celebrated, their troops looked up through the smoky haze to a clear blue sky. There they saw a bright star (the planet Venus). The army, officers and men alike, regarded the unusual phenomenon as a happy omen, "sure it was the star of peace," "Immediate Peace." They called it "Sherman's star."[15]

It was a happy day for Sherman. He prepared a congratulatory order for the army:

> The General commanding announces to this army that yesterday it beat, on its chosen ground, the concentrated armies of our enemy, who has fled in disorder leaving his dead, wounded and prisoners in our hands and burning the bridges on his retreat.
>
> On the same day Maj. Gen. Schofield from New Berne entered and occupied Goldsboro and Maj. Genl. Terry from Wilmington secured Cox's Bridge crossing and laid a pontoon bridge across Neuse River.[16]

No one could accuse him of overstatement.

As soon as Sherman sent orders to Terry and Schofield and satisfied himself that Slocum and the ambulance train were well on their way, he bid his subordinates good-bye and set out with his staff for Cox's Bridge, just as he had three days earlier. After crossing Falling Creek, Sherman rode on to Cox's Bridge, arriving there late Wednesday afternoon. Supper with Terry, whom he had never met, followed. Then Sherman retired to his tent to write to his friend, Ulysses S. Grant. It was an upbeat letter. He reviewed the events of the past week and proudly concluded:

> We have over 2,000 prisoners from this affair and the one at Averasborough, and am satisfied that Johnston's army was so roughly handled yesterday that we could march right on to Raleigh, but we have now been out six weeks, living precariously upon the collections of our foragers, our men 'dirty, ragged, and saucy,' and we must rest and fix up a little. . . . I limited the pursuit this morning to Mill Creek, and will forthwith march the army to Goldsborough to rest, reclothe, and get some rations.[17]

On Thursday morning, March 23, Sherman crossed the Neuse and rode into Goldsboro accompanied by Terry. There they met with Schofield, congratulated each other on the end of the campaign, and began planning for the arrival of Slocum and Howard. The Left Wing marched in later that day, followed by the Right Wing on March 24. Once in Goldsboro the first order of business for each wing was a review by the commanding general. Sherman stood in front of his headquarters with Slocum, Schofield, Terry, and Howard beside him. The ragged veterans of the march from Savannah straightened up and stepped out. As they passed in review, the victorious troops fastened their eyes on their commander adoringly. Sherman received their "present arms" formally, but with scarcely concealed joy and affection. Maj. Gen. Jacob D. Cox observed, "[Sherman] is full of health and spirits, and is confident that his army is now able to meet the combined forces of Lee and Johnston as necessary." The whole army, though bedraggled and bone weary, seemed to agree.[18]

Sure as Sherman had promised, his troops received a long rest. First they feasted on rations hurried forward from Kinston, "the best the Grainerys of the north can aforde."[19] They got a new issue of clothing and shoes, then money—being paid for the first time in three months. Then precious mail was distributed: "we were in the heart of the rebel country where there was not much to do but fight and march and naire of our people did not know where we were and were so anxious about us that when we got our mail every boy got a lot of letters especially from our sweet hearts and they were so loving and sweet we just wanted to go home and hug those girls."[20]

Sherman knew his men. He knew what he could ask of them. "I would like to see them [rebels] whaled," thought one Federal, "but would like to wait till we refit. You see that too much of a good thing gets *old*, and one don't enjoy even campaigning after 50 or 60 days of it together." Another exclaimed, "Hurrah for mail and clean clothes." It was time for a break.[21]

On March 25, as soon as all his troops had reached Goldsboro and encamped, Sherman placed Schofield in charge of the combined army and set out for City Point, Virginia. There he would meet with General Grant and President Lincoln to plan the final campaign against Robert E. Lee and Joe Johnston.

For the Union casualties, the ride to Goldsboro was no festive, victorious parade. After Howard's and Slocum's wounded had been collected and examined by surgeons, they were placed in ambulances, "lying flat on the bottom side by side, for a ride of twenty miles to Goldsboro." The roads were incredibly bad, excruciating for the movement of wounded. "It was much of the way corduroyed. . . . High water having misplaced many of the logs, our ambulance dropped through between them striking on the axle forcing us both with a bump against the head board, and then as the hind wheels followed, our heads striking the foot board, then a side lurch shaking us from side to side and against each other all that weary day and far into the night. May I never have another such ride."[22]

All the Union wounded were removed to Goldsboro, where the brick schoolhouse was converted into a hospital. Conditions for the sufferers improved greatly. A plucky Henry H. Nurs, 86th Illinois, wrote his father from the hospital. It had been a week since he was wounded:

> Your letter found me laying on my back taking care of my stump. I am doing well & am in good health and fine spirits and my leg is in fine condition. It could not do any better if I was at home . . . I will be able to get around first rate. . . .
>
> As soon as I get well I can get a cork leg and then I shall get a furlough and come home. You must not get scared and think I am going to die. We have a good place.[23]

It was harder for the Confederates. Johnston, lacking ambulances, had to leave many of his severely wounded behind at the crude field hospital—to the mercy of the enemy. A young girl at the time, Dora Hood recalled seventy-five years later that her father's washhouse was used for amputations. Their home itself served as the main hospital, although her young brother lay inside dying with measles. "I can almost hear the groans of the wounded men, even yet," Dora said.[24]

Those Confederates fortunate enough to get away had to endure the ordeal of being carried over corduroy roads in makeshift ambulances. Col. John D. Taylor, 36th Regiment North Carolina Troops, Hagood's Brigade, could not stand the bouncing. He climbed out of the wagon, found himself a horse, and rode on to Smithfield—all this despite his arm just having been amputated.[25]

Things got somewhat better once the wounded crowded aboard one of the trains for Raleigh. But in that city the overburdened facilities failed almost immediately. "When the hospitals filled up, the churches, public buildings, and some private homes became improvised aid stations. men lay everywhere—on benches, church pews, piles of straw."[26] Some men traveled on, through Hillsborough to Greensboro, where the courthouse had been turned into a hospital: "200 of us were laid off in rows on the floor, with only the blankets that we had brought." One remembered that he had an "armful of hay for his bed and two bricks for my pillow."[27]

For those Confederates abandoned at Bentonville, help came in the form of an unidentified high-ranking Union officer (probably Charles R. Woods or Oliver O. Howard), who "ordered his quartermaster to supply them with both rations and medicine."[28] When a Confederate scout returned to the area a week later, he found no Union casualties or surgeons. All had been moved to Goldsboro. He found Confederates, however, who had been gathered and taken to the home of Mr. and Mrs. John Harper by the Union ambulance corps. There they had been treated by Fourteenth Corps surgeons. When the Union army left, the care of all these Confederates fell upon the Harpers. The scout reported: "They are in a suffering condition for the want of proper supplies, and there is no surgeon to attend them. Mr. Harper and family are doing all their limited means will allow for the sufferers."[29] For three months the Harper family nursed about 50 Confederates; 31 recovered and went home, and 23 died, 20 of whom were buried on the place.[30]

Confederate casualties had run high. Although accounts vary, the total loss of Johnston's army was about 240 killed and 1,700 wounded. The number of missing is difficult to determine but ranged well beyond the 600 Johnston reported. Howard and Slocum claimed over 1,600 captured; 1,500 would seem a fair number. One should bear in mind not only the men in the Army of Tennessee cut off and captured by Cogswell's counterattack, but also the number who deserted on the field of battle. Many Union reports and diaries mention the Confederates wandering in to surrender, "taken in out of the wet," as the Federals would say. This high percentage of prisoners is significant. Often, if not generally, the ratio of casualties to prisoners reveals the effectiveness of the enemy army. It seems that Sherman's army, hour by hour, was destroying the Confederate will to resist.

The proportion of Confederate casualties was most uneven. The Army of Tennessee, with less than one-third of Johnston's infantry strength, suffered about one-half of the casualties. Lee's Corps, commanded by Hill, lost nearly 20 percent killed and wounded. The brigades of Colquitt (40 killed, 177 wounded out of 1,170 troops), Daniel H. Reynolds (41 killed and wounded out of 178 troops), and Joseph B. Palmer (13 killed, 121 wounded out of 468 troops) suffered similarly. Some regiments, the 40th Alabama and the 36th Regiment North Carolina Troops, for instance, suffered "frightful losses," well above 50 percent.[31]

Sherman's army lost 1,527 men—194 killed, 1,112 wounded, and 221 missing. The largest number of casualties in Howard's wing were those of Charles R. Woods's division, Fifteenth Corps, and Joseph A. Mower's division, Seventeenth Corps. But Howard's losses pale when compared to Slocum's. The Twentieth Corps lost almost as many men as the entire Right Wing. Davis's Fourteenth Corps endured over 50 percent of the total Union casualties, with the highest losses, of course, in Carlin's and Morgan's divisions.[32]

Considering the size of their armies, there is little question that Johnston suffered proportionately far heavier losses than Sherman.

There were other casualties following Bentonville as the armies regrouped and prepared for a last campaign. In Sherman's army Alpheus Williams was replaced as commander of the Twentieth Corps by Joseph A. Mower, Williams quietly assuming division command. William P. Carlin was sacked and replaced by an able brigade commander of Charles R. Woods, Brig. Gen. Charles C. Walcutt, who had been wounded on the March to the Sea. It was "a change gratifying to all of us,"[33] confided one of Carlin's men. Carlin himself later wrote: "I was prostrated by sickness, the result of exposure and fatigue on the march, and especially in the battle of Bentonville." "My physician advised my leaving the field for a month. On Surgeon's certificate of disability I obtained leave of absence for 30 days. This severed my connection with Sherman's army."[34]

Johnston's army underwent a massive reorganization in early April. Divisions were dissolved, brigades and regiments consolidated. The quartermaster sergeant of the 57th Alabama thought that the changes "resulted in about half of the officers going home." Conspicuous among the names that would be missing were Henry D. Clayton, Evander M. Law, William B. Taliaferro, William B. Bate, Lafayette McLaws, and Braxton Bragg.[35] "Discipline is already much stricter in all respects," reported a Confederate. Johnston promised that the troops would be paid. That lifted spirits. Old Joe always took care of his men. One of Johnston's soldiers went so far as to write: "my face looks bright and cheerful. You need not doubt our ability to whip Sherman."[36]

Sherman returned from City Point on March 30 and found that "all things were working well." He established his base firmly at Goldsboro, collected the necessary "forage and food for another march," and prepared to move his army of 88,000 men north of the Roanoke River. From there he might strike north against Lee or south against Johnston. Sherman's timetable was upset, however, by a lightning-fast series of events: Richmond fell on April 3 and Lee surrendered on April 9. Sherman took the field at once (April 10), changing his objective to Johnston's army. Johnston retreated from Smithfield toward Raleigh with Sherman in unhurried, methodical pursuit. Sherman pressed Johnston to and beyond Raleigh, which was captured without a fight on April 13. The next day the two generals began negotiations for the surrender of Johnston's army, a tortuous and controversial process that continued for two weeks.

14

The Angel of the Covenant Whispered to Our Commander

BENTONVILLE SHOULD NOT have been fought. We can say that with as-surance a century and a half later. Of course, seated in comfortable arm-chairs, armed with field returns, we know Sherman's strengths and we know Johnston's weaknesses. We know that Schofield awaited Sherman at Golds-boro with an army equal to Johnston's. We know the futility of it all.

It is improbable that Johnston could have defeated Sherman in battle regardless of how he had conducted it. He could not even defeat Slocum's isolated Left Wing. Indeed, did not Johnston know this himself? Report-edly he admitted to Sherman a few weeks after Bentonville "that he had known for months [since the reelection of Lincoln] that their cause was hopeless—that they must succumb, sooner or later."[1] So Johnston could not win; Sherman could not lose. On that basis, one might argue, Johnston becomes a culprit of sorts, a leader who allowed his army to bare its breast and fling itself upon the spears of an invincible enemy.

We know better. Johnston was no fool. When Gen. Thomas L. Clingman later proposed a last stand near Smithfield, a Thermopylae in effect, John-ston apparently rejected the idea out of hand. "I am not in the Thermopylae business," he is reported to have replied to Clingman.[2] Johnston also loved his men. This was the driving force, some would argue, behind the suc-cesses of his generalship, his ability to bind men to him. To throw away soldiers' lives recklessly contradicts his past.

Maybe the situation in March 1865 held little hope for victory, but John-ston fought at Bentonville because he saw an opportunity, albeit slim, to wrest the initiative from Sherman and wound his army. A limited victory at Bentonville, Johnston believed, might throw Sherman's advancing columns into disarray; a major victory might destroy a corps, a column. If he were to succeed in this unexpected battle south of the Neuse, then at work would be

Johnston's "combinations," not Sherman's. In fact, easy success by Sherman in his Carolinas Campaign might be forfeited less than twenty miles from his objective. If Johnston permitted Sherman to join Schofield at Goldsboro without a fight, then he (and Robert E. Lee) surely would confront a juggernaut.

Certainly Johnston looked over his shoulder at Richmond. This most human of generals longed for an occasion to confound his critics. Despite his conviction that the war was lost, despite his doubts about the assignment of "driving back Sherman," President Davis, Lee, and history had given Johnston another chance. He had the opportunity in March 1865, if he wished to avail himself of it, to demonstrate that he was capable of conducting successful offensive operations, that he had used defense in the past merely as a temporary expedient. Furthermore, Johnston (like Sherman) believed that successful military campaigns, indeed victory, must begin with an army's confidence, its morale. He must demonstrate to his men, particularly to the battered and gun-shy Army of Tennessee, that a calculated offensive thrust, though limited in resources and objectives, could yield important results. Johnston ached, perhaps more than his men themselves, to restore their reputation, their pride—anything to disprove the slanders of John Bell Hood. Johnston knew his men. Bentonville would be their tonic.

Credit Joe Johnston for achieving surprise. After four months of constant retreat, the Confederates crossed the Neuse and massed at a battle site chosen for its advantage to the attacker. Slocum stumbled into this trap, and, thanks to two audacious commanders, William P. Carlin and Jefferson C. Davis, the Federals even cooperated with Johnston's design—launching not one but two assaults. Their second (at noon on March 19 in division strength) in effect placed Carlin's head into the jaws of the Confederate position. This made Johnston's task still easier and helped offset his slowness and clumsiness in massing his own strike force.

Johnston revealed other shortcomings as a battlefield commander on the nineteenth. When the Confederates at last seized the tactical initiative they coveted, Johnston delivered piecemeal, poorly coordinated attacks and, for the most part, made limited and unimaginative use of available cavalry and artillery. The fact that he remained on the field in the face of a greatly superior enemy during March 20–21, after surprise had been lost, appears to have been an unreasonable risk, totally uncharacteristic of him. Johnston's rationale (removal of the wounded) seems contrived. Perhaps he did wish to invite assaults on his strong defensive position, as has been contended, but surely Johnston knew the peril of that course. His position had serious flaws, and an attack (if skillfully and resolutely conducted) could have destroyed the Confederate army.

Johnston entrusted the main attack on the nineteenth to Hardee, then seriously weakened his subordinate's strike force by allowing Braxton Bragg to siphon off McLaws's Division. The Confederates clearly lacked unity of command, although their commander was on the field. At sundown, at the crucial moment of the offensive, Bragg went over to the defensive; Harvey Hill, hoping to exploit an advantage, attacked Morgan's rear; and Hardee continued pressing down the Goldsboro road, attempting to mass forces for an all-out attack on Slocum's blocking position. Meanwhile, Johnston himself remained near the Cole house chatting with McLaws, Stewart, and others, apparently issuing no tactical orders, although he could see McLaws's men all about him, gathering rifles scattered here and there on the ground. Did he not understand that success in this most desperate of ventures required that momentum be maintained at all costs? It seems almost as though he had surrendered conduct of the battle.

His misuse of his reserve (McLaws) on offense (March 19) seems such a contrast to his bold, resourceful employment of reserves on defense (March 20–21). And by permitting Bragg and Hardee to work at cross-purposes on the nineteenth by not intervening personally, Johnston sacrificed not only unity of command but also unity of effort. To succeed at Bentonville, Johnston must have known that he must reach beyond himself—be present everywhere, exert maximum energy, utilize every resource. It was a moment for inspired military leadership, a moment for greatness. Otherwise, with an inferior force—many untrained, many unarmed, operating in most instances with unfamiliar organizational structures, maneuvering over tricky terrain— failure and death in the swamp had been prescribed by the returned hero, the diffident Old Joe so many of the Confederates worshipped.

On March 20 and 21, however, Johnston displayed high skill in occupying and fortifying defensible terrain where the enemy would have to attack. In restructuring his fortified perimeter on the twentieth (retiring Hoke's line over 90 degrees) and again on the twenty-first (when he placed his army on line facing east), Johnston showed flexibility: the ability to adapt, the willingness to gamble, the inclination to entrust subordinates with discretionary orders. Outnumbered three to one, Johnston used superior knowledge of the ground to his advantage. Moreover, he constantly shuttled small units back and forth along interior lines—always presenting the prying enemy with fieldworks bristling with graybacks. He used his thin reserves judiciously. Although Mower disclosed Johnston's poor hand on the afternoon of the twenty-first, the Confederate leader got away with his bluff. His disengagement on the night of the twenty-first was masterful. In all, Johnston demonstrated aggressiveness and risk taking that fooled Sherman. Johnston's actions at Bentonville contradicted the predictable, cautious pattern Sherman had come to know in North Georgia. Johnston, perhaps, knew Sherman better than Sherman knew Johnston.

When one considers Johnston's subordinates, it seems evident that cavalry commanders Hampton and Wheeler handled their responsibilities creditably. Hampton played a crucial role on the eighteenth, choosing the battle site and suggesting the plan of attack; he also displayed initiative and boldness on the twenty-first when resisting Mower. Wheeler contributed little on the nineteenth, though he acted promptly and aggressively on the twentieth, thereby securing sufficient time for Hoke to redeploy. On the twenty-first he and his troops did well helping to contain and throw back Mower.

Bragg played a negative role at Bentonville, disrupting Johnston's plan of battle and interfering with Hoke's attack on Morgan's division. Johnston's comment to Hoke five years after the battle, "It was a great weakness on my part, not to send him [Bragg] to Raleigh on the 18th," says much. The attack by the heavily weighted Confederate left (Bragg's sector) was tardy and, with the exception of Zachry's brigade, conducted in halfhearted, amateurish fashion. Bragg displayed poor battlefield presence. On three separate occasions, he braked Confederate momentum. He distracted Johnston, inhibited Hoke, and rushed McLaws back and forth in the bush like a favorite bird dog.

A. P. Stewart drew little comment and attracted little attention with his action or inaction throughout the battle. Apparently he held back, willing to give Harvey Hill and Hardee prominent roles. Hill, on the other hand, threw himself into the fight and demonstrated positive combat leadership. His decision to attack the rear of Morgan's position may have weakened Hardee's assault against the Twentieth Corps line, but it appears to have been sound tactically. In fact, perhaps the entire right wing of the Confederate attack, certainly most of it, should have been thrown against Morgan, thereby bringing to bear overwhelming combat power against that isolated fraction of Slocum's force.

Hardee, the good lieutenant, seems to have understood Johnston's intent without specific instructions, but his slow, disorganized pursuit of Carlin undermined the Confederate chance for victory. One can justify Hardee's course of action easily—uncertain terrain, a faulty command structure, thousands of artillerymen playing infantry, Taliaferro's deployment difficulties, Bragg's having robbed the right wing of crucial offensive weight. As a prudent commander Hardee felt that he needed to stop and re-form more than once. He had witnessed successful but weakened attacking bodies mauled by counterattack (Atlanta, Murfreesboro). His command had become disoriented and disorganized by easy success over Carlin, so he halted his troops. This cost precious momentum, but Hardee deemed control more important. It was a difficult judgment he had to make in a darkened, smoke-filled wilderness, and it seems presumptuous to second-guess him. Yet one might argue that even had another Federal division been broken up, in its place would have appeared more high-quality reserves. Would it have made any difference, really? Nevertheless, the faltering, sputtering, stop-and-go Confederate attack allowed the enemy time to dig in, time to regroup, thereby ensuring defeat. Victory, however remote, required that nothing be allowed to halt the impetus of the assault.

In fairness, Hardee, the consummate professional, did his best on March 19. He should be credited with persistence, energy, and personal leadership. His quick reaction on the afternoon of the twenty-first was decisive—a splendid curtain call for "Old Reliable."

Based on the limited evidence available, Hoke on March 19 hardly seems to have demonstrated the leadership expected of a fine division commander. It was a great disappointment. Without question, Braxton Bragg, not Robert F. Hoke, was the dominating presence on the Confederate left that afternoon. One can only surmise what Hoke's role must have been. Seemingly, utterly thwarted, he had had to defer to Bragg at every turn. What else could he have done? Is it reasonable to have expected Hoke once again to have "vehemently disagreed" with Bragg? Would it have mattered? To offset this disappointing showing, Hoke did solid work on the twentieth and twenty-first, once Bragg had been moved to the rear. Indeed, Hoke and his men seem to have been the mainstay of the Confederate defense.

Subordinate infantry commanders Walthall, Kirkland, Pettus, Zachry, and Henderson performed well, very well, as has been pointed out. Loring, Stevenson, and Clayton, on the other hand, seem to have been unexceptional in the execution of their missions. Bate and Taliaferro proved disappointing. McLaws, despite his vast combat experience and his big division, floundered about on the nineteenth, displaying a lack of initiative and energy. He ended the day as a sort of inert reserve commander, an administrator, watching as others plucked brigades from his division, committing them here and there. McLaws appeared distracted, almost uninterested. He, like

Hoke, seems to have done much better on the last two days. Perhaps the dubious fighting quality of his command discouraged McLaws. Perhaps he knew his days were numbered. One can only wonder what might have happened if his division had been led by an aggressive Harvey Hill, a leader with fire in his eyes.

Sherman's subordinates did well for the most part. Kilpatrick, as an exception, stood by with 4,000 men, in effect holding Slocum's coat. In fairness, however, apparently no one ordered him (until March 21) to take a more active role than to deploy on the left of the Federal line. The tangled battlefield did not lend itself to cavalry action (although this did not seem to daunt Wheeler and Hampton on March 21). One cannot help but wonder what impact even a dismounted division of Kilpatrick's cavalry might have had if it had been pressed hard against Johnston's left in the vicinity of Blackman's Pond throughout March 21.

William Passmore Carlin, West Pointer, paid the price for impetuosity. It is ironic that this quality, which Sherman prized in his subordinates, would become the rationalization for Carlin's dismissal from command. Had Bentonville been Missionary Ridge, perhaps it would have set things right, but on March 19 Carlin's division had been mangled in embarrassing fashion. Buell and Hobart, Carlin's brigade commanders above the Goldsboro road, did as well as they could but were victims of a rebel tidal wave. It is true that the sacrifice of Carlin's division allowed time for Morgan to burrow in and for Slocum to concentrate and fortify, but William Passmore Carlin got whipped, and Davis and Slocum and Sherman did not see fit to redeem him.

Why? In their official battle reports Carlin's superiors virtually ignore him. Had he really done that badly? He had merely followed orders and standard practice in his attempts to develop and drive the enemy. He had attacked with more force than Davis had ordered, it is true, and somewhat later he had disregarded Davis's order to "make demonstrations." Thus he provided ample excuse to his old enemy Davis to recommend that he be sacked for not following orders. Moreover, Carlin probably sacrificed whatever support he might have expected from Slocum when he took it upon himself, "after the first attacks had failed," to dismiss Slocum's advice (given through a staff officer) to fall back and fortify.

Doubtless there was more to it than that. Davis and Slocum and Sherman had blundered into an ambush at Bentonville. Carlin provided a convenient scapegoat, diverting attention from his superiors and offering an opportunity to reward Joseph Anthony Mower, a non–West Pointer, for his impetuosity, the very quality that had led to Carlin's undoing. William P. Carlin was a most unlucky soldier.

This daredevil of Perryville, this darling of the Army of the Cumberland and respected subordinate of George H. Thomas, should have been leading a trailing division in the left column that fateful Sunday morning. How would Morgan have fared as the point division? What would have happened to Mower had he had the assignment?

Fate and Sherman, Slocum, and Davis decided otherwise. Morgan and Mower became heroes of the Carolinas Campaign, and Carlin, proven combat leader of twenty fields, drifted off into obscurity.

Brigade commanders Robinson, Miles, and Vandever can be both complimented and criticized, as can Jefferson C. Davis, who ordered Carlin's mindless reactive noon attack. Davis, however, contributed much to ultimate Union success by ordering the counterattacks by Fearing and Cogswell. Doubtlessly, one can contend that Davis won the battle of March 19 by his prompt, aggressive resumption of the offensive. Colonel Fearing bodyblocked Hardee's advancing columns while Cogswell's six big regiments smashed Hill's Confederates who were greedily encircling Morgan.

Division commander Morgan knew when to fortify. He provided the anchor by which the Left Wing was able to stabilize itself. He transformed his division into a veritable sea urchin, bristling with sharp, poisonous needles that discouraged Bragg and held off Hill. Morgan must receive credit for his tenacious defense—excellent work by two dangerously positioned brigades. Also, Morgan's third brigade—Fearing's—conducted a violent, all-consuming counterattack fundamental to the successful outcome of the battle. Thus, Morgan's whole division contributed in exemplary fashion. Perhaps his best subordinate that day was John G. Mitchell. Mitchell performed in outstanding fashion. Attacked from three sides, he displayed magnificent battlefield presence and personal leadership. If his brigade had crumbled, Slocum's improvised defense line along the Goldsboro road north of the Morris house would have rolled up like a Venetian blind.

Although Alpheus S. Williams, commander of the Twentieth Corps, was replaced following Bentonville, his actions there appear to have been competent and timely. His division commanders also seem to have performed well enough. Mostly they worked to build a formidable position while individual brigades (Cogswell and Robinson, for instance) were detached from time to time and fed into the fight supporting the Fourteenth Corps. Williams, apparently unambitious militarily and politically, seemed content with doing his job. He reminds one of George Thomas.

One should not overlook Henry W. Slocum. Surprised—indeed ambushed—Slocum reacted quickly and intelligently once he learned that he was opposed in force. Letting Davis fight off the assault, Slocum rushed forward the Twentieth Corps and began constructing a hasty defense in depth that eventually ruined Hardee's best efforts. Slocum kept his head and defeated Johnston without assistance from Sherman. Truly the battle of the nineteenth was his fight. He proved himself worthy of Sherman's trust.

Slocum's counterpart, Oliver O. Howard, did well also. He carried out every order promptly and fully. In massing his wing and moving it to Slocum's support, Howard moved quickly and decisively. It is difficult to imagine another officer doing better. He reacted aggressively when Mower ran into trouble on the afternoon of the twenty-first and saw the opportunity for a knockout. He disagreed with Sherman's decision to break off the attack, but, ever the professional, Howard supported his commander totally once the course of action had been determined. Howard, almost to a fault, understood and tried to practice the precept of subordination of self.

Logan seems to have performed somewhat better than Blair in the capacity of corps commander. Apparently Blair's command was fragmented organizationally and in regard to objective. Manning F. Force and Giles A. Smith, although they performed creditably, fade in the sunlight of Mower's impetuosity. In fact, Logan's entire Fifteenth Corps merits recognition. Each of his divisions did their work very well. Hazen and Woods had difficult assignments but handled them commendably. C. R. Woods's men, particularly, excelled during the nasty, dangerous skirmishing in the swamp; they also skillfully handled the Confederate attempt to interdict the battlefield below Flowers' house. The Fifteenth Corps throughout behaved most professionally, a tribute to its most unprofessional leader.

As usual, Federal artillery played an active role, batteries in both wings being placed well forward to support infantry. Both Slocum and Howard used their artillery productively, offensively and defensively. The contrast with the limited, almost inert, employment of artillery by the Confederates is striking. Indeed, it reminds one sharply that superiority of Federal artillery remained a constant in the West from Belmont to Bentonville.[3]

At Bentonville Sherman probably forfeited his chance for even greater fame. By following up Mower's probe on March 21 (as Sherman acknowledged himself), he probably could have destroyed Johnston's army and won for himself a special place in American military history, concluding a brilliant operational year with a smashing tactical victory.

Sherman, however, kept a perspective. He knew that he held the winning hand. All he had to do was fend off Johnston and continue his march to Goldsboro. Once combined with Schofield, he could lever Johnston easily from any position he chose. North Carolina, indeed Virginia, would be his. Besides, Sherman had never before committed his entire army in battle. Why should he do so now? Why should he sacrifice the lives of his troops needlessly? If one might win by maneuver, why fight? Viewed in this light, Sherman's failure to press the fight at Bentonville is the capstone of his magnificent Carolinas Campaign.[4]

Sherman, as he had done since the spring of 1864, kept his ultimate objective paramount and showed admirable restraint at Bentonville. In fact, as Weymouth Jordan has pointed out, "he seemed almost indifferent to the matter at hand." Johnston's ambush was a nuisance, albeit dangerous, but only a nuisance nevertheless. Slocum had handled the situation. Sherman made up his mind not to play Johnston's game. He would have marched on to Goldsboro on March 22 regardless of whether Johnston remained south of the Neuse. Sherman's idea of military success was to capture Charleston "without going within a hundred miles of it." Bentonville nicely fit such a concept.[5]

Fault Sherman for carelessness and overconfidence. Perhaps take issue with him for lacking killer instinct, for being "a general who did not like to fight," but acknowledge he never lost sight of his objective. He kept his operational priorities clear. "His game," according to his admirer Jacob D. Cox, "was a perfectly sure one with patience."[6]

Oliver O. Howard added cosmic perspective: "Possibly the Angel of the Covenant whispered to our commander . . . 'Let us have peace.' "[7]

Some Confederates might claim victory at Bentonville—but not Johnston. His telegrams to Lee have a hollow sound, as indeed do writings of partisans thirty years later. In reality, in unvarnished terms, the Confederates got whipped at Bentonville. Granted, Johnston smashed Carlin's division and roughed up Davis's Fourteenth Corps; granted, the assault on March 19 was conducted in high style and achieved tactical surprise; and granted, the Confederates' final charge against Mower was as well synchronized and as dramatic as any in the war. Nevertheless, it stands that Slocum prevailed against everything Johnston threw at him. By early morning on the twentieth, reinforced by Hazen and Baird and Geary, Slocum could have defended his position for a month. If he had been so inclined, he probably could have driven Johnston across Mill Creek without help from Howard and Sherman.

So Bentonville remains—a monument to Sherman's restraint and single-mindedness and a last fieldstone to memorialize Confederate gallantry. The battle did not save the capital of North Carolina or Lee's back door; it did not even deflect Sherman's march to Goldsboro. It represents the best the South could do to stop Sherman and to punish him for his daring punitive march through Georgia and the Carolinas. It demonstrated clearly the futility of the Confederacy continuing the war.

Was it a final battle of Titans—Johnston goes forth to slay Sherman, or the other way around—an American Achilles-Hector encounter? Hardly, for no two warriors more reluctantly encountered each other. From the Confederate perspective Bentonville was brave and bold and sad. Veteran soldiers went into this battle with tight throats. All, except perhaps the Red Infantry or the young Willie Hardees, understood the odds of muzzle-loading Enfields against Henry repeating rifles. Veterans expected to die, and they did. Their suffering and courage dignified this desperate fight in the muck.

For those enamored of instructive historical patterns and themes, Bentonville might stand as a metaphor for the Confederacy itself—bright hopes drowned in dark swamp water. Why the Confederates continued to fight when all was lost, the question posed in the Preface, remains a rhetorical question, worthy of examination in itself, but a question that goes to the heart of a nation, an inquiry that must range far beyond and beneath the confines of this battle study.

The Southern Confederacy, one is reminded, represents a failed democratic revolution conducted by millions of men and women who were careful to base their actions on constitutional principles and obliged to call upon God as their support. They received a ration of dust for their sacrifice. This is as it should be, it has been argued and accepted.

When Mary Chesnut heard the news of Bentonville—that Sherman had been defeated, but that Johnston had withdrawn to Smithfield—she knew what it meant. She had read such lines before. Off in the distance she heard

Johnston's soldiers singing. She folded her arms and listened: "The camp songs of these men were a heartbreak—so sad, yet so stirring. They would have warmed the blood of an Icelander. . . . so I sat down as women have done before when they hung up their harps by strange streams, and I wept."[8]

Appendix 1

Organization of Forces at the Battle of Bentonville

Confederate Forces
Gen. Joseph E. Johnston, Infantry

Army of Tennessee: Lt. Gen. Alexander P. Stewart

CHEATHAM'S CORPS: Maj. Gen. William B. Bate

Cleburne's Division: Brig. Gen. James A. Smith
  Smith's Brigade: Capt. J. R. Bonner
    54th, 57th, 63d Georgia; 1st Georgia Volunteers
  [a]Lowry's Brigade: Lt. Col. John F. Smith
    16th & 33d & 45th Alabama; 8th & 32d Mississippi; 5th Mississippi & 3d Mississippi Battalion
  Govan's Brigade: Col. Peter V. Green
    1st & 2d & 5th & 13th & 15th & 24th Arkansas; 6th & 7th Arkansas; 8th & 19th Arkansas
  [a]Granbury's Brigade: Maj. William A. Ryan
    5th Confederate; 35th Tennessee; 7th, 10th Texas; 6th & 15th Texas; 17th & 18th Texas Cavalry (dismounted); 24th & 25th Texas Cavalry (dismounted); Nutt's Louisiana Cavalry Company (dismounted)

Bate's Division: Col. Daniel L. Kenan (w/19)
  Tyler's Brigade: Maj. William H. Wilkinson (k/19); Capt. Henry Rice
    4th Georgia Sharpshooter Battalion; 37th Georgia; 2d & 10th & 20th Tennessee
  Finley's Brigade: Lt. Col. Elisha Washburn
    1st & 3d Florida; 6th & 7th Florida; 1st Florida Cavalry (dismounted) & 4th Florida

[a,b]Brown's Division:
  Gist's Brigade: Col. Hume R. Field
    2d Georgia Sharpshooter Battalion; 46th Georgia; 6th Georgia & 8th Georgia Battalion; 16th, 24th South Carolina State Troops
  Maney's Brigade: Lt. Col. Christopher C. McKinney
    4th Confederate & 6th & 9th & 50th Tennessee; 1st & 27th Tennessee; 8th & 16th & 28th Tennessee
  Strahl's Brigade: Col. Carrick W. Heiskell
    4th & 5th & 31st & 33d & 38th Tennessee; 19th & 24th & 41st Tennessee
  Vaughan's Brigade: Col. William P. Bishop
    11th & 29th Tennessee; 12th & 47th Tennessee; 13th & 51st & 52d & 54th Tennessee

LEE'S CORPS: Maj. Gen. Daniel H. Hill

Stevenson's Division: Maj. Gen. Carter L. Stevenson
    ªCumming's Brigade: Col. Robert J. Henderson
        34th, 36th, 39th, 56th Georgia
    Pettus's Brigade: Brig. Gen. Edmund W. Pettus (w/19)
        20th, 23d, 30th, 31st, 46th Alabama
    Palmer's Brigade: Brig. Gen. Joseph B. Palmer (w/19)
        "Tennessee Consolidation" (32d Tennessee, 3d & 18th Tennessee, 23d & 26th &
        45th Tennessee); 54th, 63d Virginia; 58th, 60th Regiments North Carolina Troops

Hill's Division: Col. John G. Coltart
    Deas's Brigade: Col. Harry T. Toulmin
        19th, 22d, 25th, 39th, 50th Alabama
    Manigault's Brigade: Lt. Col. John C. Carter
        10th, 19th South Carolina State Troops

Clayton's Division: Maj. Gen. Henry D. Clayton
    Stovall's Brigade: Col. Henry C. Kellogg
        40th, 41st, 42d, 43d, 52d Georgia
    Baker's Brigade: Brig. Gen. Alpheus Baker
        22d, 54th Alabama; 37th & 40th & 42d Alabama
    Jackson's Brigade: Col. Osceola Kyle
        1st Georgia Sharpshooter Battalion; 1st Georgia (Confederate) & 66th Georgia; 25th
        Georgia; 29th & 30th Georgia

STEWART'S CORPS: Maj. Gen. William W. Loring (sick/20)

Loring's Division: Col. James Jackson
    Featherston's Brigade: Maj. Martin A. Oatis
        1st, 3d, 22d, 31st, 33d, 40th Mississippi; 1st Mississippi Battalion
    Lowry's Brigade: Lt. Col. Robert J. Lawrence
        6th, 14th, 15th, 20th, 23d, 43d Mississippi
    Scott's Brigade: Capt. John A. Dixon
        12th Louisiana; 55th, 57th Alabama; 27th & 35th & 49th Alabama

Walthall's Division: Maj. Gen. Edward C. Walthall
    Quarles's Brigade: Brig. Gen. George D. Johnston
        1st, 25th Alabama; 48th Tennessee; 42d & 46th & 49th & 53d & 55th Tennessee
    Reynolds's Brigade: Brig. Gen. Daniel H. Reynolds (w/19)
                        Col. Henry G. Bunn (w/19)
        1st & 2d Arkansas Mounted Rifles (dismounted); 4th, 9th, 25th Arkansas

Department of North Carolina: Gen. Braxton Bragg

Hoke's Division: Maj. Gen. Robert F. Hoke
    Clingman's Brigade: Col. William S. Devane (w/20)

8th Regiment North Carolina State Troops; 31st, 51st, 61st Regiments North Carolina Troops

Colquitt's Brigade: Col. Charles T. Zachry
6th, 9th, 19th, 23d, 27th, 28th Georgia

Hagood's Brigade: Brig. Gen. Johnson Hagood
7th, 11th, 21st, 25th, 27th South Carolina State Troops; 36th Regiment North Carolina Troops (2d Regiment North Carolina Artillery) & 1st Battalion North Carolina Heavy Artillery (3 companies); ᶜ40th North Carolina Troops 3d Regiment, North Carolina (3d Regiment North Carolina Artillery) (6 companies)

Kirkland's Brigade: Brig. Gen. William W. Kirkland
17th, 42d, 66th Regiments North Carolina Troops

First Brigade, Junior Reserves: Col. John H. Nethercutt
1st, 2d, 3d Regiments North Carolina Junior Reserves (70th, 71st, 72d Regiments North Carolina Troops); 1st Battalion North Carolina Junior Reserves (D. T. Millard's)

Artillery: Lt. Col. Joseph B. Starr
10th Regiment North Carolina State Troops (1st North Carolina Artillery) (1 company); 13th Battalion North Carolina Light Artillery (3 companies); 3d Battalion North Carolina Light Artillery (3 companies); Cap t. James I. Kelly's South Carolina Battery (Chesterfield Artillery)

ᵈJackson's Brigade: Col. George Jackson
19th Regiment North Carolina Troops; Maj. Peter Mallett's Battalion (Camp Guard); 8th Regiment North Carolina Senior Reserves (78th Regiment North Carolina Troops)

Department of South Carolina, Georgia, and Florida:
Lt. Gen. William J. Hardee

McLaws's Division: Maj. Gen. Lafayette McLaws
Conner's Brigade: Brig. Gen. John D. Kennedy
2d, 3d, 7th, 8th, 15th, 20th South Carolina State Troops; 3d Battalion South Carolina State Troops

Harrison's Brigade: Col. George P. Harrison, Jr.
5th, 32d, 47th Georgia

Fiser's Brigade: Col. John C. Fiser
1st Georgia Regulars; 1st Georgia Reserve Regiment; 27th Georgia Battalion & Cobb Guards

Hardy's Brigade: Col. Washington M. Hardy
50th Regiment North Carolina Troops; 77th Regiment North Carolina Senior Reserves; 10th Battalion North Carolina Light Artillery

Blanchard's Brigade: Brig. Gen. Albert G. Blanchard
1st, 2d, 6th, 7th South Carolina Reserve Battalions

Taliaferro's Division: Brig. Gen. William B. Taliaferro
Rhett's Brigade: Col. William Butler

1st South Carolina Regulars; 1st South Carolina Heavy Artillery; 15th Battalion South Carolina State Troops

Elliott's Brigade: Brig. Gen. Stephen Elliott, Jr.

22d, 27th Georgia Heavy Artillery Battalions; 2d South Carolina Heavy Artillery Regiment; Manigault's Battalion (19th South Carolina Militia Regiment)

Cavalry: Lt. Gen. Wade Hampton

Butler's Division: Maj. Gen. Matthew C. Butler (sick/20); Brig. Gen. Evander M. Law

Butler's Brigade: Brig. Gen. Evander M. Law (commanding on March 19), Brig. Gen. Thomas M. Logan

4th, 5th, 6th South Carolina Cavalry

Young's Brigade: Col. Gilbert J. Wright

7th Georgia Cavalry; Cobb's Legion; Phillips's Legion; Jeff Davis's Legion & 20th Georgia Cavalry Battalion; 10th Georgia

Horse Artillery:

Hart's Battery; Earle's Battery

WHEELER'S CORPS: Maj. Gen. Joseph Wheeler

Humes's Division: Col. Henry M. Ashby

Ashby's Brigade: Lt. Col. James H. Lewis

1st, 2d, 5th, 9th Tennessee Cavalry

Harrison's Brigade: Col. Baxter Smith

3d Arkansas Cavalry; 8th Tennessee Cavalry[e]; 8th, 11th Texas Cavalry

Dibrell's Division: Brig. Gen. George G. Dibrell

Dibrell's Brigade: Brig. Gen. William S. McLemore

4th (Murray's),[f] 13th Tennessee Cavalry[g]; Shaw's Battalion (including Allison's Tennessee Squadron)

Lewis's Brigade: Col. William C. P. Breckinridge

1st, 3d, 9th Kentucky Cavalry

Allen's Division: Brig. Gen. William W. Allen

Anderson's Brigade: Brig. Gen. Robert H. Anderson

3d, 8th, 10th Confederate Cavalry; 5th Georgia Cavalry

Hagan's Brigade: Lt. Col. D. G. White

1st, 3d, 51st Alabama Cavalry

Federal Forces

Maj. Gen. William T. Sherman, Infantry

Headquarters Guard: 7th Company, Ohio Sharpshooters

Engineers and Mechanics: Battalion (5 companies) of 1st Michigan Engineers and Mechanics; 1st Missouri

[a]**Right Wing:** Maj. Gen. Oliver O. Howard

Escort: 15th Illinois Cavalry, Company K; 4th Company, Ohio Cavalry

[a]FIFTEENTH ARMY CORPS: Maj. Gen. John A. Logan

First Division: Bvt. Maj. Gen. Charles R. Woods
   [h]First Brigade: Bvt. Brig. Gen. William B. Woods
      12th Indiana; 26th Iowa; 27th Missouri; 31st & 32d Missouri Battalion (6 companies); 76th Ohio
   Second Brigade: Col. Robert F. Catterson
      26th, 40th, 103d Illinois; 97th, 100th Indiana; 6th Iowa; 46th Ohio
   Third Brigade: Col. George A. Stone
      4th, 9th, 25th, 30th, 31st Iowa

Second Division: Maj. Gen. William B. Hazen
   First Brigade: Col. Theodore Jones
      55th, 116th, 127th Illinois; 6th Missouri (Companies A and B, 8th Missouri, attached); 30th, 57th Ohio
   Second Brigade: Col. Wells S. Jones
      111th Illinois; 83d Indiana; 37th, 47th, 53d, 54th Ohio
   Third Brigade: Brig. Gen. John M. Oliver
      48th, 90th Illinois; 99th Indiana; 15th Michigan; 70th Ohio

Third Division: Bvt. Maj. Gen. John E. Smith
   First Brigade: Brig. Gen. William T. Clark
      63d, 93d Illinois; 48th, 59th Indiana[i]
   Second Brigade: Col. Clark R. Wever
      56th Illinois; 10th, 17th Iowa (1 company); 4th Minnesota; 26th Missouri (2 companies with detachment of 10th Missouri attached); 80th Ohio

Fourth Division: Bvt. Maj. Gen. John M. Corse
   First Brigade: Brig. Gen. Elliott W. Rice
      52d Illinois; 66th Indiana; 2d, 7th Iowa
   Second Brigade: Col. Robert N. Adams
      12th, 66th Illinois; 81st Ohio
   Third Brigade: Lt. Col. Frederick J. Hurlbut
      7th, 50th, 57th Illinois; 39th Iowa
   Unassigned (in Fourth Div.): 110th U.S. Colored Troops

Artillery Brigade: Lt. Col. William H. Ross
   1st Illinois Light, Battery H; 1st Michigan Light, Battery B; 1st Missouri Light, Battery H; Wisconsin Light, 12th Battery

Unassigned (Fifteenth Corps)
   29th Missouri (mounted)

[a]SEVENTEENTH ARMY CORPS: Maj. Gen. Frank P. Blair, Jr.
Escort: 11th Illinois Cavalry, Company G

First Division: Maj. Gen. Joseph A. Mower
  First Brigade: Brig. Gen. John W. Fuller
    64th Illinois; 18th Missouri; 27th, 39th Ohio
  Second Brigade: Col. Milton Montgomery
    ʲ35th New Jersey; 43d, 63d Ohio; 25th Wisconsin
  Third Brigade: Col. John Tillson
    10th Illinois; 25th Indiana; 32d Wisconsin

Third Division: Brig. Gen. Manning F. Force
  Provost Guard: 20th Illinois
  First Brigade: Col. Cassius Fairchild
    30th, 31st, 45th Illinois; 12th, 16th Wisconsin
  Second Brigade: Col. Greenberry F. Wiles
    20th, 68th, 78th Ohio; 17th Wisconsin

Fourth Division: Bvt. Maj. Gen Giles A. Smith
  First Brigade: Brig. Gen. Benjamin F. Potts
    14th and 15th Illinois (Battalion), 53d Illinois; 23d, 53d Indiana; 32d Ohio
  Third Brigade: Brig. Gen. William W. Belknap
    32d Illinois; 11th, 13th, 15th, 16th Iowa

Artillery
  1st Michigan Light, Battery C; Minnesota Light, 1st Battery; Ohio Light, 15th Battery

Unassigned
  9th Illinois (mounted)

Left Wing: Maj. Gen. Henry W. Slocum

ᵃPontoniers: 58th Indiana

FOURTEENTH ARMY CORPS: Bvt. Maj. Gen. Jefferson C. Davis

First Division: Brig. Gen. William P. Carlin
  First Brigade: Bvt. Brig. Gen. Harrison C. Hobart
    104th Illinois; 42d, 88th Indiana; 33d, 94th Ohio; 21st Wisconsin
  Second Brigade: Bvt. Brig. Gen. George P. Buell
    13th, 21st Michigan; 69th Ohio
  Third Brigade: Lt. Col. David Miles (w/19)
    38th Indiana; 21st, 74th Ohio; 79th Pennsylvania

Second Division: Brig. Gen. James D. Morgan
  First Brigade: Brig. Gen. William Vandever
    16th, 60th Illinois: 10th, 14th Michigan; 17th New York
  Second Brigade: Brig. John G. Mitchell
    34th, 78th Illinois; 98th, 108th, 113th, 121st Ohio

[k]Third Brigade: Bvt. Brig. Gen. Benjamin D. Fearing (w/19); Lt. Col. James W. Langley
86th, 110th (battalion), 125th Illinois; 22d Indiana, 37th Indiana (1 company); 52d Ohio

[a]Third Division: Bvt. Maj. Gen. Absalom Baird
First Brigade: Col. Morton C. Hunter
82d Indiana; 23d Missouri (4 companies); 11th Ohio (4 companies); 17th, 31st, 70th, 89th, 89th, 92d Ohio
Second Brigade: Lt. Col. Thomas Doan
75th, 87th, 101st Indiana; 2d Minnesota; 105th Ohio
[a]Third Brigade: Col. George P. Este (guarding supply train)
Artillery: Maj. Charles Houghtaling
1st Illinois Light, Battery C; 2d Illinois Light, Battery I; Indiana Light, 19th Battery; Wisconsin Light, 5th Battery

TWENTIETH ARMY CORPS: Bvt. Maj. Gen. Alpheus S. Williams

Engineers: Battalion of 1st Michigan Engineers and Mechanics

First Division: Brig. Gen. Nathaniel J. Jackson
First Brigade: Col. James L. Selfridge
5th Connecticut; 123d, 141 New York; 46th Pennsylvania
Second Brigade: Col. William Hawley
2d Massachusetts; 13th New Jersey; 107th, 150th New York; 3d Wisconsin
Third Brigade: Brig. Gen. James S. Robinson
82d, 101st Illinois; 143d New York; 61st, 82d Ohio; 31st Wisconsin

[a]Second Division: Bvt. Maj. Gen. John W. Geary
First Brigade: Bvt. Brig. Gen. Ario Pardee, Jr.
5th, 29th, 66th Ohio; 28th, 147th Pennsylvania
[l]Second Brigade: Col. George W. Mindil
33d New Jersey; 119th, 134th, 154th New York; 73d, 109th Pennsylvania
Third Brigade: Bvt. Brig. Gen. Henry A. Barnum
60th, 102d, 137th, 149th New York; 29th, 111th Pennsylvania

Third Division: Bvt. Maj. Gen. William T. Ward
First Brigade: Col. Henry Case
102d, 105th, 129th Illinois; 70th Indiana; 79th Ohio
Second Brigade: Col. Daniel Dustin
33d, 85th Indiana; 19th Michigan; 22d Wisconsin
Third Brigade: Bvt. Brig. Gen. William Cogswell
20th Connecticut; 33d Massachusetts; 136th New York; 55th, 73d Ohio; 26th Wisconsin

Artillery: Maj. John A. Reynolds
1st New York, Light, Battery I; 1st New York, Light, Battery M; 1st Ohio Light, Battery C; Pennsylvania Light, Battery E

Cavalry

THIRD CAVALRY DIVISION: Bvt. Maj. Gen. Judson Kilpatrick

First Brigade: Col. Thomas J. Jordan
    3d Indiana Battalion; 8th Indiana; 2d, 3d Kentucky; 9th Pennsylvania
Second Brigade: Bvt. Brig. Gen. Smith D. Atkins
    92d Illinois (mounted Infantry); 9th Michigan; 9th, 10th Ohio, McLaughlin's (Ohio) Squadron

Third Brigade: Col. George E. Spencer
    1st Alabama; 5th Kentucky; 5th Ohio

[m]Fourth Brigade: Lt. Col. William B. Way
    1st, 2d, 3d Regiments

Artillery
    Wisconsin Light, 10th Battery

[a]Pontoon Train: Lt. Col. Joseph Moore

NOTES

Ampersands (&) indicate units that have been consolidated.

w/19 = wounded, March 19, 1865.

k/19 = killed, March 19, 1865.

[a]Arrived March 20–21, 1865.

[b]See Chapter 12, n. 59.

[c]The 3d Battalion North Carolina Light Artillery may have been functioning as Red Infantry at Bentonville, combined with the 40th Regiment North Carolina Troops rather than serving under Starr.

[d]Believed to have been at Smithfield.

[e]Baxter Smith's 8th Tennessee Cavalry usually was called the 4th Tennessee Cavalry.

[f]There were two 4th Tennessee Cavalry regiments: Murray's and the Starnes-McLemore regiment. Both were at Bentonville.

[g]Usually known as the 8th Tennessee Cavalry.

[h]W. B. Woods's brigade was guarding Fifteenth Corps wagons and did not reach the battlefield until the morning of March 21, 1865.

[i]The 18th Wisconsin was on veteran furlough during the battle.

[j]The 35th New Jersey and the 43d and 63d Ohio were with Seventeenth Corps trains.

[k]The 85th Illinois was also in Fearing's brigade but remained on train guard duty.

[l]Mindil's brigade remained on train guard duty.

[m]Provisionally organized from dismounted men in three other cavalry brigades.

Appendix 2

Beyond Bentonville

ASHBY, HENRY M., would be gunned down on the streets of Knoxville by a lawyer of questionable reputation three years after Bentonville.

BAIRD, ABSALOM, would revert to major in the regular army. At the close of his career (1887) he would serve as an observer in France and be awarded (with the concurrence of the U.S. Congress) the Legion of Honor.

BAKER, ALPHEUS, would move to Louisville, Kentucky, where he would become "a universal social favorite." A multidimensional man, Baker would not only succeed at the law, but also enjoy a local reputation as a painter and a musician.

BELKNAP, WILLIAM WORTH, would become secretary of war in 1869 at the age of forty, but he would be impeached and his name become synonymous with the corruption characterizing the postwar period.

BUELL, GEORGE PEARSON, would remain in the army for the rest of his life, commanding frontier posts and conducting expeditions against the Apache and Cheyenne.

BUNN, HENRY GASTON, would lead his Arkansas brigade across the mountains to Greenville, Tennessee, then by rail and water to Little Rock. He would resume his study of law that the war had interrupted, practice in Camden, Arkansas, and become chief justice of the state in 1893.

CARLIN, WILLIAM PASSMORE, would remain with the regular army, helping Howard as assistant commissioner of the Freedmen's Bureau in Tennessee, then spend most of the next twenty-five years on the frontier, grinding slowly up the promotional ladder. He would die aboard a train in Montana in 1903.

CATTERSON, ROBERT FRANCIS, would not return to his medical practice but go to Arkansas in an attempt to make his fortune in cotton. This venture failed so Catterson turned soldier again, commanding Negro troops against the Ku Klux Klan. He even became mayor of Little Rock. When Reconstruction ended he went to Minnesota and sold plows.

CLARK, WALTER, would become a North Carolina Supreme Court justice and compile an exemplary, multivolumed history of the Confederate soldiers of his state.

COGSWELL, WILLIAM, would return to his law practice in Salem, Massachusetts, and serve as mayor for five years. Enormously popular, he would be elected time and time again to the Massachusetts House and Senate and then, in 1886, to Congress, where he would remain until his death in 1895.

COLTART, JOHN G., temporary commander of Hill's Corps at Bentonville, would die almost exactly three years later in the Lunatic Asylum at Tuscaloosa, where he had been taken a few weeks before at his own request.

APPENDIX 2

FEARING, BENJAMIN DANA, would attempt to return to the business world in Cincinnati, but his Chickamauga and Bentonville wounds tormented him and he retired to his home in Hamar, Ohio, where he would die in 1881.

FISER, JOHN CALVIN, II, would resume his career in Memphis as a merchant. His wounds, however, left him disabled and vulnerable to disease. He would die there in 1876 at the age of thirty-eight.

FORAKER, JOSEPH BENSON, would become a lawyer and a judge. He would be elected governor of Ohio and later serve two terms in the U.S. Senate.

FULLER, JOHN WALLACE, would return to Ohio, become a boot and shoe merchant, then serve as collector of customs.

GRUMMOND, GEORGE WASHINGTON, as 2d Lieutenant, 18th Infantry, would dash to the relief of a wood train accompanying his commanding officer, Capt. William J. Fetterman, on December 21, 1866. They and their party of eighty would run smack into an ambush by Sioux, Cheyenne, and Arapaho warriors and be slaughtered to a man.

HARDEE, WILLIAM JOSEPH, would try unenthusiastically planting and railroading until his death in 1873.

HENDERSON, ROBERT JOHNSON, would return to Newton County, Georgia, and resume flour milling and farming.

JOHNSTON, JOSEPH EGGLESTON, would retire to Selma, Alabama, and spend long, enjoyable evenings in the company of his friend Hardee. Johnston eventually returned to Virginia and again became a public figure—U.S. congressman and commissioner of railroads under Grover Cleveland. He would die in 1891 from a cold contracted five weeks earlier while marching bareheaded in the funeral procession honoring his friend Sherman.

KENNEDY, JOHN DOBY, would be paroled at age twenty-five, return to his law practice at Camden, South Carolina, become a powerful figure in the national Democratic Party, and be named consul to Shanghai by Grover Cleveland.

KYLE, OSCEOLA, would practice law in Wetumpka, Alabama, marry twice, and write a history of "Old Wetumpka" before his death at the age of fifty-one.

LAW, EVANDER MCIVOR, would establish a military school in Bartow, Florida, then be instrumental in the development of Florida's public education system. He would edit a newspaper, write about his war experiences, and outlive most of his contemporaries.

MCLAWS, LAFAYETTE, would be banished by Johnston and "sent back to Georgia to organize trains, etc."

MORGAN, JAMES DADA, would return to Quincy, Illinois, become a banker, and organize several companies, a hotel, and a railroad. Eternally active, he would involve himself in veterans' activities and "endow a fund for the bestowment of prizes for scholarship in the public schools" before his death in 1896.

MOWER, JOSEPH ANTHONY, would remain in the army and in 1870 die of pneumonia in New Orleans at the age of forty-two.

NASH, FRANCIS H., would return "broke" to Alpharetta, Georgia, where he found his wife and five children in desperate straits. They left for a new life in Texas, where Nash would die in 1913.

NETHERCUTT, JOHN H., would return home to his family only to be murdered before their eyes by two men in 1867.

ROBINSON, JAMES SIDNEY, would become a postmaster, build a railroad, and serve two terms in Congress.

ROY, THOMAS BENTON, would remain faithful to his chief, Hardee, following him to Selma, Alabama, and marrying his daughter Sallie. In Selma Roy would edit a newspaper and practice law until deafness forced him to abandon the profession. He would live abroad for the remainder of his life.

SLOCUM, HENRY WARNER, would resign from the army in September 1865 and return to the practice of law in Brooklyn. Fiercely independent, this prewar Republican would forego privilege and position by becoming a Democrat for "causes that took political pacification and not personal success into account." Slocum would remain Sherman's friend and would help him celebrate his seventieth birthday at home.

TALIAFERRO, WILLIAM BOOTH, would return to Virginia, serve in the state legislature, and become a member of the board of visitors of his alma mater, William and Mary College.

TOULMIN, HARRY THEOPHILUS, would resume his law practice in Mobile and enjoy a long, distinguished career as a lawyer and judge.

VANDEVER, WILLIAM, would resume his law practice in Iowa, serve for four years as an Indian inspector, then relocate to California, where he would be elected to Congress once again.

WILLIAMS, ALPHEUS STARKEY, would be removed as commander of the Twentieth Corps. According to historian John G. Barrett, Williams "was not aggressive enough for his superiors." Andrew Johnson, who learned to appreciate nonaggressive individuals, would name him minister to Salvador. Williams would enter Congress as a Democrat in 1874 and die in Washington during his second term.

ZACHRY, CHARLES THORNTON, would become a Georgia legislator and die at McDonough, Georgia, in 1906 at the age of seventy-eight.

Notes

Abbreviations

ALA	Alabama State Department of Archives and History, Montgomery
BCL	Bowdoin College Library, Brunswick, Maine
B&L	Robert Underwood Johnson and Clarence Clough Buel, eds., *Battles and Leaders of the Civil War*. 4 vols. New York, 1884–87.
BL/UM	Bentley Library, University of Michigan, Ann Arbor
CCNMP	Chickamauga and Chattanooga National Military Park, Fort Oglethorpe, Ga.
CL/UM	Clements Library, University of Michigan, Ann Arbor
CV	*Confederate Veteran*
CWTI	*Civil War Times Illustrated*
DAB	*Dictionary of American Biography*
DU	Duke University, William R. Perkins Library, Durham, N.C.
GAH	Georgia Department of Archives and History, Athens
HL	Huntington Library, San Marino, Calif.
HPC	Hayes Presidential Center, Fremont, Ohio
HSP	Historical Society of Pennsylvania, Philadelphia
HTT	Howard-Tilton Memorial Library, Tulane University, New Orleans, La.
IHS	Indiana Historical Society, Indianapolis
ISHL	Illinois State Historical Library, Springfield
ISL	Indiana State Library, Indianapolis
KMNP	Kennesaw Mountain National Park, Marietta, Ga.
LC	Library of Congress, Washington, D.C.
MSR	Military Service Record
NARS	National Archives, Washington, D.C.
NCA	North Carolina State Archives, Raleigh
NYHS	New-York Historical Society, New York City
OHS	Ohio Historical Society, Columbus
OR	U.S. Government, *The War of the Rebellion: A Compilation of the Official Records of the Union and Confederate Armies*, 128 vols., Washington, D.C., 1880–1901. *OR* citations take the following form: volume number (part number, where applicable): page number. Unless otherwise indicated, all volumes cited throughout notes are from series 1.
SHC	Southern Historical Collection, University of North Carolina, Chapel Hill
SHSP	*Southern Historical Society Papers*
SHSW	State Historical Society of Wisconsin, Madison
TSLA	Tennessee State Library and Archives, Nashville
UAL	University of Arkansas Libraries, Fayetteville
UGL	University of Georgia Library, Athens
USAMHI	U.S. Army Military History Institute, Carlisle, Pa.

UVA   University of Virginia Library, Charlottesville
WHC   Western Historical Collection, University of Missouri at Columbia

Preface

1. McLaws to wife, Mar. 23, 1865, McLaws Papers, SHC.
2. See Hay, *Hood's Tennessee Campaign*, pp. 190, 193.

Chapter 1

1. Sherman, *Memoirs*, 2:224 (Sherman); *OR* 44:740, 742 (Grant).
2. Sherman, *Memoirs*, 2:213 (quotation); Barrett, *Sherman's March*, pp. 25–26.
3. Liddell-Hart, *Sherman*, p. 358.
4. Sherman, *Memoirs*, 2:225. Sherman seems to have confused his rivers. Raleigh is located about sixty miles below the Roanoke, which flows east along the Virginia–North Carolina border, then turns southeast to empty into Albemarle Sound.
5. A previous attempt to seize this critically important seaport had been made by Maj. Gen. Benjamin F. Butler in December 1864 with disastrous results. Terry's effort, happily for Grant, thus would serve a double purpose.
6. Grant did even more: "I took the precaution to provide for Sherman's army, in case he should be forced to turn in toward the sea coast before reaching North Carolina, by forwarding supplies to every place where he was liable to have to make such a deflection from his projected march." Schofield and the 23d Corps moved from Tennessee to the North Carolina coast in January–February 1865; once there, Schofield used his own and Terry's troops to capture Wilmington. Terry with 8,000 men had been detached from the Army of the James. Grant also canceled Thomas's movement south to Alabama and instead ordered him to "send Stoneman through East Tennessee toward Columbia, South Carolina, in support of Sherman." Grant, *Memoirs*, pp. 518–19.
7. Both the Wilmington and New Bern roads would require extensive repair, but, given the expertise and material available to Sherman, this did not present a formidable problem.
8. *OR* 47(1):17–18. See also Barrett, *Sherman's March*, pp. 30–39; Oakey, "Marching through Georgia," p. 674; Lewis, *Sherman*, pp. 477–85; Henry W. Slocum, "Sherman's March," *B&L* 4:683.
9. Society of the Army of the Tennessee, *Report of the Proceedings*, 14:115–16 (quotation); J. S. Robinson to "Friend Hunt," Apr. 20, 1865, Robinson Papers, OHS.
10. Hardee, "Memoranda of the Operations," HL; *OR* 47(1):22–23, 202 (quotation), 47(2):681; Spencer, *Last Ninety Days*, p. 73.
11. *OR* 47(1):23, 47(2):735; Roesch Memorandum, Roesch Papers, TSLA.
12. *OR* 47(2):703. Regarding the fate of South Carolina, division commander Geary wrote: "In many places there does not remain a single dwelling, and the inhabitants are in a state of starvation, many of whom must die of hunger. In this general devastation, in many instances disgraceful to humanity, you may rest assured that my hands are perfectly clean." John W. Geary to Mary Geary, Mar. 26, 1865, Geary Family Correspondence, HSP.
13. Aten, *History of the Eighty-fifth Illinois*, p. 285; *OR* 47(2):703, 717–19 (quotation, p.

719), 721. Despite Howard's and Slocum's best intentions, Federal foraging operations continued unabated during the march through North Carolina.

14. Shiman, "Engineering Sherman's March," p. 624. Fearing's quotations are from *OR* 47(1):532 (first), 203 (second, fifth), 47(2):741 (third), 47(1):532 (fourth).

15. John W. Geary to Mary Geary, Mar. 26, 1865, Geary Family Correspondence, HSP.

16. The Confederates abandoned enormous quantities of ordnance at Columbia, Cheraw, and Fayetteville: 97 cannon, 18,857 small arms, and 70,850 pounds of powder. The loss is magnified when one considers that as many as 1,000 Confederates began the Battle of Bentonville without arms and as many as 2,500 were poorly armed. On the field they eagerly would exchange their Austrian muskets for shiny Yankee rifles or, if lucky, one of the fabled "16 shooters." *OR* 47(1):171, 183-84.

17. *OR* 47(1):123 (quotation); Henry W. Slocum, "Sherman's March from Savannah to Bentonville," p. 690; John W. Geary to Mary Geary, Mar. 14, 1865, Geary Family Correspondence, HSP.

18. Sherman's troops were not pretty as armies go, Phillip Roesch, 25th Wisconsin, admitted. They were a "hard looking lot of soldiers. Lots of the men were bare-footed and we wore clothes of all kinds and descriptions. Some wore caps, some straw hats, stovepipe hats, ladies' hats, and some nothing on their heads at all. But there was never a more healthy lot of men, ready to go anywhere." Roesch Memorandum, Roesch Papers, TSLA.

19. Slocum believed that the refugees and freedmen together were "almost equal in numbers to the army." Henry W. Slocum, "Sherman's March," *B&L* 4:689. The receiving officer at Wilmington put their number at 8,000-10,000. *OR* 47(2):978.

20. Osborn, *Trials and Triumphs*, p. 196; *OR* 47(1):23, 204, 233, 188; Oakey, "Marching through Georgia," p. 673; Henry W. Slocum, "Sherman's March," *B&L* 4:687, 689; *OR* 53:54-55; Howard, "Bentonville," Howard Papers, BCL; Sherman, *Memoirs*, 2:299.

21. Pratt to parents, Mar. 31, 1865, Pratt Letters, Civil War Miscellaneous Collection, USAMHI.

22. The low incidence of disease in Sherman's army was remarkable during the tramp through the Carolinas. The troops grew healthier through privation, it seemed. Joseph Glatthaar analyzes this phenomenon thoroughly in his fine work, *The March to the Sea and Beyond*, pp. 19-20, 196-99.

23. John A. Logan's chief of artillery, Lt. Col. William H. Ross, hauled along a battery of twenty-pounder Parrotts, preferring their additional firepower despite the increased weight.

24. *OR* 47(1):42-43, 47(2):817-18; Cox, *March to the Sea*, p. 197; Jordan, *Bentonville*, p. 15n; Herring, "Bentonville," p. 7; Howard, "Bentonville," Howard Papers, BCL.

25. *OR* 47(3):21. Blair's arrow was not officially adopted until March 25. Alonzo Miller to father, Apr. 5, 1865, Miller Letters, KMNP; Albion Gross to wife, Mar. 30, 1865, Gross Letters, Civil War Miscellaneous Collection, USAMHI.

26. James P. Jones, "Battle of Atlanta"; Barrett, *Sherman's March*, pp. 32-33.

27. After a century and a half, distinctions, once crisp, have become blurred. Thus the Federal practice of naming armies for rivers (the Army of the Tennessee) and the Confederate fondness for states or regions (Army of Tennessee) tend to trip even the careful reader.

28. Tucker, *High Tide at Gettysburg*, p. 320.

29. Oliver Otis Howard, "Slocum," p. 39.

30. Sheridan, *Memoirs*, 1:10–11; Oliver Otis Howard, "Slocum," p. 39.

31. Marszalek, *Sherman*, p. 279; Cleaves, *Rock of Chickamauga*, p. 235. Sherman's selection of Howard angered not only Hooker, but Logan and most of the Army of the Tennessee as well. The westerners regarded Howard as an outsider and believed that Logan was McPherson's legitimate successor. Sherman chose Howard because he considered him a thorough professional, whereas Logan, a non–West Pointer, a mere "volunteer," was first and foremost a politician.

32. Catton, *This Hallowed Ground*, p. 352; Oliver Otis Howard, "Slocum," p. 41; Nichols, "Story of the Great March," p. 271; Executive Committee for the Army Reunion, *Army Reunion*, p. 99.

33. Eaton, "Diary of an Officer in Sherman's Army," p. 251.

34. Thomas W. Osborn, *Fiery Trail*, pp. 198–99.

35. The preceding sketch of Slocum was drawn from Cleaves, *Rock of Chickamauga*, pp. 234–35; Catton, *This Hallowed Ground*, p. 352; Nichols, *Story of the Great March*, p. 271; New York Monuments Commission, *In Memoriam*, pp. 76, 84, 89; Slocum MSR, NARS; Eaton, "Diary of an Officer in Sherman's Army," p. 251; Thomas W. Osborn, *Fiery Trail*, pp. 98, 199; Herbert, *Hooker*, p. 176; Executive Committee for the Army Reunion, *Army Reunion*, p. 99; Oliver Otis Howard, "Slocum," pp. 39–41; Shiman, "Engineering Sherman's March," p. 665; Barrett, *Sherman's March*, p. 32; Morris, *Sheridan*, p. 17; Fletcher, *Sherman*, pp. 292–94.

36. During the campaign in the Carolinas, Slocum's Army of the Cumberland was called the Left Wing and was "commonly known as the Army of Georgia." Welcher, *Union Army*, 2:174.

37. Oakey, "Marching through Georgia," p. 671; Glatthaar, *March to the Sea*, pp. 18, 30–31.

38. Morse, *Civil War Diaries*, pp. 193–94.

39. This was the famous Sept. 9, 1862, order in which Lee outlined his plans for the invasion of Maryland. Its discovery changed the course of the Antietam Campaign. Oakey, "Marching through Georgia," p. 671; *DAB* 20:247; Barrett, *Sherman's March*, p. 33; Herbert, *Hooker*, p. 176; Sears, *McClellan*, pp. 267, 281.

40. Oakey, "Marching through Georgia," p. 671.

41. Glatthaar, *March to the Sea*, p. 18.

42. Most, if not all, companies in the 17th New York wore the Zouave uniform.

43. Executive Committee for the Army Reunion, *Army Reunion*, p. 94.

44. Cleaves, *Rock of Chickamauga*, pp. 245, 266, 222–23; McNeil, *Personal Recollections*, p. 38; Stewart, *Dan McCook's Regiment*, p. 164; Glatthaar, *March to the Sea*, p. 18; Palumbo, *Thomas*, p. 126; Executive Committee for the Army Reunion, *Army Reunion*, p. 94.

45. Glatthaar, *March to the Sea*, pp. 17, 21; Leander E. Davis to Susan Davis, Mar. 25, 1865, Davis Letters, Civil War Miscellaneous Collection, USAMHI; Monnett, " 'Awfulest Time I Ever Seen,' " p. 289.

46. Grant believed that Sherman learned of Johnston's appointment while in Columbia. It seems more likely that Sherman found out somewhat later, probably while at Cheraw. Because he was not yet in communication with Terry and Schofield, Sherman's source must have been either one of his far-ranging scouts, a prisoner, or a deserter. His references to Johnston nevertheless begin to appear in dispatches and letters on March 5. Grant, *Memoirs*, p. 520; *OR* 47(2):703, 691.

47. Sherman, *Home Letters*, p. 333.

48. Sherman, *Memoirs*, 2:298.

49. "Unencumbered" or "light" meant "with only wagons sufficient to fight a battle." This minimum allowance of vehicles and animals included ambulances, ammunition wagons, organic tool wagons, etc. *OR* 47(1):204.

50. *OR* 47(1):204, 47(2):869–70, 871.

51. Slocum's two remaining divisions under John W. Geary (Twentieth Corps) and Absalom Baird (Fourteenth Corps) moved in a single column with the trains of their respective corps "in the direction of Goldsborough, crossing South River at Graham's or New Bridge, and from there to move to a point near Troublefield's Store." "My train was very long," reported Geary, "containing over 1,000 vehicles." On March 19 Geary marched at 6:00 A.M., "following the Tarborough road to Newton Grove Post-Office at Doctor Monk's house; there turned to the right on the Goldsborough new road, and encamped at Canaan Church," about five miles to the right (east) of the main body of the Left Wing. *OR* 47(1):551, 691, 693.

52. *OR* 47(2):822.

53. *OR* 47(2):949. Schofield and Jacob Cox had defeated Braxton Bragg at the Battle of Kinston (Wise's Forks) on March 8–10. Schofield could not push on to Goldsboro, however, because he lacked pontoons.

54. Howard, "Bentonville," Howard Papers, BCL; *OR* 53:54–55, 47(2):821–23, 833, 845, 47(1):24; Cox, *March to the Sea*, p. 162; Aten, *History of 85th Illinois*, p. 286; Mar. 16, 1865, entry, Bierce Diary, UVA.

55. Benjamin F. Hunter Memoir, *CWTI* Collection, USAMHI.

56. *OR* 47(1):24–25, 422, 665, 949, 47(2):869–71 (quotation, p. 871), 949, 53:55; Toombs, *Reminiscences*, pp. 213–16; Hughes, *Hardee*, pp. 281–85.

57. See Barrett, *Sherman's March*, p. 158.

58. Orendorff, *We Are Sherman's Men*, p. 198; Mar. 17, 1865, entry, Fahnestock Diary, KMNP. See also Thomas W. Osborn, *Fiery Trail*, p. 188; Oakey, "Marching through Georgia," p. 679; *OR* 47(1):24–25, 434, 784, 47(2):869–71.

59. As shown on Plate No. 138, *Official Atlas of the Civil War*, some seven miles east of Black River is a stream called Black Creek. The two should not be confused.

60. Mar. 17, 1865, entry, Fahnestock Diary, Fahnestock Papers, ISHL.

61. *OR* 47(2):877, 47(1):172, 434, 448, 456; Nichols, *Story of the Great March*, p. 260; Mar. 17, 1865, entry, Fahnestock Diary, Fahnestock Papers, ISHL; Bircher, *Drummer-Boy's Diary*, p. 193; Mar. 17, 1865, entry, Williams Diary, Detroit Public Library.

62. Nichols, *Story of the Great March*, p. 262.

63. Shiman, "Engineering Sherman's March," p. 594. A German civil engineer, "Bergholz accompanied Sherman's columns to Goldsboro, and from that point he probably rejoined his family in New York. If Bergholz had remained behind in Columbia, he would have been *most unwelcome*." M. Bradley to N. C. Hughes, May 31, 1994.

64. Shiman, "Engineering Sherman's March," pp. 594, 585, 598–603; Nichols, *Story of the Great March*, p. 262; Johnston, *Narrative*, p. 385; Herring, "Bentonville," p. 30.

65. *OR* 47(2):886.

66. Nichols, *Story of the Great March*, p. 262; *OR* 47(2):886; Barrett, *Sherman's March*, pp. 160–61; Liddell-Hart, *Sherman*, p. 375; Robert W. Barnwell, "Bentonville," p. 48; Cox,

March to the Sea, p. 185; Canfield, *21st . . . Ohio*, p. 183; Hunter, *Eighty-second Indiana*, pp. 159–60.

67. This was essentially the same tactic that William P. Carlin would employ on the morning of March 19.

68. *OR* 47(1):434, 493, 525; Mar. 18, 1865, entry, Purdum Diary, OHS.

69. *OR* 47(1):586, 600 (quotation), 784; Barrett, *Sherman's March*, p. 161; Toombs, *Reminiscences*, pp. 213–16.

70. Carlin, "Military Memoirs."

71. *OR* 47(1):671.

72. Mar. 18, 1865, entry, Isaac Kittinger Diary, Hess Collection, USAMHI.

73. Carlin, "Military Memoirs."

74. Belknap rode back to his foragers with a new countersign for the next five days and orders to move out at 3:00 A.M. on March 19. He was to meet Carlin at Cox's Bridge that night. "If you cannot drive the enemy," Carlin told him, "flank them." Charles E. Belknap, "Bentonville," p. 61.

75. Carlin, "Military Memoirs"; Marcus W. Bates, "Bentonville," p. 141; Barrett, *Sherman's March*, p. 161; Charles E. Belknap, "Bentonville," p. 6; Carlin, "Bentonville," p. 235 (quotation); Charles E. Slocum, *Slocum*, p. 274.

76. Howard, "Bentonville," Howard Papers, BCL.

77. *OR* 47(1):448, 484, 493, 423, 205, 341, 47(2):886–87; James T. Holmes, *52nd O.V.I.*, p. 25; Howard, "Bentonville," Howard Papers, BCL; Fryer, *Eightieth Ohio*, p. 20 (quotation); Henry H. Wright, *Sixth Iowa*, pp. 428–29.

78. Oakey, "Marching through Georgia," pp. 677–78; Barrett, *Sherman's March*, p. 161.

79. *OR* 47(2):886.

80. Nichols, *Story of the Great March*, p. 261.

Chapter 2

1. Govan and Livingood maintain that Beauregard's health was satisfactory and that he used illness for emotional cover, at least that seemed to characterize the conversations between Beauregard and Johnston when Johnston assumed command. Govan and Livingood, *Johnston*, p. 347.

2. *OR* 47(2):1238.

3. "In his new position," Davis rationalized to Col. James Phelan (former Confederate congressman from Mississippi), "those defects which I found manifested by him when serving as an independent commander will be remedied by the control of the general-in-chief." *OR* 47(2):1303.

4. William Palfrey to Moses Greenwood, Mar. 3, 1865, Greenwood Papers, Historic New Orleans Collection.

5. Hay, *Hood's Tennessee Campaign*, 193. See Parrish, *Richard Taylor*, 429–30.

6. Symonds, *Johnston*, p. 341; *OR* 47(2):1247–48 (first quotation, p. 1247); Johnston, "My Negotiations," p. 183 (second quotation); Thomas L. Connelly, *Autumn of Glory*, p. 518; Vance, *Last Days*, pp. 8–9.

7. Spencer, *Last Ninety Days*, p. 73; France, *Bentonville*, p. 1; *OR* 47(2):1256–57.

8. Johnston, *Narrative*, p. 371; Thomas B. Hampton to wife Jestin C. Hampton, Feb. 26,

1865, Hampton Letters, Center for American History, University of Texas, Austin (quotation); *OR* 47(2):1284; *CV* 39:62; Harper, *Fifty-eighth Regiment*, pp. 14, 17.

9. Johnston requested that Bragg be put under his control once he determined that "the first serious opposition to General Sherman's progress was to be in North Carolina." Bragg reacted immediately to Davis: "For this and other reasons which present themselves to your mind as forcibly as I could express them, I beg that you will relieve me from the embarrassing position. I seek no command or position, and only desire to be ordered to await assignment to duty at some point in Georgia or Alabama. The circumstances constraining me to make this request are painful in the extreme, but I cannot blindly disregard them." *OR* 47(2):1328, 1334.

10. Barrett, *Sherman's March*, p. 113; Johnston, *Narrative*, p. 378; *OR* 47(2):1298, 1218; Wade Hampton, "Bentonville," *B&L* 4:700-701. This operational concept seems to have been devised, or first articulated, by Wade Hampton in a February 18 dispatch to Beauregard.

11. Indeed, Johnston ordered all staff officers from army headquarters to join him except the "Chief of Artillery and his staff." William Palfrey to Moses Greenwood, Mar. 3, 1865, Greenwood Papers, Historic New Orleans Collection.

12. *OR* 47(2):1286 (first quotation); "History of 10th South Carolina," p. 130, CCNMP (second quotation); James L. Lynch to wife, Mar. 15, 1865, Lynch Letters, GAH; Stephenson, *Civil War Memoir*, 347, 353; William Palfrey to Moses Greenwood, Feb. 22, 1865, Greenwood Papers, Historic New Orleans Collection.

13. R. W. Simmons, "The Last Battle," *CV* Papers, DU (first quotation); Stephenson, "My War Autobiography," Louisiana and Lower Mississippi Valley Collections, Louisiana State University Libraries, Baton Rouge (second quotation); W. W. Mackall to J. E. Johnston, Feb. 16, 1865, Johnston Collection, Earl Gregg Swem Library, College of William and Mary, Williamsburg, Va.; Ratchford, *Some Reminiscences*, p. 38; Gibson, *Those 163 Days*, p. 187.

14. Stephen Lee had been wounded in a rear guard action during Hood's retreat from Tennessee. Hobbling about on crutches, Lee married in Columbus, Miss., on February 9, then made his way toward Johnston, gathering troops as he went. He arrived too late to participate in the fighting at Bentonville.

15. Jan. 20-Feb. 23, 1865, entries, Nash Diary, UGL; Willett, *40th Alabama*, p. 86; Howell, *Going to Meet the Yankees*, p. 260; Thomas L. Connelly, *Autumn of Glory*, p. 514; Seaton, *Bugle Softly Blows*, pp. 62-63; Ridley, *Battles and Sketches*, p. 455; Reddick, *Seventy-seven Years*, p. 35; *OR* 47(1):1080-83, 1047; *CV* 18:332; Johnston, *Narrative*, pp. 372-75.

16. Trotter, *Silk Flags and Cold Steel*, pp. 227-28. "By March 11, 120 carloads of men, guns, and wagons clogged the freight yards." Ibid., p. 228. See also Losson, *Tennessee's Forgotten Warriors*, p. 246.

17. Johnston, *Narrative*, pp. 372-74; *OR* 47(2):1194; Thomas L. Connelly, *Autumn of Glory*, p. 521; Lazarus, "A Civil War Biography" (quotation); Trotter, *Silk Flags and Cold Steel*, p. 227.

18. Johnston had been placed in charge of Bragg's forces by Robert E. Lee on February 23 but did not assume operational control for two weeks.

19. "Contrary to established practices for the naming of battles, Union sources refer to the geographical title, Wise's Forks, while Southern accounts seem to prefer Southwest Creek."

J. C. Goode to N. C. Hughes, Feb. 16, 1994. The quotation in the text is from Thomas L. Connelly, *Autumn of Glory*, p. 524.

20. Johnston, *Narrative*, pp. 378-79; *OR* 47(2):1334-40, 47(1):1045; Symonds, *Johnston*, pp. 346-47. See also Bridges, *Hill*, pp. 231-45; Cozzens, *This Terrible Sound*, pp. 518-33.

21. Thomas L. Connelly, *Autumn of Glory*, p. 155.

22. *OR* 47(2):1377.

23. Johnston, *Narrative*, p. 377; *OR* 47(2):1298-99, 1364.

24. *OR* 47(1):1050-52 (quotation, p. 1051), 47(2):1318, 1321; Symonds, *Johnston*, pp. 346-47.

25. *OR* 47(2):1372.

26. Hallock, *Bragg*, pp. 236-41; Symonds, *Johnston*, p. 346; "History of 10th South Carolina," CCNMP, p. 133. Kinston fell on March 14. Goldsboro itself, the object of Sherman's campaign, would be abandoned without a fight on March 21.

27. Robert W. Barnwell, "Bentonville," p. 47; Symonds, *Johnston*, p. 347; D. H. Sale to D. H. Hill, Mar. 13, 1865, Stevenson Papers, NARS; Johnston, *Narrative*, pp. 378, 382; *OR* 47(2):1372, 1388; Thomas L. Connelly, *Autumn of Glory*, p. 522.

28. *OR* 47(2):1181, 1202, 47(1):1048. Desperately ill with typhoid, Hardee surrendered command of Charleston to Lafayette McLaws and "had to be sent off to Kingstree." Actually it was McLaws who led the column out of the city. Feb. 14, 1865, entries, Roy Diary, ALA; *OR* 47(2):1205, 1223.

29. Hardee, "Memoranda of the Operations," HL; *OR* 47(1):1053; Jordan, *Bentonville*, p. 7.

30. Ford, "Last Battles," p. 140.

31. Sanders, "More about . . . Bentonville," p. 461.

32. Hughes, *Hardee*, p. 481; *OR* 44:1004; McMurray, *Twentieth Tennessee*, p. 148.

33. Hardee entrusted movement of the field guns to his chief of artillery at Charleston, the old Cuban revolutionary Ambrosio José Gonzales. Ironically, Johnston would make Gonzales army chief of artillery, a position long sought by the Cuban and long denied by President Davis. See Cova, "Ambrosio José Gonzales," pp. 326-32.

34. Ford, "Last Battles of Hardee's Corps," pp. 140-41. See also Cova, "Ambrosio José Gonzales," pp. 331-32.

35. Feb. 20, 1865, entry, Roy Diary, ALA.

36. Hardee was one of those rare individuals who admired both Davis and Johnston professionally and was devoted to both personally. Somehow he managed to hold the tensions of their relationship apart from himself. He could be critical, no doubt about that— witness his comments about Sidney Johnston's management of the army in February 1862 and Bragg's fiascoes in Kentucky and at Murfreesboro.

37. *OR* 47(1):1044, 1048-49, 1071-72, 47(2):1205; Johnson, "Confederate Defense of Fort Sumter," *B&L* 4:26; Johnson, *This They Remembered*, p. 124; Hardee, "Memoranda of the Operations," HL; Ford, "Last Battles," p. 140; Barrett, *Sherman's March*, p. 109; James Griffin to Leila, Feb. 27, 1865, *CWTI* Collection, USAMHI (quotation); Hagood, *Memoirs*, p. 364; Feb. 18-25, 1865, entries, Roy Diary, ALA.

38. Johnston, *Narrative of Operations*, p. 376.

39. *OR* 47(2):1320.

40. *OR* 47(2):1332–33, 1335–36 (first quotation, p. 1335), 1135 (second quotation); Ford, "Last Battles," p. 141; Johnston, *Narrative*, pp. 376, 380; Barrett, *Sherman's March*, p. 108.

41. Barrett, *Sherman's March*, p. 150; *OR* 47(2):1323, 1361; Ford, "Last Battles," p. 141; C. W. Hutson to sister, Mar. 12, 1865, Hutson Family Papers, HTT; Johnston, *Narrative*, p. 382. When Wright's Division was broken up on February 22, Gen. Hugh W. Mercer left also, reporting to Howell Cobb at Macon. Feb. 22, 1865, entry, Roy Diary, ALA.

42. Mar. 6–11, 1865, entries, Roy Diary, ALA; *OR* 47(2):1362–63.

43. *OR* 47(2):1375.

44. *OR* 47(2):1397.

45. Skirmishing began at Averasboro on the same day.

46. Hughes, *Hardee*, p. 285. See also Cozzens, *Shipwreck of Their Hopes*, p. 270.

47. The bulk of Hardee's command appears to have avoided Averasboro, although he left his seriously wounded in the village.

48. *OR* 47(2):1401–2; Hughes, *Hardee*, pp. 281–85; Oakey, "Marching through Georgia," pp. 678–79; Barrett, *Sherman's March*, p. 154; Mar. 16, 1865, entry, Roy Diary, ALA. If Johnston had sent "a force" or merely staff to Elevation as Hardee requested, the serious miscalculations about distance that occurred on Mar. 17–19 might have been avoided. It is not known why Johnston did not do so. *OR* 47(1):1073.

49. Hardee, "Memoranda of the Operations," HL.

50. Ibid.; McLaws Order Book, McLaws Papers, SHC.

51. *OR* 47(2):1411.

52. Hardee, "Memoranda of the Operations," HL; Gibson, *Those 163 Days*, p. 218; Robert W. Barnwell, "Bentonville," p. 48; Shiman, "Engineering Sherman's March," p. 588;

53. Hunter, *History of the Eighty-second Indiana*, pp. 159–60; Canfield, *21st . . . Ohio*, p. 183.

54. Hardee fortunately had started his trains on their way long in advance. Fifty-two "surplus" cannon, which he had guarded zealously on the retirement from Charleston through Cheraw through Fayetteville, he sent toward Smithfield on another road to the north (via Leachburg). Undoubtedly Hardee had these pieces in the custody of his friend and staff officer, the old Cuban revolutionary, Col. Ambrosio J. Gonzales.

55. McMurry, *Footprints*, p. 173.

56. See McLaws Papers, SHC, particularly the correspondence of Charles J. Colcock, John C. Fiser, T. B. Roy, and L. P. Yandell, Jan. 15–Feb. 1, 1865. The quotation in the text is from T. B. Roy to L. McLaws, Jan. 28, 1865.

57. Although this order has not been found, the context of Hardee's message to Johnston suggests that it dealt with the reassignment of McLaws. Furthermore, it is not known if Hardee placed the document in McLaws's hands before Bentonville. *OR* 47(1):1075.

58. The brigade, now commanded by Col. Baxter Smith, included what remained of the 8th Texas Cavalry (Terry's Texas Rangers), 11th Texas Cavalry, 3d Arkansas Cavalry, and 4th Tennessee Cavalry.

59. Hampton worried about Kilpatrick's cavalry as well. He had encountered only small bodies in advance of the infantry. Perhaps they intended "to strike at our trains or to reach the railroad at Raleigh. Some disposition should be made to counteract such a movement." *OR* 47(2):1415.

60. Hughes, *Hardee*, p. 551; *OR* 47(2):1411.

61. McLaws Order Book, McLaws Papers, SHC; McMurry, *Footprints*, p. 173; Johnston, *Narrative*, p. 383; Sanders, "Battle of Averasboro, *CV* 34:216 (quotation); Ford, "Last Battles," p. 141.

62. *OR* 47(1):1075.

63. *OR* 47(2):1410.

64. *OR* 47(1):1075 (quotations), 47(2):1410; Barrett, *Sherman's March*, p. 157; Hughes, *Hardee*, pp. 549-51.

65. Most secondary accounts of Bentonville agree that Johnston knew early on March 18 that Sherman's Right Wing was now separated by "a half day's march" from the trailing Left Wing. Armed with this intelligence, Johnston issued marching orders to his force at 6:45 A.M. to proceed to Bentonville. This is what Hampton himself contends in his article on Bentonville: "I replied at once, telling him [Johnston] that the Fourteenth Corps (Davis's) was in my immediate front; the Twentieth Corps (Williams's) was on the same road, five or six miles in the rear; while the two other corps (Logan's and Blair's) were on a road some miles to the south, which ran parallel to the one on which we were." Hampton, "Bentonville," *B&L* 4:701.

Actually the dispatches from Hampton during the seventeenth and past noon on the eighteenth indicate that the enemy force confronting him and its direction of march were not sufficiently defined. "I have not yet learned the strength of the force opposed to me, nor what force it is," Hampton reported to Johnston at 2:30 P.M. on March 18, "but I hope to get some prisoners soon. I think the Fifteenth and Seventeenth Corps camped near Beaman's Cross-Roads last night." Certainly, as late as 8:45 on the morning of the eighteenth Johnston, with a show of some uncertainty, told Hardee that he must abort the move to Bentonville if he discovered Federal forces advancing up the Averasboro-Smithfield road. If that were to develop, "on receiving prompt notice from you, all our columns could be turned on that force." *OR* 47(2):1406-36.

It appears conclusive that it was Hardee's dispatch to Hampton of 7:00 A.M. on March 18 that triggered Hampton's recommendation to Johnston. As Hardee wrote: "The Fourteenth and Twentieth Corps advanced yesterday to Averasborough and moved out about two miles on the Smithfield and Raleigh roads, but retired back to Averasborough in the afternoon. If your information be correct that the Seventeenth and Fifteenth Corps are moving on Goldsborough, we may reasonably conclude that the force at Averasborough will move to-day in the same direction. I can't think that two corps would move on Raleigh; if so, General Johnston will concentrate and whip them." *OR* 47(2):1429.

66. *OR* 47(1):1126-27, 1130, 47(2):1410-11, 1413-16, 1422; Johnston, *Narrative*, p. 383; Barrett, *Sherman's March*, pp. 156-57; Hartley, "Bentonville," p. 29; Govan and Livingood, *Johnston*, p. 354; Hughes, *Hardee*, p. 551.

67. An infuriated Cheatham did everything in his power to get his troops on their way and at one time resorted to smashing a conductor with his fist, knocking the man off the train. Losson, *Tennessee's Forgotten Warriors*, p. 246.

68. *OR* 47(2):1374.

69. Lash, *Destroyer of the Iron Horse*, pp. 170, 168. Johnston rationalized the situation, blaming the "slow working of the railroad." On March 17 he wrote Lee: "Cheatham's rolling stock only conveys about 500 men a day. . . . The Tennessee troops are not all up yet,

although the movement commenced eight days ago." *OR* 47(1):1054. For a full discussion of Johnston's role, see Lash, *Destroyer of the Iron Horse*, pp. 164-70. On the other hand, perhaps this judgment is unfair to Johnston and does not take into account sufficiently the catastrophic times in which Johnston found himself and the context of Confederate military and political policy and practice. For counterarguments see Robert C. Black, *Railroads of the Confederacy*, p. 276ff., and George E. Turner, *Victory Rode the Rails*, p. 365ff.

70. *OR* 47(2):1385-88, 47(1):1079; Mar. 13-17, 1865, entries, Nash Diary, UGL; Mar. 15, 1865, entry, Reynolds Diary, UAL; Mar. 11-17, 1865, entries, J. W. Taylor Diary, NCA.

71. *OR* 47(2):1396-97, 1399, 1402, 1412.

72. Mar. 15, 1865, entry, Reynolds Diary, UAL.

73. Ridley, *Battles and Sketches*, p. 452.

Chapter 3

1. *OR* 47(2):1414-15, 1429.

2. *OR* 47(2):1429.

3. An act disturbingly reminiscent of Tupelo, Miss., in July 1862 (Bragg took command of the Army of Tennessee on June 27 and immediately cracked down hard), apparently occurred at Smithfield on March 16. Perhaps for the sake of discipline, in this chaotic time of splintered units and loosening loyalties, Hoke or Bragg ordered a private in Colquitt's Brigade executed for mutiny. Hinsdale, *72nd . . . North Carolina*, p. 24.

4. The Army of Tennessee suffered from a disturbing penchant on the part of their commanders, certainly Braxton Bragg, for tampering with field command structure on the eve of battle. Bragg did so at Murfreesboro, Chickamauga, and Missionary Ridge with most unfortunate consequences.

5. Bragg expanded on Johnston's order in credible fashion. He dispatched a battery from Starr's artillery battalion to Cox's Bridge. These guns were to support Col. John N. Whitford's Brigade (67th and 68th Regiments North Carolina Troops), about 1,000 men. Whitford was to defend that critical approach to Goldsboro and, if driven back, to destroy the bridge across the Neuse. Cavalry would have to oppose any advance of Schofield's men from Kinston. *OR* 47(2):1424, 1436.

6. One is reminded of Johnston's indecisive visits to the Army of Tennessee in the spring of 1863. Fully empowered to replace Bragg, he equivocated.

7. *OR* 47(2):1427-29, 1435-36; Johnston, *Narrative*, p. 385.

8. Sometimes a sixth brigade (Col. George Jackson's) is listed as a part of Hoke's force. It was composed of Col. Peter Mallett's Battalion (Camp Guard), 19th Regiment North Carolina Troops (2d Regiment North Carolina Cavalry), and the 78th Senior Reserves (8th North Carolina Reserves). It appears that some of these troops remained, as did Jackson himself, in Smithfield during the battle. *OR* 47(2):1450-51; Walter Clark, *Regiments . . . from North Carolina*, 4:108.

9. Starr's command was comprised of the 3d (Maj. J. W. Moore) and 13th North Carolina Light Artillery Battalions (Capt. George B. Atkins), the 10th Battalion North Carolina Heavy Artillery, and the Chesterfield Artillery (Kelly's South Carolina Battery). For Whitford's two regiments at Cox's Bridge, see n. 4 above.

10. In May 1863 he had performed creditably at the Battle of Salem Church. His arm was

shattered in this engagement, however, and perhaps this wound had an effect on his perfor-mance thereafter.

11. Evans, *Confederate Military History*, 5:246. See also W. Glenn Robertson, *Back Door to Richmond*, pp. 146–98; D. W. Barefoot to W. T. Jordan, November 1994. There are those who disagree with such a positive assessment of Hoke. Richard A. Summers and Douglas S. Freeman believe that Hoke could not be counted on to cooperate with his fellow com-manders once he reached the level of division commander, pointing to five disappointing performances in 1864 that demonstrated a lack of teamwork. Sommers, *Richmond Re-deemed*, pp. 116–17; Freeman, *Lee's Lieutenants*, 3:592–93.

12. Gragg, *Confederate Goliath*, pp. 127, 188–89.

13. Kirkland spent a portion of 1862 with the Army of Tennessee as a volunteer aide to Har-dee, his relative by marriage. Just before the Battle of Murfreesboro he is shown with Har-dee's chief subordinate, P. R. Cleburne, as chief of staff. A fellow townsman from Hillsbor-ough, L. H. Mangum, was a Cleburne aide. Buck, *Cleburne and His Command*, pp. 22, 22n.

14. Hagood, *Memoirs*, p. 356; Mar. 11–18, 1865, entries, J. W. Taylor Diary, NCA; Walter Clark, *Regiments . . . from North Carolina*, 4:547; Mar. 18, 1865, entry, Calder Diary, DU (quotations); *OR* 47(2):1422, 1436.

15. *OR* 47(1):1106 (first quotation); Mar. 18, 1865, entry, Reynolds Diary, UAL; Corn, "In Enemy's Lines," p. 507; Ridley, *Battles and Sketches*, p. 452 (second quotation); Mar. 18, 1865, entry, Sloan Diary, TSLA.

16. Simmons, "Analysis"; Johnston, *Narrative*, p. 384.

17. Vaughan, *13th Tennessee*, p. 35.

18. Simmons, "Analysis"; Johnston, *Narrative*, p. 384; Watkins, *Company Aytch*, p. 227; Vaughan, *13th Tennessee*, p. 35; Sanders, "Battle of Averasboro," p. 216; Howell, *Going to Meet the Yankees*, p. 264; Daniel P. Smith, *Company K*, pp. 129–30; Fort, History and Memoirs, p. 27, USAMHI (first quotation); *Smithfield Herald*, Feb. 14, 1958; T. B. Hampton to Jestin Hampton, Feb. 3, 1865, Hampton Letters, Center for American History, University of Texas, Austin (second quotation).

19. W. A. Roher to Cousin Susan, Roher Letters, Feb. 2, 1864, KMNP.

20. *OR* 47(1):1106, 1093; Mar. 18, 1865, entry, Nash Diary, UGL.

21. *OR* 47(1):1075.

22. *OR* 47(2):1427, 1431.

23. Johnston, *Narrative*, p. 385.

24. Mar. 17–18, 1865, entries, Johnson Diary, DU.

25. Mar. 18, 1865, entry, C. W. Hutson Diary, Hutson Family Papers, HTT; Mar. 18, 1865, entry, William A. Johnson Diary, Atlanta *Journal*, Dec. 21, 1901.

26. *OR* 47(2):1410, 1428–29, 1431.

27. Mar. 18, 1865, entry, C. W. Hutson Diary, Hutson Family Papers, HTT.

28. *OR* 47(2):1431.

29. McLaws Order Book, McLaws Papers, SHC; Mar. 18, 1865, entry, William A. John-son Diary, Atlanta *Journal*, Dec. 21, 1901.

30. Johnston, *Narrative*, p. 385; *OR* 47(1):1056. The maps that were so disruptive to the Confederate plans (and that deceived Sherman as well) appear not to have been updated since 1854. Mar. 18, 1865, entry, Roy Diary, ALA; Nichols, *Story of the Great March*, p. 262; Bradley T. Johnson, *Johnston*, p. 213; Herring, "Bentonville," p. 30.

31. Wade Hampton, "Bentonville," *B&L* 4:701.

32. Ford, *Life in the Confederate Army*, p. 54. Hardee was referring to the rout of Rhett's Brigade, artillerists who had their baptism of fire as infantrymen on March 16.

33. Ford, *Life in the Confederate Army*, p. 54.

34. Sneed's house was about 4-6 miles from Bentonville; its locaton is otherwise unknown.

35. Mar. 18, 1865, entry, Johnson Diary, DU; *OR* 47(2):1427-28.

36. *OR* 47(2):1428.

37. Johnston, *Narrative*, p. 384.

38. *OR* 47(2):1429-33, 1439-40; Johnston, *Narrative*, p. 384; Govan and Livingood, *Johnston*, p. 354; Johnson, *Johnston*, pp. 213-14.

39. Controversy over the effectiveness of Joe Wheeler has never been resolved. Historians have tended to minimize his services and highlight the poor discipline of his command. Hardee, however, consistently supported Wheeler, and Hardee knew as well as anyone what a good cavalry commander should be. Wheeler's cavalry "is a well organized and efficient body," he informed President Davis in January 1865. "The reports of its disorganization and demoralization are without foundation, and the depredations ascribed to his command can generally be traced to bands of marauders claiming to belong to it." *OR* 47(2):1000. Supporting Hardee in this opinion were leaders such as D. H. Hill and Governor Andrew G. Magrath, neither of whom were known for diffidence in evaluating military capability or performance.

40. Wade Hampton, "Bentonville," *B&L* 4:701.

41. Ibid., pp. 701-2. See also *OR* 47(2):1429-33; Walter Clark, *Regiments . . . from North Carolina*, 3:195; Barrett, *Sherman's March*, p. 162; Orendorff et al., *103d Illinois*, p. 199; Beach, "Bentonville," p. 26; Johnston, *Narrative*, pp. 385-86.

42. Wade Hampton, "Bentonville," *B&L* 4:703.

43. Ibid., pp. 702-3; Luvaas, "Johnston's Last Stand," pp. 335-36; Govan and Livingood, *Johnston*, p. 355; Barrett, *Sherman's March*, p. 162; Herring, "Bentonville," p. 32; Liddell-Hart, *Sherman*, pp. 374-75; *OR* 47(1):1054-56; Symonds, *Johnston*, p. 348; Howard, "Bentonville," Howard Papers, BCL.

44. Thanks to the helpful and courageous work of Nancy S. King, who braved the wilds of a Bentonville swamp with a sharp saw, the author has a one-foot section of such terrible, dangerous, painful briar mounted on the wall of his study. He keeps it there, he likes to think, to remind him of the obstacles and endurance of Civil War warriors. He also keeps it there to scare the daylights out of the curious exploring their grandfather's study.

45. Howard, "Bentonville," Howard Papers, BCL.

46. *OR* 47(2):1428-29.

47. D. H. Hill to daughter, Mar. 23, 1865, Hill Family Papers, USAMHI.

Chapter 4

1. L. McLaws to wife, Mar. 23, 1865, McLaws Papers, SHC; *OR* 47(2):1444.

2. Nine sources place Hardee's troops in Bentonville in the morning, the earliest at eight and the latest at ten. One additional source has him arriving at 3:00 P.M., but this is contradicted by all other sources.

3. Mar. 19, 1865, entry, Carpenter, *Diary*; Mar. 19, 1865, entry, Johnson Diary, DU; McLaws Order Book, McLaws Papers, SHC.

4. Mar. 18, 1865, entry, Hutson Diary, Hutson Family Papers, HTT; Mar. 19, 1865, entry, Roy Diary, ALA; *OR* 47(2):1428; McLaws Order Book, McLaws Papers, SHC; Carpenter, *Diary*, p. 16; Hughes, *Hardee*, p. 551; Barrett, *Sherman's March*, pp. 159-60; Mar. 19, 1865, entry, William A. Johnson Diary, Atlanta *Journal*, Dec. 21, 1901; Mar. 19, 1865, entry, Johnson Diary, DU; Gibson, *Those 163 Days*, p. 219.

5. Johnston, *Narrative*, pp. 385-86.

6. *OR* 47(1):1103.

7. Johnston, *Narrative*, p. 385.

8. McLaws Order Book, McLaws Papers, SHC. Veteran Bentonville battle site director, John C. Goode, agrees with McLaws, believing it quite possible for Johnston's units to have been backed up all the way to Bentonville itself. *OR* 47(1):1089, 1093, 1103; D. H. Hill to daughter, Mar. 23, 1865, Hill Family Papers, USAMHI; Mar. 19, 1865, entry, Reynolds Diary, UAL; Mar. 19, 1865, entry, Calder Diary, DU; France, *Bentonville*, p. 7.

9. Mar. 19, 1865, entry, Calder Diary, DU.

10. Atlanta *Journal*, Sept. 7, 1901; Robinson, "Johnston," p. 366; Corn, "In Enemy Lines," p. 507; Dickert, *Kershaw's Brigade*, p. 523.

11. Atlanta *Journal*, Apr. 13, 1901. See also Thomas, "Their Last Battle," pp. 218-20, and "Bentonville"; Avery, "Reminiscences," GAH.

12. D. H. Hill to daughter, Mar. 23, 1865, Hill Family Papers, USAMHI.

13. Mar. 19, 1865, entry, Reynolds Diary, UAL. The shell then struck and killed the horse of Capt. Robert Davis Smith, an ordnance officer in George D. Johnston's (Quarles's) Brigade. Evans, *Confederate Military History*, 10:718.

14. Mar. 19, 1865, entry, Reynolds Diary, UAL. "The operation was performed by Dr. John T. Darby, Med. Dr. Army Tenn. assisted by my own Surgeons & others. My orderly, V. King, got my saddle & bridle & brought them off the field." Ibid. See also Dacus, *Reminiscences*, n.p.

15. See Hay, *Hood's Tennessee Campaign*, pp. 173-75.

16. One of Reynolds's men placed the blame for the misfortune squarely on division commander Walthall, who yielded to the entreaties of the Alabama brigade (Johnston's) in his division. Just "as at Nashville," the troops' position was more exposed, and they entreated Walthall to have "Reynolds to swap places wit them again." In the process of exchanging positions, Reynolds was hit. The official report of Col. Henry Bunn, who succeeded Reynolds, would appear to support this contention. Dacus, *Reminiscences*, n.p.; *OR* 47(1):1104-5. Lt. Col. Bromfield L. Ridley of Stewart's staff echoed the sentiments of many: "His [Reynolds's] loss is much lamented. He is the idol of his brigade." Ridley, *Battles and Sketches*, p. 452.

17. Dacus, *Reminiscences*, n.p. Despite Walthall's dramatic gesture, Reynolds's Brigade seems to have been led ably by Col. Henry G. Bunn, veteran commander of the 4th Arkansas. Ibid.

18. Halsey, "Last Duel," p. 31 (quotation); Robinson, "Johnston," p. 366; Hart, "Hart's ... Battery," p. 131; *OR* 47(1):1104-5; Wade Hampton, "Bentonville," *B&L* 4:703; Markens, *Hebrews in America*, p. 137. Hampton's light guns were badly mismatched, of course, against the Federal Napoleons and three-inch rifles.

19. Robert Lowry commanded Adams's Brigade at Nashville and was succeeded by Lieutenant Colonel Lawrence, then by Col. Richard Harrison in North Carolina. R. Hugh Simmons, in his exhaustive study of units and strength in the Army of Tennessee in 1865, concludes: the "1864 command structure [of Loring's Division] was present under junior commanders. Adams was killed and Scott severely wounded at Franklin, Tennessee. Featherston had remained behind in Tupelo to collect the men on furlough, and rejoined the army in early April. Adams', Scott's, and Featherston's brigades were present and on the field at Bentonville although in a sadly depleted condition." Simmons to N. C. Hughes, Oct. 25, 1993; *OR* 47(3):698, 734.

20. France, *Bentonville*, p. 7; Barrett, *Sherman's March*, p. 164; James W. Bell, *43rd Georgia*, p. 39; *OR* 47(1):1089, 1093; Robinson, "Johnston," p. 366; Cox, *March to the Sea*, pp. 188–89.

21. Walter Clark, *Regiments . . . from North Carolina*, 4:351, places the 72d North Carolina (Junior Reserves) on the right of Starr.

22. Barrett, *Sherman's March*, p. 164; J. P. Smith, "Bentonville"; Walter Clark, *Regiments . . . from North Carolina*, 4:56, 351, 547; Hagood, *Memoirs*, p. 358 (second, third quotations); Manarin, *North Carolina Troops*, 1:585; France, *Bentonville*, p. 7; Beach, "Bentonville," p. 25; Hinsdale, *72nd . . . North Carolina*, p. 25.

23. Johnston, *Narrative*, p. 385; Barrett, *Sherman's March*, p. 164; Mrs. John H. Anderson, "Memorial," p. 367; Jordan, *Bentonville*, p. 16 (quotation); Luvaas, "Bentonville," *CWTI*, p. 6.

24. *OR* 47(1):1057–58, 1089, 47(2):999–1000, 1397, 1408, 1460–61, 47(3):687; J. E. Johnston to R. E. Lee, Mar. 27, 1865, Johnston Papers, HL; Livermore, *Numbers and Losses*, p. 135. It is impossible to determine Johnston's numbers with accuracy. Perhaps the best that can be done is to use his "rough" field returns of March 17 and add 500 for men from Cheatham's Corps gained by the Army of Tennessee after that count. Hardee, however, had lost an undetermined number through straggling and desertion on his march from Elevation. The figure 15,400 may be somewhat inflated. Indeed, the estimate Johnston used twenty years later—14,100—may have been the closest for March 19. Johnston, *Narrative*, p. 392.

25. Dyer, *Reminiscences*, p. 288; Mar. 19, 1865, entry, Waring Diary, SHC; Mar. 19, 1865, entry, Johnson Diary, DU; Cox, *March to the Sea*, p. 187; John Witherspoon DuBose, *Wheeler*, p. 350; Hagood, *Memoirs*, p. 358; Mar. 19, 1865, entry, Calder Diary, DU; Watson, "In the Battle of Bentonville"; Ridley, *Battles and Sketches*, p. 452; *OR* 47(1):1089, 1099; Beach, "Bentonville," p. 26.

26. McGuire, "Greek Meeting Greek," p. 549.

27. Ibid.

28. Mar. 19, 1865, entry, Calder Diary, DU; *OR* 47(1):1093, 1099 (first quotation); Avery, "Reminiscences," GAH; Fort, "1st Georgia," pp. 26–27, USAMHI; Corn, "In Enemy's Lines," p. 507.

29. They were members of the class of 1842, as was Lafayette McLaws.

30. McGuire, "Greek Meets Greek," p. 549.

31. Ibid.

32. Ibid. The 32d Tennessee had reason to remember Chickamauga. McGuire, then a major, had commanded the regiment and had been wounded. The regiment itself lost 165 of 361 engaged. Corn, "In Enemy's Lines," p. 507.

33. *OR* 47(1):1089-90, 1093-94 (quotations, p. 1094), 1108.

34. *OR* 47(1):1089, 1094; Thomas, "Bentonville."

35. Hagood, *Memoirs*, p. 358 (quotation); *OR* 47(1):1089-90, 1093-94, 1099; James W. Bell, *43rd Georgia*, p. 39; Watson, "In the Battle of Bentonville"; Mar. 19, 1865, entry, Nash Diary, UGL; Atlanta *Journal*, Apr. 13, 1901; Bogle, *40th Ga. Regiment*, p. 213; Thomas L. Connelly, *Autumn of Glory*, p. 527.

36. Walter A. Clark, *Under the Stars and Bars*, pp. 167 (first quotation), 192; *OR* 47(2): 1437 (second quotation), 47(1):1106; Ridley, *Battles and Sketches*, p. 452; Johnston, *Narrative*, p. 387; Reddick, *Seventy-seven Years*, pp. 36-37.

37. *OR* 47(1):1056; Hagood, *Memoirs*, pp. 358-60 (first quotation, p. 358); Walter Clark, *Regiments . . . from North Carolina*, 3:698-700, 4:547; Mar. 19, 1865, entry, Calder Diary, DU; D. H. Hill to daughter, Mar. 23, 1865, Hill Family Papers, USAMHI; Luvaas, "Bentonville," p. 38; Horn, *Army of Tennessee*, p. 425; Mar. 19, 1865, entry, C. W. Hutson Diary, Hutson Family Papers, HTT (last quotation).

38. No evidence has been found indicating that either Hoke or Kirkland called for reinforcements.

39. *OR* 47(1):1056; Walter Clark, *Histories*, 4:547; Jordan, *Bentonville*, p. 17; Luvaas, "Bentonville," p. 38; Hughes, *Hardee*, p. 553; Symonds, *Johnston*, p. 350; Dickert, *Kershaw's Brigade*, p. 523; Hallock, *Bragg*, p. 253; Wade Hampton, "Bentonville," *B&L* 4:703; Johnston, *Narrative*, p. 386; J. E. Johnston to R. Hoke, Jan. 27, 1871, Hoke Papers, NCA.

40. McLaws Order Book, McLaws Papers, SHC.

41. Dickert, *Kershaw's Brigade*, p. 523.

42. Stackhouse's 3d South Carolina was not organic to Fiser's Brigade, but to Conner's.

43. Mar. 19, 1865, entry, Johnson Diary, DU; McLaws Order Book, McLaws Papers, SHC; Johnston, *Narrative*, p. 386. The location of Blanchard's small brigade of reserves is unknown. Probably it was held at the church as a deep reserve or placed on the eastern fork of the Bentonville road to help interdict the battlefield. Yet all the time it might have been at Hannah's Creek, where Hardee positioned it on March 17 to guard a bridge.

44. McLaws Order Book, McLaws Papers, SHC (quotation); Hutson Reminiscences, SHC; Mar. 19, 1865, entry, William A. Johnston Diary, Atlanta *Journal*, Dec. 21, 1901; France, *Bentonville*, p. 12.

45. Ford, *Life in the Confederate Army*, p. 55.

46. Loring would retire from the field on March 20, turning over command of the corps to Walthall.

47. *OR* 47(1):1106.

48. Ford, "Last Battles," p. 141; Ford, *Life in the Confederate Army*, p. 55; Mar. 19, 1865, entry, Roy Diary, ALA; Hardee, "Memoranda of the Operations," HL; D. H. Hill to daughter, Mar. 23, 1865, Hill Family Papers, USAMHI; *OR* 47(1):1056, 1090, 1094, 1106; France, *Bentonville*, p. 12; Barrett, *Sherman's March*, pp. 168-69; Sanders, "Bentonville," *CV* 34:299; Ridley, *Battles and Sketches*, p. 452.

49. *OR* 47(2):437-38; Johnston, *Narrative*, p. 386; Wade Hampton, "Bentonville," *B&L* 4:703-4.

50. Johnston, *Narrative*, p. 387; Ford, "Last Battles," p. 141; *OR* 47(1):1106; Thomas L. Connelly, *Autumn of Glory*, p. 527.

51. Mar. 19, 1865, entry, Calder Diary, DU; Walter Clark, *Regiments . . . from North Carolina*, 3:698.

52. Hinsdale, *72nd . . . North Carolina*, p. 25 (quotation); Walter Clark, *Regiments . . . from North Carolina*, 4:37, 351.

53. Some shells fell close to Hart's Battery, and Halsey called for volunteers to toss them away before they could explode. Dr. Marx E. Cohen, of Charleston, twenty-one and a gunner, was one of three men who rushed out. Cohen was shot dead in the attempt. Halsey, "Last Duel," 1:31; Markens, *Hebrews in America*, p. 137.

54. Ford, *Life in the Confederate Army*, p. 60.

55. Wade Hampton, "Bentonville," *B&L* 4:703; Halcott P. Jones Journal, NCA; Hinsdale, *72nd . . . North Carolina*, p. 25; Ford, *Life in the Confederate Army*, p. 60; France, *Bentonville*, pp. 12–13; Herring, "Bentonville," p. 107.

Chapter 5

1. Johnson, "Through the Carolinas," Johnson Papers, LC (quotation); Dozer, "Marching with Sherman," p. 468; Brant, *Eighty-fifth Indiana*, p. 107; Marvin, *Fifth . . . Connecticut*, p. 373; Thomas W. Connolly, *Seventieth Ohio*, p. 153; Dougall, "Bentonville," p. 214.

2. Also known as "Old 100th" and "Old Hundredth," this tune traditionally has been used when the 100th Psalm is paraphrased. It also is often the music for a familiar form of the "Doxology."

3. Nichols, *Story of the Great March*, p. 261.

4. Carlin, "Bentonville," p. 233.

5. Morris, *Sheridan*, p. 106.

6. Carlin, "Military Memoirs"; Gordon Whitney to N. C. Hughes, Feb. 11, 1994; Warner, *Generals in Blue*, p. 70. See also Hafendorfer, *Perryville*; Cozzens, *This Terrible Sound* and *Shipwreck of Their Hopes*; Richard W. Johnson, *Memoir of George H. Thomas*, pp. 84, 117, 126.

7. Charles E. Belknap, "Bentonville," 12:6–7.

8. Privates and company grade officers, North and South, frequently estimated distance in rods (5.5 yards) rather than yards or meters. It might be helpful to the contemporary reader to think of a rod in terms of about six yards or meters.

9. Belknap, "Bentonville," 12:6–7.

10. Ibid., 12:6–8; Mar. 19, 1865, entry, Boltz Diary, DU; Charles E. Benton, *As Seen from the Ranks*, p. 270 (quotation); Barrett, *Sherman's March*, p. 163.

11. Belknap, "Bentonville," 12:8.

12. Payne, *Thirty-fourth . . . Illinois*, p. 199 (quotations); Westervelt, *Light and Shadows*, p. 94; Mar. 19, 1865, entry, Fahnestock Diary, Fahnestock Papers, ISHL; *OR* 47(1):423, 434, 47(2):949–50.

13. Calkins, *One Hundred and Fourth . . . Illinois*, pp. 300, 299, 308. The wings of Hobart's brigade will be referred to as Briant's wing and Fitch's wing, although in battle reports they were called the right and left wings. Because the right wing would fight on the left, and the left wing on the right, clarity demands some relabeling.

14. J. Herr to sister, Mar. 26, 1865, Herr Papers, DU; *OR* 47(1):448, 463 (quotation); Mar.

19, 1865, entry, Boltz Diary, DU; Carlin, "Military Memoirs"; Howard, "Bentonville," Howard Papers, BCL; Calkins, *One Hundred and Fourth . . . Illinois*, pp. 299–300, 307–8.

15. McClurg, "Last Chance," pp. 391, 398–99; Henry W. Slocum, "Sherman's March," *B&L* 4:692; *OR* 47(1):25.

16. *OR* 47(2):908–9; McClurg, "Last Chance," pp. 391, 398–99; Foraker, *Notes*, 1:59; Barrett, *Sherman's March*, p. 164; Glatthaar, *March to the Sea*, p. 169. It is easy to blame Kilpatrick for allowing Sherman to stumble into Johnston's trap. Sherman himself, however, must bear responsibility for being surprised at Bentonville. He knew Kilpatrick's capabilities and shortcomings. Overconfident and impatient, Sherman depended for intelligence on the cloud of foragers that insulated his columns as much as he did on Kilpatrick. Now, in March 1865, he was relying more and more on instinct. Sherman knew better. Later on March 19, Kilpatrick, in another dispatch, attempted to correct his mistake. But it was too late.

17. Carlin, "Bentonville," p. 236.

18. This was the home of the prosperous Reddick Morris, age fifty-seven, and his fifty-three-year-old wife Allie. North Carolina Census, Johnston County, 1860, p. 767.

19. Fitch, *Echoes*, pp. 253–55; Beach, "Bentonville," p. 27; Calkins, *One Hundred and Fourth . . . Illinois*, pp. 299 (first quotation), 301; Carlin, "Bentonville," p. 236 (second quotation); Bowman Memoir, *CWTI* Collection, USAMHI (last quotation).

20. J. B. Foraker to H. W. Slocum, n.d., quoted in Foraker, *Notes*, 1:63.

21. Foraker, *Notes*, 1:59–60; *OR* 47(1):456; Hinson, "Bentonville."

22. J. Hoffhines to wife Nancy Hoffhines, Mar. 27, 1865, Hoffhines Letters, OHS.

23. Initially Carlin had Miles deploy the 79th Pennsylvania left of the road in support of Lt. Palmer F. Scovel's Battery. By the time of the general advance, however, Miles had recalled this regiment and placed it on the extreme right, connecting it with the right of the 38th Indiana.

24. *OR* 47(1):434–35, 448, 453, 473; Carlin, "Bentonville," pp. 233–37; Mar. 19, 1865, entry, Boltz Diary, DU; J. Hoffhines to wife Nancy Hoffhines, Mar. 27, 1865, Hoffhines Letters, OHS; Marcus W. Bates, "Bentonville," p. 142; France, "Bentonville," p. 11; Dougall, "Bentonville," p. 215; Ohio Infantry, *History of the Thirty-seventh*, pp. 88–89; Calkins, *One Hundred and Fourth . . . Illinois*, p. 302; Hinson, "Bentonville."

25. *OR* 47(1):575–77, 448, 434; Eicker Memoir, Eicker Papers, Harrisburg Civil War Roundtable Collection, USAMHI; Fitch, *Echoes*, p. 253; Calkins, *One Hundred and Fourth . . . Illinois*, p. 302. Early in the artillery duel, one shot struck a rebel limber and blew it up, killing and injuring those nearby.

26. *OR* 47(1):434 (first quotation), 448, 467; McClurg, "Last Chance," p. 391; Bryant, *Third . . . Wisconsin*, p. 322; Gordon Whitney to N. C. Hughes, Feb. 11, 1994 (second quotation); Bowman Memoir, Bowman Family Papers, USAMHI.

27. Wing commander Fitch maintained that he was never informed of the attack. Carlin acted peremptorily, attacking on the northern side of the road with Buell and Briant (accompanied by Hobart). Fitch all the while believed that Hobart's brigade straddled the road with Briant's wing immediately to the left of Scovel's battery. Fitch, *Echoes*, p. 260.

28. In the warm glow of hindsight, Carlin would change his story somewhat from the account in his official report, attributing the order of a general attack to Slocum: "It was General Slocum's object to develop the position of the enemy by making repeated [and

'isolated'] assaults at different points along the front." Carlin, "Bentonville," pp. 238 (quotation), 233. See also *OR* 47(1):448; *Army and Navy Journal*, Apr. 1, 1865.

29. Dougall, "Bentonville," p. 215.

30. Marcus W. Bates, "Bentonville," p. 143.

31. Ibid., p. 142 (first quotation); W. Carroll to brother and sister, Mar. 30, 1865, Carroll Diary and Letters, BL/UM (second quotation); C. S. Brown to mother and Etta Brown, Apr. 18, 1865, Brown Papers, DU (last quotation); Mar. 19, 1865, entry, Purdum Diary, OHS; *OR* 47(1):460; Eicker Memoir, Eicker Papers, Harrisburg Civil War Roundtable Collection, USAMHI.

32. Buell's brigade had not yet reached its position on Briant's left.

33. *OR* 47(1):473 (first quotation), 448 (second quotation), 476; Mar. 19, 1865, entry, Schaum Diary, Schaum Papers, DU; Perry, *Thirty-eighth . . . Indiana*, p. 213; Carlin, "Bentonville," pp. 233, 244; McClurg, "Last Chance," p. 391; Eicker Memoir, Eicker Papers, Harrisburg Civil War Roundtable Collection, USAMHI.

34. Bryant, *Third . . . Wisconsin*, p. 322; Marcus W. Bates, "Bentonville," p. 145.

35. Carlin, "Bentonville," p. 238; Bryant, *Third . . . Wisconsin*, p. 322; Dougall, "Bentonville," p. 215; Gordon Whitney to N. C. Hughes, Feb. 11, 1994; W. A. Van Horne to J. G. Mitchell, June 20, 1865, Mitchell Collection, HPC; C. S. Brown to Mother and Etta Brown, Apr. 18, 1865, Brown Papers, DU (first quotation); W. Carroll to brother and sister, Mar. 30, 1865, Carroll Diary and Letters, BL/UM (second quotation); Marcus W. Bates, "Bentonville," pp. 145-47; *OR* 47(1):448 (last quotation), 434, 467.

36. Beatty, *Memoirs*, pp. 146, 210, 234-37; Hunt and Brown, *Brevet Brigadier Generals*, p. 286; Love, *Wisconsin in the War*, p. 992.

37. Mar. 19, 1865, entry, Boltz Diary, DU; J. Hoffhines to Nancy Hoffhines, Mar. 27, 1865, Hoffhines Letters, OHS (first quotation); Hinson, "Bentonville"; Dougall, "Bentonville," pp. 215-16 (last two quotations, p. 216); *OR* 47(1):453, 460.

38. Marcus W. Bates, "Bentonville," p. 145.

39. W. P. Carlin to J. C. Davis, Mar. 19, 1865, Dearborn Collection, Houghton Library, Harvard University, Cambridge; Carlin, "Bentonville," pp. 239-40.

40. Henry W. Slocum, "Sherman's March," *B&L* 4:692-95 (first quotation, p. 692); James D. Morgan Journal, Morgan Papers, Quincy and Adams County Historical Society, Quincy, Ill.; McClurg, "Last Chance," p. 393 (second quotation).

41. Henry W. Slocum, "Sherman's March," *B&L* 4:692 (quotations); *OR* 47(1):423; Carlin, "Military Memoirs."

42. Following the repulse of his noontime assault, Carlin moved Scovel's battery from the Union center to the left to help anchor that flank. It was apparently done with Slocum's knowledge. This deprived the Union center of badly needed firepower during the major Confederate 3:00 P.M. attack. But despite the help it would have offered, Scovel's battery probably would have been overrun if it had remained in its original position. *OR* 47(1):575, 577, 424.

43. Bryant, *Third . . . Wisconsin*, p. 323; Marcus W. Bates, "Bentonville," p. 143; *OR* 47(1):600, 637, 47(2):575-80, 587; Van Horne, *Army of the Cumberland*, p. 317; Mar. 19, 1865, entry, Williams Diary, Detroit Public Library; J. S. Robinson to E. K. Buttrick, Mar. 27, 1865, Robinson Papers, OHS. A third regiment, the 101st Illinois, had been detached

early that morning to guard a crossroads. With the transfer of the two regiments to Hawley, this reduced Robinson's brigade from six to three regiments.

44. *OR* 47(1):424.

45. *OR* 47(1):450 (quotation); Shiman, "Engineering Sherman's March," p. 22.

46. New York Monuments Commission, *In Memoriam*, p. 100.

47. J. B. Foraker to H. W. Slocum, n.d., quoted in Foraker, *Notes*, 1:63; New York Monuments Commission, *In Memoriam*, p. 100. The 1861 Battle of Ball's Bluff had become synonymous with recklessness and tactical imbecility.

48. There is no evidence, however, that Scovel ever unlimbered once he reached Buell's position.

49. *OR* 47(1):496, 467. When the action grew heavy, Davis halted what there was of the corps train and placed it well back. Then he sent Vandever's brigade, which had been guarding the wagons, forward and to the right, where it took position on Mitchell's right. Vandever deployed four of his regiments in a double line and a fifth, the 60th Illinois, "well to the front" as skirmishers, with instructions to "feel to my right for the left flank of the enemy." Van Horne, *Army of the Cumberland*, pp. 317–18.

50. France, *Bentonville*, p. 12; Jordan, *Bentonville*, pp. 17–18. Briant's wing was north of Robinson but facing almost at a right angle to the left, leaving Robinson's front uncovered.

51. Carlin dubbed it "a pretty substantial fortress around his division." Carlin, "Bentonville," p. 239.

52. *OR* 47(1):434, 449.

53. *OR* 47(2):903–4. Slocum had sent another dispatch, dated 1:30 P.M., that lacked the urgency of this dispatch, dated 2:00 P.M.

54. Henry W. Slocum, "Sherman's March," *B&L* 4:693; J. B. Foraker to H. W. Slocum, quoted in Foraker, *Notes*, 1:62–63; Luvaas, *Johnston's Last Stand*, p. 7.

Chapter 6

1. Marcus W. Bates, "Bentonville," p. 148. "The Captain was on detail staff duty." Ibid.

2. *OR* 47(1):448. This adjustment by Carlin (actually the orders were given by Buell, with Carlin by his side "superintending movements") made his line impossibly thin and contributed to the defeat of his division. On the other hand, it gave the appearance of an extended Federal front. It was this skirmish line (not more than 250 men) that caught Gen. William B. Bate's eye and ultimately led to a redeployment of Taliaferro's Division and a 15–30 minute delay in the Confederate general attack. *OR* 47(1):468.

3. Marcus W. Bates, "Bentonville," p. 148.

4. *OR* 47(1):467, 448–50; Barrett, *Sherman's March*, p. 169; Bryant, *Third . . . Wisconsin*, p. 322; C. S. Brown to Etta Brown, Apr. 18, 1865, Brown Papers, DU (last quotation).

5. *OR* 47(1):468.

6. C. S. Brown to "his folks and anyone else," April 1865, Brown Papers, DU. "But he [Carlin] was proud of the 21st & they of him and he remarked to one of his staff, 'If I had known what a fighting Regt the 21st was I never would have punished them for stealing hard tack,'" said Carlin, referring to an incident that winter. Ibid.

7. Marcus W. Bates, "Bentonville," p. 148; Carlin, "Bentonville," p. 240.

8. Carlin, "Bentonville," p. 240.

9. Ibid.

10. *OR* 47(1):468 (quotation), 471; Marcus W. Bates, "Bentonville," p. 145; Wilson, *Memoirs*, p. 427.

11. *OR* 47(1):470.

12. *OR* 47(1):468, 471; C. S. Brown to Etta Brown, Apr. 18, 1865, Brown Papers, DU; Apr. 19, 1865, entry, Carroll Diary and Letters, UM.

13. Carlin, "Bentonville," p. 241. To round out the account regarding Buell, Carlin, in his official report written a week after the debacle, gave Buell credit for having rendered "more important service than any other brigade commander." Not for Buell's actions on March 19, however, but for having "constructed nearly all the bridges on our line of march." Nevertheless, it is obvious by comparing Carlin's report with his accounts written twenty years later that he grew bitter as he reflected about the battle. He would become more and more critical of Buell. *OR* 47(1):451.

14. Carlin, "Bentonville," p. 241; France, *Bentonville*, p. 13; Barrett, *Sherman's March*, p. 169.

15. Hinson, "Bentonville." These were probably James Robinson's troops.

16. Calkins, *One Hundred and Fourth . . . Illinois*, p. 308.

17. Hinson, "Bentonville."

18. Ibid.; Mar. 19, 1865, entry, Boltz Diary, DU.

19. Hinson, "Bentonville."

20. Ibid. (quotation); *OR* 47(1):448, 453, 459–62; Mar. 19, 1865, entry, Boltz Diary, DU; Dougall, "Bentonville," p. 217; Hurst, *Seventy-third Ohio*, p. 174; *Army and Navy Journal*, Apr. 1, 1865.

21. Robinson reports that he set out at 2:00 P.M. from Mingo Creek and reached his position "about an hour" later. *OR* 47(1):665.

22. J. S. Robinson to E. K. Buttrick, Mar. 27, 1865, Robinson Papers, OHS; *OR* 47(1):424, 587, 600.

23. J. S. Robinson to "Friend Hunt," Apr. 20, 1865, Robinson Papers, OHS.

24. A newspaperman and an avid Republican, Robinson proved to be a wonderful citizen soldier. Enlisting as a private in April 1861, he was a captain a month later and steadily rose in rank, becoming a brigadier general in January 1865. He had participated in the fighting from Bull Run to Chancellorsville to Gettysburg to Atlanta.

25. J. S. Robinson to E. K. Buttrick, 27 Mar. 1865, Robinson Papers, OHS.

26. Jordan, *Bentonville*, p. 18.

27. *OR* 47(1):665.

28. *OR* 47(1):666.

29. Carlin, "Bentonville," p. 241 (quotation); *OR* 47(1):435, 449–50, 679; Wallace, *Sixty-first Ohio*, p. 32; New York Monuments Committee, *Slocum*, p. 308; Shiman, "Engineering Sherman's March," p. 674.

30. *OR* 47(1):679 (quotation), 1043, 575–76, 178; Mar. 19, 1865, entry, Schaum Diary, Schaum Papers, DU.

31. McClurg, "Last Chance," p. 393.

32. *OR* 47(1):463; Fitch, *Echoes*, p. 255.

33. Fitch's skirmishers rushed from tree to tree, exchanging shots with the rebels, many of whom were in blue uniforms. This proved confusing and resulted in casualties. Maj. John H.

Widmer, commanding the 104th Illinois, was among those hit. "One of the boys called out, 'Major, are you hurt?' 'N-o-o,' he replied, with a look of disgust I shall never forget." Setting an example of determination, Widmer remained in command until nightfall. Calkins, *One Hundred and Fourth . . . Illinois*, pp. 307–8.

34. Ibid., p. 303 (first quotation); Fitch, *Echoes*, p. 257 (second quotation).

35. Fitch, *Echoes*, p. 257–58.

36. Ibid.

37. *OR* 47(1):459, 463–64; Fitch, *Echoes*, pp. 256–57, 260; Marsh, "Regimental Record," ISHL; Calkins, *One Hundred and Fourth . . . Illinois*, pp. 303–5.

38. Canfield, *21st . . . Ohio*, p. 182.

39. Ibid., pp. 182–83; Mar. 19, 1865, entry, Schaum Diary, Schaum Papers, DU; *OR* 47(1):473–74, 476, 480. According to Chickamauga historian Peter Cozzens, McMahan was responsible for making the crucial six-hour stand on Horseshoe Ridge at Chickamauga "the most distinguished service rendered by any single regiment" in that battle. Cozzens, *This Terrible Sound*, p. 505.

40. McClurg, "Last Chance," p. 393; Mar. 19, 1865, entry, Meffert Diary, Meffert Papers, SHSW.

41. "The broken remnants of the Second Brigade [Buell's]." *OR* 47(1):671.

42. *OR* 47(1):645; Toombs, *Reminiscences*, pp. 213–16.

43. C. S. Brown to "his folks and anyone else," April 1865, Brown Papers, DU. See also Mar. 19, 1865, entry, Miller Journal, IHS; Kinnear, *Eighty-sixth . . . Illinois*, p. 105.

44. Mar. 19, 1865, entry, Humphrey Journal, Chicago Public Library (first quotation); Charles E. Benton, *As Seen from the Ranks*, pp. 268–70; Bates, "Bentonville," p. 145 (second quotation); Kinnear, *Eighty-sixth . . . Illinois*, p. 105; Bowman Memoir, Bowman Family Papers, USAMHI; William Carroll to brother and sister, Mar. 30, 1865, W. Carroll Diary and Letters, BL/UM (last quotation).

45. Hinson, "Bentonville."

46. J. Hoffhines to Nancy Hoffhines, Mar. 27, 1865, Hoffhines Letters, OHS.

47. Hinson, "Bentonville." See also *OR* 47(1):461, 624, 629, 645; Mar. 19, 1865, entry, Allen Diary, BL/UM; Mar. 19, 1865, entry, Button Diary, Tripp Papers, SHSW; Luvaas, *Bentonville*, pp. 13–14; Jordan, *Bentonville*, p. 19.

48. Carlin, "Bentonville," pp. 243–47, and "Military Memoirs."

49. Carlin, "Bentonville," pp. 243–47, and "Military Memoirs"; C. S. Brown to "his folks and anyone else," April 1865, Brown Papers, DU.

50. Carlin, Bentonville," pp. 243–47, and "Military Memoirs." This Don Quixote–Sancho Panza vision probably represents the presence of one of the South Carolina or Georgia heavy artillery units (Taliaferro's men most likely) advancing as infantry.

51. Carlin, "Bentonville," pp. 243–47, and "Military Memoirs"; Barrett, *Sherman's March*, p. 170.

52. The Battle of Bentonville carried several names other than this mockery. Among them were "Harper's Farm," "Mill Creek," and "Troublefield's Swamp." S. C. Duncan to Bill Duncan, Mar. 31, 1865, Duncan Papers, New Jersey Historical Society, Newark; R. Rey to Lizzie, Mar. 28, 1865, Rey Letters, NYHS; Payne, *Thirty-fourth . . . Illinois*, p. 199; *OR* 47(1):485.

53. W. A. Van Horne to J. G. Mitchell, June 20, 1865, Mitchell Papers, HPC; J. S. Robinson to "Friend Hunt," Apr. 20, 1865, Robinson Papers, OHS.

54. McClurg, "Last Chance," p. 392.

Chapter 7

1. Beatty, *Memoirs*, p. 293; Collins, "Morgan," pp. 274–75.

2. Collins, "Morgan," pp. 274–79.

3. Cleaves, *Rock of Chickamauga*, p. 281; *OR* 47(1):487.

4. *OR* 47(1):487; Pepper, *Personal Recollections*, p. 379; Glatthaar, *March to the Sea*, p. 27; Collins, "Morgan," pp. 274–79; Beatty, *Memoirs*, p. 293; Hicken, *Illinois in the Civil War*, p. 297; *DAB* 13:171.

5. McAdams, *Every-day Soldier Life*, p. 144.

6. *OR* 47(1):423, 434, 485; Marcus W. Bates, "Bentonville," p. 149; McClurg, "Last Chance," p. 393; McAdams, *Every-day Soldier Life*, p. 144.

7. *OR* 47(1):525.

8. *OR* 47(1):534, 485, 503–4, 516; Payne, *Thirty-fourth . . . Illinois*, p. 200; Mar. 19, 1865, entry, James D. Morgan Journal, Morgan Papers, Quincy and Adams County Historical Society, Quincy, Ill.

9. *OR* 47(1):485, 434–35, 503; Westervelt, *Light and Shadows*, p. 94; Mar. 19, 1865, entry, Fahnestock Diary, NCA; W. Garrett to sister, Mar. 29, 1865, Garrett Letters, Harrisburg Civil War Roundtable Collection, USAMHI.

10. Robbins Reminiscences, Robbins Papers, SHSW.

11. *OR* 47(1):522, 526, 496, 498–99, 504, 520; Glatthaar, *March to the Sea*, p. 158; Charles E. Benton, *As Seen from the Ranks*, p. 271; Fitch, *Echoes*, p. 258; Mar. 19, 1865, entry, Fahnestock Diary, Fahnestock Papers, ISHL; McAdams, *Every-day Soldier Life*, pp. 144–45 (quotations); Jordan, *Bentonville*, p. 17.

12. McAdams, *Every-day Soldier Life*, p. 144; W. Van Horne to J. G. Mitchell, June 20, 1865, Mitchell Collection, HPC; Mar. 19, 1865, entry, Morgan Journal, Gibson County Civil War Papers, Lilly Library, Indiana University, Bloomington; *OR* 47(1):514 (Walker); France, *Bentonville*, p. 15.

13. McClurg, "Last Chance," pp. 393–94.

14. *OR* 47(1):485.

15. McClurg, "Last Chance," p. 394.

16. *OR* 47(1):485, 434–35; Mar. 19, 1865, entry, Fahnestock Diary, KMNP; Van Horne, *Army of the Cumberland*, 2:318; McClurg, "Last Chance," pp. 393–94 (quotation, p. 394); Bryant, *Third . . . Wisconsin*, p. 322; Barrett, *Sherman's March*, p. 173; France, *Bentonville*, p. 14.

17. *OR* 47(1):485.

18. *OR* 47(1):485–86, 511; W. Van Horne to J. G. Mitchell, June 20, 1865, Mitchell Collection, HPC.

19. Monsarrat, "John G. Mitchell," HPC.

20. Payne, *Thirty-fourth . . . Illinois*, p. 201.

21. Mitchell may have used some men from Miles's command as well, probably companies

of the 79th Pennsylvania, but it is vague as to which of Carlin's units he put into line other than Fitch's wing. The wounding of Miles seems to have demoralized his brigade, which had performed so well up until the time of the massive rebel attack.

22. Payne, *Thirty-fourth . . . Illinois*, p. 201.

23. Thus the left leg of Morgan's defense line (right to left) was Mitchell's 98th Ohio, 34th Illinois; Fitch's 21st Wisconsin, 42d Indiana, 104th Illinois; and Mitchell's 121st Ohio. Miles's 79th Pennsylvania is difficult to place, if indeed it retained a semblance of regimental order at this time. The best guess is that it occupied a portion of Mitchell's left, hooking itself to the 34th Illinois's left flank and remaining there until relieved by Vandever's 17th New York. Several accounts, including Mitchell's, mention its presence. *OR* 47(1):457, 464, 480; Payne, *Thirty-fourth . . . Illinois*, pp. 200-202; Fitch, *Echoes*, p. 258.

24. *OR* 47(1):511, 526, 464.

25. *OR* 47(1):518.

26. *OR* 47(1):160.

27. Ball quickly found himself in a sea of rebels, but he soon discovered that the enemy was disoriented and disorganized. Adding a half-dozen stray Union soldiers to his command, Ball went on the offensive and began capturing Confederate stragglers. Soon he had a group of thirty-five in hand which he marched back to division headquarters. Two of Ball's men, Cpl. Simeon Woodruff and Pvt. Almon Hollister, encountered a squad of rebels led by two officers and an orderly sergeant. They were escorting a sole prisoner, a woebegone private of the 34th Illinois. Woodruff ordered the rebels to surrender, which they did, the senior lieutenant yielding his sword. As a reward for his "meritorious services" Woodruff was allowed to keep the sword. *OR* 47(1):528-29.

28. *OR* 47(1):526-27; J. G. Mitchell to T. Wiseman, Mar. 30, 1865, Mitchell Collection, OHS; Barrett, *Sherman's March*, pp. 173-74; Fitch, *Echoes*, p. 258.

29. *OR* 47(1):511; Fitch, *Echoes*, p. 259. Morgan himself seems to have been instrumental in rallying a portion of these troops and forming still another line some 300-400 yards to the rear.

30. *OR* 47(1):511, 526-27, 529, 457, 459, 464, 520; Fitch, *Echoes*, p. 258; Beach, "Bentonville," p. 29.

31. W. C. Robinson to R. P. Robinson, Mar. 24, 1865, Robinson Papers, ISHL; *OR* 47(1):522; J. G. Mitchell to T. Wiseman, Mar. 30, 1865, Mitchell Collection, OHS; McAdams, *Every-day Soldier Life*, p. 144; Payne, *Thirty-fourth . . . Illinois*, p. 202. It appears that details sent back earlier for fresh ammunition never returned.

32. *OR* 47(1):437, 485-86, 514, 516, 522, 525, 527 (last quotation); Jordan, *Bentonville*, p. 19 (first quotation); Reid, *Ohio in the War*, 1:912, 2:583; Mar. 19, 1865, entry, Batchelor Diary, Batchelor Papers, ISHL (second quotation); Mar. 19, 1865, entry, Widney Diary, KMNP (third quotation); A. Miller to father, Mar. 27, 1865, Miller Letters, SHSW; Barrett, *Sherman's March*, pp. 172-73.

33. W. C. Robinson to father, Mar. 24, 1865, Robinson Papers, ISHL.

34. Stewart, *Dan McCook's Regiment*, pp. 162-63.

35. W. C. Johnson, "Through the Carolinas," Johnson Papers, LC.

36. *OR* 47(1):511.

37. This letter to Branum's family was reproduced in Branum, *Letters*, p. 48.

38. Barrett, *Sherman's March*, p. 174.

39. Lossing, *Pictorial History*, 3:501.

40. J. G. Mitchell to T. Wiseman, Mar. 30, 1865, Mitchell Collection, OHS; *OR* 47(1):485, 503, 516–17, 520, 522, 525.

41. McAdams, *Every-day Soldier Life*, pp. 144–45 (quotation, p. 144); *OR* 47(1):516–17, 504, 502.

42. *OR* 47(1):471, 496 (first quotation), 485, 504; Robertson, *Michigan in the War*, pp. 350–51 (second quotation, p. 351); Beyer and Keydel, *Deeds of Valor*, p. 491; Ferguson Reminiscences, *CWTI* Collection, USAMHI. Plant would be promoted to sergeant and color-bearer.

43. Beyer and Keydel, *Deeds of Valor*, p. 491. "Why didn't you kill that rebel," Clute's company commander demanded. "'Because I had no ammunition,' I replied." During a subsequent rebel attack on this front Clute saw the same lieutenant again. This time his adversary had a pistol and shot Clute in the arm. Beyer and Keydel, *Deeds of Valor*, p. 491; Robertson, *Michigan in the War*, p. 351.

44. Westervelt, *Light and Shadows*, p. 94.

45. *OR* 47(1):497. Vandever's second line (10th Michigan and 17th New York) was commanded by Col. Charles M. Lum, 10th Michigan. Although Vandever credits Lum with "distinguished gallantry," he does not mention him in the details of the attacks on, and counterattacks of, the second line. Instead, he conspicuously relates the role of Marshall and compliments the 10th's commander, Capt. William H. Dunphy. Lum himself applauds the work of Dunphy.

46. *OR* 471:496–97 (first two quotations, p. 497), 502–3, 508; Westervelt, *Light and Shadows*, p. 94; Stewart, *Dan McCook's Regiment*, pp. 162, 164 (last quotation).

47. *OR* 471:497, 508 (second and last quotations), 502. This may have been the moment McClurg relates: "It is even rumored that while at one time the regimental commanders of one brigade were considering whether their duty to their men did not demand a surrender, their deliberations were cut short by the action of a gigantic sergeant-major, who sprang forward with a cheer, and called for a charge, which was successfully made." McClurg, "Last Chance," p. 399.

48. *OR* 47(1):496–97, 508; Westervelt, *Light and Shadows*, p. 94; Robertson, *Michigan in the War*, p. 309; Shiman, "Engineering Sherman's March," p. 674.

49. *OR* 47(1):497 (quotation), 437, 485–86, 498–99, 504, 514, 516, 522, 525; C. S. Brown to mother and Etta, Apr. 18, 1865, Brown Papers, DU; Robertson, *Michigan in the War*, pp. 350–51; Jordan, *Bentonville*, p. 19; Reid, *Ohio in the War*, 1:912, 2:583; F. Marion to sister, Mar. 29, 1865, Marion Letters, ISHL; Mar. 19, 1865, entry, Batchelor Diary, Batchelor Papers, ISHL; Mar. 19, 1865, entry, Widney Diary, KMNP; A. Miller to father, Mar. 27, 1865, Miller Letters, SHSW; Barrett, *Sherman's March*, pp. 172–73; Westervelt, *Light and Shadows*, p. 94. Vandever mistakenly reported that Hoke was captured here but escaped in the melee.

50. *OR* 47(1):539.

51. *OR* 47(1):534–35 (quotation, p. 534), 541; Mar. 19, 1865, entry, Fahnestock Diary, Fahnestock Papers, ISHL.

52. Reid, *Ohio in the War*, 1:940–41; Mathews, *Washington County*, pp. 493–96.

53. *OR* 47(1):534.

54. *OR* 47(1):535.

55. *OR* 47(1):534–35 (fourth quotation, p. 535), 541, 548; Mar. 19, 1865, entry, Fahnestock Diary, KMNP (first two quotations); Mar. 19, 1865, entry, Ross Diary, ISHL; Mar. 19, 1865, entry, Burkhalter Diary, Burkhalter Papers, ISHL (third quotation); A. M. Ayers to wife, Mar. 25, 1865, Ayers Papers, Woodruff Library, Emory University, Atlanta (last two quotations).

56. *OR* 47(1):548.

57. *OR* 47(1):537.

58. Mar. 19, 1865, entry, Inskeep Diary, OHS; J. L. Burkhalter to E. M. Stanton, Apr. 26, 1865, and Mar. 19, 1865, entry, Burkhalter Diary, Burkhalter Papers, ISHL; Reid, *Ohio in the War*, p. 341; Mar. 19, 1865, entry, Fahnestock Diary, KMNP; A. M. Ayers to wife, Mar. 25, 1865, Ayers Papers, Woodruff Library, Emory University, Atlanta; Beach, "Bentonville," p. 28; Stewart, *Dan McCook's Brigade*, p. 160; James Taylor Holmes, *52nd O.V.I.*, p. 25; Van Horne, *Army of the Cumberland*, 2:318; *OR* 47(1):537 (quotations).

59. *OR* 47(1):537-38.

60. Mar. 19, 1865, entry, Fahnestock Diary, Fahnestock Papers, ISHL; J. L. Austin to wife, Mar. 27, 1865, Austin Correspondence, BL/UM; G. M. Trowbridge to Libby Trowbridge, Mar. 19, 1865, Trowbridge Letters, CL/UM; Mar. 19, 1865, entry, Dickinson Diary, Dickinson Papers, SHSW; Kinnear, *Eighty-sixth . . . Illinois*, p. 104; *OR* 47(1):435, 645, 665, 672, 679; Wallace, *Sixty-first Ohio*, p. 32; Jordan, *Bentonville*, p. 19; Marcus W. Bates, "Bentonville," p. 148; *Record of the Ninety-fourth . . . Ohio*, p. 91; Rogers, *125th . . . Illinois*, pp. 119–20; *OR* 47(1):671 (quotation).

61. Strong, *A Yankee Private's Civil War*, pp. 192–93.

62. This line undoubtedly was bolstered by fragments of Carlin's division and fortified, thus presenting a formidable fire wall, certainly more than a skirmish line might suggest.

63. Originally Selfridge had been placed on the extreme left of the main line, beyond Hawley.

64. Strong, *A Yankee Private's Civil War*, p. 193.

65. The Confederates did appear in force and threaten the left, which became Ward's responsibility to defend, but instead of advancing their columns, they retired, turning south and joining in the assault on the Union center. These were probably Taliaferro's men. *OR* 47(1):587, 600–601, 612, 637, 665, 667, 784, 809; Mar. 19, 1865, entry, A. S. Williams Diary, Detroit Public Library; Van Horne, *Army of the Cumberland*, 2:317; Marcus W. Bates, "Bentonville," p. 145; Toombs, *Reminiscences*, p. 216; Wilson, *Memoirs*, p. 427; McBride, *Thirty-third Indiana*, pp. 173–74; Mar. 19, 1865, entry, Congleton Diary, LC; Ward, Civil War Service, Filson Club, Louisville, Ky.; Bauer, *Soldiering*, p. 230.

66. C. S. Brown to mother and Etta Brown, Apr. 18, 1865, Brown Papers, DU (first quotation); Bryant, *Third . . . Wisconsin*, p. 323 (second quotation); Mar. 19, 1865, entry, Meffert Diary, Meffert Papers, SHSW; Putney Memoir, CL/UM; Walton, *Civil War Courtship*, p. 137; Harryman Manuscript, Harryman Papers, ISL; L. E. Davis to Susan Davis, Davis Letters, Civil War Miscellaneous Collection, USAMHI; *OR* 47(1):435, 574–81, 846–50, 852, 854; Jordan, *Bentonville*, p. 19.

67. *National Cyclopedia*, 4:466; *OR* 47(1):827. His own regiment, the 2d Massachusetts, remained with its old brigade (Hawley's).

68. Storrs, *Twentieth Connecticut*, p. 164.

69. *OR* 47(1):846.

70. Carlin, "Bentonville," pp. 249–50.

71. Ibid.

72. Ibid., p. 250.

73. Connecticut War Record, April 1865; Underwoood, *Three Years' Service*, pp. 283–84.

74. Hurst, *Seventy-Third Ohio*, p. 175.

75. Actually it was the consolidated 23d, 26th, 45th Tennessee Regiment, Palmer's Brigade.

76. Cogswell lost 11 killed, 113 wounded.

77. New Haven *Connecticut War Record*, April 1865.

78. Carlin, "Bentonville," pp. 249–50; *OR* 47(1):434–35, 537 (last quotation), 784, 826, 834, 838, 840–45, 538, 435; New Haven *Connecticut War Record*, April 1865; Storrs, *Twentieth Connecticut*, p. 164; Mar. 19, 1865, entry, Burkhalter Diary, Burkhalter Papers, ISHL; Boies, *Thirty-third Massachusetts*, p. 116; Hurst, *Seventy-third Ohio*, pp. 173–75 (first two quotations, p. 175); Underwood, *Thirty-third Mass. Infantry Regiment*, pp. 283–84; Glatthaar, *March to the Sea*, p. 170; Barrett, *Sherman's March*, pp. 174–75; New York Monuments Commission, *In Memoriam*, p. 308; McClurg, "Last Chance," p. 395; Beach, "Bentonville," p. 29; Bradley, *Star Corps*, p. 273; France, *Bentonville*, pp. 14–15; Luvaas, "Johnston's Last Stand," p. 350.

Chapter 8

1. Hardee says 3:00 P.M. Some place the time at 2:45; Harvey Hill and others set it at 3:15. Hardee, "Memoranda," HL; *OR* 47(1):1103, 1090.

2. Walter Clark, *Regiments . . . from North Carolina*, 4:21.

3. Mrs. John H. Anderson, "Boy Soldiers at . . . Bentonville," p. 175.

4. J. P. Smith, "Bentonville"; Walter Clark, *Regiments . . . from North Carolina*, 4:21; France, *Bentonville*, p. 13; Symonds, *Johnston*, p. 350.

5. When Johnston reorganized the army following Bentonville, the 1st Arkansas Regiment consisted of the former 1st, 2d, 5th, 6th, 7th, 8th, 13th, 15th, 19th, and 24th Arkansas Volunteer Infantry and the 3d Confederate.

6. Walter A. Clark, *Under the Stars and Bars*, p. 193.

7. Ibid., pp. 192–93.

8. Taliaferro's South Carolinians appear to have missed the 3:00 P.M. attack altogether, apparently spending the time thrashing about behind the Confederate right. One soldier reported that he thought they were being held in reserve, so he felt free to take a nap. Another had them lightly engaged in a running scrap with Federal vedettes but primarily concerned with finding their way through the "thick forest." C. W. Hutson Reminiscences, SHC; Ford, "Last Battles," p. 141.

9. *OR* 47(1):1056, 1106, 1108; Johnston, *Narrative*, p. 387; Roy, "Hardee"; Unidentified clipping in Hardee Family Papers, in possession of Mrs. H. Bowen, Birmingham, Ala.; McMurry, *Footprints*, p. 173; John W. Jones, "Hardee," p. 442; Dickert, *Kershaw's Brigade*, p. 523.

10. Walter A. Clark, *Under the Stars and Bars*, pp. 192–93.

11. Brewer, *Forty-sixth Alabama*, p. 38.

12. *OR* 47(1):1090. See also D. H. Hill to daughter, Mar. 23, 1865, Hill Family Papers,

USAMHI; Harper, *Fifty-eighth . . . North Carolina*, p. 14; *OR* 47(1):1094, 1099; Brewer, *Forty-sixth Alabama*, p. 38.

13. Watson, "In the Battle of Bentonville," p. 95.

14. Corn, "In Enemy's Lines," p. 507; *OR* 47(1):1098; Lambert, "Bentonville," p. 221; Fort, History and Memoirs, USAMHI; Mar. 19, 1865, entry, Nash Diary, UGL; Brewer, *Forty-sixth Alabama*, p. 36; Hiram Smith Williams, *War So Horrible*, p. 127; Calhoun, *42d . . . Georgia*, p. 40; Adamson, *Thirtieth Georgia*, p. 48; James W. Bell, *43rd Georgia*, p. 39; H. R. Jackson to B. F. Cheatham, Dec. 10, 1864, Cheatham Papers, University of the South.

15. Bunn, a native of North Carolina, was a student at Davidson College when the war began. Evans, *Confederate Military History*, 14:436-37.

16. See Sword, *Embrace an Angry Wind*, pp. 417-22.

17. *OR* 47(1):1101-3; Ridley, *Battles and Sketches*, pp. 452-53; Dacus, *Reminiscences*, n.p.

18. *OR* 47(1):1101; Zorn, *29th Alabama*, p. 153.

19. Dacus, *Reminiscences*, n.p.

20. Mar. 19, 1865, entry, Jones Journal, NCA.

21. *OR* 47(1):1090-91 (quotation, p. 1091), 1094, 1099, 1101, 1104, 1108; Harper, *Fifty-eighth . . . North Carolina*, p. 14; Barrett, *Sherman's March*, p. 171; Corn, "In Enemy's Lines," p. 507; Ridley, *Battles and Sketches*, p. 452; Lambert, "In the Battle of Bentonville," p. 221.

22. Roy, "Hardee."

23. Livermore places the Left Wing's numbers (4 divisions factored at 93 percent, less 603 lost on March 16) at 16,127. Jordan gives average Federal division strength at 3,700 and brigade at 1,300. Livermore, *Numbers and Losses*, p. 134; Jordan, *Bentonville*, p. 15n.

24. *OR* 47(1):1105.

25. Hagood, *Memoirs*, p. 360.

26. An uncorroborated story appeared in 1927 from another North Carolina participant, a member of Atkins's Battery which was giving fire support for Walthall's attack. He heard a mounted Alabama soldier (probably in one of George Johnston's regiments) shout, "there's some killed." The soldier, braving the fire of Federal sharpshooters, rode forward to a wounded man, helped lift him into the saddle, and with "most profound resoluteness" brought him back and laid him near Atkins's Battery. The wounded soldier died. Then, to the gunner's astonishment, he discovered that the rescuer was a woman—the wounded man's wife. She had disguised herself and served undiscovered with her husband in the Alabama regiment since 1862. Greensboro *Daily News*, Mar. 20, 1927.

27. *OR* 47(1):1105.

28. *OR* 47(1):1101.

29. *OR* 47(1):1101-5.

30. J. E. Johnston to R. F. Hoke, Jan. 27, 1871, Hoke Papers, NCA.

31. Hagood, *Memoirs*, p. 360.

32. Ibid. (quotations); *OR* 47(1):1091.

33. Croom, *War History*, pp. 28-29; Robert G. Johnson, "Gilmer Blues," pp. 22-23; Mar. 19, 1865, entry, Calder Diary, DU.

34. Taylor's command consisted of a fragment of the 36th North Carolina State Troops

(2d Regiment North Carolina Artillery and three companies of the 1st North Carolina Battalion Heavy Artillery).

35. John D. Taylor Reminiscences, Taylor Papers, NCA; Hagood, *Memoirs*, p. 360; Walter Clark, *Regiments . . . from North Carolina*, 2:651, 630, 4:312. Taylor lost his left arm as a result of this wound.

36. Walter Clark, *Regiments . . . from North Carolina*, 2:763-64.

37. It is unclear whether Mallett was killed in this sharp repulse on March 19 or in defending the Confederate left on the twenty-first. Walter Clark, *Regiments . . . from North Carolina*, 2:763-64.

38. On March 19 Hagood lost 4 killed, 127 wounded, 139 missing; Kirkland lost 3 killed, 41 wounded, and 13 missing; and Clingman's Brigade lost 1 killed, 18 wounded, and 1 missing. *OR* 47(1):1080.

39. Hagood, *Memoirs*, p. 361.

40. Ibid.; *OR* 47(1):1091; Luvaas, "Bentonville," pp. 42-43.

41. *OR* 47(2):1397.

42. McLaws Order Book, McLaws Papers, SHC.

43. Ibid.; Hutson Reminiscences, SHC; France, *Bentonville*, p. 15.

44. *OR* 47(1):1106-8.

45. *OR* 47(1):1094.

46. *OR* 47(1):1100, 1090-94; Ogilvie, "Days and Nights," p. 361.

47. *OR* 47(1):1100.

48. *OR* 47(1):1090.

49. Watson, "In the Battle of Bentonville," p. 95 (quotation); *OR* 47(1):1090-91; "History of 10th South Carolina Infantry," p. 134, CCNMP; Emanuel, *Georgetown Rifle Guards*, p. 28.

50. Col. Henry C. Kellogg commanded Marcellus A. Stovall's Brigade. The 42d Georgia constituted one-half of the diminished brigade.

51. *OR* 47(1):1091, 1094-95, 1102; Mar. 19, 1865, entry, Nash Diary, UGL; Calhoun, *42d . . . Georgia*, p. 40.

52. Hill, "Palmer's Brigade," p. 332.

53. Oates, *The War*, p. 455.

54. Hiram Smith Williams, *War So Horrible*, p. 127; Oates, *The War*, p. 455; Lambert, "In the Battle of Bentonville," pp. 221-22.

55. Lambert, "In the Battle of Bentonville," p. 222.

56. Ibid., pp. 221-22. See also Oates, *The War*, p. 455.

57. Lambert, "In the Battle of Bentonville," p. 222.

58. Harper, *Fifty-eighth . . . North Carolina*, p. 15.

59. Ibid.; Neff, *Tennessee's Battered Brigadier*, p. 149.

60. Lambert, "In the Battle of Bentonville," p. 222.

61. France, *Bentonville*, p. 15; Beach, "Bentonville," p. 29; Luvaas, "Johnston's Last Stand," p. 13.

62. *CV* 5:125; Hiram Smith Williams, *War So Horrible*, p. 129.

63. *OR* 47(1):1091; Walker, *10th Regiment S.C.*, p. 134; Willett, *History of Company B*, p. 88 (quotation).

64. Palmer's right wing was cut in half. It is remarkable that he did not suffer a greater loss

of men captured (he lost 5 percent). In all, Palmer's Brigade suffered heavily that day in its attacks—about 20 wounded killed and wounded, about the same as Zachry's (Colquitt's) battered brigade.

65. Corn, "In Enemy's Lines," p. 507.

66. Most of the men appear to have been members of Brown's Tennessee Brigade, specifically soldiers from the 18th (Palmer's old regiment) and 45th Tennessee, although troops from Alabama and South Carolina regiments were mixed with them.

67. Mar. 19-26, 1865, entries, Ogilvie Diary, TSLA.

68. Corn, "In Enemy's Lines," p. 507.

69. Mar. 19-24, 1865, entries, Ogilvie Diary, TSLA (quotations); *OR* 47(1):1090-91, 1099; *CV* 8:263, 5:125; South Carolina Division, United Daughters of the Confederacy, *Recollections and Reminiscences*, 1:189-90; Watson, "In the Battle of Bentonville," p. 95; Ogilvie, "Days and Nights," p. 361; Willett, *History of Company B*, p. 88; McMurray, *Twentieth Tennessee*, p. 357; Corn, "In Enemy's Lines," p. 507; Harper, *Fifty-eighth . . . North Carolina*, p. 16; Walker, *10th Regiment S.C.*, p. 134; Lindsley, *Annals*, p. 367.

70. *OR* 47(1):1098.

71. Ibid.

72. *OR* 47(1):1091.

73. *OR* 47(1):1095.

74. *OR* 47(1):1098-99, 1091, 1094-95 (quotation, p. 1094); Evans, *Confederate Military History*, 12:438.

75. *OR* 47(1):1091, 1100-1105; Johnston, *Narrative*, p. 388.

76. McLaws Order Book, McLaws Papers, SHC.

77. Ibid.; *OR* 47(1):1109.

78. *OR* 47(1):1107.

79. Walter A. Clark, *Under the Stars and Bars*, p. 196.

80. Ibid., pp. 194-95.

81. Ibid., p. 196.

82. Ibid., pp. 167, 196-97; *OR* 47 (1):1106.

83. Ford, *Life in the Confederate Army*, p. 56.

84. Ford, "Last Battles," p. 142.

85. Sanders, "Battle of Bentonville," p. 299.

86. Mar. 19, 1865, entry, J. W. Brown Diary, GAH.

87. Ravenel, "Ask the Survivors."

88. Ford, *Life in the Confederate Army*, p. 56.

89. Ibid.

90. Ibid.

91. Ibid.

92. Mar. 19, 1865, entry, Brown Diary, GAH; Mar. 19, 1865, entry, Hutson Diary, SHC; Whaley Reminiscences, DU (first quotation); Ford, "Last Battles," p. 141 (second quotation); Sanders, "Battle of Bentonville," p. 299; Barrett, *Sherman's March*, p. 175; *OR* 47(1): 1109-10, 601, 1107; Herring, "Bentonville," p. 135.

93. McLaws Order Book, McLaws Papers, SHC.

94. *OR* 47(1):1109.

95. Ibid.

96. *OR* 47(1):1110, 1102–3.

97. *OR* 47(1):1102 (quotation), 1104–5, 1110; France, *Bentonville*, p. 15; Beach, "Bentonville," pp. 29–30.

98. Mar. 19, 1865, entry, W. A. Johnson Diary, Atlanta *Journal*, Dec. 21, 1901.

99. Ibid.

100. Ibid.

101. No one could question Harrison's courage. Three times wounded and cited repeatedly by his superiors for personal gallantry, he had been an important figure in the defense of Charleston in 1863 and at the Battle of Olustee in 1864. While recuperating from his Olustee wound, Harrison was assigned "command of the post of Florence, South Carolina, and the prison there. His humane treatment of prisoners won praise from the Union troops imprisoned there." Allardice, *More Generals in Gray*, p. 123.

102. *OR* 47(1):1107. Also killed at this time was Harrison's acting assistant adjutant general, Lt. George M. Blount. John Lipscomb Johnson, *University Memorial*, pp. 704–8.

103. Fort, History and Memoirs, *CWTI* Collection, USAMHI.

104. Ibid.

105. France, *Bentonville*, p. 15.

106. Payne, *Thirty-fourth . . . Illinois*, p. 201.

107. Barrett, *Sherman's March*, p. 175.

108. Walter Clark, *Regiments . . . from North Carolina*, 4:104–5; McClurg, "Last Chance," p. 397 (quotations).

109. McClurg, "Last Chance," p. 397; Stewart, *Dan McCook's Regiment*, pp. 164–65.

110. Walter Clark, *Regiments . . . from North Carolina*, 1:512, 4:336; Jordan, *North Carolina Troops*, 12:145–47.

111. Mar. 19, 1865, entry, Sloan Diary, TSLA. Gardiner probably was Capt. William T. Gardner, Company E, 50th North Carolina Troops. Edmundson probably was Jesse W. Edmundson, adjutant of the 50th Regiment North Carolina Troops. Ibid.

112. McClurg, "Last Chance," p. 397 (first quotation); Walter Clark, *Regiments . . . from North Carolina*, 4:104–5 (second quotation, p. 104). Although Wortham's fate following Bentonville is unknown, presumably he was court-martialed. His superior, "Wash" Hardy, "to the gratification of all," was relieved of command at Smithfield. France, *Bentonville*, p. 16; Osborn, *Fifty-fifth Ohio*, p. 202; Payne, *Thirty-fourth . . . Illinois*, p. 208; Hutson Reminiscences, SHC; Barrett, *Sherman's March*, p. 175.

113. McLaws Order Book, McLaws Papers, SHC.

114. Mar. 19, 1865, entry, Sloan Diary, TSLA.

115. *OR* 47(1):1091, 1095, 1094 (first quotation), 1055 (second quotation); Symonds, *Johnston*, p. 109; France, *Bentonville*, p. 16.

116. Mar. 21, 1865, Batchelor Diary, Batchelor Papers, ISHL.

Chapter 9

1. Foraker, *Notes*, p. 62.

2. W. T. Sherman to J. B. Foraker, September 1889, in Foraker, *Notes*, pp. 63–64. Foraker's ride also inspired a poem that was published years later in a Cincinnati newspaper.

3. Foraker, *Notes*, p. 64.

4. William E. Strong, Reminiscences, ISHL.

5. *OR* 47(2):910.

6. Sladen, "Service with General Howard," Sladen Family Papers, USAMHI (first quotation); Osborn Journal, Colgate University Library, Hamilton, N.Y. (second quotation); *OR* 47(2):910; Luvaas, *Johnston's Last Stand*, p. 15.

7. Thomas W. Osborn, *Fiery Trail*, pp. 192–93.

8. Present U.S. Highway 13.

9. Thomas W. Osborn, *Fiery Trail*, pp. 192–93.

10. These roads "ran nearly parallel to ours." William E. Strong, Reminiscences, ISHL.

11. On March 18 the Seventeenth Corps had marched from Beaman's Crossroads to Troublefield's Store. The corps divided at that point using two roads for the sake of mobility. McClurg, "Last Chance," p. 398; *OR* 47(2):25, 889; Osborn Journal, Colgate University Library, Hamilton, N.Y.; Barrett, *Sherman's March*, p. 176.

12. Mar. 20, 1865, entry, Brower Diary, Civil War Miscellaneous Collection, USAMHI; Thomas W. Osborn, *Fiery Trail*, pp. 192–93.

13. Beach, "Bentonville," p. 30; William E. Strong, Reminiscences, ISHL.

14. William E. Strong, Reminiscences, ISHL.

15. Ibid.

16. *OR* 47(1):205, 234.

17. Meanwhile, Capt. William Duncan, Howard's chief scout, led an advance party toward Goldsboro to check out the other main bridge and to establish contact with Schofield. Duncan met rebels instead. Duncan's party drove the enemy off, however, forcing the Confederates to destroy the "Old State" bridge over the Neuse. Sladen, "Service with General Howard," Sladen Family Papers, USAMHI; *OR* 47(1):205–6, 223, 234, 321, 47(2): 898–900; Mar. 19, 1865, entry, Platter Diary, Platter Papers, UGL.

18. Osborn Journal, Colgate University Library, Hamilton, N.Y.

19. Foraker got back to Slocum after midnight. "The ride back being so much longer in point of time because the road was full of troops, it was dark, and my 'horse-flesh' was used up!" J. B. Foraker to H. W. Slocum, n.d., quoted in *B&L* 4:693, Foraker, *Notes*, p. 63, and *OR* 47(2):905.

20. *OR* 47(2):898.

21. Anders, *Eighteenth Missouri*, pp. 314–15; William E. Strong, Reminiscences, ISHL; *OR* 47(1):205, 47(2):897–99 (quotation, p. 897), 901; Barrett, *Sherman's March*, p. 177.

22. *OR* 47(1):25.

23. *OR* 47(1):25, 918–19; Sherman, *Memoirs*, 2:203; William E. Strong, Reminiscences, ISHL.

24. *OR* 47(1):918.

25. Earlier he had worried that Johnston might march down the old Goldsboro road and attack Howard at Cox's Bridge as he prepared to cross the Neuse. *OR* 47(2)905.

26. *OR* 47(2):918–19.

27. *OR* 47(2):922, 924–25.

28. Mar. 20, 1865, entry, Parmater Diary, OHS.

29. Grecian, *Eighty-third . . . Indiana*, pp. 79–80.

30. *OR* 47(2):899, 47(1):273–74, 288, 303; Mar. 20, 1865, entry, Hazen Journal, Hazen Papers, USAMHI; Henry W. Slocum, "Sherman's March," *B&L* 4:695; Mar. 20, 1865,

entry, Parmater Diary, OHS; I. T. Dillon to wife, Mar. 22, 1865, Dillon Papers, ISHL; Hazen, *Narrative*, p. 359; Grecian, *Eighty-third . . . Indiana*, pp. 79–80; Trimble, *Ninety-third . . . Illinois*, p. 184; C. B. Tompkins to wife, Mar. 22, 1865, Tompkins Letters, DU; Mar. 19, 1865, entry, Schweitzer Diary, *CWTI* Collection, USAMHI; Hedley, *Marching through Georgia*, p. 406; Cox, *March to the Sea*, p. 194; Pittenger Diary, OHS.

31. C. B. Tompkins to wife, Mar. 22, 1865, Tompkins Letters, DU (first quotation); Dozer, "Marching with Sherman," p. 468; Mar. 20, 1865, entry, Inskeep Diary, OHS; Bauer, *Soldiering*, p. 231; Mar. 20, 1865, entry, Kittinger Diary, Hess Collection, USAMHI.

32. Duke, *Fifty-third . . . Ohio*, p. 185; *OR* 47(1):274, 487 (quotation), 47(2):915; C. B. Tompkins to wife, Mar. 22, 1865, Tompkins Letters, DU; Ohio Infantry, *94th Ohio*, p. 92.

33. *OR* 47(2):921, 47(1):424.

34. The 5th Wisconsin Light (left section) fired twenty rounds of solid shot "but was not replied to by the enemy's batteries," reported Capt. Joseph McKnight, battery commander. *OR* 47(1):581.

35. *OR* 47(1):588, 753, 624, 694, 554, 708, 856, 575; Trimble, *Ninety-third . . . Illinois*, p. 184; McAdams, *Every-day Soldier Life*, p. 146; New York Monuments Commission, *In Memoriam*, p. 309; Morse, *Civil War Diaries*, p. 195.

36. A perplexing question arises with Baird. Why did he end the war as only a brigadier general? He did hold the brevet rank of major general, but his record seems to have entitled him to higher rank. "His commanders [Rosecrans, Thomas, and Sherman] repeatedly—but unavailingly—recommended him for promotion." Faust, Patricia L., ed. *Historical Times Illustrated Encyclopedia of the Civil War*, p. 34.

37. A member of Fearing's brigade disagreed. Carlin's division is "still terribly demoralized," he confided to his diary. Mar. 20, 1865, entry, Burkhalter Diary, Burkhalter Papers, ISHL.

38. *OR* 47(1):826, 436, 453, 645, 486–87, 47(2):917–18 (quotation, p. 917); Mar. 20, 1865, entry, Fritz Diary, IHS; Mar. 20, 1865, entry, Williams Diary, Detroit Public Library.

39. That morning the wagon train was all aflutter—"great excitement . . . no reports can be relied on." Then Col. George W. Mindil moved the train east to Thornton's Plantation near Falling Creek. There he had the wagons parked and ordered his brigade and the teamsters to dig, entrenching themselves and the wagons in a work "strong enough to resist a formidable assault from any force." Feeling secure, the teamsters and commissary soldiers "had a stag dance in the evening on the ground." Capt. Dexter Horton, onetime postmaster turned leader of soldiers, reported: "Drew a barrel of apple jack and issued it." *OR* 47(1):729; McCain, *A Soldier's Diary*, p. 50; Eaton, "Diary," pp. 249–50. See also *OR* 47(2):919.

40. Mar. 20, 1865, entry, Rugg Diary, Connecticut State Library, Hartford; James Taylor Holmes, *52nd O.V.I.*, p. 25; *OR* 47(1):624, 679; Marvin, *Fifth . . . Connecticut*, p. 374; Mar. 20, 1865, entry, Kittinger Diary, Hess Collection, USAMHI; Mar. 20, 1865, entry, Fahnestock Diary, Fahnestock Papers, ISHL.

41. Orendorff, *Reminiscences*, p. 200.

42. *OR* 47(2):920 (quotation), 47(1):436; Ohio Infantry, *94th Ohio*, p. 92; Bauer, *Soldiering*, p. 231.

43. Mar. 20, 1865, entry, Brower Diary, Civil War Miscellaneous Collection, USAMHI.

44. Mar. 20, 1865, entry, Inskeep Diary, OHS; W. C. Johnson, "Through the Carolinas," Johnson Papers, LC.

45. Mar. 20, 1865, entry, Miller Journal, IHS. See also *OR* 47(1):575, 581; Mar. 20, 1865, entry, Kittinger Diary, Hess Collection, USAMHI. The loss of the horses would indicate effective work by Confederate sharpshooters, close up, or that the section was stationed well forward, without cover, close to or on the skirmish line, conducting in effect an "artillery charge."

46. Mar. 20, 1865, entry, Miller Journal, IHS. See also Illinois Infantry, *Fifty-fifth . . . Illinois*, pp. 413–15; W. C. Johnson, "Through the Carolinas," Johnson Papers, LC; *OR* 47(1):436, 552, 554; *Army and Navy Journal* 2, no. 32, Apr. 1, 1865; Mar. 20, 1865, entry, Inskeep Diary, OHS; Mar. 20, 1865, entry, Brower Diary, Civil War Miscellaneous Collection, USAMHI.

47. Fleharty, *102d Illinois*, p. 161.

48. Ibid., pp. 161–62. The assault scheduled for the morning of March 21 (if actually ordered) never took place. One source, however, even has Baird saying to Slocum "that he could not make a charge on his own responsibility for he believed it to be a well constructed slaughter pen, and you will have to be responsible." Fodrea, "101st Indiana," ISL.

49. *OR* 47(1):588. See also *OR* 47(1):601, 629, 809; Mar. 20, 1865, entry, Finley Diary, Civil War Miscellaneous Collection, USAMHI; Mar. 20, 1865, entry, Rilea Diary, ISHL; Mar. 20, 1865, entry, Pierce Diary, *CWTI* Collection, USAMHI.

50. Payne, *Thirty-fourth . . . Illinois*, p. 204.

51. Ibid.; *OR* 47(1):494, 512; McAdams, *Every-day Soldier Life*, p. 146; Mar. 20, 1865, entry, Batchelor Diary, Batchelor Papers, ISHL.

52. *OR* 47(1):538; Mar. 20, 1865, entry, Burkhalter Diary, Burkhalter Papers, ISHL.

53. *OR* 47(1):538, 47(2):472.

54. *OR* 47(1):499.

55. *OR* 47(1):497, 499.

56. Grummond maintained that Vandever ordered him to make the disastrous attack, and that he did so employing a strong skirmish line. He is contradicted, however, by Vandever, the commander of the 16th Illinois (Capt. Herman Lund), and one of Grummond's own company commanders (Capt. J. Walter Myers). *OR* 47(1):497, 499–500, 503, 505–7; Westervelt, *Lights and Shadows*, p. 94; Robertson, *Michigan in the War*, pp. 35–51; France, *Bentonville*, p. 17.

57. Mar. 20, 1865, entry, Kittinger Diary, Hess Collection, USAMHI.

58. Mar. 20, 1865, entry, Hunter Diary, and Hickenlooper Memoirs, *CWTI* Collection, USAMHI; Mar. 20, 1865, entry, Perry Diary, WHC; Anders, *Eighteenth Missouri*, pp. 314–15; *OR* 47(2):903.

59. Mar. 20, 1865, entry, Sladen Diary, USAMHI; William W. Belknap, *Fifteenth . . . Iowa*, p. 467; *OR* 47(1):383, 409, 47(2):903; R. S. Finley to family, n.d., 1865, Finley Letters, SHC; William E. Strong, Reminiscences, ISHL; Nichols, *Story of the Great March*, p. 264; Mar. 20, 1865, entry, Nilson Diary, IHS; Mar. 20, 1865, entry, Bates Diary, USAMHI; Adair, *Forty-fifth Illinois*, p. 161.

60. *OR* 47(1):321. Both Sherman and Johnston wanted Cox's Bridge destroyed—Sherman, to clear his flank as he moved toward Bentonville. Johnston similarly had ordered that Cox's Bridge be destroyed "at all hazards" in the event his men were driven from their position below the river. This was a necessary precaution to prevent a Yankee dash into Goldsboro from the west. It also guarded against a flanking movement by Howard down the

northern side of the Neuse toward Smithfield and Johnston's vulnerable rear. *OR* 47(2):1436, 47(1):235; Barrett, *Sherman's March*, p. 177.

61. The trains of both the Fifteenth and Seventeenth Corps would be parked at Buck Creek, 8 miles from Dudley Station, guarded by a brigade from Mower's division. *OR* 47(1):206, 235, 321, 47(2):916.

62. *OR* 47(1):206.

63. Monnett, "'Awfulest Time I Ever Seen,'" p. 287.

64. Henry H. Wright, *Sixth Iowa*, p. 429 (quotation); Monnett, "'Awfulest Time I Ever Seen,'" p. 287; *OR* 47(1):259, 262; Mar. 20, 1865, entry, McKee Diary, Civil War Miscellaneous Collection, USAMHI; Mar. 20, 1865, entry, Armstrong Diary, IHS; Dozer, "Marching with Sherman," p. 470; N. C. Hughes conversation with John C. Goode, Oct. 9, 1993. It appears that all, or portions of all, of Catterson's regiments were armed with repeaters.

65. "Capt Pratt" probably was Capt. William B. Pratt of Logan's staff.

66. The "off mule" was the off-side animal in a brace of two, the one without a driver or rider.

67. Upson, *With Sherman to the Sea*, p. 159.

68. Logan, Woods, and others who were "up close behind the skirmish line." Strong, Reminiscences, ISHL.

69. *OR* 47(1):246, 259, 262; Hubert, *Fiftieth . . . Illinois*, p. 370; Upson, *With Sherman to the Sea*, p. 159; Sherlock, *One Hundredth . . . Indiana*, pp. 208–10; William E. Strong, Reminiscences, ISHL.

70. Upson, *With Sherman to the Sea*, p. 160.

71. *OR* 47(1):235. Evidently this primitive signaling device failed. Howard had listened closely but in vain at 7:00 A.M. for Slocum's guns, which would have signified that Johnston "had fallen back." Likewise there is no mention in the reports of Slocum or his subordinates hearing the periodic cannon fire from Howard's column.

72. *OR* 47(1):206. See also *OR* 47(1):26, 206, 235, 365–66, 47(2):914, 916; Mar. 20, 1865, entry, Walters Diary, IHS; Grigsby, "History of 53rd Indiana," Grigsby-McDonald Papers, IHS; Mar. 20, 1865, entry, McKee Diary, Civil War Miscellaneous Collection, USAMHI; Mar. 20, 1865, entry, Bean Diary, SHC; Thomas W. Osborn, *Fiery Trail*, p. 195; Nichols, *Story of the Great March*, p. 264. The Confederate strong point was located at the intersection of the old Goldsboro road and the road leading north through Bentonville to Smithfield. Just north was the home of ancient Nathan Flowers, age 89; his wife Delana, 87; and his daughter Adda, 54. North Carolina Census, Johnston County, 1860, p. 132.

73. *OR* 47(1):26, 206, 235, 365–66, 409, 47(2):914, 916; Mar. 20, 1865, entry, Walters Diary, IHS; Grigsby, "History of 53rd Indiana," Grigsby-McDonald Papers, IHS; Mar. 20, 1865, entry, McKee Diary, Civil War Miscellaneous Collection, USAMHI; Mar. 20, 1865, entry, Bean Diary, SHC; Thomas W. Osborn, *Fiery Trail*, p. 195; Nichols, *Story of the Great March*, p. 264; Henry W. Slocum, "Sherman's March," *B&L* 4:695.

74. Belknap, *Fifteenth . . . Iowa*, p. 468. See also *OR* 47(1):26, 206, 262, 266, 47(2):1443; Henry H. Wright, *Sixth Iowa*, p. 431; Thomas W. Osborn, *Fiery Trail*, pp. 195–96; Nichols, *Story of the Great March*, p. 264; Sherlock, *One Hundredth . . . Indiana*, p. 209.

75. Mar. 20, 1865, entry, Platter Diary, UGL.

76. Brown, *Fourth . . . Minnesota*, p. 392.

77. Hubert, *Fiftieth . . . Illinois*, p. 371.

78. *OR* 47(1):235 (first quotation); Hubert, *Fiftieth . . . Illinois*, pp. 370-71 (second quotation). See also Henry H. Wright, *Sixth Iowa*, p. 431; *OR* 47(1):235; Thomas W. Osborn, *Fiery Trail*, p. 196; Hazen, *Narrative*, pp. 359-60, 366; *OR* 47(1):288, 294, 259.

79. *OR* 47(1):263.

80. *OR* 47(1):267, 206, 246, 274, 294.

81. *OR* 47(1):206, 235, 383, 47(2):914; Belknap, *Fifteenth . . . Iowa*, p. 469; Henry H. Wright, *Sixth Iowa*, p. 431; Nichols, *Story of the Great March*, p. 264; Oliver Otis Howard, *Autobiography*, 2:148; William E. Strong Reminiscences, ISHL; Hickenlooper Memoirs, *CWTI* Collection, USAMHI; Ambrose, *7th . . . Illinois*, p. 300; Mar. 20, 1865, entry, Brush Diary, Brush Family Papers, ISHL; Mar. 20, 1865, entry, Sladen Diary, USAMHI.

82. Oliver Otis Howard, *Autobiography*, 2:149.

83. *OR* 47(1):262 (first quotation), 235 (second quotation), 26 (third quotation), 206, 341, 366, 47(2):916; W. T. Sherman to H. W. Slocum, Mar. 20, 1865, Schoff Civil War Collections, CL/UM (last quotation).

84. Belknap, *Fifteenth . . . Iowa*, p. 467.

85. *OR* 47(1):259, 267, 235 (second quotation); Dozer, "Marching with Sherman," p. 468; Sladen, "Service with General Howard," Sladen Family Papers, USAMHI; Henry H. Wright, *Sixth Iowa*, p. 432 (first quotation); Sherwood, "50th Illinois . . . Journal," Hess Collection, USAMHI.

86. Hagood, *Memoirs*, p. 361; *OR* 47(2):925.

87. W. T. Sherman to H. W. Slocum, Mar. 20, 1865, Schoff Collection, CL/UM.

88. Schofield would take possession of Goldsboro on the afternoon of March 21.

89. *OR* 47(2):925.

90. Barrett, *Sherman's March*, pp. 178-79; France, *Bentonville*, p. 17; Luvaas, *Johnston's Last Stand*, p. 17; Liddell-Hart, *Sherman*, p. 377.

Chapter 10

1. Ford, "Last Battles," p. 141.

2. James W. Bell, *43rd Georgia*, p. 40; Ford, "Last Battles," p. 142.

3. This probably was Capt. Bernard Sweetman, an artillery officer with some experience in engineering who had been active in the defense of Wilmington. Taylor Reminiscences, NCA.

4. *OR* 47(2):1442-44.

5. *OR* 47(1):1054-56, 47(2):1454.

6. *OR* 47(1):1056.

7. Although the elevations differ appreciably, the term *plateau* is an exaggeration for the sake of clarity.

8. Mar. 20, 1865, entry, Johnson Diary, DU; McLaws Order Book, McLaws Papers, SHC. In 1995 the route that concerned Hardee is secondary road 1136 (Overshot Road). The mill and pond are designated on U.S. geodetic maps as Blackman's Pond.

9. Fort, History and Memoirs, USAMHI; Mar. 20, 1865, entry, Jones Journal, NCA; Manarin, *North Carolina Troops*, 1:585.

10. *OR* 47(2):1446-47; Graber, *A Terry Texas Ranger*, pp. 224-25.

11. Graber, *A Terry Texas Ranger*, pp. 224–25, quoting an 1897 letter from McLaws.

12. Mar. 20, 1865, entry, Waring Diary, SHC; *OR* 47(2):1443; Johnston, *Narrative*, p. 389.

13. McLaws Order Book, McLaws Papers, SHC. This plan would prove impossible with their thin manpower, so eventually Wheeler's and Mully Logan's dismounted troopers fell back and filled in between the left flank of the infantry and the swamp.

14. It is difficult and sometimes misleading to reconstruct the Confederate cavalry organization at this time. Even the editors of the *Official Records* gave up, hiding behind such phrases as "embracing, in part, the following-named organizations," then proceeding to lump twenty-seven cavalry regiments without brigade or division designation and then listing ten division and brigade commanders without specific commands.

15. *OR* 47(2):1436, 1445.

16. *OR* 47(2):1443 (quotation); Johnston, *Narrative*, p. 389; Wade Hampton, "Bentonville," *B&L* 4:704–5; Hartley, "Bentonville," p. 32.

17. McMurry, *Footprints*, p. 174.

18. Dodson, *Wheeler*, pp. 350–51.

19. *OR* 47(2):1443.

20. Mar. 20, 1865, entry, Calder Diary, DU; Mar. 20, 1865, entry, Jones Journal, NCA; *OR* 47(2):1442; Johnston, *Narrative*, pp. 389–90; Hagood, *Memoirs*, p. 361; Barrett, *Sherman's March*, pp. 177–78; Hughes, *Hardee*, p. 561.

21. Evidence is conflicting in regard to Lowry's and Granbury's Brigades. Some reports have them arriving not on March 20 but late in the afternoon of the twenty-first. *OR* 47(1):1108, 1097, 1082–83, 47(2):1441, 1444; Johnston, *Narrative*, p. 393; Horn, *Army of Tennessee*, p. 425.

22. *OR* 47(2):1443.

23. Ford, "Last Battles," p. 142.

24. The incidence of illness, at least as reported, within the Confederate general officer corps is noteworthy: Beauregard, Hardee, Hill, Loring, and Butler. Perhaps there were more. *OR* 47(2):1442; Ridley, *Battles and Sketches*, p. 453.

25. In his report and communications Hill's attitude toward his West Point classmate Stewart appears to be one of thinly disguised disapproval, if not lack of confidence.

26. *OR* 47(1):1091; Mar. 20, 1865, entry, Jones Journal, NCA.

27. Mar. 20, 1865, entry, Nash diary, UGA; James W. Bell, *43rd Georgia*, p. 40; Ridley, *Battles and Sketches*, p. 453; *OR* 47(1):1091, 1095; France, *Bentonville*, p. 17.

28. Walter Clark, *Regiments . . . from North Carolina*, 4:548.

29. *OR* 47(1):1056, 1091, 1131; Walter Clark, *Regiments . . . from North Carolina*, 2:13, 4:57, 698–99, 197, 548–49 (quotation, p. 548); Hagood, *Memoirs*, pp. 361–62; Powell Reminiscences, SHC; Jones Journal, NCA; Jordan, *Bentonville*, p. 23; Mar. 20, 1865, entry, Baldwin Diary, SHC; Hinsdale, *72nd . . . North Carolina*, pp. 25–26; Johnston, *Narrative*, p. 390; Mar. 20, 1865, entry, Sloan Diary, TSLA.

30. Mrs. John H. Anderson, "Boy Soldiers at . . . Bentonville," p. 175; W. Clark to mother, Mar. 27, 1865, in Brooks and Lefler, *Papers of Walter Clark*, 1:136–37.

31. A man helping Kirkland in the capacity of aide-de-camp was Maj. Fraz Joseph Hahr, an "accomplished" Swede who had participated in the defense of Wilmington. Hahr distinguished himself for his coolness and effectiveness under fire. Manarin, *North Carolina Troops*, 3:3, 32; Walter Clark, *Regiments . . . from North Carolina*, 4:383, 548.

32. Fort, Memoirs, USAMHI.

33. Ibid. There was no soldier named "Gilham" in Fort's company, but there were two named "Gillham" in Rutherford's company, at least one of whom, Pvt. George W. Gillham, was alive at the time of Bentonville. Henderson, *Roster of . . . Soldiers of Georgia*, 1:357, 362, 363.

34. The photograph was of a "Florida beauty." Alas, she married another, but "Augustus consoled himself in the charms of a young widow." Fort, Memoirs, USAMHI.

35. France, *Bentonville*, p. 17.

36. Howard, "Bentonville," Howard Papers, BCL; Johnston, *Narrative*, pp. 389–90; Hagood, *Memoirs*, p. 361.

37. Hagood, *Memoirs*, p. 361.

38. Such a calamity would occur in Mobile three weeks later when Maj. Gen. Edward R. S. Canby assaulted Fort Blakely's breastworks with overwhelming force.

39. Boggy land, marsh.

40. Hagood, *Memoirs*, p. 361; Watson, "In the Battle of Bentonville," p. 95.

41. Wade Hampton, "Bentonville," *B&L* 4:704.

42. *OR* 47(2):1442; Mar. 20, 1865, entry, Calder Diary, DU.

43. Erik D. France and Johnston biographer R. M. Hughes argue that Johnston remained the extra day first to "disprove slanders" made against him personally by Davis, Bragg, and Hood in the past and second to disprove slanders made against the Army of Tennessee for Chattanooga and Nashville—in other words, for the sake of his and "his" army's honor. The Army of Tennessee as well as its commander wanted to show that they were not afraid to stand and fight. "Most of the less sanguine had already deserted. The cause was already all but hopeless—why not go down fighting?" E. D. France to N. C. Hughes, Oct. 26, 1994; R. M. Hughes, *Johnston*, p. 270.

Chapter 11

1. Mar. 21, 1865, entry, Roseberry Diary, BL/UM; Mar. 21, 1865, entry, Lynch Diary, WHC; Johnson, "Through the Carolinas," Johnson Papers, LC; Hubert, *50th Illinois*, p. 370; Eaton, "Diary," p. 250; McKinney Diary, Bentonville Battlefield Historical Site, Newton Grove, N.C.; Nichols, *Story of the Great March*, p. 265 (first quotation); *OR* 47(2):944–45 (second quotation, p. 945), 47(1):27.

2. *OR* 47(2):942.

3. *OR* 47(2):930–31.

4. Erik France poses the question: "Didn't Sherman's plan to draw off Slocum's wing . . . give Johnston, in effect, another escape route to the west, south of Mill Creek? . . . In other words, perhaps Johnston's predicament was not solely dependent on the actual retreat route taken over the Mill Creek bridges close by Bentonville." E. France to N. C. Hughes, Jan. 5, 1995.

5. The Confederates "are forced to guard against [Howard] upon their flank and rear." Thus they might counterattack to alleviate this threat. Nichols, *Story of the Great March*, pp. 265–66.

6. *OR* 47(2):942.

7. Mar. 21, 1865, entry, Kittinger Diary, Hess Collection, USAMHI; Mar. 21, 1865, entry,

Fateley Diary, IHS; *OR* 47(1):441, 694, 47(2):937; Mar. 21, 1865, entry, Bruce Diary, ISL; Mar. 21, 1865, entry, Michael Diary, IHS.

8. Mar. 21, 1865, entry, Childress Diary, ISHL.

9. Bowman Memoir, Bowman Family Papers, USAMHI.

10. Mar. 21, 1865, entry, Childress Diary, ISHL; *OR* 47(2):939; Bowman Memoir, Bowman Family Papers, USAMHI (quotations); Mar. 21, 1865, entry, Inskeep Diary, OHS.

11. In his history of the 52d Ohio, James T. Holmes maintains that these sharpshooters were from the 22d Indiana, Fearing's brigade. Holmes, *52nd O.V.I.*, p. 25.

12. Payne, *Thirty-fourth . . . Illinois*, p. 205.

13. *OR* 47(1):500, 508, 512, 538; Payne, *Thirty-fourth . . . Illinois*, pp. 204-5. See also Mar. 21, 1865, entry, Fahnestock Diary, Fahnestock Papers, ISHL; Cheverell, *Twenty-ninth Ohio*, p. 146.

14. Holmes, *52nd O.V.I.*, p. 25.

15. Ibid.; *OR* 47(1):538, 47(2):939; Mar. 21, 1865, entry, Fahnestock Diary, Fahnestock Papers, ISHL; Mar. 21, 1865, entry, Burkhalter Diary, Burkhalter Papers, ISHL.

16. *OR* 47(2):937; Mar. 21, 1865, entry, Patton Diary, Civil War Miscellaneous Collection, USAMHI.

17. Bauer, *Soldiering*, p. 231.

18. *OR* 47(1):667, 601, 653; Mar. 21, 1865, entry, Finley Diary, Civil War Miscellaneous Collection, USAMHI; Mar. 21, 1865, entry, West Diary, USAMHI; Marvin, *Fifth . . . Connecticut*, p. 374; Mar. 21, 1865, entry, Patton Diary, Civil War Miscellaneous Collection, USAMHI.

19. Mar. 21, 1865, entry, Miller Journal, IHS. It is only fair to point out that these Confederates were replaying their disastrous assault of two days before—maneuvering over the same ground, charging the same batteries. It is little wonder that they advanced without precision. Furthermore, some of the bodies seen by Miller may have been those of Taliaferro's men killed on the nineteenth.

20. It is unclear whether Strong was referring to Noel B. Howard, Charles Henry Howard, or Jacob M. Howard, all of whom served as General Howard's staff officers in the last year of the war.

21. William E. Strong, Reminiscences, ISHL.

22. Hickenlooper Memoirs, *CWTI* Collection, USAMHI.

23. Official Diary, Sladen Family Papers, USAMHI; *OR* 47(2):913-24.

24. *OR* 47(1):206, 235-36, 274, 283, 298 (second quotation), 304, 341 (first quotation), 354, 366, 47(2):933-34, 915; Oliver Otis Howard, *Autobiography*, 2:149-50; Mar. 21, 1865, entry, Schweitzer Diary, *CWTI* Collection, USAMHI; Rowe Recollections, IHS; C. B. Tompkins to wife, Mar. 22, 1865, Tompkins Letters, DU.

25. Hubert, *Fiftieth . . . Illinois*, p. 371 (first, second quotations); Cluett, *57th . . . Illinois*, p. 98 (third quotation); Ambrose, *7th . . . Illinois*, p. 300; Mar. 21, 1865, entry, Risedorph Diary, Minnesota Historical Society, St. Paul; Mar. 21, 1865, entry, Bean Diary, SHC. The 7th was armed with Henry rifles, "magazine guns," characterized by a tube under the barrel. Thomas Wilhelm noted that it "as now [1881] improved is known as the *Winchester*, and is sold in every part of the globe." Wilhelm, *Military Dictionary*, p. 295.

26. R. B. Hoadley to Cousin Em, Apr. 8, 1865, Hoadley Papers, DU.

27. Henry H. Wright, *Sixth Iowa*, pp. 432-33.

28. *OR* 47(1):268.

29. Orendorff, *Reminiscences*, p. 201.

30. *OR* 47(1):253, 257, 261, 267-68, 341, 935; Mar. 21, 1865, entry, Stratton Diary, ISL; Nichols, *Story of the Great March*, p. 265; Mar. 21, 1865, entry, McKee Diary, Civil War Miscellaneous Collection, USAMHI; Mar. 21, 1865, entry, Platter Diary, Platter Papers, UGA; Mar. 21, 1865, entry, Armstrong Diary, IHS; Mar. 21, 1865, entry, Thayer Diary, NCA.

31. *OR* 47(1):354, 356, 366, 368, 373; Grecian, *Eighty-third . . . Indiana*, pp. 79-80.

32. *OR* 47(1):372.

33. *OR* 47(1):178. See also *OR* 47(1):935, 372; Henry H. Wright, *Sixth Iowa*, p. 433; Mar. 21, 1865, entry, Walters Diary, IHS; Nichols, *Story of the Great March*, p. 265.

34. Belknap, *Fifteenth . . . Iowa*, p. 469.

35. *OR* 47(1):409, 415-17; Mar. 21, 1865, entry, Hunter Diary, *CWTI* Collection, USAMHI.

36. *OR* 47(2):936-37.

37. *OR* 47(1):694, 47(2):936-40. It seems unlikely, certainly uncharacteristic, that Sherman intended to mass the Left Wing behind Howard's right flank to support a heavy attack on Johnston's left flank.

38. *OR* 32(3):325.

39. *OR* 47(1):383; Anders, *Eighteenth Missouri*, p. 316.

40. Anders, *Eighteenth Missouri*, pp. 316-17 (quotations); *OR* 47(1):391. In an unsubstantiated accusation, Maj. Thomas W. Osborn, Howard's chief of artillery, states that he "understood General Sherman ordered Mower in person to make the advance and neither General Blair, or General Howard knew of it, and were not responsible for failing to support him. The moment General Howard heard of Mower's condition, he ordered the Corps to his assistance, but he [Mower] had returned before the Corps could move. Had General Sherman given General Howard the order instead of doing the unsoldierly thing of giving a division commander orders direct, we should have gained a splendid victory, instead of a repulse." Osborn, *Fiery Trail*, p. 197.

41. *OR* 47(1):391, 395, 397, 403; Charles H. Smith, *Fuller's Ohio Brigade*, p. 273; Anders, *Eighteenth Missouri*, pp. 317-18; Official Diary, Sladen Family Papers, USAMHI.

42. Mar. 21, 1865, entry, Nilson Diary, IHS; Charles H. Smith, *Fuller's Ohio Brigade*, p. 273 (quotations); Jamison, *Recollections*, n.p.

43. *OR* 47(1):391.

44. Ibid.

45. The remainder of Mower's Second Brigade was far to the rear at Buck Creek guarding the wagon train. *OR* 47(1):253, 391, 395, 403.

46. *OR* 47(1):391. See also Mar. 21, 1865, entry, Perry Diary, WHC; Anders, *Eighteenth Missouri*, pp. 318-19; Wilson, *Memoirs*, p. 430.

47. *OR* 47(1):403.

48. *OR* 47(1):395, 403-4, Oliver Otis Howard, *Autobiography*, 2:149; Anders, *Eighteenth Missouri*, p. 319 (quotation); Sweet, "27th Ohio," WHC; Mar. 21, 1865, entry, Pittenger Diary, OHS; Roesch Journal, Civil War Miscellaneous Collection, USAMHI; Mar. 21, 1865, entry, Martin Journal, IHS; A. M. Bly to Anna Bly, Mar. 29, 1865, Bly Papers, SHSW.

49. *OR* 47(1):383, 391, 395-96, 403, 207, 47(2):950; Howard, "Bentonville," Howard Papers, BCL; Hickenlooper Memoirs, *CWTI* Collection, USAMHI; Cox, *March to the Sea*,

p. 195; Hitchcock, *Marching with Sherman*, pp. 276–77; Gage, *From Vicksburg to Raleigh*, p. 298; Nichols, *Story of the Great March*, pp. 267–68; Liddell-Hart, *Sherman*, p. 377; William E. Strong, Reminiscences, ISHL.

50. Anders, *Eighteenth Missouri*, p. 319; Oliver Otis Howard, *Autobiography*, 2:149–50; *OR* 47(1):207; William E. Strong, Reminiscences, ISHL.

51. Howard, "Bentonville," Howard Papers, BCL.

52. Anders, *Eighteenth Missouri*, p. 319.

53. William T. Sherman, *Memoirs*, 2:304. See also Cox, *March to the Sea*, p. 195; Liddell-Hart, *Sherman*, p. 377.

54. Howard, "Bentonville," Howard Papers, BCL.

55. Oliver Otis Howard, *Autobiography*, 2:150.

56. *OR* 47(2):941.

57. *OR* 47(2):937; Mar. 21, 1865, entry, Rilea Diary, ISHL.

58. *OR* 47(1):601, 785, 588, 424, 436.

59. Nichols, *Story of the Great March*, p. 265.

60. *OR* 47(2):236, 47(1):247, 268, 383; Belknap, *Fifteenth . . . Iowa*, p. 470; Wilson, *Memoirs*, p. 430; Nichols, *Story of the Great March*, p. 265; Mar. 21, 1865, entry, Lynch Diary, WHC; Mar. 21, 1865, entry, Schweitzer Diary, *CWTI* Collection, USAMHI; Dozer, "Marching with Sherman," pp. 468–69; Official Diary, Sladen Family Papers, USAMHI; Thomas W. Osborn, *Fiery Trail*, p. 198; Mar. 21, 1865, entry, Bean Diary, SHC.

61. Hedley, *Marching through Georgia*, p. 406.

62. Ibid.

63. *OR* 47(2):934; Brown, *Fourth . . . Minnesota*, p. 392; Mar. 21, 1865, entry, Lynch Diary, WHC; Belknap, *Fifteenth . . . Iowa*, p. 470 (quotation); Mar. 21, 1865, entry, Childress Diary, ISHL; I. T. Dillon to wife, Mar. 22, 1865, Dillon Papers, ISHL.

64. *OR* 47(1):372–73, 253; Henry H. Wright, *Sixth Iowa*, p. 432; Howard, "Bentonville," Howard Papers, BCL.

65. Brown, *Fourth . . . Minnesota*, p. 392; Mar. 21, 1865, entry, Fahnestock Diary, KMNP (first quotation); Mar. 21, 1865, entry, Schweitzer Diary, *CWTI* Collection, USAMHI (second quotation); Ambrose, *7th . . . Illinois*, p. 300; Dozer, "Marching with Sherman," pp. 468–69; Canfield, *21st . . . Ohio*, p. 183; Mar. 21, 1865, entry, Childress Diary, ISHL.

Chapter 12

1. Former First Sergeant Curtis, 13th Battalion North Carolina Light Artillery, a four-year veteran from Hillsborough and only twenty-two, died the next morning. Manarin, *North Carolina Troops*, 1:446, 587.

2. Mar. 20–21, 1865, entries, Jones Journal, NCA.

3. *OR* 47(1):1446.

4. *OR* 47(1):1057, 1092, 1095; Johnston, *Narrative*, p. 390.

5. *OR* 47(1):1057. Johnston's analysis was correct. Sherman did plan to withdraw the army on March 22, beginning on the left flank with the Twentieth Corps.

6. See Law to Hampton, 2:00 A.M., March 21, *OR* 47(2):1447.

7. This left Kennedy with four regiments as McLaws's and Hoke's reserve.

8. McLaws Order Book, McLaws Papers, SHC.

9. Ibid.; Johnston, *Narrative*, p. 391; *OR* 47(2):1447.

10. McMurry, *Footprints*, p. 174.

11. In helping repel one of the charges against Fiser, the commander of the North Carolinians hung back: "a venerable old gray-beard, riding a white horse, as soon as bullets began to pelt pines, took refuge behind a large tree." Dickert, *Kershaw's Brigade*, p. 524.

12. McMurry, *Footprints*, p. 174.

13. Ibid.

14. Second Lt. J. C. Ellington, regimental historian for the 50th Regiment North Carolina Troops, recalled the following counterattack by Hardy's Brigade on March 21. But it appears that Ellington was mistaken about the date and probably the circumstances, confusing the incident with Hardy's disastrous probe into Mitchell's position as the fighting closed on the nineteenth.

According to Ellington, the 50th and the 10th Regiments North Carolina State Troops attacked late in the afternoon of March 21, suffering frightful losses from Yankee muskets and direct artillery fire. In "five minutes" Hardy lost one-third of his command. When it looked as though all were lost, when the survivors faced death or capture, Colonel Hardy "saved the day." Leading the assault himself, "dressed in a suit of sky blue broadcloth and broad-brimmed slouch hat, he might easily be taken for a Federal officer." Hardy ran forward to the enemy line. Within sight of everyone, gray and blue alike, he "paced up and down and ordered them to cease firing." Federal officers, astonished, shouted for their men to resume shooting. "Utterly confused," the Yankees hesitated. Before they could react some of Hardy's men had "crawled out of the swamp and made their escape." Hardy himself "walked off without a scratch." Walter Clark, *Regiments . . . from North Carolina*, 3:198 (quotations); Jordan, *North Carolina Troops*, 12:147; Mark Bradley to N. C. Hughes, Nov. 26, 1994; Mar. 19, 1865, entry, Sloan Diary, TSLA.

15. *OR* 47(1):1055; Mar. 21, 1865, entry, Hutson Diary, Hutson Family Papers, HTT; Mar. 21, 1865, entry, Calder Diary, DU; Mar. 21, 1865, entry, Nash Diary, UGA; Ridley, *Battles and Sketches*, p. 453; Holman, "Concerning the Battle at Bentonville," p. 153.

16. Evidently Wheeler had withdrawn to the rear and right after Monday's fight at Flowers' Crossroads.

17. McLaws that morning had Col. John S. Prather's 8th Confederate Cavalry (Anderson's Brigade, Allen's Division) screening his front. *OR* 47(2):1448.

18. *OR* 47(1):1113, 1131, 47(2):1447-48; James G. Holmes, "Artillery at Bentonville"; Mar. 21, 1865, entry, Gordon Diary, Gordon Papers, SHC; Guild, *Fourth Tennessee Cavalry*, p. 132; Dodson, *Wheeler*, p. 351. It is assumed that Dibrell's Brigade (Ashby's division) guarded Bate's right flank in the vicinity of Blackman's Pond or was held in deep reserve across Mill Creek. A. P. Stewart, writing in 1904, placed Dibrell's Brigade, or part of it led by Maj. Moses H. Clift, in the counterattack against Mower. Stewart appears to have been mistaken. *CV* 20:132.

19. The whereabouts and activities of Mully Logan's Brigade (4th, 5th, and 6th South Carolina Cavalry), not to speak of his individual regiments, is impossible to determine from the handful of Confederate reports and dispatches. Law made no report himself, nor did Logan, Wright, Butler, or Hampton. It is plausible that at least one of Logan's regiments crossed Mill Creek acting as the force Law reported to Hampton that he had stationed north of Mill Creek to counter any movement by Federal cavalry from Cox's Bridge toward

Smithfield. On the other hand, one or more of Logan's regiments may have been the force Hampton sent to the right to help picket the approach via Blackman's Pond. Some, perhaps all, of Logan's command seems to have been present, however, because of the caustic comments made about the "South Carolina cavalry." Mar. 21, 1865, entry, Waring Diary, SHC; *OR* 47(2):1447; Friend, "Rangers at Bentonville."

20. James G. Holmes, "Artillery at Bentonville" (quotation); Wade Hampton, "Bentonville," *B&L* 4:704.

21. James G. Holmes, "Artillery at Bentonville" (quotation); L. Maness to mother, Mar. 28, 1865, Maness Collection, NCA; Mar. 21, 1865, entry, Gordon Diary, Gordon Papers, SHC; Mar. 21, 1865, entry, Waring Diary, SHC; Graber, *A Terry Texas Ranger*, p. 226; Holman, "Concerning the Battle at Bentonville," p. 153. Lt. Pride Jones of Atkins's battery recorded that the cavalry "ran in the greatest confusion clear past the village." W. R. Friend met a brigade of Butler's cavalry at the bridge, "a disorderly mob" that said it had been attacked by at least a corps of infantry. "They were sure the enemy had gained the high bank on the opposite side of the creek and had cut off the only line of retreat." Mar. 21, 1865, entry, Jones Journal, NCA; Friend, "Rangers at Bentonville."

22. The exact location of Johnston's headquarters is unknown. It is likely that he used either Benton's log house or a tent or tents pitched nearby.

23. A period name for the Bentonville-Smithfield road.

24. The author must admit that, had he been there with the Yankee skirmishers, he could not have seen the bridge. A curve in the Bentonville-Smithfield road plus the sharp dropoff down to the creek itself would have made the bridge impossible to see until one was "at it." The author, however, could see the general site of the bridge. His imagination did the rest. Of course, it helps to possess visionary powers fortified by historical hindsight.

25. Interview with John C. Goode and Mark Bradley, Oct. 8, 1993; James G. Holmes, "Artillery at Bentonville"; *OR* 47(1):1131, 1057; Hagood, *Memoirs*, p. 362; Johnston, *Narrative*, p. 390; Mar. 21, 1865, entry, Roy Diary, ALA.

26. Mar. 21, 1865, entry, Sloan Diary, TSLA.

27. Stuart's battery was part of Rhett's artillery battalion. Another cavalry officer acting as an artilleryman in the emergency was Capt. Edwin W. Moise, commander of the 10th Georgia Cavalry.

28. Mar. 21, 1865, entry, Jones Diary, NCA; *OR* 47(1):1057; Johnston, *Narrative*, p. 391; C. W. Hutson to Em, Mar. 22, 1865, Hutson Family Papers, HTT; James G. Holmes, "Artillery at Bentonville"; Elzas, *Jews of South Carolina*, p. 249; Wade Hampton, "Bentonville," *B&L* 4:704–5.

29. James G. Holmes, "Artillery at Bentonville."

30. Estimates range from 150 to 300 troops—down from about 1,000–1,500 in 1862.

31. Allardice, *More Generals in Gray*, pp. 127–28.

32. Mar. 21, 1865, entry, Roy Diary, ALA; *OR* 47(1):1097; Fort, History and Memoirs, USAMHI; M. J. Davis, "Eighth Texas Cavalry at Bentonville"; Mathes, *Old Guard in Gray*, p. 125; Johnston, *Narrative*, p. 391; Hardee, "Memoranda of the Operations," HL; Wade Hampton, "Bentonville," *B&L* 4:704–5; Hughes, *Hardee*, p. 562; Ridley, *Battles and Sketches*, p. 453.

33. Guild, *Fourth Tennessee Cavalry*, p. 132. Smith's two other regiments—the 3d Arkansas and the 11th Texas Cavalry—were dismounted and skirmishing beside McLaws's infantry.

34. Guild, *Fourth Tennessee Cavalry*, pp. 132–34; *OR* 47(1):1092.

35. Allardice, *More Generals in Gray*, p. 239.

36. Mar. 21, 1865, entry, J. F. Waring Diary, SHC (first quotation); James G. Holmes, "Artillery at Bentonville" (second quotation). Although a staff officer of Law's and present at the fight, Maj. James G. Holmes views the Union "left" from the Confederate vantage point. Holmes, "Artillery at Bentonville."

37. Saffell's coat, vest, sash, and sword were removed by friends to be sent home to his sister. Then he and Boggess were buried in a common grave with dozens of other Confederates. *OR* 47(1):1096; Miner, "'A Brave Officer,'" p. 18; Lindsley, *Annals*, p. 413; Mar. 21, 1865, entry, Gordon Diary, Gordon Papers, SHC.

38. Immediately in command of Hagan's Brigade was Lt. Col. D. G. White, inspector of cavalry for Hardee's Department of South Carolina, Georgia, and Florida. Roy, "Hardee," in possession of Hardee Chambliss, Jr., Fairfax, Va.

39. James G. Holmes, "Artillery at Bentonville"; Mar. 21, 1865, entry, Gordon Diary, Gordon Papers, SHC; *OR* 47(1):1057, 1131; Allen Memoirs, TSLA; James K. P. Blackburn, "Reminiscences," p. 169; Dodson, *Wheeler*, pp. 351–52; *OR* 47(1):1131; J. A. Jones, "An Incident of Bentonville" (quotation); Johnston, *Narrative*, p. 391; Mar. 21, 1865, entry, Sloan Diary, TSLA.

40. M. J. Davis, "Eighth Texas Cavalry at Bentonville."

41. *OR* 47(1):1097.

42. *OR* 47(1):1095–98 (quotation, p. 1095); Ridley, *Battles and Sketches*, p. 453; Fuller, "Battle at Averysboro"; Wade Hampton, "Bentonville," *B&L* 4:704; Johnston, *Narrative*, p. 391; M. J. Davis, "Eighth Texas Cavalry at Bentonville"; Ford, "Last Battles," p. 142. Henderson lost four killed and eighteen wounded in the attack on Mower.

43. M. J. Davis, "Eighth Texas Cavalry at Bentonville."

44. Guild, *Fourth Tennessee Cavalry*, p. 134.

45. Ibid., pp. 130–32; Smith, "History of the 8th Tennessee Cavalry," Civil War Miscellaneous Collection, USAMHI; Scoggins, "Fourth Tennessee Cavalry at Bentonville."

46. Lawson, *Wheeler's Last Raid*, p. 374. Lt. W. R. Friend, 8th Texas Cavalry, returning to the army after convalescing from wounds received during the Atlanta Campaign, passed through Raleigh where he visited his old adjutant (Capt. Billy Sayers) and brigade commander (Thomas Harrison), both wounded at Bentonville. As he journeyed on he met Major Jarmon and Colonel Cook, both commanders of the 8th Texas and both also wounded at Bentonville. Friend, "Rangers at Bentonville."

47. Oliver Otis Howard, *Autobiography*, 2:151; Roy, "Hardee," in possession of Hardee Chambliss, Jr., Fairfax, Va.; Pickett, *Hardee*, pp. 43–44.

48. The Confederacy treated the "enlistment" of sixteen-year-olds informally. Although carried on unit rolls, they could transfer without the formalities required of an eighteen-year-old. See Stephenson, "My War Autobiography," Louisiana and Lower Mississippi Valley Collections, Louisiana State University Libraries. Half the sources mentioning Willie have him enlisting on Monday, the twentieth; the others, including Roy, maintain that he came over on Tuesday afternoon.

49. James K. P. Blackburn, "Reminiscences," p. 170.

50. Giles, *Terry's Texas Rangers*, p. 96.

51. Ibid.

52. Ibid., p. 97.

53. M. J. Davis, "Eighth Texas Cavalry at Bentonville" (first two quotations); *OR* 47(1): 1131 (third, fourth quotations); *CV* 3:71; Giles, *Terry's Texas Rangers*, pp. 95-98; Harcourt, "Terry's Texas Rangers," p. 96; Wade Hampton, "Bentonville," *B&L* 4:705; Holman, "Concerning the Battle at Bentonville," p. 153; Oliver Otis Howard, *Autobiography*, 2:151; Hutson Reminiscences, SHC; Johnston, *Narrative*, p. 391; James K. P. Blackburn, "Reminiscences," p. 169; Roy, "General Hardee," *SHSP* 8:346-47; Mar. 21, 1865, entry, Roy Diary, ALA; Fitzhugh, *Terry's Texas Rangers*, p. 19; Fletcher, *Rebel Private*, p. 144; Fort, History, USAMHI; Friend, "Rangers at Bentonville"; Graber, *A Terry Texas Ranger*, pp. 226-28 (last quotation, p. 227).

54. Wade Hampton, "Bentonville," *B&L* 4:705; Robinson, "Johnston," p. 367; Capers, *Soldier-Bishop*, p. 117;

55. C. W. Hutson to Em, Mar. 21, 1865, Hutson Family Papers, HTT; Amele [last name unknown] to C. W. Hutson, Mar. 28, 1865, Hutson Papers, SHC; Friend, "Rangers at Bentonville" (quotation); Jordan, *Bentonville*, p. 24. Willie's older sister, Anna Hardee, wrote General Howard informing him of Willie's death and, "recalling old times," asking Howard for "protection for her Kirkland friends. . . . I hardly need to say that it was a pleasure to do anything that might properly be done thus to soften the asperity of war." Howard, of course, was happy to comply. Anna Hardee to O. O. Howard, Apr. 14, 1865, and Howard, "Bentonville," both in Howard Papers, BCL.

56. Mar. 24, 1865, entry, Roy Diary, ALA.

57. *CV* 3:71.

58. Worsham, *Old Nineteenth Regiment*, p. 193; Graber, *A Terry Texas Ranger*, p. 226.

59. To reconstruct the handfuls of troops that constituted the shattered regiments and brigades of Brown's Division at Bentonville is almost impossible. It appears that Brown's Division did not fight as a division and probably saw action as individual brigades. Brown himself, severely wounded at Franklin, would not arrive at Johnston's headquarters until April. Brig. Gen. Roswell S. Ripley is shown in command of Brown's Division on Mar. 26 and again on Mar. 31, but it is doubtful that Ripley was on the field in a command capacity on March 21. *OR* 47(3):698, 735.

60. Apparently Cheatham did not take part in the repulse of Mower, nor did his division. Bate noted that "they did not arrive until after the battle." Cheatham's Corps acting assistant adjutant general, Maj. Henry Hampton, entered in the Corps Itinerary somewhat vaguely that Mower's attack was "handsomely driven from the field by our cavalry and infantry," implying that the work was done by other units. Christopher Losson, biographer of Cheatham and chronicler of the campaigns of his division, commented emphatically that "Cheatham was not present." *OR* 47(1):1106, 1083; Losson, *Tennessee's Forgotten Warriors*, p. 246.

61. *OR* 47(1):1095; Lindsley, *Annals*, p. 438; *OR* 47(1):1092; Mathes, *Old Guard in Gray*, p. 125; Hagood, *Memoirs*, p. 362.

62. Lambert, "Bentonville," p. 222 (quotation); Hagood, *Memoirs*, p. 362; Weeks, "University of North Carolina," p. 19; Mar. 21, 1865, entry, Calder Diary, DU; B. S. Williams to mother, Mar. 23, 1865, Williams Papers, DU. It is unclear whether Lt. Col. Edward Mallett, 61st Regiment North Carolina Troops, was killed in this action or in Hagood's attack on the nineteenth.

63. Fort, Memoirs, *CWTI* Collection, USAMHI. It was extremely hazardous along

McLaws's line. Gratz Cohen had been president of the Jefferson Society at the University of Virginia and known for his poetry and a novel he had written as an undergraduate. This twenty-year-old, perhaps a cousin of Marx Cohen killed two days before, was serving as a volunteer on the staff of Gen. George P. Harrison and had just ridden up to report to his commanding officer when he was killed by a bullet through the head. John Lipscomb Johnson, *University Memorial*, pp. 704–8.

64. Fort, Memoirs, *CWTI* Collection, USAMHI.

65. Ibid.

66. Mar. 21, 1865, entry, Calder Diary, DU.

67. Graber, *A Terry Texas Ranger*, p. 228; Johnston, "My Negotiations," p. 185; *OR* 47(2):1446. Johnston also knew that telegraphic communication with Goldsboro had ceased at 2:00 P.M., meaning that the office there had been closed or the line cut. One could infer that the enemy had seized the town. Weymouth Jordan believes that this was decisive: "Schofield's force alone was larger than Johnston's, and it was at most a two-day march from either Bentonville or Smithfield. Not only was Smithfield Johnston's base, his only withdrawal route led there. Johnston had no choice but to retreat." Jordan, *Bentonville*, p. 26.

68. C. W. Hutson to Em, Mar. 22, 1865, Hutson Family Papers, HTT.

69. *OR* 47(1):1092; Mar. 21, 1865, entry, Nash Diary, UGA; James W. Bell, *43rd Georgia*, p. 41; Mar. 21, 1865, entry, Purdum Diary, OHS; Hughes, "Hardee," p. 565; W. K. Pilsbring to J. W. Eldridge, Nov. 20, 1897, HL (first quotation); Hutson Reminiscences, SHC (second quotation); Ludwig Memoirs, Ludwig Papers, SHC; Fort, Memoirs, *CWTI* Collection, USAMHI (last quotation).

70. Lindsley, *Annals*, p. 438 (quotation); *OR* 47(2):931–32.

71. Tedder, "Fort Sumter to Bentonville," SHC; *OR* 47(1):1131, 1113, 1083.

72. Ludwig Memoirs, Ludwig Papers, SHC; *OR* 47(1):1131–32, 1113, 1083, 1092, 47(2): 1452; Lindsley, *Annals*, pp. 438, 895; Mar. 22, 1865, entry, Gordon Diary, Gordon Papers, SHC; Johnston, *Narrative*, p. 392; Mar. 22, 1865, entry, Waring Diary, SHC; Mar. 22, 1865, entry, Johnson Diary, DU; Ford, *Life in the Confederate Army*, p. 62; Wade Hampton, "Bentonville," *B&L* 4:705.

73. *OR* 47(1):1055, 1057, 1076 (third quotation), 1083; Hagood, *Memoirs*, pp. 362–63; Mar. 22, 1865, entry, Nash Diary, UGA; Mar. 22, 1865, entry, Harper Diary, Harper Papers, SHC (first quotation); Johnson, "Through the Carolinas," Johnson Papers, LC (second quotation); Mar. 22, 1865, entry, Calder Diary, DU; D. H. Hill to family, Mar. 23, 1865, Hill Family Papers, USAMHI.

74. J. E. Johnston to R. E. Lee, Mar. 23, 1865, Johnston Papers, HL.

Chapter 13

1. It was also Braxton Bragg's forty-eighth birthday.

2. Dozer, "Marching with Sherman," p. 469; *OR* 47(1):236, 247, 259, 268 (quotation); Mar. 22, 1865, entry, Childress Diary, ISHL.

3. *OR* 47(1):259.

4. There were two bridges over Mill Creek at Bentonville, but only one that was capable of handling wagons and artillery. The other was a small footbridge. *OR* 47(1):259, 27, 47(2): 955–56, 964; Henry H. Wright, *Sixth Iowa*, p. 433; Mar. 22, 1865, entry, Walters Diary, IHS.

5. *OR* 47(1):215–18 (quotations, p. 217); Official Diary, Sladen Family Papers, USAMHI.

6. Some of Mower's troops also entered Bentonville early that morning, but they were ordered back to their trench line.

7. Mar. 22, 1865, entry, Nilson Diary, IHS (last quotation); Mar. 22, 1865, entry, Walters Diary, IHS; *OR* 47(2):958; Mar. 22, 1865, entry, Roesch Journal, Civil War Miscellaneous Collection, USAMHI; Sherlock, *Memorabilia*, p. 212 (first quotation); Matthews, "Civil War Diary," p. 311 (second quotation); Johnson, "Through the Carolinas," Johnson Papers, LC (third quotation); Mar. 22, 1865, entry, Bowman Diary, Bowman Family Papers, USAMHI; Dozer, "Marching with Sherman," p. 469.

8. Mar. 22, 1865, entry, Miller Journal, IHS.

9. Henry H. Wright, *Sixth Iowa*, pp. 433–34 (quotation, p. 434); Sherlock, *Memorabilia*, p. 211; Dozer, "Marching with Sherman," p. 469; Upson, *With Sherman to the Sea*, p. 160.

10. Johnson, "Through the Carolinas," Johnson Papers, LC (quotations); Mar. 22, 1865, entry, Bean Diary, SHC; Mar. 22, 1865, entry, Nelson Diary, USAMHI.

11. *OR* 47(2):952.

12. Barrett, *Sherman's March*, p. 185; *OR* 47(2):952–53, 47(1):28.

13. Early that morning, although pleased that Johnston had withdrawn, the wary Howard became concerned that the rebels might be crossing Mill Creek "to go after Schofield." Or Johnston might be leaving a bridgehead at the Mill Creek crossing. In that event, Howard ordered Logan to "have all your artillery brought forward and brought to bear on it." These worries of Howard's were dispelled by noon. *OR* 47(2):950, 953; Thomas W. Osborn, *Fiery Trail*, p. 199.

14. *OR* 47(2):959–61, 47(1):27; Foraker, *Notes*, 1:65–66.

15. Fleharty, *102d Illinois*, p. 162; Omaha, Nebr., *World-Herald*, Mar. 21, 1965.

16. W. T. Sherman, Congratulatory Order, Sherman Papers, Mar. 22, 1865, Chicago Historical Society.

17. *OR* 47(2):950. "Our combinations were such," Sherman proudly stated, "that Schofield entered Goldsborough from New Berne, Terry got Cox's Bridge with pontoons laid and a brigade across entrenched, and we whipped Joe Johnston, all on the same day." Ibid.

18. *OR* 47(1):436, 522, 935 (quotation); Barrett, *Sherman's March*, pp. 186–87.

19. Mar. 22, 1865, entry, Sherwood, "50th Illinois . . . Journal," Hess Collection, USAMHI.

20. Ferguson Reminiscences, USAMHI.

21. Orendorff, *Reminiscences*, p. 201; Wills, *Army Life*, p. 365. Another welcome sight in Goldsboro was reinforcements. The 79th Pennsylvania, for instance, one of Carlin's regiments that had been badly mauled, received two hundred recruits. Heisey, "The Gallant Seventy-ninth Regiment," p. 20.

22. Marcus W. Bates, "Bentonville," p. 151. The ride proved fatal for some. Abner Smith, 20th Connecticut, had his leg amputated satisfactorily at Harper House but died of "exhaustion in being transported." A. Smith to Mrs. A. C. Smith, Mar. 23, 1865, and C. N. Lyman to Mrs. Abner C. Smith, Mar. 29, 1865, Smith Letters, Connecticut State Library, Hartford.

23. H. H. Nurs to father, Mar. 28, 1865, Nurs Letters, ISHL. See also Eicker Memoir, Eicker Papers, Harrisburg Civil War Roundtable Collection, USAMHI.

24. Raleigh *News and Observer*, July 21, 1940.

25. J. D. Taylor Reminiscences, Taylor Papers, NCA.

26. Trotter, *Silk Flags and Cold Steel*, pp. 132–33.

27. Ford, *Life in the Confederate Army*, p. 63.

28. Sanders, "More about . . . Bentonville," p. 461.

29. *OR* 47(3):705 (quotation); *Charlotte Observer*, Mar. 23, 1941; *CV* 2:200; John C. Goode to N. C. Hughes, Nov. 27, 1994.

30. In 1893 some 360 Confederate dead were gathered from burial places scattered across the battlefield and reburied in a common grave near the Harper house. *CV* 3:232; H. V. Rose to W. T. Leeper, Sept. 19, 1950, Leeper Papers, UAL; Darley, *Harper Journey of Faith*, p. 38.

31. *OR* 47(1):1057, 1059–60, 1080, 1092–93, 1096, 114; Livermore, *Numbers and Losses*, pp. 135, 144; Mar. 27, 1865, entry, Reynolds Diary, Reynolds Papers, UAL; A. P. Stewart, "Report of Casualties," HUL; Charlotte *Daily Bulletin*, Mar. 26–27, 1865; Bauer, *Soldiering*, p. 232; *CV* 5:125.

32. *OR* 47(1):67–76, 188, 27, 1059, 1077, 47(3):687, 690–91; Livermore, *Numbers and Losses*, p. 75.

33. Mar. 23, 1865, entry, Boltz Diary, DU.

34. Carlin, "Bentonville," p. 251, and "Military Memoirs."

35. Bragg appears to have been gone by March 26 because as of that date Hoke's Division is shown within Hardee's Corps. *OR* 47(3):697.

36. Murphree, "Autobiography," p. 171; C. W. Hutson to sister, Mar. 31, 1865, Hutson Family Papers, HTT; G. W. Peddy to Kitty Peddy, Mar. 23, 1865, Peddy Family Papers, Woodruff Library, Emory University, Atlanta.

Chapter 14

1. J. S. Robinson to "Friend Hunt," Apr. 20, 1865, Robinson Papers, OHS.

2. *Philadelphia Times*, Oct. 10, 1896, as reprinted in *SHSP* 14:308.

3. For an enlightened discussion of this subject, see Larry J. Daniel's *Cannoneers in Gray*.

4. Actually Sherman's decision to allow Johnston to depart in peace duplicates his action exactly ninety days earlier. With the opportunity at hand and possessing the power to easily smash Hardee's army as it evacuated Savannah, Sherman held back, displaying remarkable forbearance. He knew the Confederates were slipping away and were vulnerable, but he never lost sight of the ultimate objective of the March to the Sea—capture of the seaport. He would never allow himself or his army to be diverted. Savannah was a dress rehearsal for the third day at Bentonville. See Hughes, "Hardee's Defense of Savannah," pp. 60–61.

5. Jordan, *Bentonville*, p. 23; Thomas W. Osborn, *Fiery Trail*, p. 203.

6. Castel, *Decision in the West*, p. 565; Cox, *March to the Sea*, p. 195.

7. Oliver Otis Howard, "To the Memory of Henry Slocum," p. 41.

8. Woodward, *Chesnut Diary*, p. 768.

Bibliography

Primary Sources

MANUSCRIPTS
Ann Arbor, Mich.
    Bentley Library, University of Michigan
        C. Emerson Allen Diary
        Justin Austin Correspondence
        Charles Butler Papers
        William Carroll Diary and Letters
        John Wesley Daniels Papers
        Isaac Roseberry Diary
        Sligh Family Correspondence
        Spaulding Family Papers
    William L. Clements Library, University of Michigan
        Schoff Civil War Collections
            William G. Putney Memoir (typescript)
            Charles G. Rogers Diary
            George M. Trowbridge Letters
Athens, Ga.
    Georgia Department of Archives and History
        James B. Avery Reminiscences
        James E. Blackshear Papers
        James W. Brown Diary
        Civil War Miscellany
        James L. Lynch Letters
        Marcellus A. Stovall Papers
    University of Georgia Library
        Francis H. Nash Diary
        C. C. Platter Papers
Atlanta, Ga.
    Robert W. Woodruff Library, Emory University
        John H. Ash Papers
        Alexander M. Ayers Papers
        William G. Baugh Letters
        James Blackshear Diaries
        Confederate Miscellany
          J. M. Culpepper Papers
        Charles H. Cox Letters
        Peddy Family Papers
        Isaac Roseberry Diary
        Jennie S. Smith Letters

William M. Tunno Papers
Union Miscellany
  Ephraim L. Girdner Letters
Austin, Tex.
  Center for American History, University of Texas
    Robert F. Bunting Papers
    Thomas B. Hampton Letters
Baton Rouge, La.
  Louisiana and Lower Mississippi Valley Collections, Louisiana State University Libraries
    Philip D. Stephenson, "My War Autobiography"
Bloomington, Ind.
  Lilly Library, Indiana University
    Gibson County Civil War Letters
    Joshua W. Williams Diary
Boston, Mass.
  Massachusetts Historical Society
    Thomas S. Howland Papers
    Charles F. Morse Papers
Brunswick, Maine
  Bowdoin College Library
    Oliver O. Howard Papers
      Howard, "Battle of Bentonville & Sketches of Carolina Campaign"
Cambridge, Mass.
  Houghton Library, Harvard University
    Frederick M. Dearborn Collection
Carlisle, Pa.
  U.S. Army Military History Institute
    Civil War Miscellaneous Collection
      Ephraim F. Brower Diary (typescript)
      Leander E. Davis Letters
      Thomas Y. Finley Diary
      Jasper P. George Memoirs
      Albion Gross Letters and Journal
      Mark P. Lowry Autobiography
      John J. McKee Diary
      Isaac C. Nelson Diary
      James H. Patton Diary
      Lorenzo N. Pratt Letters
      Philip Roesch Journal
      Baxter Smith, "History of the 8th Tennessee Cavalry"
      Samuel Smith Diary
    Civil War Times Illustrated Collection
      Charles F. Bowman Memoir
      George W. Cheney, "Cruel War: An Account of the 105th Ohio Infantry Regiment, 1862–1865"

Frank L. Ferguson, "Battle of Bentonville, N. Carolina"

John Porter Fort, History and Memoirs

Peter W. Funk Diary

James Griffin Letter

Andrew Hickenlooper Memoirs

Benjamin F. Hunter Diary

Henry Hurter Diary

Andrew J. Ostrum Diary

Thomas E. Pierce Diary

Edward E. Schweitzer Diaries and Correspondence

Harrisburg Civil War Roundtable Collection

John Eicker Papers

William Garrett Letters (typescripts)

David Nichol Letters and Diary

William B. Hazen Papers

Earl M. Hess Collection

Isaac Kittinger Diary

Frederick Sherwood, "50th Illinois Regimental Journal"

Daniel Harvey Hill Family Papers

New York Infantry Collection

150th New York

Sladen Family Papers

Official Diary of the Army of the Tennessee

Chapel Hill, N.C.

Southern Historical Collection, University of North Carolina

James W. Albright Diary

John K. Baldwin Diary

Jesse S. Bean Diary

Henderson Deans Reminiscences

Franklin H. Elmore Papers

Robert S. Finley Letters

William W. Gordon Papers

George W. F. Harper Papers

Heyward-Ferguson Papers and Books

Robert F. Hoke Papers

Charles W. Hutson Reminiscences

Henry T. J. Ludwig Papers

Lafayette McLaws Papers

Charles S. Powell Manuscript (typed copy), "A Confederate Soldier's Account of the Last Days of the War in Ga. and the Carolinas"

Augustine T. Smythe Letters

Marcellus A. Stovall Papers

Lawrence W. Taylor Reminiscences

Daniel M. Tedder, "Fort Sumter to Bentonville"

C. Irvine Walker, "Sketch of the Career of the 10th and 19th South Carolina Regiments"
Joseph F. Waring Diary
Charlottesville, Va.
University of Virginia Library
Ambrose Bierce Diary
Chattanooga, Tenn.
Special Collections, Chattanooga Bi-Centennial Library
George W. McKenzie Papers
Regimental Headquarters Order Book, 5th Tennessee Cavalry
Chicago, Ill.
Chicago Historical Society
William T. Sherman Papers
Chicago Public Library
William T. Humphrey Papers
University of Chicago Library
Ezra Warner Correspondence and Research File
Cleveland, Ohio
Western Reserve
Lafayette McLaws Papers
Columbia, Mo.
Western Historical Manuscript Collection, University of Missouri at Columbia
William H. Lynch Diary
Elias Perry Diary
Benjamin F. Sweet Memoir
Columbia, S.C.
University of South Carolina Library
Matthew C. Butler Papers
William J. Holt Papers
R. Y. Woodlief Diary
Columbus, Ohio
Ohio Historical Society
Lyman D. Ames Papers
Robt. M. Atkinson (George W. Duffield) Papers
J. W. Baldwin Papers
Robert N. Elder Letters
John W. Griffith Papers
Lyde Harriman (Green and Wesleyn Southard)
Samuel B. Herrington Papers
George H. Hildt (Daniel G. and George H. Hildt)
Joseph Hoffhines Letters
John D. Inskeep Diary
William Joslin Papers
Lewis Family (Harry Lewis) Letters
A. R. Mead, "A Farm Boy and the 68th Ohio Volunteer Infantry, 1862–1865"
John G. Mitchell Collection

Martin Mock Papers
Luke Murray and Aaron D. Riker Papers
James M. Naylor Papers
Robert Norris Papers
Nathaniel L. Parmater Diary
William H. Pittenger Diary
Styles W. Porter Diary
Nelson Purdum Diary
James S. Robinson Papers
James M. Scott Papers
Robert H. Scott Papers
James H. Smith Papers
James R. Stillwell Papers
Joseph M. Strickling Papers
Lynne S. Sullivan Papers
Thomas T. Taylor Papers (S. T. Bonner, T. T. Taylor)
John Vail Papers
Veteran Banner
Cropwell, Ala.
In possession of Mrs. Margaret Butler
Thomas B. Roy Papers
Des Moines, Iowa
Vance Family Papers
Detroit, Mich.
Detroit Public Library
Alpheus S. Williams Diary (typescript)
Durham, N.C.
William R. Perkins Library, Duke University
Ferdinand F. Boltz Diary
Charles S. Brown Papers
Matthew C. Butler Papers
William Calder Diary and Papers
Thomas L. Clingman Papers
Confederate States of America Papers
Confederate Veteran Papers
John Herr Papers
Robert B. Hoadley Papers
John Johnson Diary
Charles S. Powell Reminiscences
William Schaum Papers
Charles B. Tompkins Letters
Herbert B. Waterman Letters
Elliott S. Welch Papers
Edward M. Whaley Reminiscences
Benjamin S. Williams Papers

Fairfax, Va.
  In possession of Hardee Chambliss, Jr.
    Thomas B. Roy, "Lieut. General William Joseph Hardee"
Fayetteville, Ark.
  University of Arkansas Libraries
    W. T. Leeper Papers
    Daniel Harris Reynolds Papers
Fort Oglethorpe, Ga.
  Chickamauga and Chattanooga National Military Park
    John W. Geary Letters (typescript)
    "History of 19th Alabama Infantry"
    "History of 10th South Carolina Infantry"
    John W. Nesbitt Manuscript
    A. H. Reed Diary
    John W. Sparkman, Jr., Diary
Fremont, Ohio
  Rutherford B. Hayes Presidential Center
    John Grant Mitchell Collection
    John Monsarrat, "John G. Mitchell in the Union Army"
Greenville, N.C.
  Joyner Library, East Carolina University
    Johnny Craig Young Collection
Hamilton, N.Y.
  Colgate University Library
    Thomas W. Osborn Letters and Journal
Hartford, Conn.
  Connecticut State Library
    Harlan P. Rugg Diary and Memorandum
    Abner C. Smith Letters
Indianapolis, Ind.
  Indiana Historical Society
    Robert Armstrong Diary
    Jefferson C. Davis Papers
    David A. Fateley Diary
    John Fritz Diary
    Grigsby-McDonald Papers
    John D. Martin Journal
    Daniel Martz Letters
    Charles C. Michael Diary
    William B. Miller Journal
    Charles F. Nelson Diary
    John Nilson Diary
    Daniel H. Rowe Recollections
    Augustus Van Dyke Papers

Amos C. Weaver Papers
Jesse B. White Letters
Sylvester S. Wills Letters
Indiana State Library
Daniel E. Bruce Diary
Jefferson C. Davis Papers and Correspondence
Levi P. Fodrea, "History of 101st Regiment of Volunteer Infantry of Indiana"
Samuel K. Harryman Papers
William H. Judkins Diary
Regimental History, 75th Indiana Volunteer Infantry Regiment
Regimental History, 101st Indiana Volunteer Infantry Regiment
Marden Sabin Memoirs
George D. Stratton Diary and Letters
Iowa City, Iowa
State Historical Society of Iowa
S. S. Farwell Papers
Charles Berry Senior Papers
7th Iowa Volunteer Infantry Regiment Papers
Louisville, Ky.
The Filson Club
Ward Family Papers
William T. Ward, Civil War Service
Madison, Wis.
State Historical Society of Wisconsin
Adelbert M. Bly Papers
Charles H. Dickinson Papers
William C. Meffert Papers
Alonzo Miller Letters
James Henry Otto, War Memoirs
James T. Reeve Papers
Henry Clay Robbins Papers
John B. Tripp Papers
Marietta, Ga.
Kennesaw Mountain National Park
Allen L. Fahnestock Diary
James W. Langley Papers
Alonzo Miller Letters
W. G. Putney Diary
W. A. Roher Letters
Charles M. Smith Letters
Lyman S. Widney Diary
Miami, Fla.
Samuel Richey Collection, University of Miami

Montgomery, Ala.
   Alabama State Department of Archives and History
     Alpheus Baker Papers
     Henry D. Clayton Papers
     William J. Hardee Papers
     "History of 23rd Alabama Infantry"
     "History of 26-50th Alabama Infantry"
     "History of 29th Alabama Infantry"
     Edmund W. Pettus Papers
     Thomas B. Roy Diary
     S. H. Sprott, "History of 40th Alabama"
     Harry T. Toulmin Papers
Nashville, Tenn.
   Tennessee State Library and Archives
     William G. Allen Memoirs
     George P. Buell and John S. Brien Papers
     William H. Ogilvie Diary
     Philip Roesch Papers
     William E. Sloan Diary
     Thomas B. Wilson, "Diary and Reminiscences" (pamphlet)
Newark, N.J.
   New Jersey Historical Society
     Sebastian C. Duncan Papers
New Orleans, La.
   Historic New Orleans Collection
     Moses Greenwood Papers
   Howard-Tilton Memorial Library, Tulane University
     Hutson Family Papers
Newton Grove, N.C.
   Bentonville Battleground Historical Site
     Stephen B. Barnwell, "The Story of an American Family"
     Oscar M. Bizzell, "Yankee Soldiers Tell about Newton Grove in March, 1865"
     Enos McKinney Diary (typescript)
New York, N.Y.
   New-York Historical Society
     Rudolph Rey Letters
     Henry W. Slocum Letters
Philadelphia, Pa.
   Historical Society of Pennsylvania
     Geary Family Correspondence
Princeton, N.J.
   Princeton University Libraries
     Kienbusch Angling Collection
     Andre De Coppet Collection

Providence, R.I.
  John Hay Library, Brown University
    Anne S. K. Brown Military Collection
Quincy, Ill.
  Quincy and Adams County Historical Society
    James D. Morgan Papers
Raleigh, N.C.
  North Carolina State Archives
    Allen L. Fahnestock Diary
    Daniel H. Hill Papers
    Robert F. Hoke Papers
    Halcott P. Jones Journal
    Thurman D. Maness Collection
    Joseph B. Starr Papers
    Alexander P. Stewart Correspondence
    John D. Taylor Papers
    John W. Taylor Diary and Papers
    William Frederick Thayer Diary
    Raymond W. Watkins, "Confederate Soldiers Killed at the Battle of Bentonville"
Richmond, Va.
  Confederate Museum
    William B. Taliaferro Papers
  Virginia Historical Society
    Thomas R. Shaw Papers
Rolla, Mo.
  Western Historical Manuscript Collection, University of Missouri-Rolla
    Thomas A. Barr Papers
St. Paul, Minn.
  Minnesota Historical Society
    Levi Nelson Green Papers
    John E. Risedorph Diary
San Marino, Calif.
  Henry E. Huntington Library and Art Gallery
    J. W. Eldridge Collection
    William J. Hardee, "Memoranda of the Operations of My Corps, while Under the Command of Genl J. E. Johnston, in the 'Dalton & Atlanta' and the 'North Carolina' Campaigns"
    Joseph E. Johnston Papers
    James M. Mullen, "Last Days of Johnston's Army"
    William B. Taliaferro, Troop Strength Report
Savannah, Ga.
  Georgia Historical Society Library
    Joseph Frederick Waring Papers

Sewanee, Tenn.
   University of the South, DuPont Library
      Cheatham Family Papers
Shiloh, Tenn.
   Shiloh National Military Park and Cemetery
      Charles Swett, "A Brief Narrative of Warren Lt. Artillery Known during the Civil War
         as Swett's Battery, Hardee's Corps, Army of Northern Kentucky, Army of Ten-
         nessee" (1908)
Springfield, Ill.
   Illinois State Historical Library
      Smith D. Atkins Papers
      John Batchelor Papers
      Brush Family Papers
      James Burkhalter Papers
      George L. Childress Diary
      I. T. Dillon Papers
      Allen L. Fahnestock Papers
      David N. Holmes Letters
      Frederick Marion Letters
      George Marsh, "Regimental Record"
      Henry H. Nurs Letters
      Matthew H. Peters Papers
      Joshua D. Rilea Diary
      William C. Robinson Papers
      Levi A. Ross Diary
      Charles E. Smith Diary
      John D. Strong Papers
      William E. Strong Reminiscences
Washington, D.C.
   Library of Congress
      William H. Bradbury Papers
      James A. Congleton Diary
      W. C. Johnson Papers
      O. M. Poe Papers
   National Archives and Record Service
      Army of Tennessee, Orders and Circulars of Lt. Gen. William J. Hardee's Corps,
         1863–65 (RG 109)
      Army of Tennessee, Special Field Orders and Special Orders, 1864–65 (RG 109)
      Department and Army of Tennessee, Orders and Circulars, 1862–65 (RG 109)
      Department of South Carolina, Georgia, and Florida, General Orders, Circulars, and
         Special Field Orders, Lt. Gen. W. J. Hardee, 1864–65 (RG 109)
      Department of South Carolina, Georgia, and Florida, Special Orders, Lt. Gen. W. J.
         Hardee, 1864–65 (RG 109)
      Lafayette McLaws Papers, 1861–65 (RG 109)
      Henry W. Slocum MSR

Carter L. Stevenson Papers (RG 109)
Territorial Commands and Administration, Unbound Documents Files (RG 98)
West Point, N.Y.
U.S. Military Academy Library
Charles T. Greene Memoir
Oliver O. Howard Papers
Williamsburg, Va.
Earl Gregg Swem Library, College of William and Mary
Joseph E. Johnston Collection
William B. Taliaferro Papers

COLLECTED WORKS, LETTERS, DIARIES, MEMOIRS,
REMINISCENCES, AND UNIT HISTORIES

Abernathy, Alonzo. *Incidents of an Iowa Soldier's Life. Annals of Iowa* 12 (1911): 401–28.

Adair, John M. *Historical Sketch of the Forty-fifth Illinois Regiment.* Lanark, Ill., 1869.

Adams, Jacob. *Diary.* Columbus, Ohio, 1930.

Adams, John. "Letters of John Adams to Catherine Varner." *North Dakota Historical Quarterly* 4 (1930): 266–70.

Adamson, Augustus P. *Brief History of the Thirtieth Georgia Volunteer Infantry.* Griffin, Ga., 1912.

Alexander, John D. *History of the Ninety-seventh Regiment of Indiana Volunteer Infantry.* Terre Haute, Ind., 1891.

Ambrose, Daniel L. *History of the 7th Regiment Illinois Volunteer Infantry.* Springfield, Ill., 1868.

Anderson, John. "Civil War Reminiscences." *Yearbook of the Swedish Historical Society* 3 (1910): 17–22.

Andrews, W. H. *Diary of W. H. Andrews, 1st Sergt. Co. M, 1st Georgia Regulars, from February, 1861, to May 2, 1865.* East Atlanta, 1891.

Arbuckle, John. *Civil War Experiences of a Foot-Soldier Who Marched with Sherman.* Columbus, Ohio, 1930.

Aten, Henry J., comp. *History of the Eighty-fifth Regiment.* Hiawatha, Kans., 1901.

Austin, J. P. *The Blue and the Gray.* Atlanta, 1899.

Bahnson, Henry T. *The Last Days of the War.* Hamlet, N.C., 1903.

Baker, Nathan M. "Extracts from Diary of Chaplain N. M. Baker, 116th Illinois." *Illinois Central Magazine* 4 (1913): 9–18.

Barnard, Harry V. *Tattered Volunteers: The Twenty-seventh Alabama Infantry Regiment, C.S.A.* Northport, Ala., 1965.

Barnes, Philander Y. *War Reminiscences.* Shiloh, Ohio, 1925.

Bartmess, Jacob W. "Civil War Letters." Edited by Donald F. Carmony. *Indiana Magazine of History* 52 (1966): 49–74, 157–86.

Bates, Marcus W. "Battle of Bentonville." *Military Order of the Loyal Legion of the United States—Minnesota.* Vol. 5, pp. 136–51.

Bates, Samuel P. *History of Pennsylvania Volunteers.* Harrisburg, 1869–71.

Battle, Kemp Plummer. *Memories of an Old-Time Tar Heel.* Edited by William J. Battle. Chapel Hill, 1945.

Bauer, K. Jack, ed. *Soldiering: Civil War Diary of Rice Bull.* San Rafael, Calif., 1977.

Beall, John B. *In Barrack and Field: Poems and Sketches of Army Life.* Nashville, 1906.

Beatty, John. *Memoirs of a Volunteer.* Edited by Harvey S. Ford. New York, 1946.

Belknap, Charles E. "Bentonville: What a Bummer Knows about It." *Military Order of the Loyal Legion of the United States—District of Columbia.* Vol. 1, War Papers, no. 12.

Belknap, William W. *History of the Fifteenth Regiment, Iowa Veteran Volunteer Infantry.* Keokuk, Iowa, 1887.

Bell, Hiram P. *Men and Things.* Atlanta, 1907.

Bell, John T. *Tramps and Triumphs of the Second Iowa Infantry.* Omaha, Nebr., 1886.

Benton, Charles E. *As Seen from the Ranks.* New York, 1902.

Bevens, William E. *Reminiscences of a Private: William E. Bevens of the First Arkansas, C.S.A.* Edited by Daniel E. Sutherland. Fayetteville, Ark., 1992.

Bircher, William. *A Drummer-Boy's Diary: Comprising Four Years of Service with the Second Regiment Minnesota Veteran Volunteers, 1861–1865.* St. Paul, Minn., 1889.

Bishop, Judson W. *The Story of a Regiment.* St. Paul, Minn., 1890.

Blackburn, James K. P. *Reminiscences of the Terry Texas Rangers.* Austin, 1919.

———. "Reminiscences of the Terry Texas Rangers." *Southwest Historical Quarterly* 22 (1919): 38–77, 143–79.

Blackburn, Theodore W. *Letters from the Front: A Union "Preacher" Regiment.* Dayton, Ohio, 1981.

Bogle, Joseph. *Some Recollections of the Civil War by a Private in the 40th Ga. Regiment, C.S.A.* Atlanta, 1900.

Bogle, Joseph, and William L. Calhoun. *Historical Sketches of Barton's (Later Stovall's) Georgia Brigade.* Edited by William S. Hoole and Martha D. Hoole. University, Ala., 1984.

Boies, Andrew J. *Record of the Thirty-third Massachusetts Volunteer Infantry.* Fitchburg, Mass., 1880.

Boies, Henry L. "The One Hundred and Fifth: Sketch of the One Hundred and Fifth Regiment Illinois Infantry Volunteers." In H. L. Boies, *History of DeKalb County, Illinois,* pp. 113–202. Chicago, 1868.

Bowman, Samuel M., and R. B. Irwin. *Sherman and His Campaigns.* New York, 1865.

Boyle, John Richards. *Soldiers True: The Story of the One Hundred and Eleventh Regiment Pennsylvania Veteran Volunteers, and of Its Campaigns in the War for the Union, 1861–1865.* New York, 1903.

Boynton, H. V. *Sherman's Historical Raid.* Cincinnati, 1875.

Bradley, George S. *The Star Corps; or, Notes of an Army Chaplain, during Sherman's Famous March to the Sea.* Milwaukee, Wis., 1865.

Brant, Jefferson E. *History of the Eighty-fifth Indiana Volunteer Infantry.* Bloomington, 1902.

Branum, John M. *Letters.* New Castle, Pa., 1897.

Brewer, George E. *History of the Forty-sixth Alabama Regiment.* Montgomery, 1902.

Briant, Cyrus E. *History of the Eighty-eighth Indiana Volunteers Infantry.* Fort Wayne, 1895.

Brooks, Aubrey L., and Hugh T. Lefler, eds. *The Papers of Walter Clark.* 2 vols. Chapel Hill, 1948–50.

Brooks, Ulysses R. *Butler and His Cavalry*. Columbia, S.C., 1909.

———. *Stories of the Confederacy*. Columbia, S.C., 1912.

Brown, Alonzo Leighton. *History of the Fourth Regiment of Minnesota Infantry Volunteers*. St. Paul, 1892.

Brunson, Joseph W. *Pee Dee Light Artillery*. University, Ala., 1983.

Bryant, Edwin E. *History of the Third Regiment of Wisconsin Veteran Volunteer Infantry, 1861–1865*. Cleveland, Ohio, 1891.

Buck, Irving. *Cleburne and His Command*. Edited by T. R. Hay. Jackson, Tenn., 1959.

Byers, Samuel H. M. *Iowa in War Times*. Des Moines, 1888.

Calhoun, William L. *History of the 42d Regiment, Georgia Volunteers, Confederate States Army*. Atlanta, 1900.

Calkins, William W. *The History of the One Hundred and Fourth Regiment of Illinois Volunteer Infantry, War of the Great Rebellion, 1862–1865*. Chicago, 1895.

Camm, William. "Diary of Colonel William Camm." *Journal of the Illinois Historical Society* 18 (1925): 793–969.

Canfield, Silas S. *History of the 21st Regiment Ohio Volunteer Infantry*. Toledo, 1893.

Capron, Thaddeus H. "War Diary." *Journal of the Illinois Historical Society* 12 (1919): 330–406.

Carlin, William P. "The Battle of Bentonville." *Military Order of the Loyal Legion of the United States—Ohio*, 3:231–52.

———. "Military Memoirs." *National Tribune*, July 30, August 6, 1885.

Carpenter, Kinchen J. *War Diary of Kinchen J. Carpenter, Company I, Fiftieth North Carolina Regiment*. Edited by Julie C. Williams. Rutherfordton, N.C., 1955.

Chamberlin, William Henry. *History of the Eighty-first Ohio Infantry Volunteers, during the War of the Rebellion*. Cincinnati, 1865.

Chandler, Josephine C. "An Episode of the Civil War: A Romance of Coincidence." *Journal of the Illinois Historical Society* 17 (1924): 352–68.

Chapman, Horatio D. *Civil War Diary: Diary of a Forty-Niner*. Hartford, 1929.

Cheverell, John H. *Journal History of the Twenty-ninth Ohio Veteran Volunteers*. Cleveland, 1883.

Clark, James H. *The Iron-hearted Regiment: Being an Account of the Battles, Marches, and Gallant Deeds Performed by the 115th Regiment N.Y. Vols*. Albany, 1865.

Clark, James I. *The Civil War of Private Cooke: A Wisconsin Boy in the Union Army*. Madison, 1955.

Clark, Walter. *Histories of the Several Regiments and Battalions from North Carolina in the Great War, 1861–1865*. 5 vols. Goldsboro, N.C., 1901.

Clark, Walter A. *Under the Stars and Bars*. Augusta, Ga., 1900.

Clement, Abram W. "Diary of Abram Clement." *South Carolina Historical Magazine* 59 (1958): 78–83.

Cluett, William W. *History of the 57th Regiment, Illinois Volunteer Infantry*. Princeton, Ill., 1886.

Cogley, Thomas S. *History of the Seventh Indiana Cavalry Volunteers*. La Porte, Ind., 1876.

Collins, George K. *An Abbreviated Account of Certain Men of Onondaga County Who Did Service in the War of 1861–1865*. Syracuse, N.Y., 1928.

———. *Memoirs of the 149th Regt. N.Y. Vol. Inf*. Syracuse, N.Y., 1891.

Connelly, Thomas W. *History of the Seventieth Ohio Regiment.* Cincinnati, 1902.

Connolly, James Austin. "Major Connolly's Letters to His Wife: 1862–1865." *Transactions of the Illinois State Historical Society* 35 (1930): 215–438.

——. *Three Years in the Army of the Cumberland.* Indianapolis, 1959.

Conyngham, David P. *Sherman's March through the South with Sketches and Incidents of the Campaign.* New York, 1865.

Cook, Charles N. "Letters of Privates Cook and [Lafayette] Ball." *Indiana Magazine of History* 27 (1941): 243–68.

Cook, Harvey T. *Sherman's March through South Carolina in 1865.* Greenville, S.C., 1938.

Cook, Stephen G., and Charles E. Benton, eds. *The "Duchess County Regiment."* Danbury, Conn., 1907.

Cooke, Chauncey H. *Soldier Boy's Letters to His Father and Mother, 1861–5.* Independence, Wis., 1915.

Corn, T. J. "In Enemy's Lines with Prisoners." *Confederate Veteran* 11 (1903): 506–7.

Crane, William E. *Bugle Blasts.* Cincinnati, 1884.

Crist, Lynda L., James T. McIntosh, and Haskell M. Monroe, Jr., eds. *Papers of Jefferson Davis.* 7 vols. Baton Rouge, La., 1971–.

Croom, Wendell D. *The War History of Company "C," Sixth Georgia Regiment.* Fort Valley, Ga., 1879.

Curry, J. H., "A History of Co. B, Fortieth Alabama Infantry." *Alabama Historical Quarterly* 17 (1953): 159–222.

Cuttino, George P., ed. *Saddle Bags and Spinning Wheel.* Macon, Ga., 1981.

Dacus, Robert H. *Reminiscences of Company "H," First Arkansas Mounted Rifles.* Dardanelle, Ark., 1897.

Davis, Jefferson. *The Rise and Fall of the Confederate Government.* 2 vols. New York, 1881.

Davis, M. J. "Eighth Texas Cavalry at Bentonville." *Confederate Veteran* 24 (1916): 184.

Deckert, D. Augusta. *History of Kershaw's Brigade.* Newberry, S.C., 1899.

DeRosier, Arthur H., ed. *Through the South with a Union Soldier.* Johnson City, Tenn., 1969.

DeVelling, C. T. *History of the Seventeenth Regiment.* Zanesville, Ohio, 1889.

Dobson, James A. C. *A Historical Sketch of Company K of the 79th Regiment Indiana Volunteers.* Plainfield, Ind., 1894.

Dodson, William Carey, ed. *Campaigns of Wheeler and His Cavalry.* Atlanta, 1899.

Dougall, Allen H. "Bentonville." *Military Order of the Loyal Legion of the United States—Indiana,* 1:212–19.

Downing, Alexander G. *Downing's Civil War Diary.* Olynthus B. Clark, ed. Des Moines, Iowa, 1916.

Dozer, Jesse L. "Marching with Sherman through Georgia and the Carolinas." Edited by Wilfred W. Black. *Georgia Historical Quarterly* 52 (1968): 308–36, 451–79.

DuBose, Henry K. *The History of Company B, Twenty-first Regiment (Infantry), South Carolina Volunteers.* Columbia, S.C., 1909.

Dudley, H. A., and R. M. Waley. *History of Company "K" of the Seventeenth Regiment, N.Y.V.* Warsaw, N.Y., n.d.

Duke, John K. *History of the Fifty-third Regiment Ohio Volunteer Infantry.* Portsmouth, Ohio, 1900.

Dunkelman, Mark H., and Michael J. Winey. *The Hardtack Regiment: An Illustrated History of the 154th Regiment, New York State Infantry Volunteers*. Rutherford, N.J., 1981.

Dunn, Jacob B. *Indiana and Indianans*. Chicago, 1919.

Dyer, John W. *Reminiscences; or, Four Years in the Confederate Army*. Evansville, Ky., 1898.

Eaton, Clement, ed. "Diary of an Officer in Sherman's Army Marching through the Carolinas." *Journal of Southern History* 9 (1943): 238–54.

Emanuel, S. *An Historical Sketch of the Georgetown Rifle Guards and as Company A of the Tenth Regiment, So. Ca. Volunteers*. Georgetown, S.C., 1909.

Executive Committee for the Army Reunion. *The Army Reunion*. Chicago, 1866.

Fitch, Michael H. *Echoes of the Civil War as I Hear Them*. New York, 1905.

Fleharty, S. F. *Our Regiment: A History of the 102d Illinois Infantry Volunteers with Sketches of the Atlanta Campaign, the Georgia Raid, and the Campaign of the Carolinas*. Chicago, 1865.

Fletcher, Thomas C. *Life and Reminiscences of General Wm. T. Sherman*. Baltimore, Md., 1891.

Fletcher, William A. *Rebel Private: Front and Rear*. Austin, Tex., 1954.

Floyd, David B. *History of the Seventy-fifth Regiment Indiana Infantry Volunteers*. Philadelphia, 1893.

Foote, Corydon E. *With Sherman to the Sea*. Edited by Olive D. Hormel. New York, 1960.

Foraker, Joseph B. *Notes of a Busy Life*. 2 vols. Cincinnati, 1916.

Ford, Arthur P. "The Last Battles of Hardee's Corps." *Southern Bivouac* 1 (1881–82): 140–43.

——. *Life in the Confederate Army*. New York, 1905.

Fowler, James A., and Miles M. Miller. *History of the Thirtieth Iowa Infantry*. Midiapolis, Iowa, 1908.

Frank, Malcolm. "'Such Is War': The Letters of an Orderly in the 7th Iowa Infantry." Edited by James I. Robertson, Jr. *Iowa Journal of History* 58 (1970): 321–56.

Friend, W. R. "Rangers at Bentonville." *Philadelphia Weekly Times*, Nov. 12, 1887.

Fry, James B. *Killed by a Brother Soldier*. New York, 1885.

Fryer, David F. *History of the Eightieth Ohio*. Newcomertown, Ohio, 1904.

Fuller, D. F. "Battle at Averysboro, N.C." *Confederate Veteran* 5 (1897): 68.

Funk, Arville L. *A Hoosier Regiment in Dixie: A History of the Thirty-eighth Indiana Volunteer Infantry Regiment*. Chicago, 1978.

Gaddis, Alfred. *Three Years of Army Life*. Lafayette, Ind., 1896.

Gage, Moses D. *From Vicksburg to Raleigh; or, A Complete History of the Twelfth Regiment Indiana Volunteer Infantry*. Chicago, 1865.

Garrison, G. C. "General Hardee's Son." *Confederate Veteran* 24 (1916): 7.

Gault, William P. *Diary of the 78th Regt., O.V.I.* Columbus, Ohio, 1901.

Geer, Allen M. *The Civil War Diary of Allen Morgan Geer, Twentieth Regiment, Illinois Volunteers*. Edited by Mary Ann Andersen. Denver, Colo. 1977.

George, Henry. *History of the Third, Seventh, Eighth, and Twelfth Kentucky, C.S.A.* Louisville, 1911.

Gilbert, Alfred West. *Colonel A. W. Gilbert: Citizen-Soldier of Cincinnati*. Edited by William E. Smith and Ophia D. Smith. Cincinnati, 1934.

Giles, Leonidas B. *Terry's Texas Rangers*. Austin, 1911.

Goodloe, Albert T. *Confederate Echoes*. Nashville, 1893.

Gorgas, Josiah. *The Civil War Diary of Josiah Gorgas*. Edited by Frank Vandiver. University, Ala., 1947.

Graber, Henry W. *A Terry Texas Ranger*. Austin, 1987.

Grant, Ulysses S. *Personal Memoirs*. Edited by E. B. Long. New York, 1982.

Grecian, Joseph. *History of the Eighty-third Regiment, Indiana Volunteer Infantry*. Cincinnati, 1865.

Gresham, Matilda. *The Life of Walter Quintin Gresham, 1832–1895*. 2 vols. Chicago, 1919.

Grigsby, Melvin. *The Smoked Yank*. Sioux Falls, S.Dak., 1888.

Griscom, George L. *Fighting with Ross' Texas Cavalry Brigade, C.S.A.* Edited by Homer L. Kerr. Hillsboro, Tex., 1976.

Guild, George B. "Battle of Bentonville: Charge of the Fourth Tennessee and Eighth Texas Cavalry." In Edwin L. Drake, ed., *Annals of the Army of Tennessee* 1 (1878): 62–64.

——. *A Brief Narrative of the Fourth Tennessee Cavalry Regiment*. Nashville, 1913.

Hagood, Johnson. *Memoirs of the War of the Secession*. Columbia, S.C., 1910.

Halliburton, Lloyd, ed. *Saddle Soldiers: The Civil War Correspondence of General William Stokes*. Orangeburg, S.C., 1993.

Hamilton, William Douglas. *Recollections of a Cavalryman of the Civil War after Fifty Years*. Columbus, Ohio, 1915.

Hampton, Wade. "The Battle of Bentonville." In Johnson and Buel, *Battles and Leaders of the Civil War*, 4:700–705.

——. "The Battle of Bentonville." *Century Magazine* 34 (October 1887): 939–45.

Harby, Lee C. "Hart's Battery . . . Dedicated to the Survivors of Hart's Battery, in Memory of My Only Brother, Dr. Marx E. Cohen, a Member of the Company Who Fell at the Battle of Bentonville, March 19, 1865." Charleston, S.C., 1898.

Harcourt, A. P. "Terry's Texas Rangers." *Southern Bivouac* 1 (1881–82): 89–97.

Harding, George C. *Miscellaneous Writings*. Indianapolis, 1882.

Harper, George W. F. "Palmer's Brigade and the Battle of Bentonville." Raleigh *News and Observer*, Dec. 20, 1887.

——. *Sketch of the Fifty-eighth Regiment (Infantry) North Carolina Troops*. Lenoir, N.C., 1901.

Hart, James F. "Hart's South Carolina Battery." *Southern Historical Society Papers* 6 (1878): 128–32.

Haskell, Orson S. *Memorandum of the Fifty-third Regiment Illinois Vet. Volunteer Infantry*. Louisville, Ky., 1865.

Hazen, William B. *A Narrative of Military Service*. Boston, 1885.

Hedley, *Marching through Georgia: Pen-Pictures of Everyday Life*. Chicago, 1885.

Heisey, M. Luther. "The Gallant Seventy-ninth Regiment." *Journal of the Lancaster County Historical Society* 46 (1942): 1–29.

Hewes, Fletcher W. *Outline of the Veteran Service of the Tenth Regiment of Michigan Veteran Infantry*. Bloomfield, N.J., 1891.

Hight, John J. *History of the Fifty-eighth Regiment of Indiana Volunteer Infantry*. Princeton, Ind., 1895.

Hill, G. W. "Palmer's Brigade in the Carolinas." *Confederate Veteran* 18 (1910): 332.

Hinkley, Julian W. *A Narrative of Service with the 3rd Wisconsin Infantry*. Madison, 1912.

Hinman, Wilbur F. *The Story of the Sherman Brigade*. Alliance, Ohio, 1897.

Hinsdale, John W. *History of the 72nd Regiment of the North Carolina Troops*. Goldsboro, N.C., 1901.

Hinson, Joseph. "Bentonville." *National Tribune*, July 8, 1886.

History of the 32nd Ohio Veteran Volunteer Infantry. Columbus, 1896.

Hitchcock, Henry. *Marching with Sherman: Passages from the Letters and Campaign Diaries of Henry Hitchcock*. Edited by M. A. DeWolfe Howe. New Haven, Conn., 1927.

Holman, J. A. "Concerning the Battle at Bentonville." *Confederate Veteran* 6 (1898): 153-54.

Holmes, James G. "The Artillery at Bentonville." *Confederate Veteran* 3 (1895): 103.

Holmes, James Taylor. *52nd O.V.I., Then and Now*. Columbus, Ohio, 1898.

Holmes, Robert M. *Kemper County Rebel: The Civil War Diary of Robert Masten Holmes, C.S.A.* Edited by Frank A. Dennis. Jackson, Miss., 1973.

Hopkins, Vivian C., ed. "Soldier of the 92nd Illinois: Letters of William H. Brown and His Fiancee, Emma Jane Frazey." *Bulletin of the New York Public Library* 73 (1969): 114-36.

Horrall, Spillard F. *History of the Forty-second Indiana Volunteer Infantry*. Chicago, 1892.

Horton, Joshua H. *A History of the Eleventh Regiment*. Dayton, Ohio, 1866.

Houghton, Edgar P., and Solomon Teverbaugh. *A History of the Eleventh Regiment (Ohio Volunteer Infantry)*. Dayton, 1866.

Howard, Oliver Otis. *Autobiography of Oliver Otis Howard, Major-General, United States Army*. 2 vols. New York, 1907.

——. "To the Memory of Henry Slocum." Edited by Thomas E. Hilton. *Civil War Times Illustrated* 21 (1982): 38-41.

Howard, Wiley C. *Sketch of Cobb Legion Cavalry and Some Incidents and Scenes Remembered*. Atlanta, 1901.

Hubert, Charles F. *History of the Fiftieth Regiment, Illinois Volunteer Infantry*. Kansas City, Mo., 1894.

Hunter, Alfred G. *History of the Eighty-second Indiana Volunteer Infantry*. Indianapolis, 1893.

Hurst, Samuel H. *Journal-History of the Seventy-third Ohio Volunteers Infantry*. Chillicothe, Ohio, 1866.

Illinois Infantry. *Ninety-second Illinois Volunteers*. Freeport, Ill., 1875.

——. *The Story of the Fifty-fifth Regiment Illinois Volunteer Infantry*. Clinton, Mass., 1887.

Ingersoll, Lurton Dunham. *Iowa and the Rebellion*. Philadelphia, 1866.

Jackson, Oscar Lawrence. *The Colonel's Diary*. Sharon, Pa., 1922.

Jamison, Matthew H. *Recollections of Pioneer and Army Life*. Kansas City, Kans., 1911.

Johnson, John. "The Confederate Defense of Fort Sumter." In Johnson and Buel, *Battles and Leaders of the Civil War*, 4:23-26.

Johnson, Robert G. "The Gilmer Blues." In Mary N. Johnson, ed., *This They Remembered*, pp. 1-40. Columbus, Ga., 1986.

Johnson, Robert Underwood, and Clarence Clough Buel, eds. *Battles and Leaders of the Civil War*. 4 vols. New York, 1884-87.

Johnson, William C. "Marching, Fighting, and Camping." Atlanta *Journal*, Nov. 9, 1901-Jan. 25, 1902.

——. *March to the Sea*. Cincinnati, 1891.

Johnston, Joseph E. "My Negotiations with General Sherman." *North American Review* 143 (1896): 183–97.

———. *Narrative of Military Operations, Directed during the Late War between the States by Joseph E. Johnston, General, C.S.A.* New York, 1874.

Jones, J. A. "An Incident of Bentonville." *Confederate Veteran* 21 (1913): 125.

Jones, Katharine M. *When Sherman Came.* New York, 1964.

Kerr, C. D. *From Atlanta to Raleigh: Military Order of the Loyal Legion of the United States—Minnesota.* 6 vols, 1:202–23. St. Paul, Minn., 1887–1909.1

Kinnear, John R. *History of the Eighty-sixth Regiment Illinois Volunteer Infantry.* Chicago, 1866.

Kremer, Wesley P. *100 Great Battles of the Rebellion.* Hoboken, N.J., 1906.

Lambert, R. A. "In the Battle of Bentonville, N.C." *Confederate Veteran* 37 (1929): 221–23.

Lankford, Nelson D., ed. *An Irishman in Dixie.* Columbia, S.C., 1988.

Lawson, Lewis A. *Wheeler's Last Raid.* Greenwood, Fla., 1986.

Leach, Floy. "Survivor Recalls Terror of Clash at Bentonville." Raleigh *News and Observer,* July 21, 1940.

Lindsley, John Berrien, ed. *The Military Annals of Tennessee.* Nashville, 1896.

Lucas, Daniel R. *History of the 99th Indiana Infantry.* Lafayette, Ind., 1865.

Lybarger, Edwin L. *Leaves from My Diary.* Coshocton, Ohio, 1910.

Lyle, William W. *Lights and Shadows of Army Life.* Cincinnati, 1865.

McAdams, F. M. *Every-day Soldier Life.* Columbus, Ohio, 1884.

McBride, John R. *History of the Thirty-third Indiana Veteran Volunteer Infantry.* Indianapolis, 1900.

McCain, Warren. *A Soldier's Diary; or, the History of Company "L," Third Indiana Cavalry.* Indianapolis, 1885.

McClurg, Alexander C. "The Last Chance of the Confederacy." *Atlantic Monthly* 50 (September 1882): 389–400.

McCutchon, Kenneth P., ed. *"Dearest Lizzie."* Evansville, Ind., 1988.

McGill, Robert M. "Diary." In R. M. McGill, *McGill Family Record,* pp. 171–244. Richmond, 1907.

McGuire, John P. "Greek Meeting Greek." *Southern Bivouac* 2 (1883–84): 549–50.

McMorries, Edward Young. *History of the First Regiment Alabama Volunteer Infantry C.S.A.* Montgomery, 1904.

McMurray, W. J. *History of the Twentieth Tennessee Regiment Volunteer Infantry, C.S.A.* Nashville, 1904.

McMurry, Richard M. *Footprints of a Regiment.* Marietta, Ga., 1992.

McNeil, Samuel A. *Personal Recollections of Service in the Army of the Cumberland and Sherman's Army, from August 17, 1861 to July 20, 1865.* Richwood, Ohio, 1910.

Mahon, John K., ed. "The Civil War Letters of Samuel Mahon Seventh Iowa Infantry." *Iowa Journal of History* 51 (1963): 233–66.

Marcy, Henry O. "Sherman's Campaign in the Carolinas." *Military Order of the Loyal Legion of the United States—Massachusetts,* 2:331–48.

Marshall, Randolph V. *An Historical Sketch of the Twenty-second Regiment Indiana Volunteers.* Madison, Ind., 1877.

Marvin, Edwin E. *The Fifth Regiment Connecticut Volunteers: A History Compiled from Diaries and Official Reports*. Hartford, 1889.

Matthews, James L. "Civil War Diary." Edited by Roger C. Hackett. *Indiana Magazine of History* 24 (1938): 306–16.

Meade, Rufus. "With Sherman through Georgia and the Carolinas." Edited by James A. Padgett. *Georgia Historical Quarterly* 32 (1948): 285–322, 33 (1949): 49–81.

Merrill, Samuel. *The Seventieth Indiana Volunteer Infantry in the War of the Rebellion*. Indianapolis, 1900.

Miller, James C. "With Sherman through the Carolinas." *Civil War Times Illustrated* 8 (1969): 42–48.

Mills, George. "The Sharp Family Civil War Letters." *Annals of Iowa* 34 (1933): 481–532.

Mims, Wilbur F. *War History of the Prattville Dragoons*. Prattville, Ala., n.d.

Miner, Mike, ed. " 'A Brave Officer': The Letters of Richard Saffell." *Military Images* 12 (1991): 16–18.

Monnett, Howard N. " 'The Awfulest Time I Ever Seen': A Letter from Sherman's Army." *Civil War History* 8 (1962): 283–89.

Moore, Frank, ed., *The Rebellion Record*. 10 vols. New York, 1861–68.

Moore, James. *Kilpatrick and Our Cavalry*. New York, 1865.

Morhous, Henry C. *Reminiscences of the 123rd Regiment*. Greenwich, N.Y., 1879.

Morris, William S., J. B. Kuykendall, and L. D. Harwell. *History of the 31st Regiment Volunteers, Organized by John A. Logan*. Evansville, Ind., 1902.

Morse, Bliss. *Civil War Diaries*. Edited by Loren J. Morse. Pittsburg, Kans., 1963.

Mullen, James M. "Last Days of Johnston's Army." *Southern Historical Society Papers* 18 (1888): 97–113.

Murphree, Joel P. "Autobiography and Civil War Letters of Joel Murfree, 1864–1865." *Alabama Historical Quarterly* 19 (1955): 170–208.

Murphy, David A. *Murphy's Battles: An Ohio Soldier's Autobiography*. Cincinnati, 1913.

Nelson, Charles F. *Diary of Charles F. Nelson*. Edited by Franklin V. Nelson. Springfield, Ill., 1958.

New York Infantry. *One Hundred and Forty-third Regiment New York Vol. Inf. Sullivan Co.* Monticello, N.Y., 1892.

New York Monuments Commission for the Battlefields of Gettysburg and Chattanooga. *In Memoriam: Henry Warner Slocum, 1826–1894*. Albany, 1904.

Nichols, George Ward. *The Story of the Great March from the Diary of a Staff Officer*. New York, 1865.

Northrop, Henry D. *Life and Deeds of General Sherman, Including the Story of His Great March to the Sea*. Philadelphia, n.d.

Oakey, Daniel. "Marching through Georgia and the Carolinas." In Johnson and Buel, *Battles and Leaders of the Civil War*, 4:671–79.

Oates, William C. *The War between the Union and the Confederacy*. Dayton, Ohio, 1985.

Ogilvie, W. H. "Days and Nights Cut Off in Swamps." *Confederate Veteran* 15 (1907): 361–62.

Ohio Infantry. *History of the Thirty-seventh Ohio Volunteer Infantry*. Columbus, 1889.

O'Neal, H. "From the Western Border of Texas." *Confederate Veteran* 5 (1897): 125.

Orendorff, Henry. *We Are Sherman's Men: The Civil War Letters of Henry Orendorff.* Edited by William M. Anderson. Macomb, Ill., 1986.

Orendorff, Henry H., et al. *Reminiscences of the Civil War from Diaries of Members of the 103d Illinois Volunteer Infantry.* Chicago, 1905.

Osborn, Hartwell. *Trials and Triumphs: The Record of the Fifty-fifth Ohio Volunteer Infantry.* Chicago, 1904.

Osborn, Thomas W. *The Fiery Trail: A Union Officer's Account of Sherman's Last Campaign.* Edited by Richard Harwell and Philip N. Racine. Knoxville, 1986.

Overholster, James F. *Diary.* N.p., n.d.

Owens, Ira S. *Greene County Soldiers in the Late War: Being a History of the Seventy-fourth O.V.I.* Xenia, Ohio, 1872.

Patton, Joseph T. *Personal Recollections.* Detroit, Mich., 1892.

Payne, Edwin W. *History of the Thirty-fourth Regiment of Illinois Volunteer Infantry.* Clinton, Iowa, 1903.

Peddycord, William F. *History of the Seventy-fourth Regiment Indiana Volunteer Infantry.* Warsaw, Ind., 1913.

Pepper, George W. *Personal Recollections of Sherman's Campaigns in Georgia and the Carolinas.* Zanesville, Ohio, 1866.

Perry, Henry F. *History of the Thirty-eighth Regiment Indiana Volunteer Infantry.* Palo Alto, Calif., 1906.

Pickett, William D. *Sketch of the Military Career of William J. Hardee, Lieutenant General C.S.A.* Lexington, Ky., 1910.

——. "Willie Hardee." *Confederate Veteran* 24 (1916): 182.

Plane, W. F. "Letters . . . to His Wife." *Georgia Historical Quarterly* 57 (1973): 215–28.

Puntenney, George H. *History of the Thirty-seventh Regiment of Indiana Infantry Volunteers.* Rushville, Ind., 1896.

Quint, Alonzo H. *The Record of the Second Massachusetts Infantry.* Boston, 1867.

Ranstead, Herbert E. *A True Story and History of the Fifty-third Regiment Illinois Veteran Volunteer Infantry.* N.p., 1910.

Ravenel, Samuel W. "Ask the Survivors of Bentonville." *Confederate Veteran* 18 (1910): 124.

Record of the Ninety-fourth Regiment Ohio Volunteer Infantry. Cincinnati, 1906.

Reddick, Henry W. *Seventy-seven Years in Dixie: The Boys in Gray of 61–65.* Santa Rosa, Fla., 1910.

Reid, Whitelaw. *Ohio in the War: Her Statesmen, Her Generals, and Soldiers.* 2 vols. Cincinnati, 1868.

Remington, Cyrus K. *A Record of Battery I, First N.Y. Light Artillery Vols.* Buffalo, 1891.

Reminiscences of the Civil War from Diaries of Members of 103d Illinois Volunteer Infantry. Chicago, 1904.

Reunion of Dan McCook's Third Brigade, 14th Army Corps. Chicago, 1901.

Ridley, Bromfield Lewis. *Battles and Sketches of the Army of Tennessee.* Mexico, Mo., 1906.

——. "Last Battles of the War." *Confederate Veteran* 3 (1895): 20, 70–71.

Robertson, John, ed. *Michigan in the War.* Lansing, 1882.

Rogers, Robert M. *The 125th Regiment Illinois Volunteer Infantry.* Champaign, Ill., 1882.

Rood, Hosea W. *Story of the Service of Company E, and of the Twelfth Wisconsin Regiment of Veteran Volunteer Infantry.* Milwaukee, 1893.

Roth, Margaret Brobst, ed. *Well Mary: Civil War Letters of a Wisconsin Volunteer.* Madison, 1960.

Roy, Thomas B. "General Hardee and the Military Operations around Atlanta." *Southern Historical Society Papers* 8 (1880): 337–87.

Rumpel, John W. "Ohiowa Soldier." Edited by H. Rosenberger. *Annals of Iowa* 36 (1935): 110–48.

Ryder, John J. *Reminiscences of Three Years' Service in the Civil War.* New Bedford, Mass., 1928.

Sanders, Robert W. "The Battle of Bentonville." *Confederate Veteran* 34 (1926): 215–16, 299–300.

———. "More about the Battle of Bentonville, N.C." *Confederate Veteran* 37 (1929): 460–62.

Scoggins, Samuel. "The Fourth Tennessee Cavalry at Bentonville, N.C." *Confederate Veteran* 25 (1917): 446.

Sheridan, Philip H. *Personal Memoirs.* 2 vols. New York, 1902.

Sherlock, Eli J. *Memorabilia of the Marches and Battles in which the One Hundredth Regiment of Indiana Infantry Volunteers Took an Active Part.* Kansas City, Mo., 1896.

Sherman, George W. *A Narrative of War Time.* Lynbrook, N.Y., 1912.

Sherman, William T. *Home Letters of General Sherman.* Edited by M. A. DeWolfe Howe. New York, 1909.

———. *Memoirs of General William T. Sherman.* 2 vols. New York, 1892.

Shoemaker, Michael. "The Michigan Thirteenth." *Michigan Historical Collections* 4 (1881): 133–68.

Sligh, Charles R. *History of the Services of the First Regiment Michigan Engineers and Mechanics, during the Civil War.* Grand Rapids, Mich., 1921.

Slocum, Henry Warner. "Final Operations of Sherman's Army." In Johnson and Buel, *Battles and Leaders of the Civil War,* 4:754–58.

———. "Marching through Georgia and the Carolinas." *Century Magazine* 34 (October 1887): 917–39.

———. *Military Lessons Taught by the War: An Address Delivered before the Long Island Historical Society.* New York, 1869.

———. "Sherman's March." *Army and Navy Journal* 2 (1865): 497, 505.

———. "Sherman's March from Savannah to Bentonville." In Johnson and Buel, *Battles and Leaders of the Civil War,* 4:681–695.

Smith, Charles H. *The History of Fuller's Ohio Brigade.* Cleveland, 1909.

Smith, Daniel P. *Company K, First Alabama Regiment; or, Three Years in the Confederate Service.* Prattville, Ala., 1885.

Smith, John H. "Civil War Diary." *Iowa Journal of History* 47 (1959): 140–70.

Snowden, Yates. *Marching with Sherman.* Columbia, S.C., 1929.

Society of the Army of the Tennessee. *Report of the Proceedings of the Society of the Army of the Tennessee.* 45 vols. Cincinnati: 1866–1922.

Soldiers' and Citizens' Album of Biographical Record [of Wisconsin] Containing Personal Sketches of Army Men and Citizens Prominent in Loyalty to the Union. Chicago, 1890.

South Carolina Division, United Daughters of the Confederacy. *Recollections and Reminiscences, 1861–1865 through World War I.* 4 vols. Columbia, 1990–93.

Spencer, Cornelia Phillips. *The Last Ninety Days of the War in North Carolina*. New York, 1866.

Stallcop, James. "Letters." *North Dakota Historical Quarterly* 4 (1930): 116–42.

Stephenson, Philip D. *Civil War Memoir*. Edited by Nathaniel C. Hughes, Jr. Conway, Ark., 1995.

Stevenson, Thomas M. *History of the 78th Regiment O.V.V.I.* Zanesville, Ohio, 1865.

Stewart, Nixon B. *Dan McCook's Regiment: 52nd O.V.I.* Alliance, Ohio, 1900.

Storrs, John W. *The Twentieth Connecticut*. Ansonia, Conn., 1886.

The Story of the Fifty-fifth Regiment Illinois Volunteer Infantry. Clinton, Mass., 1887.

Strong, Robert H. *A Yankee Private's Civil War*. Edited by Ashley Halsey. Chicago, 1961.

Sweet, Benjamin F. "Civil War Experiences." Edited by Vivian K. McLarty. *Missouri Historical Review* 43 (1948): 237–50.

Sykes, Edward T. "Walthall's Brigade." *Mississippi Historical Society Publications* 1 (1896): 477–623.

Thomas, Lorick P. "Bentonville." Atlanta *Journal*. April 13, 1901.

——. "Their Last Battle, Fight at Bentonville, North Carolina between Sherman and Johnston, Some Personal Observations." *Southern Historical Society Papers* 29 (1897): 215–22.

Thompson, Edwin P. *History of the Orphan Brigade*. Louisville, Ky., 1898.

Toombs, Samuel. *Reminiscences of the War: Comprising a Detailed Account of the Experiences of the Thirteenth Regiment New Jersey Volunteers*. Orange, N.J., 1878.

Tourgée, Albion W. *The Story of a Thousand: Being a History of the Service of the 105th Ohio Volunteer Infantry*. Buffalo, N.Y., 1896.

Trimble, Harvey M. *History of the Ninety-third Regiment, Illinois Volunteer Infantry*. Chicago, 1898.

Tucker, William H. *The Fourteenth Wisconsin Vet. Vol. Infantry*. Indianapolis, 1892.

Underwood, Adin B. *The Three Years' Service of the Thirty-third Mass. Infantry Regiment, 1862–1865*. Boston, 1881.

Upson, Theodore F. *With Sherman to the Sea*. Edited by Oscar O. Winther. Bloomington, Ind., 1958.

Vance, Zebulon B. *The Last Days of the War in North Carolina: An Address*. Baltimore, 1885.

Vaughan, Alfred J. *Personal Record of the Thirteenth Regiment Tennessee Infantry*. Memphis, 1897.

Veale, Moses. *The One Hundred and Ninth Regiment Pennsylvania Volunteers*. Philadelphia, 1890.

Waddell, Alfred M. *Last Year of the War in North Carolina, including Plymouth, Fort Fisher, and Bentonville*. Richmond, 1888.

Walker, Cornelius I. *10th Regiment S.C. Vols., Confederate States Army: Rolls and Sketch*. Charleston, 1881.

Wallace, Frederick S. *The Sixty-first Ohio Volunteers*. Marysville, Ohio, 1902.

Wallace, William. "Operations of Second South Carolina Regiment in Campaigns of 1864 and 1865." *Southern Historical Society Papers* 7 (1879): 128–31.

Walton, William, ed. *A Civil War Courtship: The Letters of Edwin Weller from Antietam to Atlanta*. New York, 1980.

Ward, Dallas T. *The Last Flag of Truce*. Franklinton, N.C., 1915.

Watkins, Sam R. *"Co. Aytch": A Sideshow of the Big Show*. New York, 1962.

Watson, B. F. "In the Battle of Bentonville." *Confederate Veteran* 37 (1929): 95.

Westervelt, William B. *Light and Shadows of Army Life*. Marlboro, N.Y., 1886.

Whittlesey, C. *War Memoranda: Cheat River to the Tennessee*. 1884.

Wilder, Theodore. *The History of Company C, Seventh Regiment, OVI*. Oberlin, Ohio, 1866.

Willett, Elbert D. *History of Company B (Originally Pickens Planters), 40th Alabama Regiment, Confederate States Army, 1862 to 1865*. Anniston, Ala., 1902.

Williams, Alpheus S. *From the Cannon's Mouth: The Civil War Letters of Alpheus S. Williams*. Edited by Milo M. Quaife. Detroit, 1959.

Williams, Hiram Smith. *This War So Horrible*. Edited by Lewis N. Wynne and Robert A. Taylor. Tuscaloosa, Ala., 1993.

Willison, Charles A. *Reminiscences of a Boy's Service with the 76th Ohio, in the Fifteenth Army Corps, under General Sherman*. Menasha, Wis., 1908.

Wills, Charles W. *Army Life of an Illinois Soldier: Letters and Diary of the Late Charles W. Wills*. Compiled by Mary E. Kellogg. Washington, D.C., 1906.

Wilson, Ephraim A. *Memoirs of the War*. Cleveland, Ohio, 1893.

Wise, George M. *Marching through South Carolina*. Edited by Wilfred W. Black. Columbus, Ohio, 1957.

Wood, David W., comp. *History of the 20th Ohio Veteran Volunteer Infantry Regiment*. Columbus, Ohio, 1876.

Woodward, C. Vann, ed. *Mary Chesnut's Civil War*. New Haven, 1981.

Worsham, William J. *Old Nineteenth Regiment, C.S.A.* Knoxville, 1902.

Worthington, Thomas. *Brief History of the Forty-sixth Ohio Volunteers*. N.p., n.d.

Wright, Charles. *A Corporal's Story*. Philadelphia, 1887.

Wright, Henry H. *A History of the Sixth Iowa Regiment*. Iowa City, 1923.

Wynne, Lewis M., and Robert A. Taylor, eds. *This War So Terrible: The Civil War Diary of Hiram Smith Williams*. Tuscaloosa, Ala., 1993.

Younce, William H. *The Adventures of a Conscript*. Cincinnati, 1901.

NEWSPAPERS

Atlanta *Journal*
Atlanta *Sunny South*
Charlotte, N.C., *Daily Bulletin*
Charlotte Observer
Greensboro, N.C., *Daily News*
Harper's Weekly; A Journal of Civilization (62 vols; New York, 1857–1916)
Hillsborough, N.C., *Recorder*
Leslie's Illustrated Weekly Newspaper (134 vols; New York, 1855–1922)
London *Army and Navy Gazette*
New Haven *Connecticut War Record*
New York Times
New York Tribune
Omaha, Nebr., *World-Herald*

Raleigh Daily Confederate
Raleigh *News and Observer*
Raleigh *North Carolina Standard*
Raleigh *North Carolinian*
Smithfield, N.C., *Smithfield Herald*
Washington, D.C., *National Tribune*

GOVERNMENT DOCUMENTS

Candler, Allen D. *The Confederate Records of the State of Georgia.* 6 vols. Atlanta, 1909–11.

Illinois Adjutant General's Office. *Report of the Adjutant General of the State of Illinois.* 10 vols. Springfield, 1900–1902.

Indiana Adjutant General's Office. *Report of the Adjutant General of the State of Indiana.* 8 vols. Indianapolis, 1865–69.

Iowa Adjutant General's Office. *Roster and Record of Iowa Soldiers in the War of the Rebellion.* 6 vols. Des Moines, 1908.

Massachusetts Civil War Centennial Committee. *Massachusetts in the Civil War.* Boston, 1960–.

Medal of Honor, 1863–1968, "In the Name of the Congress of the United States." Washington, D.C., 1968.

Michigan Adjutant General's Department. *Michigan in the War.* Lansing, 1882.

Minnesota Civil and Indian Wars Commission. *Minnesota in the Civil and Indian Wars, 1861–1865.* St. Paul, 1890–93.

New Jersey Adjutant General's Office. *Record of Officers and Men of New Jersey in the Civil War.* Trenton, 1876.

New York Adjutant General's Office. *A Record of the Commissioned Officers, Non-commissioned Officers, and Privates of the Regiments.* Albany, 1864–68.

Official Roster of the Soldiers of the State of Ohio in the War of the Rebellion and in the War with Mexico. 12 vols. Akron, Cincinnati, and Norwalk, Ohio, 1886–95.

"Report of Major General William T. Sherman to the Hon. Committee on the Conduct of the War." *U.S. 38th Congress, 2d sess., Joint Committee on the Conduct of the War, Supplemental Report . . .* 2 vols. Washington, D.C., 1866.

U.S. Adjutant General's Office. *Campaign of the Carolinas: Organization of the Union Forces (Commanded by Major-General William T. Sherman) January–April, 1865.* Washington, D.C., n.d.

U.S. Government. *Atlas to Accompany the Official Records of the Union and Confederate Armies.* Washington, D.C., 1891–95.

——. *Biographical Directory of the American Congress, 1774–1949.* Washington, D.C., 1950.

——. Census of Smith County, North Carolina, 1860.

——. *War of the Rebellion: A Compilation of the Official Records of the Union and Confederate Armies.* 128 vols. Washington, D.C., 1880–1901.

Wisconsin Adjutant General's Office. *Annual Report.* Madison, 1861–65.

MAPS

Library of Congress
Battle of Bentonville

Robert M. McDowell Maps

Thomas B. Van Horne Maps

National Archives

L145(G145): Maps Illustrating Battle of Bentonville . . . Compiled under the direction of
Col. O. M. Poe by Maj. E. F. Hoffman

L143 (G32): 10 Maps: Line of March of Twentieth Corps from Savannah, Ga., to Goldsboro, N.C., with Plans of Battlefields of Averasboro and Bentonville

Secondary Sources

BOOKS

Achorn, Edgar D. *Major General Oliver Otis Howard*. Cumberland Gap, Tenn., 1910.

Allardice, Bruce S. *More Generals in Gray*. Baton Rouge, La., 1995.

Anders, Leslie. *The Eighteenth Missouri*. Indianapolis, 1968.

Anderson, William M. *They Died to Make Men Free: A History of the 9th Michigan Infantry
in the Civil War*. Berrien Springs, Mich., 1980.

Arnett, Ethel S. *Confederate Guns Were Stacked, Greensboro, North Carolina*. Greensboro,
1965.

Baird, John A. *Profile of a Hero: The Story of Absalom Baird*. Philadelphia, 1977.

Baldwin, Elmer T. *History of LaSalle County, Illinois*. 2 vols. Chicago, 1886.

Barnes, William H. *Lives of Ulysses S. Grant and Hon. Henry Wilson, Together with
Sketches of Republican Candidates for Congress in Indiana*. New York, 1872.

Barnhill, Floyd R., Sr., and Calvin L. Collier. *The Fighting Fifth, Pat Cleburne's Cutting
Edge: The Fifth Arkansas Infantry Regiment C.S.A.* Jonesboro, Ark., 1990.

Barrett, John G. *The Civil War in North Carolina*. Chapel Hill, 1963.

——. *North Carolina as a Civil War Battleground, 1861–1865*. Raleigh, 1991.

——. *Sherman's March through the Carolinas*. Chapel Hill, 1956.

Barrett, John G., and W. Buck Yearns. *North Carolina Civil War Documentary*. Chapel
Hill, 1980.

Bates, Samuel P. *History of Pennsylvania Volunteers*. 5 vols. Harrisburg, 1869.

Bell, James W. *The 43rd Georgia Infantry Regiment*. Duluth, Ga., 1990.

Beyer, W. F., and O. F. Keydel, eds. *Deeds of Valor: How America's Civil War Heroes Won
the Congressional Medal of Honor*. Stamford, Conn., 1992.

Birdsong, James C. *Brief Sketches of the North Carolina State Troops in the War between
the States*. Raleigh, 1894.

Black, Robert C. *The Railroads of the Confederacy*. Chapel Hill, 1952.

Brewer, Willis. *Brief Historical Sketches of Military Organizations Raised in Alabama during the Civil War*. University, Ala., 1962.

Bridges, Leonard Hal. *Lee's Maverick General: Daniel Harvey Hill*. New York, 1961.

Burne, Alfred H. *Lee, Grant, and Sherman: A Study of Leadership in the 1864–1865 Campaign*. New York, 1938.

Capers, Walter B. *The Soldier-Bishop: Ellison Capers*. New York, 1912.

Carpenter, John A. *Sword and Olive Branch: Oliver Otis Howard*. Pittsburgh, Pa., 1964.

Castel, Albert. *Decision in the West: The Atlanta Campaign of 1864*. Lawrence, Kans.,
1992.

Catton, Bruce. *Never Call Retreat*. Garden City, N.Y., 1965.

——. *This Hallowed Ground*. New York, 1956.

Cist, Henry Martyn. *The Army of the Cumberland*. New York, 1882.

Cleaves, Freeman. *Rock of Chickamauga: The Life of General George H. Thomas*. Norman, Okla., 1986.

Collier, Calvin L. *First In, Last Out: The Capitol Guards, Ark. Brigade*. Little Rock, 1961.

——. *"They'll Do To Tie To!" The Story of the Third Regiment Arkansas Infantry*. Little Rock, 1959.

——. *The War Child's Children: The Story of the 3rd Regiment Arkansas Cavalry*. Little Rock, 1965

Connelly, Thomas Lawrence. *Autumn of Glory*. Baton Rouge, La., 1971.

Cox, Jacob D. *The March to the Sea*. New York, 1906.

Cozzens, Peter. *The Shipwreck of Their Hopes*. Chicago, 1994.

——. *This Terrible Sound*. Urbana, Ill., 1992.

Daniel, Larry J. *Cannoneers in Gray: The Field Artillery of the Army of Tennessee, 1861–1865*. University, Ala., 1984.

Darley, Pat P. Harper. *Harper Journey of Faith*. Cordele, Ga., 1988.

Davis, Burke. *Sherman's March*. New York, 1980.

Dickert, D. Augustus. *History of Kershaw's Brigade*. Dayton, Ohio, 1973.

DuBose, John Witherspoon. *General Joseph Wheeler and the Army of Tennessee*. New York, 1912.

Dunlop, William S. *Lee's Sharpshooters*. Little Rock, 1899.

Dyer, John Percy. *"Fightin' Joe" Wheeler*. Baton Rouge: Louisiana State University Press, 1941.

Eddy, Thomas Mears. *The Patriotism of Illinois*. 2 vols. Chicago, 1865–66.

Eisenschimel, Otto, and Ralph Newman. *The American Iliad*. Indianapolis, 1947.

Elzas, Barnett A. *The Jews of South Carolina*. Philadelphia, 1905.

Evans, Clement Anselm. *Confederate Military History*. Expanded ed. 12 vols. Atlanta, 1899.

Faust, Patricia L., ed. *Historical Times Illustrated Encyclopedia of the Civil War*. New York, 1986.

Fitzhugh, Lester N. *Terry's Texas Rangers: 8th Texas Cavalry, C.S.A.* Dallas, 1958.

France, Erik. *The Battle of Bentonville*. Board game with commentary. [Lexington, Va.], ca. 1980.

Freeman, Douglas S. *Lee's Lieutenants: A Study in Command*. 3 vols. New York, 1942–44.

Gibson, John M. *Those 163 Days*. New York, 1961.

Glatthaar, Joseph T. *The March to the Sea and Beyond: Sherman's Troops in the Savannah and Carolinas Campaigns*. New York, 1985.

Govan, Gilbert E., and James W. Livingood. *A Different Valor: The Story of General Joseph E. Johnston, C.S.A.* Indianapolis, 1956.

Gragg, Rod. *Confederate Goliath: The Battle of Fort Fisher*. New York, 1991.

Hafendorfer, Kenneth A. *Perryville: Battle for Kentucky*. Louisville, 1981.

Hallock, Judith L. *Braxton Bragg and Confederate Defeat*. Tuscaloosa, Ala., 1991.

Hay, Thomas R. *Hood's Tennessee Campaign*. New York, 1929.

Henderson, Lillian, comp. *Roster of the Confederate Soldiers of Georgia*. 6 vols. Hapeville, Ga., 1959–.

Herbert, Walter H. *Fighting Joe Hooker*. New York, 1944.

Heritage of Johnston County Book Committee. *The Heritage of Johnston County, North Carolina*. Winston Salem, 1985.

Hicken, Victor. *Illinois in the Civil War*. Urbana, 1966.

Hill, Daniel H. *History of North Carolina in the War between the States*. 2 vols. Raleigh, 1926.

Hoole, William S. *Vizetelly Covers the Confederacy*. Tuscaloosa, Ala., 1957.

Horn, Stanley F. *The Army of Tennessee: A Military History*. Indianapolis, 1940.

Howell, H. Grady, Jr. *Going to Meet the Yankees: A History of the "Bloody Sixth" Mississippi Infantry, C.S.A.* Jackson, 1981.

Hughes, Nathaniel Cheairs, Jr. *General William J. Hardee: Old Reliable*. Baton Rouge, La., 1965.

Hunt, Roger D., and Jack R. Brown. *Brevet Brigadier Generals in Blue*. Gaithersburg, Md., 1990.

Jeffries, Charlie C. *Terry's Rangers*. New York, 1961.

Johnson, Allen, and Dumas Malone, eds. *Dictionary of American Biography*. 21 vols. New York, 1928–37.

Johnson, Bradley T. *Memoirs of J. E. Johnston*. Baltimore, 1891.

Johnson, John Lipscomb. *The University Memorial Biographical Sketches of Alumni of the University of Virginia Who Fell in the Confederate War*. Baltimore, 1871.

Johnson, Richard W. *Memoir of George H. Thomas*. 1881.

Jordan, Weymouth T., Jr. *The Battle of Bentonville*. Wilmington, N.C., 1990.

———, comp. *North Carolina Troops, 1861–1865: A Roster*. Vols. 4–13. Raleigh, 1973–.

Kinney, William L. *Sherman's March: A Review*. Bennettsville, S.C., 1961.

Kohler, Minnie I. *A Twentieth-Century History of Hardin County, Ohio*. Chicago, 1910.

Lash, Jeffrey N. *Destroyer of the Iron Horse: General Joseph E. Johnston and Confedrate Rail Transport, 1861–1865*. Kent, Ohio, 1991.

Leeper, Wesley T. *Rebels Valiant: Second Arkansas Mounted Rifles*. Little Rock, 1964.

Lewis, Lloyd. *Sherman: Fighting Prophet*. New York, 1932.

Liddell-Hart, Basil Henry. *Sherman: Soldier, Realist, American*. New York, 1929.

Livermore, Thomas Leonard. *Numbers and Losses in the Civil War in America, 1861–1865*. New York, 1901.

Lossing, Benjamin J. *Pictorial History of the Civil War, 1861–65*. Philadelphia, 1866–68.

Losson, Christopher. *Tennessee's Forgotten Warriors: Frank Cheatham and His Confederate Division*. Knoxville, 1990.

Love, William DeLoss. *Wisconsin in the War of the Rebellion*. Chicago, 1866.

Luvaas, Jay. *Johnston's Last Stand—Bentonville*. Smithfield, N.C., 1978.

McDonough, James L. *Schofield: Union General in the Civil War and Reconstruction*. Tallahassee, Fla., 1972.

Manarin, Louis H., comp. *North Carolina Troops, 1861–1865: A Roster*. Vols. 1–3. Raleigh, 1966–71.

Markens, Isaac. *The Hebrews in America*. New York, 1888.

Marshall, Park. *A Life of William B. Bate*. Nashville, 1908.

Marszalek, John F. *Sherman: A Soldier's Passion for Order*. New York, 1992.

Mathews, Alfred. *History of Washington County, Ohio*. Cleveland, 1881.

Merrill, Catharine. *The Soldier of Indiana in the War for the Union.* 2 vols. Indianapolis, 1866–69.

Merrill, James M. *William Tecumseh Sherman.* Chicago, 1971.

Miles, Jim. *To the Sea: A History and Tour Guide of Sherman's March.* Nashville, 1989.

Miller, Rex. *The Forgotten Regiment: A Day-by-Day Account of the 55th Alabama.* Williamsville, N.Y., 1984.

Morris, Roy, Jr. *Sheridan.* New York, 1992.

Neff, Robert O. *Tennessee's Battered Brigadier.* Nashville, 1988.

Palumbo, Frank A. *George Henry Thomas: The Dependable General.* Dayton, Ohio, 1983.

Parrish, T. Michael. *Richard Taylor: Soldier Prince of Dixie.* Chapel Hill, 1992.

Phisterer, Frederick. *New York in the War of the Rebellion.* 5 vols. Albany, 1912.

Quiner, Edwin B. *The Military History of Wisconsin.* Chicago, 1866.

Ratchford, J. W. *Some Reminiscences of Persons and Incidents of the Civil War.* Austin, Tex., n.d.

Reston, James, Jr. *Sherman's March and Vietnam.* New York, 1984.

Robertson, William G. *Back Door to Richmond: The Burmuda Hundred Campaign, April–June 1864.* Newark, Del., 1987.

Roman, Alfred. *The Military Operations of General Beauregard.* 2 vols. New York, 1884.

Rowell, John W. *Yankee Cavalrymen: Through the Civil War with the Ninth Pennsylvania Cavalry.* Knoxville, Tenn., 1971.

Sears, Stephen W. *George B. McClellan the Young Napoleon.* New York, 1988.

Seaton, Benjamin M. *The Bugle Softly Blows.* Edited by Harold B. Simpson. Waco, Tex., 1965.

Seitz, Don Carlos. *Braxton Bragg: General of the Confederacy.* Columbia, S.C., 1924.

Shepherd, Rebecca A., C. W. Calhoun, E. S. Shoemaker, and A. F. January, comps. *A Biographical Directory of the Indiana General Assembly.* 2 vols. Indianapolis, 1980–84.

Sievers, Harry J. *Benjamin Harrison, Hoosier Warrior, through the Civil War Years.* New York, 1960.

Slocum, Charles Elihu. *The Life and Services of Major-General Henry Warner Slocum.* Toledo, Ohio, 1913.

Smith, Frank. *History of Maury County, Tennessee.* Columbia, Tenn., 1969.

Sommers, Richard J. *Richmond Redeemed: The Siege at Petersburg.* Garden City, N.Y., 1981.

Starr, Stephen Z. *The Union Cavalry in the Civil War.* 3 vols. Baton Rouge, La., 1985.

Stuart, Addison A. *Iowa Colonels and Regiments: Being a History of Iowa Regiments in the War of the Rebellion.* Des Moines, 1865.

Sword, Wiley. *Embrace an Angry Wind.* New York, 1992.

Symonds, Craig L. *Joseph E. Johnston: A Civil War Biography.* New York, 1992.

Taylor, John S. *Sixteenth South Carolina Regiment, CSA, from Greenville County, S.C.* N.p., 1963.

Terrell, W. H. H. *Indiana in the War of the Rebellion.* Indianapolis, 1960.

Tinkcom, Harry Marlin. *John White Geary: Soldier-Statesman, 1819–1873.* Philadelphia, 1940.

Todd, George T. *First Texas Regiment.* Waco, 1963.

Trimble, Harvey M. *History of the Ninety-third Regiment.* Chicago, 1898.

Trotter, William R. *Silk Flags and Cold Steel: The Civil War in North Carolina: The Piedmont*. Winston-Salem, 1988.

Tucker, Glenn. *Chickamauga: Bloody Battle in the West*. Indianapolis, 1961.

——. *High Tide at Gettysburg*. Indianapolis, 1958.

——. *Zeb Vance: Champion of Personal Freedom*. Indianapolis, 1965.

Turner, George E. *Victory Rode the Rails*. Indianapolis, 1953.

Van Horne, Thomas B. *History of the Army of the Cumberland*. 2 vols. Cincinnati, 1875.

Walters, John B. *Merchant of Terror: General Sherman and Total War*. Indianapolis, 1973.

Walton, Clyde C., ed. *Behind the Guns: The History of Battery I, 2nd Regiment Illinois Light Artillery, by Sgt. Thaddeus C. S. Brown, Sgt. Samuel J. Murphy, and Bugler William G. Putney*. Carbondale, 1965.

Warner, Ezra J. *Generals in Blue: Lives of the Union Commanders*. Baton Rouge, La., 1964.

——. *Generals in Gray: Lives of the Confederate Commanders*. Baton Rouge, La., 1959.

Welcher, Frank J. *The Union Army, 1861–1865*. 2 vols. Bloomington, Ind., 1989–93.

Wellman, Manley Wade. *Giant in Gray: A Biography of Wade Hampton of South Carolina*. New York, 1949.

Wells, Edward Laight. *Hampton and His Cavalry in '64*. Richmond, 1899.

Wessels, William M. *Born to Be a Soldier: The Military Career of William Wing Loring*. Fort Worth, Tex., 1971.

Wheeler, Richard, ed. *Sherman's March to the Sea*. New York, 1991.

White County Historical Society. *History of White County, Illinois*. Chicago, 1883.

Wilhelm, Thomas. *A Military Dictionary*. Philadelphia, 1881.

Williams, Alfred B. *Hampton and His Red Shirts*. Charleston, S.C., 1935.

Williams, Kenneth P. *Lincoln Finds a General*. 5 vols. New York, 1949–59.

Williams, Thomas Harry. *P. G. T. Beauregard: Napoleon in Gray*. Baton Rouge, La., 1954.

Zorn, William A. *Hold at All Hazards: The Story of the 29th Alabama Infantry Regiment, 1861–65*. Jesup, Ga., 1987.

ARTICLES AND PARTS OF BOOKS

Anderson, Mrs. John H. "Last Days of the Confederacy in North Carolina." *Confederate Veteran* 39 (1931): 20–24.

——. "Memorial on the Battle Field of Bentonville." *Confederate Veteran* 35 (1927): 367–68.

——. "North Carolina Boy Soldiers at the Battle of Bentonville." *Confederate Veteran* 35 (1927): 174–76.

Barnett, John G. "Bentonville." In Frances H. Kennedy, ed., *The Civil War Battlefield Guide*, pp. 268–72. Boston, 1990.

Barnwell, Robert W. "Bentonville—The Last Battle of Johnston and Sherman." *Proceedings of the South Carolina Historical Association* 13 (1944): 42–54.

Beach, Lansing H. "The Civil War Battle of Bentonville." *Military Engineer* 21 (1929): 24–30.

Benton, Barbara. "The Thin Gray Line." *Quarterly Journal of Military History* 3 (1987): 76–79.

"Bentonville Recalls the Horrors of War." *Southern Living*, March 1991.

Bragg, Nick. "Johnston vs. Sherman in Bentonville Battle." Raleigh *News and Observer*, Sept. 18, 1961.

"Brigadier General Stephen Elliott." *Land We Love* 4 (1867): 453–58.

Carley, Kenneth. "The Second Minnesota in the West." *Minnesota History* 38 (1953): 258–73.

Castel, Albert. "The Life of a Rising Son." *Civil War Times Illustrated* 19 (1980): 10–21.

Cates, C. Pat. "A Long Road to Bentonville: The First Confederate Regiment Georgia Volunteers." *Civil War Regiments* 1 (1990): 42–73.

Charnley, Jeffrey G. "Michigan's General A. S. Williams and Civil War Historians: A Century of Neglect." *Michigan Historical Review* 12 (1986): 1–28.

Collins, William H. "Biographical Sketch of Maj. Gen. James D. Morgan." *Publications of the Illinois State Historical Library* 9 (1908): 85.

———. "Biographical Sketch of Maj. Gen. James D. Morgan." *Transactions of the Illinois Historical Society* 11 (1906): 274–85.

Doyle, J. E. Parker. "Sherman's Sixty Days in the Carolinas." *United States Service Magazine* 3 (1865): 511–14.

Dugan, Gene. "The North Carolina Junior Reserves Fought with a Fierceness That Belied Their Youth." *America's Civil War* 6 (1993): 12–24.

Fonvielle, Chris E., Jr. "The Last Rays of Departing Hope: The Fall of Wilmington, including the Campaign against Fort Fisher." *Blue and Gray Magazine* 7 (1990): 10–21.

Goode, Johnny C. "They Don't Drive Worth a Damn." *United Daughters of the Confederacy Magazine* 53 (1991): 18–34.

Hagerman, Edward. "Field Transportation and Strategic Mobility in the Union Armies." *Civil War History* 34 (1988): 143–71.

Halsey, Ashley, Jr. "The Last Duel of the Confederacy." *Civil War Times Illustrated* 1 (1962): 6–8, 31.

Hartley, Chris. "Bentonville." *America's Civil War* 1 (1988): 27–33.

Herbert, Sidney. "A Life Long Soldier: Brilliant Career of William Wing Loring of North Carolina." *At Home Abroad* 3 (1893): 281–85.

Hughes, Nathaniel C., Jr. "Hardee's Defense of Savannah." *Georgia Historical Quarterly* 47 (1963): 43–67.

Jones, James P. "The Battle of Atlanta and McPherson's Successor." *Civil War History* 7 (1961): 393–405.

———. "General Jeff C. Davis, U.S.A., and Sherman's Georgia Campaign." *Georgia Historical Quarterly* 47 (1963): 231–48.

Jones, John W. "William J. Hardee." In Julian A. C. Chandler et al., *The South in the Building of the Nation*, 11:441–43. 13 vols. Richmond, 1909–13.

Lazarus, Lyn. "A Civil War Biography—William R. Talley." Jacksonville, Fla., *Times-Union and Journal*, Feb. 6, 1975.

Luvaas, Jay. "Bentonville—Last Chance to Stop Sherman." *Civil War Times Illustrated* 2 (1963): 6–9, 38–42.

———. "Johnston's Last Stand—Bentonville." *North Carolina Historical Review* 33 (1956): 332–58.

———. "Lee and the Operational Art: The Right Place, the Right Time." *Parameters* 22 (1993): 2–18.

McNeill, William J. "A Survey of Confederate Soldiers' Morale during Sherman's Campaign through Georgia and the Carolinas." *Georgia Historical Quarterly* 55 (1971): 1–25.

Olds, Fred A. "The Last Big Battle." *Confederate Veteran* 37 (1929): 50-51, 75.

Quillen, Martha. "Emotions Stirred in Re-enactment of Bentonville." Raleigh *News and Observer*, Mar. 18, 1990.

Rhett, Claudine. "Frank H. Harleston—A Hero of Ft. Sumter." *Southern Historical Society Papers* 10 (1882): 307-20.

Robinson, Leigh. "General Joseph E. Johnston." *Southern Historical Society Papers* 19 (1889): 337-70.

Salter, William. "Major-General John M. Corse." *Annals of Iowa* 2 (1896): 1-19, 105-45, 278-304.

Smith, J. P. "The Battle of Bentonville." *Smithfield Herald*, Mar. 19, 1936.

Weeks, Stephen B. "The University of North Carolina in the Civil War." *Southern Historical Society Papers* 24: 1-38.

Wellman, Manley W. "Bentonville—The Last Might-Have-Been." *The State Magazine*, Aug. 9, 1958.

UNPUBLISHED STUDIES

Babits, Larry E. "Exploratory Archaeology at Bentonville Battleground State Historic Site." Raleigh, 1976.

Barrett, John G. "General William T. Sherman's Military Operations in North Carolina, March 4, 1865-March 25, 1865." M.A. thesis, University of North Carolina, 1949.

Carpenter, John A. "An Account of the Civil War Career of Oliver Otis Howard Based on His Private Letters." Ph.D. dissertation, Columbia University, 1954.

Charnley, Jeffrey G. "Neglected Honor: The Life of General A. S. Williams of Michigan (1810-1878)." Ph.D. dissertation, Michigan State University, 1983.

Cooper, Fleeta F. "The Triumverate of Colquitt, Gordon, and Brown." M.A. thesis, Emory University, 1931.

Cova, Antonio de la. "Ambrosio José Gonzales: A Cuban Confederate Colonel." Ph.D. thesis, West Virginia University, 1994.

Cross, Jerry L. "Historical Research Report for the Harper House, Bentonville, North Carolina." 1975.

France, Erik D. " 'To Uphold Our Valor': The Confederate Stand at Bentonville." [ca. 1980.]

Harsch, Robert M. "Ninety-seventh Regiment, Indiana Volunteer Infantry, 1862-1865." M.A. thesis, West Texas State University, 1967.

Hendricks, Howard O. "Imperilled City: The Movements of the Union and Confederate Armies toward Greensboro in the Closing Days of the Civil War." M.A. thesis, University of North Carolina at Greensboro, 1987.

Herring, William B., III. "The Battle of Bentonville: March 19-21, 1865." M.A. thesis, East Carolina University, 1982.

King, George Wayne. "The Civil War Career of Hugh Judson Kilpatrick." Ph.D. dissertation, University of South Carolina, 1969.

Shiman, Philip L. "Engineering Sherman's March: Army Engineers and the Management of Modern War, 1862-1865." Ph.D. dissertation, Duke University, 1991.

Simmons, R. Hugh. "Analysis of Historical Data Pertaining to Stewart's Corps, the Confederate Army of Tennessee in North Carolina in 1865." (1993; in possession of author.)

——. "The Story of the 12th Louisiana Infantry in the Final Campaign in North Carolina with the Confederate Army of Tennessee–January to April, 1865." (1993; in possession of author.)

Torrence, James E. "The Strategic Significance of Sherman's Campaign through Georgia and the Carolinas in the Last Year of the American Civil War." M.A. thesis, Duke University, 1967.

AUTHOR'S INTERVIEWS AND BATTLEFIELD TOURS

Hiram Cole, resident of Johnston County, N.C., near Bentonville, N.C., Apr. 28, 1956.

John Goode, Director of Bentonville Battleground State Historic Site, at Bentonville Battleground, Oct. 8–9, 1993, May 19, 1994.

Herschell V. Rose, County Court Clerk, Johnston County, N.C., Apr. 28, 1956.

Index

Black, Samuel L., 196

Black Creek, N.C., 211, 249 (n. 59)

Blackman's Pond, 227, 280 (n. 8), 286 (n. 18), 287 (n. 19)

Black River, N.C., 14–15, 17, 33–37, 249 (n. 59)

Blair, Francis P., Jr., 6, 19, 152, 154, 161, 183, 186–87, 192–93, 198, 215, 229, 247 (n. 13), 284 (n. 40)

Blanchard, Albert G., 51; Blanchard's Brigade, 51, 168–69, 260 (n. 43)

Blasland, Capt., 118

Blaylock, John, 146–47

Blount, George M., 275 (n. 102)

Boltz, Ferd F., 74

Boggess, Abijah, 201, 288 (n. 37)

Bonner, J. R., 55, 59, 120–21

Boston, Mass., 94

Bradley, Mark L., xv

Bragg, Braxton, 25–29, 32, 35, 37–41, 53, 60–61, 72, 125–26, 128, 130–31, 136, 168, 220, 224–26, 228, 249 (n. 53), 251 (n. 14), 252 (n. 36), 255 (nn. 3, 5), 290 (n. 1), 292 (n. 35)

Branum, John M., 105

Breckinridge, William C. P., 46

Briant, Cyrus E., 67, 93, 262 (n. 27); Briant's wing, 67–71, 84–88, 261 (n. 13), 264 (n. 50)

Broadfoot, Charles W., 120

Brown, Charles S., 81, 83, 90, 92

Brown, John C., 135; Brown's Brigade, 274 (n. 66); Brown's Division, 171, 207, 289 (n. 59)

Brown, Joseph E., 32, 51

Buck Creek, 279 (n. 61), 284 (n. 45)

Buell, Don Carlos, 69

Buell, George P., 69, 73–75, 79, 81–84, 93, 227, 241, 262 (n. 27), 264 (n. 2), 265 (n. 13); Buell's Brigade, 57, 69–75, 81, 83, 89–90, 96, 124–25, 157, 266 (n. 41)

Bunn, Henry G., 123, 125–26, 145, 241, 258 (nn. 16, 17), 272 (n. 15)

Butler, Benjamin F., 246 (n. 5)

Butler, Matthew C., 46, 49, 170, 281

(n. 24), 286 (n. 19); Butler's Brigade, 45, 198; Butler's Division, 287 (n. 21)

Butler, William, 141, 143

Buzzard's Roost Gap, 101

Cairo, Ill., 95

Callahan, Charles M., 186

Camden, Ark., 241

Camden, S.C., 242

Canby, Edward R. S., 282 (n. 38)

Cape Fear River, 4–5, 14, 28, 31–33

Carlin, William P., 17–19, 65–69, 71–77, 79–81, 83–85, 91–94, 98, 116–18, 157, 160–61, 220, 223, 225–28, 241, 250 (nn. 67, 74), 262 (nn. 23, 27, 28), 263 (n. 42), 264 (nn. 51, 6), 265 (n. 13), 268 (n. 21); Carlin's Division, 71–89, 96, 100, 102–3, 106, 109, 114, 125, 138, 156, 181, 220, 225, 230, 277 (n. 37), 291 (n. 21)

Carter, John C., 129; Carter's Brigade, 132

Catterson, Robert F., 163–64, 212, 214–15, 241; Catterson's Brigade, 162, 164, 185, 212–13, 279 (n. 64)

Chancellorsville, Battle of, 90

Charleston, S.C., 3, 21, 29–31, 35, 182, 230

Charleston and Savannah Railroad, 35

Charlotte, N.C., 22, 24–25

Cheatham, Benjamin F., 25, 37, 43, 171, 254 (nn. 67, 69), 289 (n. 60); Cheatham's Corps, 43–44, 120, 207, 259 (n. 24)

Cheraw, S.C., 3, 29–32, 247 (n. 13), 253 (n. 54)

Chesnut, Mary, 231–32

Chester, S.C., 37

Chesterfield, S.C., 3

Chickamauga, Battle of, 11, 51, 58, 65, 73, 101, 242, 259 (n. 32), 266 (n. 39)

Cincinnati, Ohio, 242

City Point, Va., 217, 220

Clark, Walter, 174, 241

Clarke, John J., 168

Clayton, Henry D., 55, 123, 220; Clayton's Division, 55, 58, 122–23, 129–30, 138, 226

Cleburne, Patrick R., 256 (n. 13); Cle-

Vandever's Brigade, 77, 98, 108–9, 118, 160, 174, 264 (n. 49)
Vernon, Maris R., 98, 106–9
Virginia troops: 54th Infantry, 109; 63d Infantry, 22

Walcutt, Charles C., 220
Walker, Peter F., 99
Walthall, Edward C., 42, 54, 123–26, 143, 144, 172, 226, 258 (nn. 16, 17), 260 (n. 46), 272 (n. 26); Walthall's Division, 54–55, 120, 123–25, 136, 143
Ward, William T., 14–15, 18, 36, 117, 270 (n. 65); Ward's Division, 115–16, 157, 159, 193
Waring, J. Fred, 170
Watson, Ben, 123
Wayne, Richard A., 146, 197, 208
Webb, Samuel D., 75, 87; Webb's Battery, 75, 77–78, 85–89
Weldon Railroad, 22, 28
Wetumpka, Ala., 242
Wever, Clark R., 161–62, 166; Wever's Brigade, 153, 162
Wheeler, Joseph, 24, 33, 36, 44–46, 65, 168–69, 189, 196, 198, 200–201, 202–3, 206–7, 210, 225, 227, 257 (n. 39), 281 (n. 13), 286 (n. 16)
White, D. G., 201, 288 (n. 37)
White, Francis, 214
Whitford, John N., 255 (nn. 5, 9)
Widmer, John H., 103, 265 (n. 33)
Wilhelm, Thomas, 283 (n. 25)
Wilkinson, William H., 140

Williams, Alpheus S., 10, 16, 75–76, 86, 114, 116–17, 154, 156, 158, 182, 186–87, 215, 220, 228–29, 243
Wilmington, N.C., 2–3, 5, 14, 19, 24–25, 30, 41, 216, 246 (n. 6), 280 (n. 3), 281 (n. 31)
Wilmington and Weldon Railroad, 2, 179
Wilson, James H., 123
Wisconsin troops: 3d Infantry, 115; 5th Light Artillery, 156, 158, 277 (n. 34); 12th Light Artillery, 184, 186; 21st Infantry, 88; 25th Infantry, 189, 247 (n. 13); 31st Infantry, 86–87; 32d Infantry, 189
Wise's Forks (Kinston), Battle of, 26–28, 41, 128, 249 (n. 53), 251 (n. 19)
Woodruff, Simeon, 268 (n. 27)
Woods, Charles R., 164, 193, 212–13, 218, 220, 229, 279 (n. 68); Woods's Division, 153, 156, 162, 165, 184–86, 193, 213–14, 219
Wortham, George W., 148, 275 (n. 112)
Wright, Ambrose R., 29, 32, 253 (n. 41); Wright's Division, 29
Wright, Gilbert J., 170, 198, 201, 286 (n. 19)
Wright, Henry, 11
Wright, W. W., 2
Wyeth, Andrew, xiv

Young's Brigade, 170, 198

Zachry, Charles T., 40, 56, 126–28, 225–26, 243, 274 (n. 64)
Zickerick, William, 186
Zouave uniform, 248 (n. 42)

973.738   Hughes, C. I
H   Cheai

        Bento

$37.50